Broadway Bodies

Broadway Bodies

A Critical History of Conformity

RYAN DONOVAN

OXFORD
UNIVERSITY PRESS

Oxford University Press is a department of the University of Oxford. It furthers
the University's objective of excellence in research, scholarship, and education
by publishing worldwide. Oxford is a registered trade mark of Oxford University
Press in the UK and certain other countries.

Published in the United States of America by Oxford University Press
198 Madison Avenue, New York, NY 10016, United States of America.

© Oxford University Press 2023

All rights reserved. No part of this publication may be reproduced, stored in
a retrieval system, or transmitted, in any form or by any means, without the
prior permission in writing of Oxford University Press, or as expressly permitted
by law, by license, or under terms agreed with the appropriate reproduction
rights organization. Inquiries concerning reproduction outside the scope of the
above should be sent to the Rights Department, Oxford University Press, at the
address above.

You must not circulate this work in any other form
and you must impose this same condition on any acquirer.

Library of Congress Cataloging-in-Publication Data
Names: Donovan, Ryan, author.
Title: Broadway bodies : a critical history of conformity / Ryan Donovan.
Description: New York : Oxford University Press, 2023. |
Includes bibliographical references and index.
Identifiers: LCCN 2022040722 (print) | LCCN 2022040723 (ebook) |
ISBN 9780197551073 (hardback) | ISBN 9780197551080 (paperback) |
ISBN 9780197551103 (epub)
Subjects: LCSH: Musicals—Casting. | Musicals—Auditions. |
Physical-appearance-based bias. | Musicals—Political aspects. |
Broadway—(New York, N.Y.)—History—20th century. |
Broadway—(New York, N.Y.)—History—21st century. |
Musicals—New York (State)—New York—20th century—History and criticism. |
Musicals—New York (State)—New York—21st century—History and criticism.
Classification: LCC ML3918.M85 .D66 2023 (print) | LCC ML3918.M85 (ebook) |
DDC 792.6089/0097471—dc23/eng/20220830
LC record available at https://lccn.loc.gov/2022040722
LC ebook record available at https://lccn.loc.gov/2022040723

DOI: 10.1093/oso/9780197551073.001.0001

This book is dedicated to anyone who has ever been told they were too fat, too short, too gay, too disabled, and otherwise too much or not enough to be in a musical.

Contents

Acknowledgments	ix
Companion Website	xiii

PART I. BROADWAY BODIES

Introduction: The Broadway Body	3
1. "I Saw What They Were Hiring": Casting and Recasting *A Chorus Line*	27

PART II. SIZE

2. *Dreamgirls*, Size, and the Body Politics of Padding	57
3. "Must Be Heavyset": Casting Fat Women in Broadway Musicals	86

PART III. SEXUALITY

4. *La Cage aux Folles* and Playing Gay	115
5. "Keeping It Gay" on The Great White Way	145

PART IV. ABILITY

6. Deaf West's *Awakening* of Broadway	179
7. Musicals, Physical Difference, and Disability	207
Epilogue: Recasting Broadway	239

Notes	247
Bibliography	275
Index	303

Acknowledgments

Work on this book began long before I had any inkling that I would ever become a scholar. Looking back, I now see that casting has confounded me ever since first grade, when I was cast not as the title character but as the campy villain Captain Hook in our class's stick puppet version of *Peter Pan*. I didn't see myself as Captain Hook and couldn't understand why Ms. O'Donnell did. If anyone is responsible for my path from there to here, it's her fault as much as anyone else's! All kidding aside, this book would not have been possible without the support and encouragement of so many people—especially from teachers.

This work began with the germ of an idea—first as a seminar paper, then a dissertation—while I was in graduate school at The Graduate Center, City University of New York. David Savran directed my dissertation along with committee members Jean Graham-Jones and Elizabeth Wollman, each of whom helped me believe that I could pull off a dissertation with interventions in four discrete fields and who pushed me to think more rigorously, to write more passionately, and to allow for complexity. I am lucky to have their ongoing support and friendship. Other mentors at The Graduate Center whose support made all the difference include Judith Milhous, whose early encouragement was crucial; Rhonda Garelick, who believed in me more than I did myself; Cathy Davidson, from whom I learned so much about teaching and learning; my colleagues at the Teaching and Learning Center; and the Theatre and Performance program's Assistant Program Officer Lynette Gibson, whose support and encouragement cannot go unmentioned and who is greatly missed.

The first person I told about my then-nascent idea for a dissertation was Norm Hirschy, who would acquire it for Oxford University Press a few years later and whose careful and thoughtful editing throughout the process from proposal to book has made me a stronger writer and a clearer thinker. Special kudos must go to Norm for coming up with the elegantly precise subtitle for this book. Without the feedback from the truly generous anonymous readers, who pushed me to clarify my thinking, check my assumptions, and be more exacting, this book would not be the same. I am indebted to all of them.

X ACKNOWLEDGMENTS

Thank you to everyone at Oxford who worked to make it a reality, especially title manager Zara Cannon-Mohammed. Copy editor Patterson Lamb and production manager Koperundevi Pugazhenthi brought this book to publication and Daniel Gundlach went above and beyond in creating the index. Rachel Perkins designed the gorgeous cover of the book.

Everyone I interviewed for this work made it possible and, hopefully, colored the narrative with their personal experiences. I appreciate your generosity and willingness to have sometimes difficult and intimate conversations with a total stranger. I extend special gratitude to those who helped connect me to interview subjects: Carl Andress, the late Jane Blass, David Engel, Stephanie Fittro, Asmeret Ghebremichael, Nina Goldman, Leon Le, Shana O'Hara, Vanessa Van Vrancken, and Blake West.

A major highlight of this project was interviewing Broadway legend Baayork Lee. Chorus dancers like Lee were always the stars in my eyes and this project honors them.

Colleagues in musical theatre studies contributed much to my conception of this book; in particular, participants at the Association for Theatre in Higher Education's (ATHE) Music Theatre/Dance Focus Group and the Song, Stage and Screen conference gave generous comments, feedback, questions, and, above all, intellectual community. The support and encouragement that I received during and since the early stages of this project from Joanna Dee Das, Liza Gennaro, Raymond Knapp, Jeff Magee, Doug Reside, Jessica Sternfeld, Dominic Symonds, Stacy Wolf, and Tamsen Wolff kept me going. I extend my appreciation to colleagues and collaborators including Margit Edwards, William Everett, Julia Foulkes, Donatella Galella, Robert Gordon, Alosha Grinenko, Barrie Gelles, Laura MacDonald, Emilio Mèndez, Hillary Miller, Ashley Pribyl, Bryan Vandevender, Samuel Yates, Catherine Young, and Kayla Yuh, among many others. David Román's encouragement has meant so much to me and speaking with his University of Southern California students about A Chorus Line made me reconsider my own positions thanks to their insights. Ariel Nereson and Lezlie Cross selected an earlier version of Chapter 3 in their special issue of the Journal of American Drama and Theatre; " 'Must Be Heavyset': Casting Women, Fat Stigma, and Broadway Bodies" was published in the Journal of American Drama and Theatre 31, no. 3 (2019) and is reproduced here with the generous permission of Frank Hentschker and the Martin E. Segal Theatre Center.

Colleagues and friends who graciously read various iterations of this book include Fidan Eylül Akinci, Joanna Dee Das, Chloë Edmonson, Andrew

ACKNOWLEDGMENTS xi

Goldberg, Phoebe Rumsey, Jennifer Thompson, Liz Wollman, and Stacy Wolf. Each of you was an important cheerleader during the various stages of this project.

This book was made possible in part by funding from The Graduate Center, CUNY, both with the Dissertation Fellowship and the Doctoral Students' Research Grant. The Interlibrary Loan team made the research process much more efficient and I am indebted to their services. The Broadway Bodies conference at Washington University in St. Louis in 2018 provided a wonderful (and aptly named) venue to share this research just as I was finishing my dissertation. Heather Nathans, Barbara Wallace Grossman, and the ATDS/ATHE Contingent Faculty Publication Development Forum held at Tufts University in February 2020 helped me refine my thinking about how I was writing and for whom.

Archivists and librarians at the Library of Congress, the New York Public Library for the Performing Arts, and Yale University's Beinecke Rare Book & Manuscript Library and Manuscripts and Archives Repository provided invaluable help finding materials, especially Tom Lisanti and Jeremy Megraw at NYPL, who always found just the right photograph. The images provided by photographers Teresa Castracane, Carol Rosegg, Joan Marcus, and Michael Lutch have made visible what this book is about. I am forever grateful to Kate Reinking and Peter Talbert for their assistance and permission in securing this work's cover image of Ann Reinking as Cassie in *A Chorus Line*. I learned so many lessons as a student of Ann's, none perhaps more prescient than "your dreams will come true, just not in the way you planned." She was right!

Students from my Disability & Theatre and Musicals & Identity courses at The New School always sparked new ideas and generated exciting conversations as I was working through the ideas that appear here. I'm especially grateful to them and to the group with whom I gathered every few weeks on Zoom in the most uncertain days of summer 2020: Isaac Grivett, Samantha Levine, Sierra Gamble, Emily McNally, Maia Gersten, and Emmy Briggs.

My research attracted attention after Michael Paulson's May 2021 *New York Times* article about the return of Broadway (inadvertently) created an outpouring of actors speaking out against body shaming in the theatre. As a result, I extend my gratitude to him and the following journalists and outlets who featured my research: Alec Hamilton and Michael Hill at WNYC, Ashley Lee at the Los Angeles *Times*, Abby Rose Morris at the *More Than Tracy Turnblad* podcast, and Gianluca Russo at *Teen Vogue*.

xii   ACKNOWLEDGMENTS

Grad school is hard, and the job market is cruel. Writing a book while surviving both of those processes would not have been possible without the support and encouragement of Margaret Mackey in grad school and especially Enid Zuckerman afterward—I'm lucky to have you in my corner.

My colleagues at Duke University's Department of Theater Studies made it feel like home right away: Neal Bell, Torry Bend, Cyndi Bunn, Alex Ferrone, Lauren Donovan Ginsberg, R. Darren Gobert, Katja Hill, Chauntee' Schuler Irving, Douglas Jones, Juliana Kleist-Mendez, Esther Kim Lee, Jody McAuliffe, Johann Montozzi-Wood, Thom Quintas, Jeffrey Storer, and Erika Weiberg. Dean William Johnson and Trinity College of Arts and Sciences provided publication subvention that helped fully realize my vision for this project, which was also supported by the American Theatre and Drama Society's 2022 Publication Subvention Award.

Friends helped me realize that readers outside of the academy might care about this work, and I want to particularly acknowledge the encouragement of fellow writers Deb Goldberg, Bill Goldstein, Deb Hiller, Colleen Hubbard, Sarah Robbins, and David Tamarkin. My family has always supported me whether it was traveling to see me perform at some regional theatre or another or encouraging—and in some cases, tolerating—my Patti LuPone obsession (which began with the *Evita* LP on repeat at my aunt Joanie Kilmon's house). My brother Wesley keeps me laughing and never lets me take myself too seriously and my sister-in-law Julie has been unfailingly encouraging. Thank you to my parents for letting me stay up late reading every night as kid—it made me a writer. My dad and my step-mom Mary took me to see my first musical on Broadway and encouraged me to pursue my dreams. But first, my mom and my stepdad Jay took me to see a touring production of *Cats* and ignited my Broadway dreams at the National Theater in Washington, D.C.

Thank you to my husband Erik for all the little things we do together that make marriage a joy.

I dedicate this book to the memory of Addison Rose Donovan, Sally Donovan, Gerald W. Donovan, and Helene Gensler. The losses I endured during the writing of this book are a daily reminder to heed Jerry Herman's lyrics to "The Best of Times":

So hold this moment fast,
And live and love
As hard as you know how,
And make this moment last,
Because the best of times is now.

Companion Website

www.oup.com/us/broadwaybodies

Oxford has created a website to accompany *Broadway Bodies*. Visual material that cannot be made available in a book is provided here, namely, brief video excerpts of musicals mentioned in the book. These video clips allow readers to see the Broadway Body in performance.

A playlist of songs from musicals mentioned in the book is also available via Spotify, a link to which can be found on the website.

PART I
BROADWAY BODIES

Introduction

The Broadway Body

I lied about my height on my résumé the entire time I was a dancer, though in truth I don't think the extra inch ever actually made a difference. In the United States, 5'6" still reads as short for a man no matter how you slice it. The reason for my deception was that height was frequently the reason I was disqualified: choreographers generally wanted taller male dancers for the ensemble and listed a minimum height requirement (often 5'11" and up) in the casting breakdown. More than once, I was disqualified before I could even set foot in the audition because I possessed an unchangeable physical characteristic that frequently made me unemployable in the industry. I was learning an object lesson in Broadway's body politics—and, of course, had I not been a white cisgender non-disabled man, the barriers to employment would have been compounded even further. I wasn't alone in feeling stuck in a catch-22. Not being cast because of your appearance, or "type" in industry lingo, is casting's status quo. The casting process openly discriminates on the basis of appearance. This truism even made its way into a song cut from *A Chorus Line* (1975) called "Broadway Boogie Woogie," which comically lists all the reasons one might not be cast: "I'm much too tall, much too short, much too thin/Much too fat, much too young for the role/I sing too high, sing too low, sing too loud."[1] *Funny Girl* (1964) put it even more bluntly: "If a Girl isn't pretty/Like a Miss Atlantic City/She should dump the stage/And try another route."[2]

In *Broadway Bodies*, I address the actor's paradox of being too much and not enough and how casting enacts this paradox through the bodies seen in Broadway musicals. Many of the histories in this book may strike you as outrageous, but they did not raise many eyebrows at the time among those with power in the Broadway industry or even in the media. Conventions change, as do perspectives on the past. In this book, I analyze intersections of musical theatre history, US cultural history, and changing body politics in the fifty-year span beginning in 1970. The complexities and contradictions of

Broadway Bodies. Ryan Donovan, Oxford University Press. © Oxford University Press 2023.
DOI: 10.1093/oso/9780197551073.003.0001

4   BROADWAY BODIES

Broadway's body politics (the hierarchical power relations of bodies to each other) led me to think critically and historically about casting and identity in this period. Since singing and dancing can tend to obscure the fact that "musicals are necessarily political, even as they appear to be only entertainment,"[3] Broadway's body politics often go unnoticed despite their visibility. And Broadway is a fundamentally conservative institution whose casting has, as this book will show, upheld ableism, fat phobia, heterosexism, misogyny, and white supremacy. Yet at the same time, Broadway is also a space that attempts to welcome people marginalized by those very same social forces that make it so conservative. Whether we are onstage or not, we all navigate body politics all the time, including those of disability, gender, sexuality, size, and race and ethnicity.

This book lays bare the fat-phobia, homophobia, and disability exclusion that ran rampant on Broadway for decades. The fifty years beginning in 1970 saw the rise of movements for equality from fat acceptance to gay rights, devastating inequality wrought by neoliberal economics, the explosion of the fitness industry, and the unprecedented economic growth of the Broadway musical industry—and all of these factors fed into the dominance of what I call the *Broadway Body*, embodied by the hyper-fit, muscular, tall, conventionally attractive, exceptionally *able* triple-threat performer (one highly skilled in acting, dancing, and singing). The Broadway Body became Broadway's ideal body as the result of a confluence of aesthetic, economic, and sociocultural factors. In *Broadway Bodies*, I study bodies that differ from this ideal but that should be considered Broadway bodies, too.

Inside the Broadway industry, Broadway Bodies are the extremely physically fit, especially able bodies that seem to announce, "I just left *Wicked* for *Hamilton* and I squeezed in some cardio and lifting, a voice lesson, and a healthy meal between the matinee and the evening show."

The Broadway Body is an early twenty-first-century iteration of the so-called ideal body, coupled with industry pressure to be a triple-threat. The paradox of the ideal body is that it must remain an unattainable ideal since even those who come close to the ideal must still strive for it, too.[4] If the ideal body is a fiction, it is one that in reality regulates our behaviors, bodies, and norms—and its impact goes beyond Broadway and into all of the media we consume.

As Broadway prepared to reopen in 2021 after over a year of being shuttered due to the COVID-19 pandemic, an article in the *New York Times* ignited a debate that took place on social media and in the press over whose bodies are Broadway Bodies. In the article's originally published version, reporter Michael Paulson wrote simply, "Some performers have gained weight," which the paper later amended to read: "Some performers need to recondition their bodies or their voices."[5] Even though both statements were factual, and Paulson was acknowledging that Broadway producers might not rehire the performers who had gained weight, the platform of the *Times* meant that industry insiders paid attention to the first version of the sentence. Actors took to social media to share experiences of body shaming in and by the industry, including fat phobia at auditions and contractual weigh-ins while performing in certain productions.[6] The open secret of Broadway's body shaming and its fat phobia spilled out into public view. While the structures that regulate bodies on Broadway did not go away (or even change that much) during the pandemic closure, one hopeful sign of size-inclusive casting news appeared when producers of the 2022 revival of *Funny Girl* (1964) cast Beanie Feldstein as Fanny Brice. Even though Feldstein's tenure in the role was short-lived and received mixed notices, most critics faulted the size of her voice and not the size of her body.

If musicals embody difference in what musical theatre scholar Stacy Wolf describes as "bodies shaped through song and dance,"[7] then what do these singing and dancing bodies signify? If, as historian Julia Foulkes contends, "musicals do not change the world, but they do shape how we see it," then how do the bodies we see onstage shape our perspectives?[8] Casting is how musicals determine this shaping because who we see onstage—and in which roles—matters. There are so few jobs in musicals that "great power lays in the hands of those deciding who gets a part and who does not. Every act of casting is then simultaneously a creative act of interpretation and also an administrative allocation of resources," as theatre scholar Brian Eugenio Herrera observes.[9] Casting fundamentally connects to labor: auditions are effectively job interviews (sometimes they are very clearly pre-screens, too). Auditions are only the middle part of the casting process, which includes the conception of a role through the writing of the role descriptions and requirements for the breakdown (or casting notice) and on through auditions and callbacks all the way to the moment the performer steps foot onstage. The casting of Broadway musicals has largely upheld the status quo of bodily norms, and when bodies that exceed these norms have broken through, they are the exceptions: we notice them because their difference stands out. This book is thus more concerned with addressing how those with marked identities navigate the space occupied freely by those with seemingly unmarked identities, or privileged non-identities. What does it mean to exist in a space made to accommodate others who do not look, move, or sound like you? This book takes a hard look at casting in order to ask how Broadway musicals stage and include difference.

I center how ability, sexuality, and size intersect with gender, race, and ethnicity in casting and performance in order to ask, How does the use of fat suits, even in ostensibly fat-positive musicals like *Hairspray*, actually stigmatize fatness? What were the political implications of casting two white heterosexual actors as the gay couple in *La Cage aux Folles* in 1983? How did Broadway respond to movements for LGBTQ+ equality and the increased presence of newly out actors? How did d/Deaf actors change the sound of musicals in Deaf West's Broadway revivals? How do musicals use the aesthetics of physical difference as metaphors for disability? What happens when non-conforming bodies attempt to fit into a system that denies them a full range of representation?

I analyze casting as a labor practice on the musical's biggest stage, Broadway, because casting is a series of aesthetic choices revealing the limits of Broadway's tolerance of many kinds of difference. Casting is an unevenly distributed resource that showcases the bodies valued not just by Broadway but by US society at large, increasingly so in the years from 1970 to today. Though musicals appear to celebrate identity onstage in song and dance, how identity is treated offstage is quite a bit messier. This contradiction is a major theme of *Broadway Bodies*, and musicals cement this contradiction since they encourage normative assimilation *and* celebrate difference—often simultaneously. This book centers on people who have been told that they could not or should or would not play certain roles or even do musicals at all because of aesthetics—how their bodies look, move, and sound. If you have ever been told you were too Black, too "ethnic," too fat, too gay, too loud, both too much *and* not enough, or that your body does not look or move in the right ways for musicals, this book is for you. But my aim is not only to preach to the converted; no matter which side of the audition table you have been on, this book is an invitation to consider how learning from Broadway's past can help create a more equitable industry.

Why Casting?

Few things in representation are as fraught as the relationship between casting and identity. The debate over who should play whom never runs out

INTRODUCTION 7

of steam. Casting controversies have historically arisen when lines around ethnic and racial representation are crossed (e.g., white actor Jonathan Pryce's casting as the biracial Engineer in *Miss Saigon*) but increasingly have turned as well toward gender, sexuality, and ability since 2010. Casting's relationship to identity is contingent on (and determined by) cultural and historical contexts, and each era approaches casting and identity differently and with different language; each subsequent chapter of this book addresses this powerful relationship in one way or another. While many actors do get the opportunity to portray their own identity onstage, there are scores who never even have the opportunity to audition for these roles—and concerns regarding the miscasting of identity have too often been ignored in the industry.

Actors' marketability is greatly affected by their perceived flexibility—whether the industry (and the country at large) sees them as *able* to play any role. As this book shows, the determination of such flexibility is not just tied to whiteness but also to ability, sexuality, and size. For instance, Broadway actress Lisa Howard has made her career by carving out a niche as the plus-sized sidekick. She told the *New York Times*, "I've gotten that my whole career—'If you would only lose 30 pounds, you'd have every lead on Broadway. What's wrong with you?'"[10] Howard's experience demonstrates Broadway's reluctance to confront its explicit biases. The message is clear about whose bodies get to be seen in leading roles and whose do not. Imagine for a moment another industry that accepts as normal (not to mention legal) someone's size keeping them from employment or promotion, because that is precisely what Broadway does.

Casting concerns are labor issues. The labor concerns around casting usually become subsumed under "artistic license," providing cover for harmful and exclusionary practices. Theatre historian Angela C. Pao's work calls our attention to "the need to consider casting practices not just in terms of discursive categories and ideological interests but also as an employment policy subject to many of the same pressures and policies as other forms of work and commerce."[11] The fact is, though, that casting has largely sidestepped the pressures and policies to which other industries are subjected. "Looking the part" determines one's employability onstage to the point that it is part of the job description—the casting breakdown. Critics and scholars have rightfully argued that race and ethnicity are often primary factors of aesthetic disqualification and discrimination on Broadway, but, as this book shows, disqualification also extends to, is compounded by, and is indeed inseparable from ability, size, and sexuality.[12]

8   BROADWAY BODIES

Most casting taxonomies have been framed around performance abilities like vocal ranges and/or dance styles and vectors of identity like appearance, gender, race, and ethnicity. There are relatively few terms coined for the kinds of difference studied in this book apart from the relatively recent term "size-blind."[13] Yet describing any casting as color-, size-, or otherwise-blind only calls attention to what is actually *most* visible about casting. The terms of casting shift and negotiate new contexts and, as of this writing, have moved toward *authentic casting* and *inclusive casting* as the most capacious descriptors. When the terms widely used to discuss identity shift, casting plays catch-up.

Sometimes audiences laud musicals for their casting practices while critics and scholars critique them; *Hamilton* is a prime example since it featured Black and brown actors playing dead white people, which critics and scholars simultaneously viewed as both progressive *and* as masking the operation of white supremacy.[14] Because white supremacy is so foundational to the United States, it makes sense that racial and ethnic differences are often the central axes on which casting seems to hinge. Race and ethnicity are the primary lenses through which critics, scholars, and spectators often view casting because of whiteness's over-representation onstage, which leaves less-discussed the over-representation of certain body types onstage. In the United States, race and ethnicity have been central concerns of debate and discourse in mainstream theatre since at least the 1960s, and they came to the foreground again as the Black Lives Matter movement forced the country to confront its structural racism in 2020.[15] Racist power dynamics have historically erased race and ethnicity for white performers, who "are given a kind of VIP pass to enter whatever character-door they want to because white America is not always presumed to be carrying its race around," while everyone who is not white *is* presumed to carry their race around.[16] In their own specific ways, Deaf actors, disabled actors, fat actors, and LGBTQ+ actors all also carry their difference into the audition space.

To mitigate the discrimination endemic in show business, Actors' Equity Association (AEA), the union for professional actors, sets rules for casting. These rules differ based on the kind of contract under which the actors will be working. AEA encourages producers to be very detailed in casting breakdowns so that actors can "type themselves." The instructions to producers also remind them of the following: "Please remember also to **ENCOURAGE PARTICIPATION BY PERFORMERS OF ALL RACES AND ETHNICITIES** and, when required by your company's agreement, to

INTRODUCTION   9

identify roles suitable for non-traditional casting in your notice."[17] Note that race, ethnicity, and "non-traditional casting" are the *only* acknowledgments of *any* kind of difference mentioned, reflecting their prevalence as the dominant frames through which the industry itself considers casting's power dynamics. Yet most of the guidelines for casting written by AEA are purely procedural and are often toothless, as producers wield more power than the union.

AEA's suggestion that actors "type themselves" dodges the inherent problems of typing and places the burden on the actor rather than addressing the larger issues of systematic appearance-based disqualification. While this aims to make casting a more efficient process, it allows inequity in casting to continue unabated. AEA's instructions on how typing should proceed are explicitly about appearance: " 'Typing' may be used by casting personnel to audition only those members the casting personnel determine to be physically right for the production."[18] Typing is a quick way for casting personnel to sift through large numbers of applicants in order to eliminate as many people as possible based precisely on their appearance. This would be unacceptable in most professions, and yet the industry has accepted it as the norm for decades. Resources and time for casting are not unlimited, and the supply of willing actors could cast every production dozens of times over, so typing remains the system that the parties involved have agreed on as the most efficient if not the most equitable.

The competing needs and desires of the artistic teams, casting personnel, and producers on one side of the audition table and the actors on the other side insistently enact a hierarchy based on bodily appearance. To see how this plays out in practice, simply see almost any Broadway musical. This bodily hierarchy is wedded to broader notions about who is allowed to perform certain roles—and not only onstage. Representation admits hard truths about life offstage, too; as ethnographer D. Soyini Madison explains, "Representation has consequences: how people are represented is how they are treated."[19] Representation thus shapes not only its subjects but its objects. Following theatre scholar Amy Cook, I am concerned in this book with "the relationship between characters and the bodies that are chosen to represent them."[20]

AEA realized that one action they could take to encourage more inclusive casting on Broadway was to reward it. In 2007, AEA inaugurated the Extraordinary Excellence in Diversity on Broadway Award, which it initially awarded to productions with notable racially and ethnically diverse casting.

The honor has largely been awarded to musicals: only four non-musical plays have been recognized since its inception. The first awards went to revivals of *110 in the Shade* (2007) and *Les Misérables* (2006) for what AEA's Equal Employment Opportunity Committee Co-Chair Christine Toy Johnson called "the kind of unique, diverse casting that we have been dreaming of for years: interracial families and diverse communities that reflected the true tapestry of America."[21] AEA honored *Billy Elliott* (2008) "due to its multi-ethnic casting of the role of the Billy's."[22] In the award citation, Johnson explained, "Though many people claim to cast the 'best person' for every role on Broadway, unspoken in that, is the reality that even if the 'best person' is of a race or ethnicity not originally imagined, they may not, in actuality, even be considered." In 2016, Deaf West's *Spring Awakening* (2016) shared the award with *Hamilton* (2015) and *Waitress* (2016), showing AEA's growing awareness of multiple forms of difference. Productions winning the award that were inclusive of LGBTQ+ representations include *If/Then* (2014) and *It Shoulda Been You* (2015).

Despite AEA's awards for diverse casting, in practice little changed. AEA's "Diversity Report," covering the years from 2016 to 2019, paints a bleak picture showing the industry's failures to cast more inclusively on the coveted Production Contract for Broadway shows, on national tours, and at regional theatres.[23] On Production Contracts, white actors received 56.47% of Principal Contracts and 50.48% of Chorus Contracts, while men took 57.28% of principal roles to 41.52% for women. Nationally, the statistics show that only 3.46% of Principal Contracts and 3.32% of Chorus Contracts went to performers who self-identify as disabled, a category that is likely underreported due to disability stigma. Only 0.51% of Principal Contracts and 0.18% of Chorus Contracts went to non-binary or transgender performers. AEA's executive director Mary McColl laments that the union can do only so much, writing, "Equity cannot control who an individual employer chooses to hire, but we can be loud and insistent in calling out a structure built on biases both implicit and overt. It is our duty to be part of the solution, to work to tear down barriers and rebuild a structure that is truly inclusive." And these figures are all contingent on the casting requirements of which specific shows are running: AEA noted that the increase in contracts for BIPOC (Black, Indigenous, and people of color) actors was due to multiple concurrent productions of *Hamilton*.[24] *Hamilton* has never been far from the center of discussions around casting, inclusion, and equity since it premiered in 2015, and that itself represents the potency of Broadway's body politics. Less acknowledged is the reality that *Hamilton*'s casting does not extend to include fat actors or actors with visible disabilities, and its depiction of King George as a fop relies on making male effeminacy a joke (no doubt heightened when played by an out gay actor like Jonathan Groff or Rory O'Malley). Even cultural zeitgeist-tapping musicals like *Hamilton* fail in one way or another to be wholly inclusive.

Casting controversies continue to persist, as ever. *Hamilton* had its own in 2016 over a casting breakdown requesting "non-white" performers, though of course no corresponding outcries were made during decades of all-white Broadway casts.[25] Casting practices have historically favored normative, white, cisgender, able bodies for most roles. Think, for instance, of all of the non-disabled actors awarded for playing disabled characters, all the heterosexual and cisgender actors awarded for playing LGBTQ+ roles, or the media free-for-all every time an ingénue dons a fat suit. The chance to audition for roles calling for an identity an actor inhabits should be a given, but it is not. Disability scholar Lennard J. Davis poignantly asks how this practice is not discrimination: "In what other profession would it be acceptable to discriminate against an identity and get away with it? In what other profession would we counsel young people to forget their hopes and dreams because of rampant prejudice against the kind of person they are?"[26]

Performers with non-conforming bodies face the double bind of being expected to only be able to represent their own identity and then not even being considered for those roles. Casting, then, writes disability scholar Carrie Sandahl, "is an important choice economically for the livelihood of disabled actors, aesthetically in terms of portraying the intimate depths and complex life experiences of the disabled character, and politically as a form of solidarity."[27] Sandahl's argument also applies to the other group identities covered in this book, since they too have historically been denied the right to play their own identities onstage (and sometimes still are).

While casting can and does harm excluded, marginalized, and oppressed people, it also contains the power to do good. Achieving parity should be casting's first goal: performers from marginalized groups should have the right to play not just their own identity but also the range of roles regularly offered to others. Casting is how the industry can start redressing its unequal distribution of roles. Removing physical descriptions and in many cases even gender from casting breakdowns and focusing instead on the other qualities of the character would represent a start. Requirements for voice type and range or specific styles of dance will likely always be primary factors in

12 BROADWAY BODIES

casting since they are constitutive of what makes musicals musicals. However, a more capacious understanding of what counts as ability and whose bodies the industry considers castable is urgently needed. But what you will find inside this book is a history, not a roadmap of how to build a more equitable industry.[28]

Representation alone is never enough to make change, and neither is awareness without action. Laws that are ineffectual or unenforceable have not undone structural discrimination against oppressed and marginalized people either—but they are at least a start. Under neoliberal capitalism, the burden of addressing structural problems falls on individuals more often than not, and in this book, I highlight individual actors and productions that represent inflection points in Broadway's dependence on difference. In that light, focusing on representation is intended to highlight what representation means to actors: a job. Lack of representation translates into different life outcomes for actors denied work because of aesthetics; this lack means little or infrequent access to health care and insurance, reliance on low-wage and part-time jobs, and dreams deferred.

Broadway and Body Conformity

In theatre, the Broadway Body ideal sets unrealistic standards enforced by industry gatekeepers—from agents and casting directors to producers and college professors. That appearance matters for performers is old news (the Ziegfeld girls were not all chosen for their dance talent in the 1910s), but Broadway's pervasive body-shaming is only beginning to be studied by scholars and openly discussed in the industry itself despite its long history. A 2019 study found that two-thirds of performers had been asked to change their appearance, and that 33% of those had been told to lose weight.[29] As a result of the pressure to look a certain way in order to be castable, a small industry of Broadway-focused fitness companies like Built for the Stage and Mark Fisher Fitness, sprang up in response. The combination of fitness and Broadway made good business sense: Broadway experienced massive financial growth over the past five decades, going from grossing $57.4 million in 1975 to a record $1.82 billion in the 2018–2019 season,[30] paralleling the rapid growth of the fitness industry into a multi-billion-dollar industry. The Broadway Body embodies the merger of these two significant sociocultural and economic shifts.

The term *Broadway Bodies* itself was popularized in part by the New York City–based personal training gym Mark Fisher Fitness, alongside a stream of *Playbill* articles. In 2011, former actor Mark Fisher opened his eponymously named gym and specifically tailored it for the Broadway community. The gym became an unqualified success, winning public acclaim from sources like *Forbes* magazine and Broadway director-choreographer Jerry Mitchell. Mark Fisher Fitness went digital in 2015 with a new brand, MyBroadwayBody.com; this allows actors to continue their fitness plans while touring (Figure I.1) and shows how the brand appeals to performers. A promotional email quotes Mitchell as saying, "If you want to be your best, go #fullout, and make it to BROADWAY, you can count on Mark Fisher Fitness! It is where I train, and they're my go to resource for myself and my casts."[31] *Backstage* noted that Mark Fisher Fitness "is particularly popular among those in the performing arts community looking to get a 'Broadway Body.'"[32] Other theatrical press picked up on the idea; an article in *Playbill* asked, "Who doesn't want a Broadway body?"[33] The Broadway Body is not merely a twenty-first century marketing ploy but an ideology grounded in an appearance-based hierarchy perpetuated by the media, Broadway-focused fitness companies, and even some notable Broadway stars alike; this ideology has a starry past. In the 1980s, original *West Side Story* star Carol Lawrence released a workout video titled *Carol Lawrence's Broadway Body Workout*, Broadway dancer Ann Reinking wrote a book called *The Dancer's Workout*, and even five-time Tony Award winner Angela Lansbury got in on the game by releasing a workout video called *Angela Lansbury's Positive Moves*. As this book will show, the Broadway Body existed as an ideal long before the term itself was coined.

Figure I.1 Screenshot of the MyBroadwayBody.com website.
Credit: Author.

14   BROADWAY BODIES

Industry channels promoted Broadway's body politics as much as the fitness companies targeting performers. The theatrical press cemented the connection between physical fitness and success as a performer. Broadway choreographer Spencer Liff was the subject of a *Playbill* feature inviting readers to "Follow Choreographer Spencer Liff's Workout Routine for a Broadway Body."[34] This article displayed Liff's hyper-fit body as he instructed readers on how to attain their own Broadway Body. Another typical *Playbill* headline reads, "Thanksgiving for a Broadway Body! How to Stay Hot and Healthy This Holiday."[35] In that article, Fisher dispensed fitness tips (e.g., "If you really want a Broadway Body, the context of your day-to-day eating habits matter most.") to help performers "keep [their] Broadway body." The subtext was clear: control yourself and you will work on Broadway.[36]

As Broadway-focused fitness companies sold the *idea* of a Broadway Body, they also endorsed body positivity. The website for the now-defunct fitness class Broadway Bodies even prominently highlighted that it was a "shame-free community." At its core, though, the Broadway fitness industry sells actors on the idea that they can become fit enough—thin enough, usually—to make it on Broadway. The reality is that many actors do seek to change their bodies to further their careers. Trainer Geoff Hemingway related an anecdote about one of his clients, saying, "When she started she was like, 'I just played Tracy Turnblad in this regional production of *Hairspray*. That was my dream role, and now I've done it and I don't want to be fat anymore.' Since coming in to Mark Fisher, she's shed about 50 pounds and is now being seen for ingénue roles."[37] Tracy Turnblad *is* an ingénue role, but Hemingway's client's size prevented the industry from seeing her as one. This actor knew that she would not be considered for many other roles if she was a "Tracy Turnblad type." But Hemingway dispelled the notion that inhabiting a Broadway Body itself will lead to more work, saying, "A lot of people get wrapped up in that stigma of a Broadway body. . . . The fitness doesn't breed work."[38] While a fit body does not suddenly beget a Production Contract, the reality of the business is such that there are more jobs for those whose bodies adhere to these norms.

While *Playbill* did its part to establish the concept of the Broadway Body, it has also nodded to bodily diversity. In a feature on the off-Broadway musical *Gigantic* (2015), *Playbill* asked, "Is there more than just one kind of 'Broadway Body?' "[39] This article featured interviews with members of the *Gigantic* (previously known as *Fat Camp*) cast, who all noted that "shows only have room for one character of their size." Actor Bonnie Milligan told *Playbill* her dream

INTRODUCTION   15

is a love story with "a big girl [that] has nothing to do with size."[40] Her wish came true in *Head Over Heels* (2018). Even when acknowledging that the Broadway Body *could* include a diverse array of body types, bodies that do not conform to the ideal are still positioned in opposition to it. Broadway *has* made strides toward integrating bodily difference, but like most progress, it has been slow, halting, and unevenly distributed.

In *Broadway Bodies*, I detail the presence of bodies that challenged norms simply by being onstage at specific historical moments. The bodies discussed in this book's subsequent sections can all be considered "non-conforming bodies."[41] Non-conforming bodies are those stigmatized by their deviation from the norm, whether in terms of appearance or behavior. Factors including ability, gender, race, and size stratify this deviation and ensure that stigmatization's effects remain uneven.[42] Bodily appearance accordingly determines one's place in aesthetic hierarchies.[43] On Broadway as elsewhere, bodily hierarchies are not only aesthetic but also economic. Broadway shows are big business, and the cultural meanings of bodies cannot be divorced from their relation to capital.

The ever-increasing demands of performing a Broadway musical eight times a week necessitate some of the changes seen in Broadway Bodies, from notably higher technical demands placed on dancers to challenging vocal tracks. Aesthetic imperatives became economic ones; musicologist Jake Johnson notes the "considerable pressure to stay fit and maintain consistent eating habits; even the slightest fluctuation in weight could require a costume refitting, an expense many producers see as unnecessary. Given the uniform size and physique of most performers, interchanging ousted performers with near-identical replacements is an easy way to cut costs."[44] The wear and tear on actors' bodies caused by repeatedly performing songs and dances requiring virtuosity increase the financial pressure and the physical toll; life offstage becomes about staying fit to prevent injury and staying ready for the next job. Actors pay more attention than ever to their bodies to remain competitive and employed.

Because the number of spots in the chorus typically outnumbers speaking roles, Broadway's bodily norms most often adhere to the body fascism of the dance and fitness worlds, which strictly regulates and disciplines the appearance and behaviors of the performer's body into thinness.[45] But these norms do not only impact those in the ensemble: *Dreamgirls* (1981) star Jennifer "Holliday's weight fluctuations were often the subject of tabloid fodder, but much of the cast felt the pressure to be unrealistically thin," including

Holliday's co-star Sheryl Lee Ralph, who "realized she was wasting away" due to this pressure.[46] Broadway's body fascism typically presents in the dominance and over-representation of the hyper-fit, muscular-yet-thin dancer (as depicted in Figure I.2). This look presents an iteration of the gay male clone look prevalent since the mid-1980s. American studies scholar Jeffry J. Iovannone describes the gay clone aesthetic as inspired by the "hyper-masculine look" of the "rugged, working-class" Marlboro Man.[47] Given that

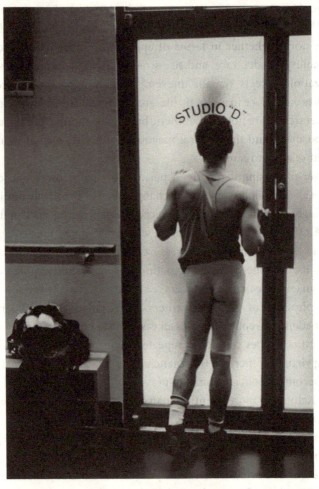

Figure I.2 *A Chorus Line* (1975–1990 Broadway). Music by Marvin Hamlisch. Lyrics by Edward Kleban. Book by James Kirkwood and Nicolas Dante. Directed and Choreographed by Michael Bennett. Shown: International tour. Credit: Photofest.

INTRODUCTION   17

white gay men have cast, directed, or choreographed so many Broadway musicals since the 1970s, it makes sense that the aesthetic choices made by those in power mirror the bodies seen by the mainstream as powerful off-stage: heterosexual, muscular, "masculine," white men. The adoption of this aesthetic is not so easily reduced to just a capitulation to dominant culture; it also attempts to outdo, parody, and redefine US culture's ideal bodies by reappropriating that which is valued.

Broadway's body culture increasingly depends on the hyper-fit bodies of its dancers, and these are often celebrated onstage in musicals and intra-industry charity events. Director-choreographer and former Broadway dancer Jerry Mitchell founded *Broadway Bares* in 1992 as a fundraiser for Broadway Cares/Equity Fights AIDS. The first event took place at the New York City gay club Splash, infamous for scantily clad go-go boys dancing in shower stalls situated around the club. *Broadway Bares* thus marks a pivotal intersection of gay male body culture, AIDS, and Broadway. Using the highly chiseled bodies of Broadway dancers to provide support to those whose bodies were wasting away from AIDS heightened the paradox underlying the clone look. The clone look replaced earlier gay male aesthetics, which went from thin to muscular as the subculture's norm. This body meant to communicate "health, cleanliness, and physical fitness in the form of muscularity."[48] The muscled body was a fragile defense first against a homophobic world and then AIDS. Writer Ken Gault noted, "Those pounds of muscle said to the world that this bad-ass body does not, cannot, will not have AIDS. That might happen to someone else, but not to me, not to this body."[49] None of the muscularity in the world could stop homophobia or AIDS, but neither could the threat of AIDS or homophobia forestall body fascism's dominance. Dancers' bodies adopted these aesthetics, too, becoming ever more sculpted (which I discuss in chapter 1).

The sculpted gay male body was not just warding off AIDS; it was also fighting off fat. Sociologist Jason Whitesel describes how size is one parameter used to create appearance-based hierarchies within body-conscious gay male communities, noting, "Historically, gay men have not enjoyed the same leeway as heterosexual men with regard to fatness. They are marginalized for not conforming to rigid bodily standards used to stratify their community by size."[50] The emphasis on fitness and size comes with attendant costs, including the marginalization of those bodies who do not comply with body fascism. On Broadway, casting is the site where these concerns come to a head.

"Whipped into Shape": Ability, Labor, and the Neoliberal Body

A central premise of this book is that casting is a labor issue inseparable from ableism. Ableism is baked into casting musicals increasingly dependent on triple-threat performers' virtuosic abilities (discussed at length in chapter 1). The concept of ability itself can be challenging to conceptualize because its ubiquity makes it hard to see; also, ability is not "distinct from sexuality, class, race, gender, and age" but is "always already so complexly intertwined with everything else."[51] Viewing Broadway musicals through the lens of ability highlights connections among and disparities between how marginalized groups have been treated and unfavorably held up to an unrealistic, unachievable norm.

Broadway is professional theatre's biggest mirror of the corporeal standards established by US society as the norm, largely through representation in popular culture. The norm itself is an embodiment of what scholars identify as white supremacist hetero-able patriarchy. In 1963, sociologist Erving Goffman defined the norm as "a young, married, white, urban, northern, heterosexual Protestant father of college education, fully employed, of good complexion, weight and height, and a recent record in sports."[52] Goffman's definition of the norm has retained its grip despite its incongruity with the diverse corporeality of the population (and now cisgender would certainly be included in an updated version of Goffman's norm). Goffman's formulation notes how race, size, sexuality, gender, and ability are themselves implicated in bodily hierarchies. Repetition (or performance) only reiterates the norm, much like it does with gender; this reiteration is how norms self-reinforce and also how this process leads to what disability theorist Robert McRuer terms "compulsory able-bodiedness."

Drawing from Adrienne Rich's theorization of compulsory heterosexuality, McRuer theorizes that able-bodiedness, coupled with heterosexuality, hegemonically produces a structure in which there is a norm and an *other*— "compulsory heterosexuality is contingent on compulsory able-bodiedness and vice versa."[53] Social structures compel actors within them toward normativity, or able-bodied heterosexuality. McRuer and Rich's theorization of compulsory normativity explicates how sociocultural structures regulate bodies and behaviors and "create an imperative to be normal,"[54] while also prompting connections between and among seemingly discrete identity groups since any norm *needs* difference to will itself into being at all.

INTRODUCTION 19

If the norm is a sociocultural construct, it is undeniably physical. Trends in the kinds of normative bodies represented in popular culture are at odds with the reality of the bodies of Americans; the Centers for Disease Control and Prevention characterizes 42% of adults in the United States as obese and notes that one in four adults lives with a disability.[55] Broadway is no different from mass media; for every visible non-conforming body on Broadway, there are scores of bodies that do conform to dominant aesthetic standards. Increasingly fit bodies whipped into shape became the norm on Broadway stages—if not in their auditoriums after 1970. Each identity group studied in *Broadway Bodies* can trace the roots of its stigmatization to the nineteenth century's changing notions of the body, which were tied to labor and physical fitness. The late nineteenth and early twentieth centuries were, not coincidentally, the period when the Broadway musical began to be recognizable as a distinct theatrical form.

Physical fitness thus became an important standard for determining ability (and so did mental fitness, though space precludes addressing that concern in this book). Like all standards, the goalpost shifted according to one's position at the outset. The connection between labor, fitness, and ability informs the questions driving this book's inquiry into casting. In the United States, labor and ability's bond began to firmly coalesce in the nineteenth century as a result of the Industrial Revolution and capital's growing need for specific kinds of laboring bodies. The nineteenth century also saw the concept of the "ideal body" replaced by the "normal body."[56] The subsequent growth, spending power, and leisure time of the middle class meant that meanings attached to bodies and bodily ideals changed profoundly during the next century. Conceptions of ideal bodies increasingly tilted toward thinness in the twentieth century to the point that what the US mainstream once considered average sized became seen as fat in a culture obsessed with weight loss. Physical fitness itself "became more closely linked to notions of virtue, moral purity, and power."[57] As the fit body became the moral body, society deemed the bodies that did not meet these standards amoral.

Fitness can refer to mental or physical abilities, and also to general readiness to perform a task or job, inevitably pointing toward labor. Labor and fitness became tied to specifically American ideas about belonging; as disability scholar Rosemarie Garland-Thomson argues, "Labor, the definitive creed of Puritan through contemporary America, transforms necessity into virtue and equates productive work with moral worth, idleness with depravity."[58] Productive workers become productive consumers; hence, productive citizens form a productive nation.[59] These ideological shifts meant that disability increasingly became viewed through a moralistic lens in early twentieth-century America.[60] Historian Sarah F. Rose describes how "people with disabilities [were rendered] unproductive citizens in the cultural imagination: a concept central to disability policy in the United States during the rest of the twentieth century," and this in turn became a self-perpetuating cycle keeping people with disabilities from full participation in the labor market, and hence, from full participation as citizens.[61] The physically different or impaired body became grounds for exclusion and disablement by society.

The US emphasis on productivity did not take long to have an impact on bodies, and the interchangeability of laborers was key to the process. Davis describes the "industrial mentality that saw workers as interchangeable and therefore sought to create a universal worker whose physical characteristics would be uniform, as would the result of their labors—a uniform product."[62] This mentality evinces itself in the well-oiled machine of a Broadway musical, which requires uniformity from its performing bodies night after night. This uniformity is not necessarily always negative; on the one hand, it is intended to ensure safety and, on the other, offer consistency for audiences no matter which performance they attend. Performing a musical eight times a week is its own kind of Fordist production, demanding machine-like precision of the performers. Performing in a Broadway musical is repetitive work.

If industrialization in the nineteenth and early twentieth centuries set the stage for remarkable changes in bodies, then the economic and labor policies of neoliberal capitalism (from the 1970s on) similarly created new demands with profound results on bodies. *Guardian* writer George Monbiot's concise explanation of neoliberalism's ideology proves helpful on this point. He writes, "Neoliberalism sees competition as the defining characteristic of human relations. It redefines citizens as consumers, whose democratic choices are best exercised by buying and selling, a process that rewards merit and punishes inefficiency."[63] Monbiot notes that it was in the 1970s that neoliberalism, which had been first formulated in the 1930s, began to hold sway. In its emphasis on the relation of personal responsibility to consumption, neoliberalism regulates not just the economy, but bodies increasingly pushed toward efficiency.

Neoliberalism intensely affected views of non-conforming bodies. The explosion of the fitness industry since the 1970s parallels the concurrent quest to reduce body size and eliminate fat. The paradox of the fat body is that it reveals a "bad" individual but a "good" consumer who can "[spend] money on becoming thin."[64] Sociologists Samantha Kwan and Jennifer Graves explain, "Neoliberalism is closely tied to personal responsibility; if individuals are able to make their own choices . . . then they must deal with the consequences of their choices."[65] The ideology of personal responsibility leads to size being perceived as a choice rather than as the resulting confluence of biological, social, and structural factors. Neoliberalism's insistence on privatization shifted both the blame and the burden from structures to individuals, and spending became the answer to all problems. Citizens will ideally choose to spend money on the "right" food and exercise, regulating their bodies by being good consumers (as I will discuss in Chapter 3).

LGBTQ+ communities also bore the impact of neoliberal ideologies, emblematized in the shift from gay liberation to corporatized gay pride. Cultural theorist Lisa Duggan explains that, as a result, "gay civil rights groups have adopted neoliberal rhetoric and corporate decision-making models" that ultimately serve "an increasingly narrow gay, moneyed elite."[66] Subsequently, instead of liberation, gay rights groups fought for assimilation into institutions that actually regulated sexuality instead, like marriage and the military. A contradiction of gay liberation when it came to bodies, though, was the fact that the dominant picture of the gay male body in the 1970s—the muscular, leather or denim-clad clone—was its own regulation of body politics. Gay liberation paradoxically made space for a decidedly conformist body to become dominant. The clones represented the desire for homogeneity from communities stigmatized for their difference and calling the men clones was an insult that harkened to their seeming interchangeability.

Interchangeability itself came to define Broadway musicals beginning in the 1970s, as Broadway became an increasingly powerful and profitable industry that adapted to and adopted neoliberal practices. The Broadway Body is the ultimate neoliberal body. Since musicals now needed to be replicable in order to maximize profits, performers needed to become more interchangeable to get cast. Broadway producers' demand for *more* led to the standardization of the Broadway Body and came at the expense of individuality. Broadway has become more homogenous even though its stars became stars because of the idiosyncrasies. As writer Johnny Oleksinski opined in the *New York Post*, "Physique-obsessed Broadway, too, would likely not make room for a Zero Mostel, Michael Crawford or a Patti LuPone anymore. Lately musculature has been prized above all else on the Great White Way."[67]

22 BROADWAY BODIES

Would anyone dare to tell LuPone or Mostel their bodies were not Broadway Bodies? Broadway stars are permitted difference, but the industry requires conformity from most everyone else.

Coming Out and Identity

The group identities covered in this book coalesced *as identities* in the late nineteenth and early twentieth centuries as a result of their stigmatization, the social process that instates an arbitrary hierarchy based on difference. In *Broadway Bodies*, I am more concerned with the *social* performance of identity and its ensuing categorizations than with identity as a *personal* truth even as one's social performance produces one's lived experience. Identity's meanings are never stable and are always contingent on their historical contexts—think, for instance, of how *queer* once was a slur and now means so much more. The social meanings of and the terms used to describe identity are flexible, not fixed.

Disabled people, d/Deaf people, fat people, and LGBTQ+ people have been oppressed, pathologized, and slated for eradication as a result of the pseudo-scientific eugenics movement since the late 1800s. Central to the fact that these identities often intersect is that eugenicists considered them all "categories of disability" that could be eliminated to shore up white supremacy.[68] In the nineteenth century, eugenicists perverted the mathematical concept of the norm to argue that the errant bodies they called out deviated from the norm. The eugenicist's desire to disqualify centered on the erroneous belief that "the lesser the ability, the lesser the human being."[69] Ability thus became a measuring stick for who counts as human.[70]

Beliefs from the nineteenth century continue to resonate culturally in material ways, from wage gaps to the effects of unconscious bias. A longitudinal study of implicit attitudes published in 2019 showed that bias decreased for sexuality and race and skin-tone, but stayed constant for age, disability, and body weight (which actually saw bias increase).[71] These attitudes show that stigmatization is a social and structural practice displaced onto individual bodies. Garland-Thomson notes, "The problems we confront are not disability, ethnicity, race, class, homosexuality, or gender; they are instead the inequalities, negative attitudes, misrepresentations, and institutional practices that result from the process of stigmatization."[72] The social movements associated with these groups (e.g., the disability rights movement) came together by the 1960s in the United States to combat stigma's corrosive effects. Goffman explains that the concept of stigma itself comes from ancient Greeks, who "originated the term *stigma* to refer to bodily signs designed to expose something unusual and bad about the moral status of the signifier."[73] This way of looking at bodies has proved remarkably durable, and it extends from the body's appearance to its behavior. In other words, bodies communicate meaning by how they act and how they look. Bodies are always performing the work of signifying identity, which is a *doing* as much as a *being*.[74]

Like LGBTQ+ people, d/Deaf and hard of hearing people, disabled people, and fat people all confront the question of whether to come out, which might seem contradictory, since coming out is often about what is secret. Coming out about something that is already audible, tangible, or visible is about claiming individual and collective power through identification.[75] Coming out is a political act, as evinced in the ways that gays and lesbians began to come out in droves to gather political muscle through visibility in the 1970s; other examples include disability scholar Rosemarie Garland-Thomson's description of coming out as a person with a disability, and queer theorist Eve Kosofsky Sedgwick's writing about coming out as fat.[76] Coming out means claiming an identity, even if the identity itself is malleable. No identity category is a monolith, however, even those we lump together in useful though always incomplete categories like "mainstream" or "marginalized" and so on; lived experience is always more complex than categorization allows. *Broadway Bodies* also explores what it means to be American and how the identity categories studied within it have been historically excluded from full participation and incorporation into the United States and the Broadway musical alike.

The embodied identities I study in this book, though, have historically been perceived as changeable, curable, or fixable. If it is hard for some to conceptualize that there is such a thing as an LGBTQ+ body, then consider how that extends to disabled, fat, gendered, and racialized bodies too—which are all social constructs as much as embodied experiences.[77] Debates regarding the changeability, curability, or fixedness of non-conforming bodies persist over cochlear implants for d/Deaf people, the very existence of gay conversion therapy, and the never-ending "war on obesity." Eugenics reappears in new guises, as fat studies scholar Kathleen LeBesco describes how anxiety over "gay" genes and "fat" genes contributes to what she terms the "new consumer eugenics movement aimed at abolishing aberrations [d]eemed

24   BROADWAY BODIES

socially or aesthetically undesirable";[78] technology's ability to detect congenital difference in utero has made this debate especially urgent to disability communities. Eugenics went from fringe pseudo-science to mainstream discourse. Stigma prevents the non-stigmatized from seeing stigmatized people as fully human.[79] Coming out and visibility matter in this environment by paradoxically naming what is already often most visible.

Overview

Questions of gender, race, and ethnicity are already woven into understandings of ability, sexuality, and size and are never far from the surface of this book's inquiries, even if they are not its primary focus.[80] This is the first scholarly book on musicals to situate ability, sexuality, and size together; gender, race, and ethnicity in musicals have each been addressed in previous book-length studies and many articles, typically focused on an identity or approach like Stacy Wolf's lesbian feminist history of Broadway musicals *Changed for Good* or Allen Woll's *Black Musical Theatre from* Coontown *to* Dreamgirls. *Broadway Bodies* builds on the insights in those and other works and aims to provoke new conversations about Broadway's histories. Musicals are my object for exploring body politics because, as Wolf notes, in performance "there's a body there. The struggle over meaning concerns how spectators make sense of that body in the cultural landscape, what that body can mean and to whom."[81] Bodies that sing and dance signify differently from those that simply act; musicals depend on this difference.

Casting is both the lens and the process through which I present the histories of Broadway's body politics that follow. If most of what I write about in these pages never rose to the level of public controversy, then that is my point: by studying what US society and Broadway previously accepted as natural, neutral, or normal, we gain a deeper understanding of contemporary bodily norms. A constant concern of this book is who gets to play whom, and how: Sandahl notes, "Convention dictates which identities are considered acceptable to take on other identities in performance."[82] Musicals intervene in this debate by adopting the use of fat suits, having actors "crip up" to play a disabled character, and by using the casting of straight actors in gay roles as a show's selling point.

Broadway Bodies is thematically organized into four parts centered, respectively, on body politics, size, sexuality, and ability. Each section contains two chapters: one in-depth case study of a specific Broadway musical and its treatment of a specific facet of identity, and a chapter surveying how musicals have historically staged that identity. The academic fields (primarily deaf studies, disability studies, fat studies, and LGBTQ+ studies) forming this book's theoretical basis all emerged after their associated social liberation movements. While these discrete fields initially sought to theorize specific identities, they have all moved toward understanding their inter-relatedness, and disability studies has led the way in this regard; the question of ability informs all of the other fields, and disability is an identity any of us may inhabit.[83]

The first section examines the construction of the Broadway Body and the triple-threat performer. The second looks at casting and size, specifically fat women. The third section focuses on LGBTQ+ representation and its stunning increase in musicals. The final section analyzes deafness and disability in Broadway musicals, questioning the concept of ability itself. While each section's focus is thematic, the book's case studies proceed in chronological order, beginning with *A Chorus Line* (1975) and concluding with Deaf West Theatre's *Spring Awakening* (2015).

Each chapter includes a "Broadway Number" section, so that readers attend to the dynamics of singing and dancing bodies. In these sections, I analyze a specific performance from a Broadway musical in order to discuss, for instance, what it meant when heterosexual *La Cage* star George Hearn performed the gay anthem "I Am What I Am" in a tuxedo rather than in costume on the Tony Awards or how American Sign Language (ASL) and gesture choreograph new modes of musical theatre performance in Deaf West's *Spring Awakening*. I selected each "Broadway Number" for its online availability, and most are from Tony Awards broadcasts, which represents the collision of Broadway and mass culture. The performances speak to what producers deemed acceptable onstage in New York versus in nationwide living rooms and to the ways that mass culture's body politics trickle down to Broadway's. Clips of the Broadway Numbers are all featured on this book's companion website in addition to video clips of many other notable performances and interviews mentioned in the book.

In this history of individuals and the institution of the Broadway musical, I seek neither to celebrate nor condemn those involved but to analyze what happened through the use of archival materials, original interviews, reviews, and scholarship. My own experience as musical theatre performer-turned-scholar gives me an insider-outsider perspective on casting. I've been there, done that, and wrote this book about it.

Musicals make meaning through their embodiment of difference. As *Los Angeles Times* critic Charles McNulty observes, representation matters because "our identities are inextricably bound with the cultural representations that are available to us. Identity is a function of identification, and a narrower range limits the imaginative possibilities."[84] As such, musicals extend the promise of "a place for us" so that you, too, might just feel free to declare "I Am Who I Am." As *Broadway Bodies* makes clear, the Broadway industry profoundly ties an actor's employability to their appearance; when an actor enters the audition room they put their body on the line: do they have a Broadway Body or not? *A Chorus Line*'s "Dance: Ten, Looks: Three" memorably musicalizes this moment when the character Val relates how her appearance prevented her from booking jobs until she had plastic surgery. Suddenly, she was castable.

Casting is exciting because it is dangerous, it is about power, it is sometimes the difference between a hit and a flop, it causes controversy, gives hope, and raises questions. Casting is about visibility. As I was writing this book, I received a text message from a friend who loves Broadway. She related how she and her wife had just seen two Broadway musicals in one day and when she got home that night, she googled "Why are there no fat people in Broadway musicals?" She went on: "God forbid there even be a token chubby or fat person that looks like me." Audiences notice the lack of representation. They see how some bodies get cast while others get cast aside. They notice the stereotypical roles into which Broadway casts marginalized individuals. When identities that cannot be removed are played by actors who can shed them along with their costume, casting perpetuates the power imbalances and discrimination that exist in mainstream society. The old adage about casting that says actors need to "fit the costume" of an existing part to play it speaks to how aesthetic considerations are also financial ones when it comes to casting. Broadway is an business every bit as much as it is the dream of many actors. Casting can and must challenge and upend stereotypes of who "fits"—and where—if parity is to be achieved. If not, perhaps Actors' Equity Association may need to rethink its middle name.

Broadway has serious body issues. It's time to recast whose bodies sing, dance, and act on Broadway.

1

"I Saw What They Were Hiring"

Casting and Recasting *A Chorus Line*

On a cold gray winter day in New York City in 2005, hundreds of dancers stood in line on West 42nd Street waiting to enter an open call for the first Broadway revival of *A Chorus Line*. A casting assistant came out to prepare the dancers for what they were about to face, saying, "We're gonna do a double pirouette. All we're looking at right now is technique and type. And then you're gonna stay or you're gonna go."[1] Once in the audition studio before director Bob Avian and choreographer Baayork Lee, dancers pirouetted their hearts out, but most still summarily ended up back on 42nd Street with the other cut dancers, left to shuffle off to their next auditions and survival jobs. Dancers who stayed learned a short section of the show's opening number before facing another cut. The show's casting procedures had solidified decades earlier once the original 1975 Broadway production had become a runaway hit and its auditions regularly drew hundreds of dancers of varying technique and type. The original ran for fifteen record-breaking years, spawning numerous concurrently running productions necessitating nearly constant recasting. When the show first opened off-Broadway in 1975, *New York Times* critic Clive Barnes gushed, "The conservative word for 'A Chorus Line' might be tremendous, or perhaps terrific."[2] There had simply never been anything quite like it before.

When the original production closed in 1990, talk show host Phil Donahue invited the original cast (minus the understudies) to appear on his popular television talk show, where he explained how type determines casting to viewers at home. He asked, "Are you too fat? Are you too thin? Are you too old? Are your breasts too big or too small? What about your hairline?"[3] *A Chorus Line* deeply embodied these very real questions onstage and off; when a *New York Times* reporter observed auditions for the show, she noted, "A few people were eliminated immediately because they were too old or too short."[4] This book starts with *A Chorus Line* not only because the dancer body became the Broadway Body against which other bodies are measured, but also

Broadway Bodies. Ryan Donovan, Oxford University Press. © Oxford University Press 2023.
DOI: 10.1093/oso/9780197551073.003.0002

28   BROADWAY BODIES

because *A Chorus Line* directly engages with the body politics and identity politics at play in casting Broadway musicals.

A Chorus Line represents an inflection point in the transition from mid-century's so-called Golden Age of Broadway to contemporary musical theatre in look, sound, and subject matter. The show came to represent Broadway itself in the years from 1975 to 1990, when it became Broadway's then-longest running show: a television commercial for New York City's "I Love New York" campaign featured the *Chorus Line* ensemble in their champagne-colored finale costumes, moving downstage in a wedge formation, as a voiceover says, "There's only one Broadway."[5] There may be only one Broadway, but there's also seemingly only one *A Chorus Line* since every major production in New York or on tour in the United States has been a recreation of the original. Because the first cast famously played composite versions of themselves (and each other), both these composites and the original cast's types became templates for reproducing the show. If *A Chorus Line* represented Broadway, the body types onstage came to do so as well.

A Chorus Line cemented the changed role of the dance ensemble in Broadway musicals and had profound impacts not just on the creation and dramaturgy of musicals but also on their economics and their aesthetics, all of which affected casting and the rise of the triple-threat performer as the new paradigm for Broadway performers. This chapter opens by historicizing the shifts from separate choruses of singers and dancers to ensembles full of triple-threats. I then detail *A Chorus Line*'s origins and its treatment of identity, where the show broke new ground in terms of representation with its text emerging from the dancers' life stories. These life stories eventually had to be recast in other performers' bodies, though. Much ink has been spilled on the show's genesis and development in the first workshop process, but there has been less focus on keeping *A Chorus Line* going from 1975 to 1990 on Broadway and since then—and what this meant for Broadway writ large. Finally, I argue that while *A Chorus Line*'s success was a love letter to Broadway dancers, it came with a cost: the musical that was supposed to individuate dancers ended up making them even more interchangeable than before.

The Ensemble from Singers and Dancers to Triple-Threats

If *A Chorus Line* was first and foremost about dance and dancers, it also solidified the industry's demand for triple-threat performers. Before the

CASTING AND RECASTING *A CHORUS LINE* 29

triple-threat, there were simply dancers or singers.[6] Throughout most of the first seven decades of the twentieth century, Broadway musicals had separate choruses—dancers didn't have to sing and singers didn't have to dance, and neither really had to act. *A Chorus Line* original cast member Baayork Lee contends that her fellow original castmates "were the major players in the forming of the triple-threat." She went on to explain, "It wasn't there before us singing, dancing and acting. There were other shows such as *Hair* before us and *Oklahoma!* had dancers and they had singers, and everything was divided. But when it came to *A Chorus Line*, we were the first to have no stars. Everybody's name was in alphabetical order. . . . We were required to sing, dance, and act."[7] Prior to *A Chorus Line*, dancers did not typically have lines to speak since these went to the singers. Despite being lower in the hierarchy of musicals than singers and actors, dancers—and dance itself—drove innovations in earlier landmark musicals like *Oklahoma!* and *West Side Story*. If dance transformed musical theatre dramaturgy, triple-threat performers revolutionized both the *shows* and the *business*. And, as Lee says, "Producers loved it."

A Chorus Line was the culmination of danced dramaturgical innovations begun decades earlier. One much-noted inflection point was Agnes de Mille's dream ballet in *Oklahoma!* (1943), "Laurey Makes Up Her Mind," widely credited by critics and scholars as being central to the so-called integrated musical because of how de Mille used dance to express character and advance plot. *Oklahoma!* relied on separate singing and dancing choruses and double cast the principal roles in the ballet, meaning that Dream Laurey was not the same performer who acted and sang Laurey in the rest of the musical. De Mille's casting of the dancers was an important part of how she changed Broadway musicals. As dance historian and choreographer Liza Gennaro explains, "De Mille's dances expanded the parameters of the libretto and disrupted the Broadway casting blueprint by knocking the iconic chorus girl, a patriarchal fabrication of female beauty and allure, off her pedestal. . . . De Mille caused an ideological shift in the function of dance on Broadway."[8] De Mille's dancers were *individuals* within an ensemble, and "she added characters that would link all of her dance numbers to one another and serve a particular function," but since these characters existed only in choreography, they don't exist in the published script.[9] Jerome Robbins drew from de Mille's methods when he created *West Side Story* (1957), where dance, in addition to the show's subject matter and presentation, proved pivotal to its dramaturgy.

30 BROADWAY BODIES

While it is overly simplistic to argue that any one show or one person changed everything, *West Side Story* was in many ways the result and the beneficiary of the changes in Broadway musicals following *Oklahoma!* The rise of the singular director-choreographer cannot be overlooked, but it too did not lead to immediate change in casting and/or dramaturgy. Though the consolidation of jobs happened on both sides of the footlights, it was an offstage innovation first. De Mille was the first to serve in both capacities for *Allegro* (1947) and she retained the conventional separation of singers and dancers. Musicals without much dancing regularly designated their chorus the *ensemble* as opposed to *dancer* or *singer* (as musicals like *Guys and Dolls* [1950] did). *Wonderful Town* (1953) listed ensemble members according to their role in the show, "Greenwich Villager," rather than their primary talent. The more dancing a show contained, the more likely it was to categorize dancers separately in the *Playbill*, e.g., in a musical like *Kismet* (1953), choreographed by Jack Cole. *The Pajama Game* (1954), choreographed by Bob Fosse and supervised by Robbins, separately classified dancers and singers. *House of Flowers* (1954) featured noted dancers Alvin Ailey, Carmen de Lavallade, and Arthur Mitchell in choreography by Herbert Ross and Geoffrey Holder but did not separate by primary talent and identified its ensemble members as "townspeople." There was not a hard and fast rule every production followed. When there was one ensemble as opposed to separate ensembles of dancers and singers, it tended to be smaller. The precedent of consolidating the ensemble had been set even in the years before *West Side Story*, and if this was not yet a consistent practice it was on its way to becoming one.

Not coincidentally, the ensemble is where the majority of jobs in Broadway musicals lie and the place that most highly demands body conformity in the twenty-first century. *West Side Story* cast one ensemble of performers who played one role for the entire show, doing all of the acting, dancing, and singing—including the principals, who danced the "Somewhere" dream ballet themselves, marking a shift from *Oklahoma!*'s double casting of its dream ballet. *West Side Story* was not the first musical to use its ensemble this way, but it was the one that shifted the paradigm.[10] Dance was the skill that tipped the scales toward triple-threats becoming the new norm in Broadway choruses. Hiring triple-threat performers carried economic implications since producers could now hire fewer performers for each show.[11] The creation of the triple-threat performer is thus directly tied to economic and labor concerns as well as artistic ones—hiring fewer performers who could

CASTING AND RECASTING *A CHORUS LINE* 31

do more meant musicals could have smaller casts and staging could be more flexible.

Even musicals without dancers per se participated in this aesthetic and economic consolidation. *Company* (1970) featured no ensemble and only one dancer (Donna McKechnie) and every member of the company performed dual functions as soloist and chorus throughout. Bob Fosse's production of *Pippin* (1972) further cemented the changed role of the chorus and marked another turning point. Fosse biographer Kevin Winkler notes, "Three years before *A Chorus Line* listed dancers' names on lobby cards and select advertisements, *Pippin* initiated the practice, a breakthrough that gave chorus performers a higher profile than ever before."[12] Numerous members of *Pippin*'s ensemble have spoken about how Fosse "used dancers as individuals rather than as anonymous members of an ensemble."[13] If this was not entirely an innovation by this time, it was still something of a rarity. Not all 1970s musicals conformed to the new trend—*Purlie* (1970), for instance, still had separate singing and dancing ensembles.

The path toward triple-threats becoming the norm was clear, though. Underlying the increasing dominance of the triple-threat lies an ableism that glorifies extraordinary ability. Triple-threats must be *hyper*-able, not merely proficient but excellent actors, dancers, and singers who can cover principal roles while performing eight shows a week in the ensemble and maintaining a fit body. Since the 1970s, the ideology of hyper-ability has increasingly been taken to extremes, which reflects increased competition for jobs in the always ultra-competitive Broadway labor market. It is not uncommon to have more than 500 performers audition for fewer than ten available spots in the ensemble. In the 1970s, amid New York City's economic downturn, Broadway and New York were in trouble and the familiar refrain that "Broadway was dying" suddenly seemed more of an actual possibility. Dancers worried that they would be the first to go under and they were tired of being seen as anonymous automatons, easily exploited and walked all over. And when Broadway dancer Michon Peacock had had enough, she decided to do something about it.

"I Really Need This Job": *A Chorus Line*'s Meta-theatricality

Peacock had just finished a particularly bruising run in a flop, *Rachael Lily Rosenbloom (And Don't You Ever Forget It)*, that made it to Broadway but

32   BROADWAY BODIES

closed in previews in December 1973. When Peacock reached out to its choreographer, Tony Stevens, the seed for what became *A Chorus Line* was planted. Many Broadway dancers did not view the early 1970s as a great time to be a Broadway dancer even though Bennett and Fosse, among others, were still alive and active. A yearlong run was then considered healthy for most musicals. Long-running smash hits were rare, and even those were closing with more frequency in the early 1970s, including *Cabaret*; *Fiddler on the Roof*; *Hello, Dolly!*; *Mame*; *Man of La Mancha*; and *Promises, Promises*—all of which closed by the end of 1972. A few musicals of the era like *Pippin* and *Grease* (1972) did have lengthy runs, but most shows ran for only a season or two or flopped quickly. Revivals were not yet the box office hits they would later become. All of these factors translated into less regular work for dancers.

Dancers were needed for musicals that centered on nostalgia like *No, No Nanette* (1971), *Follies* (1971), and *Over Here!* (1974), but new musicals like *Company* and other Sondheim musicals did not need trained dancers. The economics of Broadway were changing, and fewer musicals opened than in prior decades: sixteen musicals opened in 1964 versus just eleven in 1974. Broadway wasn't dying, but it was shrinking, and this squeeze was keenly felt by dancers.[14] Bennett later explained that this is why dancers were willing to participate at all in the workshops that ultimately produced *A Chorus Line*: "The thing is, in 1974, there wasn't other work. If there'd been work, they wouldn't have been at the Shakespeare Festival for $100 a week. No one's that noble."[15] Dancers *really did* need that job.

The workshops only began after Peacock and Stevens mentioned to Bennett their ideas for gathering and discussing the issues facing dancers.[16] Peacock and Stevens discussed forming a company of dancers who would produce their own work as a way to ensure that dancers had jobs first of all and then that choreographers were valued contributors, too. *A Chorus Line* biographer Denny Martin Flinn explains, "This dancers' repertory company seemed like a viable way to avoid the ridiculous ineptitude under which they so often suffered."[17] Not only was *A Chorus Line* sparked by the idea that dancers needed more opportunities to work, it was created out of their personal lives—their identities as dancers, as Puerto Rican, as gay, as adult children of divorced parents, and so on. A late-night rap session-cum-group therapy followed Peacock and Steven's meeting with Bennett, which gave him ideas about how to reconcile his nascent concept for a show about dancers with what Peacock and Stevens were proposing. The tapes of these

CASTING AND RECASTING *A CHORUS LINE*   33

rap sessions became the raw material from which *A Chorus Line* was fashioned into a musical during its workshops by co-choreographer Bob Avian, Bennett, co-librettist Nicholas Dante, composer Marvin Hamlisch, co-librettist James Kirkwood, lyricist Edward Kleban, with an uncredited assist by playwright Neil Simon. Along the way, though, Peacock and Stevens both left for positions working with Fosse on *Chicago*, which seemed more of a sure thing than whatever these workshops might produce. Over the series of workshops at off-Broadway's The Public Theater, the show came together and opened there in April 1975.[18] It was an overnight sensation and transferred to Broadway that summer.

A Chorus Line is a quintessential backstage musical. Its setting and concept also make it a prototypical metatheatrical musical, too: a musical about an audition for a musical was unusual even in a form populated by backstage shows like *Gypsy*. The concept is simple: at an audition, dancers vie for eight spots in the chorus, "four boys, four girls" in the show's lingo. At the audition, the director of this musical, Zach, alternately bullies, cajoles, and coaxes the dancers into revealing their life stories (this is how the material from the taped rap sessions figured in). Seventeen dancers make it past the first cut in the opening number ("I Hope I Get It"), which gives a whiff of authenticity to what is decidedly a non-realistic take on the audition process. Though this is supposed to be the final callback of a big Broadway musical, the cut dancers never would have made it that far, especially Vicki (who has no ballet training) or Lois (who can *only* dance ballet). Additionally, we never hear the dancers sing anything at this audition that is not part of an inner monologue until late in the show. Yet realism isn't the point, which here is that the first cut raises the stakes for the dancers and the audience. However, *A Chorus Line* never reveals anything about the show the dancers are auditioning for beyond the fact that Zach is looking to hire four men and four women adept at multiple styles of dance. That the musical they are auditioning for is so generic it is rarely mentioned is also part of *A Chorus Line*'s point: the dancers and their bodies are what remain visible and specific. The dancers *perform* their specific individual differences for Zach and for each other as they tread the line between conformity and individuality.

The musical progresses through a series of solos and ensemble numbers in which each member of the line is given a spot to shine, if only for a moment. The dancers' shared life stories progress chronologically, beginning in childhood (Mike's "I Can Do That" and Sheila, Bebe, and Maggie's "At the Ballet"), then charting their way through adolescence (the company's "Hello Twelve,

34 BROADWAY BODIES

Hello Thirteen, Hello Love" and Diana's "Nothing"), and culminating in adulthood (Cassie's "The Music and the Mirror"). The show notably explores the concept of what kinds of bodies are seen on Broadway in Val's "Dance: Ten, Looks: Three" (pictured in Figure 1.1). Body type is specifically tied to employability: Val says, "But, after a while I caught on. I mean, I had eyes.... I saw what they were hiring."[19] [Clip 1.2] When the original cast reunited on his talk show, Donahue artfully described Val's song as "the lament of a talented young woman who wanted to be thought of as more than just a body."[20] Val had plastic surgery in order to make her body conform to contemporary dominant sexist standards of beauty so that producers and casting directors would recognize her talent, which she suggests her plainness previously masked. The upbeat tempo and jaunty melody are at odds with the experiences described in her song and the sad truths underlying them. This song encapsulates the body politics performers contend with in the industry.

Since *A Chorus Line* is about an audition, it builds toward the final cut where Zach will select the eight dancers for his show. Just before this cut can happen, Paul injures himself learning one of the dance combinations and must receive medical attention, giving up his chance at the job. This prompts the dancers to reflect poignantly on the brevity of their chosen careers ("What

Figure 1.1 Pamela Blair performing "Dance: Ten, Looks: Three" in a scene from the Broadway musical *A Chorus Line* (New York). 1975. Credit: Martha Swope. © The New York Public Library for the Performing Arts.

CASTING AND RECASTING *A CHORUS LINE*   35

I Did for Love"). Zach begins to make his selections and asks six dancers to step forward, allowing them and the audience to think for a second that they have been chosen. When Zach dismisses them instead, the remaining eight dancers and the audience both realize who has booked the job. There is a blackout and when the lights come up again, it is for the finale/bows ("One"), heartbreak swiftly followed by celebration. *A Chorus Line*'s structure is somewhat circular: the show's narrative opens with Zach's first cut and it ends with the final one.

Broadway Number: "I Hope I Get It"

A Chorus Line begins in the middle of an audition for an unnamed Broadway musical. The opening number, "I Hope I Get It," artfully stages its examination of casting and identity. Lights come up on a group of dancers facing upstage, using the mirrors there to pick up the audition combination.[a] Director-choreographer Zach drills them as he studies how each dancer moves. The dancers appear hesitant as they learn the steps and make mistakes as they go, standing out for an arm akimbo or being a beat behind. No one is in unison yet; they are all distinctly individuals even if they are still anonymous. This sequence gives audiences the perspective of what it is like to stand at the back of the room in a dance call. Zach instructs the dancers to do the combination facing away from the mirrors. [Clip 1.2] The dancers suddenly turn downstage, and, as the audience sees their faces for the first time, the orchestra kicks in (heretofore only a piano had been playing) and the combination brings one of Broadway's most thrilling sequences to life.

Zach counts out "5, 6, 7, 8" and the hopefuls dance the jazz combination we have just seen them learning. The show's audition situation is highly compressed and unrealistic, and the deception begins with the "5, 6, 7, 8" since the music is not in a 4/4 signature, but a 6/8, meaning that the dancers should really be counted in with "4, 5, 6." Additionally, neither of the combinations that the dancers learn here has anything to do with the style of the show for which they are auditioning, which we learn later is more of a 1930s style. The jazz combination's choreography is low to the ground, muscular, awkward to perform, and difficult—it is designed to weed out those without

36 BROADWAY BODIES

technique. Its style is very 1970s and matches the dancers' lithe bodies well. This is followed by a ballet combination, which is different for the men and the women. At this point, it starts to become clear that Zach knows some dancers better than others, since he refers to some by name (Diana) and some by items of clothing ("boy in the head-band"). The dancers begin to sing "I Hope I Get It" as Zach gives corrections to some dancers, and the song expresses their internal dialogue, anxieties, and hopes during the audition. The lyrics show how the dancers' inner feelings contradict the need to outwardly project confidence in the audition. The dancers perform the jazz and ballet combinations in groups of six, allowing audiences their first chance to start watching and evaluating certain dancers more closely. Some dancers don't pick up the choreography's nuance, some don't have ballet technique, others fall out of their turns—this almost feels like a real audition, especially when Zach begins to choose which dancers will continue on to the next round.

Zach makes the first cut, calling out the dancers by the numbers on their audition cards, winnowing the group down to just seventeen dancers. This cut dramatizes the moment when some dancers' dreams get to live on while others are dashed short. The cut dancers register their disappointment, grab their dance bags, and exit the stage. The remaining dancers gather their headshots from their dance bags and come downstage when suddenly there's a blackout. The lights come up with the dancers standing toe to toe on the white line across the front of the stage, holding their headshots in front of their faces. This moment emblematizes the paradox of *A Chorus Line*: there's the version of the dancer on the headshot and then there's the real person behind the show business smile on the 8 × 10. And to further complicate matters, there's the real person on whom the role was based. Zach's first cut builds to this moment since the audition itself is a demonstration of who can figure out the correct balance between being themselves and being what Zach wants. And this is the contradiction of being a performer that *A Chorus Line* profoundly exploits as the dancers ask, "Who am I anyway?"

[a] This analysis is based on the show's segment on the 1976 Tony Awards. MrPoochSmooch, "A Chorus Line 1976 Tony Awards."

"Who Am I Anyway?" Identities on the *Line*

A Chorus Line is the ur-Broadway musical of this book for many reasons, the foremost of which is that it is a musical about casting a Broadway show but also, crucially, it is about how the performance of identity informs the casting process both within the narrative and the production, too. *A Chorus Line* broke new ground in 1975 with its onstage frankness about and inclusion of racial, ethnic, and sexual minorities all within the same narrative—the vast majority of musicals up to that point had been mostly white-cast musicals—apart from the heyday of Black musicals in the 1920s and the few Black musicals of the 1970s (*Purlie* [1970], *Ain't Supposed to Die a Natural Death* [1971], *Don't Bother Me, I Can't Cope* [1972], *Raisin* [1973], and *The Wiz* [1975]). If in the 1970s it was possible to see an all-Black cast of a previously all-white cast musical like *Hello, Dolly!* or *Guys and Dolls* on Broadway, that was then considered progress by some observers and participants at the time because Broadway had been segregated for the better part of its history (though others felt all-Black shows were perhaps just as segregating as all-white ones).

On top of its notable addressing of racial and ethnic identities, *A Chorus Line* also notably tackled then-taboo subjects. Lee explains that the mid 1970s were a time "when nobody talked about being homosexual onstage or being molested onstage or a father being alcoholic."[21] These were new subjects for a Broadway musical and it used humor *and* pathos to address these taboos. Since *A Chorus Line*'s original cast was performing versions of their own life stories and/or those of their fellow cast members, there was more than a soupçon of authenticity that the show could never again regain. When casting the 2006 Broadway revival, Lee quipped, "Do I get a chance to say who I want to play my life?"[22] In the original production, everyone had to audition—even to play the show's version of their life story. Original cast member Wayne Cilento later recalled, "The strange thing about it was that people walked into that room and auditioned for their life and didn't get it. They walked out of that room not getting the part."[23]

But even those in the original cast were not exactly playing their own lives because many roles were composites of several dancers' stories. Richie's story, for instance, was not original cast member Ron Dennis's life but largely that of Tony Stevens. Dennis joined the line only after Candy Brown decided not to continue with the workshops in order to join Fosse's *Chicago*, and

38 BROADWAY BODIES

here the show's inclusion of and casual indifference toward race played out as Bennett replaced one Black dancer with another, although of a different gender. Dennis's experience of joining the musical later in its development and not having his life story incorporated into it, coupled with being the only Black performer on the line, informed his feelings about the show and led him to quip that the show was about "A Group of White Dancers."[24] On the other hand, Dennis later noted that his casting at all was remarkable, saying, "When I came to New York in 1964, the dancers of color being hired for Broadway were all fair skinned so they could blend in. When I started getting roles as a darker-skinned dancer, and being short on top of it, it was a radical new thing at the time."[25]

A Chorus Line attended to race and ethnicity in ways that had not yet been done in Broadway musicals—especially those by white creators—and this was due to the direct involvement of the dancers represented. This involvement allowed glimpses into how dancers like Priscilla Lopez, who played Diana, experienced their racial and ethnic identities in the United States. In Diana's story, the show examined what it meant to be a Puerto Rican student at the High School of Performing Arts; in Connie's story the audience learns about her wish to be a prima ballerina but winding up in The King and I, implicitly commenting on racist boundaries in show business. Dennis's pointed joke was true—Broadway shows were mostly white. In addition to Dennis as Ritchie, the show and the original cast also featured three other roles but only two other performers of color: Lee and Lopez (who are Asian American and Latinx, respectively) played versions of themselves in the show, and both had previously appeared in several shows for Bennett. Lee later noted that "short Orientals were not being hired either" in response to Dennis's comments about how his dark skin kept him from being cast (Lee herself had appeared in ten Broadway shows prior to A Chorus Line, sometimes as the only Asian American cast member).[26] Lee's solo moment came in the "Hello, Twelve, Hello Thirteen" montage and is called "Four Foot Ten." Her song and dialogue are about being short and feeling left behind as an adolescent while everyone else grew taller. When the cast was on Donahue, a studio audience member asked Lee, "How did a short lady like you ever get to be such a successful dancer? I understand you're all supposed to be tall and slim."[27] Lee gamely responded that she had played a lot of kids in her career, but also that Bennett cast her when others didn't, whether in platform shoes in Seesaw or as a dancing receptionist in Promises, Promises. While Lee's height precluded her from being a showgirl type, it allowed her to find

CASTING AND RECASTING *A CHORUS LINE* 39

work even if the work was limited by the industry's inability to let go of type and stereotype. Even though she began her Broadway career as Orientalized "Asian" characters in Rodgers and Hammerstein musicals like *The King and I* and *Flower Drum Song*, Lee's presence challenged Broadway's status quo for both Asian American performers and short dancers.

An initially overlooked aspect of the show's importance is that co-librettist Nicholas Dante's contribution helped create "the first Latino crossover theatrical piece on the Great White Way."[28] The experience former dancer-turned-writer Dante shared at the first rap session in 1974 became Paul's monologue. He would later feel that he was allowed to continue to write the musical despite his lack of experience as a professional writer only because Bennett needed that monologue. Paul's story was crucial to the show's success, in addition to its groundbreaking portrayal of a gay Latinx man. But were some of these Latinx characters simply tokens, as some have argued?[29] Some critics find *A Chorus Line*'s minority representation affirmative while others find it tokenizing; perhaps it is both at once. Theatre scholar David Román notes that the show actually challenged stereotypes: "It is also worth mentioning that [Diana] was not a mother, daughter, or wife either, that she was not represented as playing any of the conventional roles that Latinas are imagined to occupy within Latino culture. The fact that Morales is an actor is central to the point."[30] Scholar Warren Hoffman counters that the show promotes "a vision that is both utopic in imagining a theatrical landscape that did not yet exist and naïve in its ability to consider the ways in which the real world's engagement with race shaped hiring practices, including on Broadway."[31] Though there had been other somewhat multi-racial Broadway musical casts earlier in the 1970s—including shows that the dancers of *A Chorus Line* had performed in—*A Chorus Line* produced new conditions of casting even as it itself was produced by existing conditions.

In *A Chorus Line*, whiteness remains unmarked while the Asian American, Black, and Puerto Rican characters perform their racial and ethnic identities. Hoffman argues, "Race and ethnicity become equal and flattened out in *A Chorus Line*; racial difference is treated no differently from any other kind of difference."[32] But neither Sheila nor Cassie, for instance, ever speak about being white in the ways that the non-white characters speak about themselves. The show's treatment of race was in line with mainstream 1970s politics of multi-culturalism, and it was a Broadway musical, not experimental theatre whose radical politics could be assumed. Given that the show was written using the words and stories of the original cast, remixed by Bennett,

Dante, and Kirkwood, it becomes tough to disentangle the dancers' self-presentations from how the writers shaped these into a musical, even more so given the cast's involvement in the workshop process. *A Chorus Line* ultimately acknowledges class, race, ethnicity, gender, and sexuality without entirely essentializing them; in the end, everyone is presented as both a dancer *and* as a member of an identity group. If the show's treatment of race can seem stuck in 1975, its depiction of gay men remains remarkable—and offers at once a time capsule of the mid-1970s and a reminder that the closet and homophobia continue to exist.

In addition to the way the character of Paul advanced more complex Latinx representation, Dante made strides for gay representation by representing him as "credible, humane, and courageous in his act of coming out." Dante's involvement ensured "that gay people be represented in an authentic way, and that gay theater be a source of self-respect, empowerment, and pride."[33] While the other gay characters, Bobby and Greg, are largely comic relief, Paul carries the musical's dramatic weight and marked a groundbreaking turning point in Broadway's representation of gay men because Paul is not a comic figure. *A Chorus Line*'s emotional peak comes not in song or dance but in Paul's monologue—and how Zach comforts Paul after he breaks down by coming to the stage and putting his arms around him; the physical intimacy between a straight man and a gay man was groundbreaking in the 1970s. Dante came to see this moment's importance, later observing, "I think the whole show hangs on that monologue and I'm thrilled with it. I think now it paved the way for *Torch Song Trilogy* and other gay material that reached Broadway."[34]

Dante later recalled that at the first rap session he was unsure about sharing his story, saying, "But something told me that this was a very important evening and that I really had to do this. It was the story of what a tortured life I'd had as an effeminate young man; how I was forced to quit school and because everybody made fun of me."[35] In the musical, Paul injures himself dancing just after delivering the monologue, dashing his hopes for getting cast by Zach and perhaps curtailing his dancing days, too. Dante "was annoyed that it had to be the gay character who also had the accident. I thought, 'Why does it always have to be the poor fucking gay character?' But we found out it had to be Paul."[36] Dramaturgically speaking, Paul has just broken the audience's collective hearts in his monologue, which made them more invested in his success and thus more devasted by his injury. In 1974, Dante was making the shift from being a dancer to a writer and decided he didn't want to be in the show, though he later played the role on tour in the mid-1980s. Dante's Latinx heritage has been largely overlooked in terms of its importance to *A*

Chorus Line—in no small part because representing homosexuality was a bigger taboo at the time. Perhaps Dante's identity was obscured because of Broadway's then-common casting practices: a white performer originated the role of Paul.

New Jersey–born Italian American Sammy Williams (pictured in Figure 1.2) won the Tony Award for his performance as Paul. Williams, too, did not play his own story in the musical—Wayne Cilento's character, Mike, was based on Williams.[37] But when Williams returned to the Broadway cast in

Figure 1.2 Sammy Williams (*right*) in a scene from the Broadway musical *A Chorus Line* (New York). 1975. Credit: Martha Swope. ©The New York Public Library for the Performing Arts.

42   BROADWAY BODIES

1983 for a two-year stint, he called attention to the musical's slippage with identity, noting, "Originally, we were those characters we played. The people now are acting what we were."[38] Of course, Williams never *was* Paul, but his rhetoric around the difference between the originals and their replacements was echoed by nearly every member of the original cast. Identity informed the roles from the start.

Williams's casting presented Paul's racial and ethnic identity in brownface (albeit without makeup). This kind of racial miscasting had been standard practice on Broadway, especially after *West Side Story* (Broadway's other dance musical notably about Puerto Ricans). In major productions, Paul has not always been played by an actor of Puerto Rican or Latinx descent; for example, the 2006 revival featured Asian American Jason Tam as Paul. Paul's sexuality has trumped his Puerto Rican identity in many productions, leading to multiple instances of brownface casting. According to theatre scholar Alberto Sandoval-Sánchez: "Paul's gayness is inscribed on the body of the actor Sammy Williams, who originated the role: his thinness, softness, and effeminate gestures were all signs that stereotypically confirmed his sexuality."[39] *A Chorus Line* needed to feature gay male characters to maintain its authenticity since there were a lot of gay male dancers in Broadway choruses. If, as Sandoval-Sánchez contends, gayness was inscribed on the body, it was in performance that the actor's body signified sexuality.

However, on the show's closing, original cast member Thommie Walsh contended that the show also "showed that the male dancer could be virile and masculine. It ended the image of the male dancer as a queer."[40] Making dancing safer for straight men was not quite the challenge to heterosexism at the time that humanizing gay men was, and the association between dance and gay men remains as strong as ever. When the show was revived in 2006, there was concern among the creative team over whether Paul's monologue would still land with audiences. Lee, who recreated Bennett's choreography, explained that director Avian was unsure since "people used to walk out on Sammy Williams and cough through his whole monologue and men would just get up and leave." But in the revival, she recalled, "you could hear a pin drop during Paul's monologue," noting that audiences had caught up with the show. Lee noted the bigger impact of the musical, saying, "So many people came out of the closet after *A Chorus Line*. That is an important movement that we helped: men coming out of the closet and admitting to their parents that they were gay and living their lives."[41]

CASTING AND RECASTING *A CHORUS LINE* 43

If *A Chorus Line* was a landmark in the Broadway musical's representation of identity and difference, the way it ultimately subsumed the dancers' hard-fought individuality in its finale challenged audiences. The finale has proved to be a point of contention, misunderstanding, and misrecognition of what *A Chorus Line* ultimately means. "One" can be read at once as the finale of *A Chorus Line*, the bows for its performers, and a fantasy-cum-dream number from the unnamed musical that the dancers have been auditioning for all evening (though "One" cannot be understood as a real performance of that musical because Zach makes clear that only eight dancers will be hired and "One" features the entire line). [Clip 1.3] Bennett wanted the number to mirror *A Chorus Line*'s paradox: that the dancers distinguish themselves as individuals during the show only to become anonymous members of an ensemble in the end. Bennett intended it "to be the most horrifying moment you will ever experience in a theatre."[42] The horror dissolves though, overshadowed by the celebratory feeling created by Bennett and Avian's choreography and the sight of everyone decked out in Theoni V. Aldredge's champagne-colored costumes. Perhaps the truly horrifying moment occurs just before "One" when Zach makes the final cut, and the reality of casting's harshness hit home. But it is overly simplistic to view the finale only as horrifying or as triumphant. Audiences want the dancers to get the job as much as they themselves want it. Musical theatre scholar Millie Taylor extends this to note that it "includes the ironic fact that a lyric about individuality, 'One,' is performed by a unified group."[43] Many, Bennett included, understood the song as the culmination of the entire musical since the dancers willingly shed their individuality to become part of an interchangeable group. What was the point of getting to know the dancers individually just to have them all disappear into a mass? Theatre journalist Ken Mandelbaum concurred, writing, "The sad irony is that these dancers who we now know are special are kicking their way into musical-comedy oblivion."[44]

Is achieving a spot in the chorus worth giving up their individuality? Musical theatre scholar Bruce Kirle contends that the dancers "fight for assimilation into insider status by ultimately losing their identities."[45] Kirle's suggestion that the characters lose their identities is provocative, but why wouldn't it also apply to any role in any musical? On a primary level, acting enacts a separation from one's self even as it also presents a heightened version of the actor. Yet casting foregrounds acting as a site of power relations because casting paradoxically makes identity *more* visible. If actors are praised for "disappearing into the role," it is only because something is understood or presumed about the actor's own identity. *A Chorus Line* blurred these lines. The insider status suggested by Kirle is actually that of being a working dancer, no small achievement. After all, the entire reason *A Chorus Line* exists at all was because Peacock and Stevens dreamed of creating work for dancers. Dancing is presented as a choice and a sacrifice on the *Line*, but one done for love above all.

Dancing in and as an ensemble is pleasurable, and ideally, the whole adds up to more than the sum of its parts. In a fame-obsessed culture, the possibility that the dancers actually did this for love was viewed by some as unrealistic. Kirle forecloses the possibility that identity may actually be liberated by performance in *A Chorus Line*. It is not assimilation the dancers are ultimately after but simply a job, albeit one that clearly reinforces their sense of identity *as dancers*. Though Kirle claims the musical espouses "not an egalitarian ideal but a demand for mediocrity," his view of the skill it takes to cohere as an ensemble is frankly insulting. Framing the original cast's success in terms of whether they achieved stardom also misses the point; Bennett biographer Kevin Kelly fell into this trap, writing, "The only star to emerge from *A Chorus Line* was Michael Bennett. The rest—with the occasionally flitting exception of Donna McKechnie—have been trapped in the chorus, frozen figures circling an endless strut beneath the pendulum of an endless clock."[46] Apart from being untrue (some went on to Tony Award–winning careers as actors while others left the business altogether and made an impact elsewhere), implying that the dancers were failures or less-than in some way because they did not achieve stardom admits a deep misunderstanding of what and who *A Chorus Line* stood for.[47] Cassie, the show's almost-star, expresses this perfectly when she tells Zach that she'd be honored to dance in the chorus.

Bennett and Avian's staging brilliantly invites the audience to experience the dancers' collective triumph in the finale as the stage mirrors reflect the musical's message to its spectators. Taylor eloquently describes this moment: "The focus of the mirrors on the audience extends that gaze so that audiences see themselves as individuals *and* as part of a larger cohort."[48] Broadway's final Cassie, Laurie Gamache, told an interviewer, "It's a metaphor about America. It's about being part of a team. It's not about seeking individual glory."[49] Broadway's second Cassie, Ann Reinking, echoed Cassie's sentiment, in her oft-repeated adage, "You're special, but so is everybody else." *A Chorus Line*'s message is suggested in its finale, embodying the motto of the United States itself, *E pluribis unum*: out of many, one.[50] However, "one" does not mean a level playing field but might be the hellscape of a never-ending audition for a position in an un-named, unseen, as yet unproduced and unrealized musical called *America*, with its attendant inequities covered in sequins, song, and dance.

Casting and Recasting the Line

If *A Chorus Line* was about getting the job, performing in it could some-times still feel like an audition itself. Initially, Bennett kept the dancers on edge by choosing different dancers each night to get cut at the end of the show. Lee recalls that "he used to stand behind Bob LuPone and whoever danced the hardest, they would get the job and every night was somebody different. And so we worked our asses off to get the job." This worked until the wardrobe mistress told Bennett this was wreaking havoc backstage for the dressers frantically trying to get the dancers back onstage for the finale.[51] Even once the cut dancers were set, the tense, audition-like atmosphere remained. Original cast member Pamela Blair later recollected, "I felt like literally every night we were auditioning for our jobs."[52] Bennett's occasional unannounced presence backstage and in the house would suddenly raise the stakes for the performers. Bennett "would often show up in town, see a per-formance, and rehearse the company in preparation for its next opening. He would not hesitate to fire dancers whose work he was dissatisfied with, or move dancers around from company to company for balance."[53] This uncer-tainty was a tool Bennett used to keep the show fresh and the dancers from getting too comfortable. Like Jerome Robbins before him, Bennett notori-ously used psychological manipulation to get the performance he wanted. At early auditions for replacements, Bennett sometimes made the auditions resemble the one depicted in the show, asking one dancer, "How did your family feel about your being in theater?"[54] The show's meta-theatricality created a self-reinforcing strange loop.

A Chorus Line needed constant recasting once its production team saw clearly that it was going to run a long time. This meant company after com-pany and replacement after replacement. The irony of the musical's emphasis on individuality is not so much that "one" erased the individual dancers, but rather that the continuous recasting of the show in the mold of the original performers did. The original production's replacements were not cast this way initially, though. For instance, Reinking's body and dancing couldn't

46 BROADWAY BODIES

have been more different from her predecessor, Donna McKechnie. In fact, one of the first auditions for replacements and understudies in June 1975 sought "all types of dancers who can sing well" rather than specifying types in its casting notice.[55] Bennett began to go into audition overdrive to keep up with the demand for new companies, and he and Avian and Lee "traveled to a dozen major cities, held cattle call after cattle call, and built up their files."[56] Just a year into its long Broadway run, the show had become such a phenomenon that the *New York Times* called *A Chorus Line* "an industry," and indeed it was swiftly on its way to one.[57] By January 1976, casting was under way for the new New York, Los Angeles, and Toronto companies, which began "with an open call in N.Y. early in January, followed by auditions in Los Angeles, San Francisco, Las Vegas and possibly Chicago" according to *Variety*.[58] By November 1976, auditions were being held in Australia and New York for the show's Australian premiere. *A Chorus Line* was now an industry, with multiple revenue-generating centers from merchandise to ticket sales, none of which would have been possible without workers—in this case, dancers.

As the number of companies proliferated, the casting procedures became more codified, as did restaging the show on new bodies. Auditions for the show began to follow a standard format: dancers first do a time step and a double pirouette, and if they make the cut then they learn jazz and ballet combinations from the opening number.[59] The first cut was an easy way to type out dancers whose appearance was deemed wrong, those who clearly didn't possess enough dance technique to meet the demands of the choreography, and it was also a way of saving everyone's time. Since auditions for the show attracted so many dancers, weeding through them needed efficiency and speed.

Despite the show's emphasis on individuality, type mattered when it came to recasting and restaging. Theatre scholar Victor Holtcamp perceptively explains, "They cast the same show again, and again, and again. To make this possible the specific stories of the original dancers had to be abstracted and condensed into character types that could then be reliably filled."[60] He notes that this required "its own scientific system" that led to the successful replication of the original.[61] Recasting the show was not only about the importance of type or even the original dancer, but it was also economic—fitting into existing costumes meant new ones did not have to be constructed for each new replacement. *A Chorus Line*'s success demonstrates how aesthetic choices on Broadway have economic implications in (and for) the long run.

CASTING AND RECASTING *A CHORUS LINE* 47

Multiple companies of *A Chorus Line* playing simultaneously made the dancers actually interchangeable, and this increasingly became a commonplace feature of the industry. *A Chorus Line* understudy Fraser Ellis later explained how this worked in practice: "Anyone who knew the role could come into the show, never having rehearsed with that company, and just go on. There was never any traffic; they had it down to a science. . . . There were charts for each character, grids showing you where to go."[62] This practice became typical of later musicals whether they had replica productions or not; dance captains and stage managers take detailed notes in rehearsals long before they know whether their show will be a hit. The point of replica productions is not to veer too far from the original. This was purposeful because, as Lee explains, Bennett wanted audiences everywhere to feel "they were seeing the show on Broadway."[63]

A Chorus Line's success and replicability came with a human cost, however. The cast noted that they started to feel like cogs in a vast machine. Michael Serrecchia, an understudy in the original cast, felt that "we were more and more becoming part of a mega-money-making machine."[64] Replacement performer Janet Wong recalled original cast member Thommie Walsh telling her, "Welcome to the Factory," when she joined the company.[65] If the production had the feel of a factory for dancers (who were its interchangeable parts), those in charge shouldered the burden of keeping those parts moving. General manager Bob Kamlot explained, "The most difficult thing during the run of the show was the revolving door, the constant replacement [of] performers."[66] McKechnie noted the newness of the situation wrought by success, saying, "When *A Chorus Line* became such a big hit, there had been no precedent set for how to maintain."[67] Even Bennett, who was getting rich from the show, reportedly told Tommy Tune that he didn't relish another big hit: "It means you have this company and that company and that company, and you eat and live and breathe it. You have to balance them all and keep them all up. It's a terrible responsibility."[68]

The machine-like nature of the production in part resulted from the need to systematize the staging to meet the demands of keeping the companies up and running, as Bennett pointed out. At one point, to ensure uniformity, the production brought together dance captains from various productions and went through the show step by step in a kind of bootcamp. Once Bennett and Avian moved on to other productions and became less involved in the day-to-day operations, the tension between individuality and conformity reached a head. Initially, the show could still be reasonably tailored to suit new cast

48   BROADWAY BODIES

members because the creative team was still taking a hands-on approach. As the show ran and ran (and sadly outlived Bennett and too many others), this tailoring became impractical and eventually impossible. The original cast's idiosyncrasy paradoxically determined their replicability. Broadway dance captain Troy Garza later said, "The main problems we had in New York were when people on the road had been directed by Joe Nelson and he had been cloning them, telling them, 'You must do this gesture here.' "[69] On Broadway, though, Garza allowed some individual variation.

The ultimate irony of *A Chorus Line*'s success is that for all its celebration of individuality, the demand to capitalize on its success led to practices of replicating facsimiles of originals who could never really be replicated or reproduced. Its approach to replica productions provided a blueprint for the megamusicals of the 1980s as they proliferated around the world. As musicologist Jake Johnson laments, "Musical theater largely has moved away from the iconic in favor of the fabricated."[70] *A Chorus Line* had played twenty-four countries by the time the Broadway production closed in 1990.[71] The scale of *A Chorus Line*'s national and global proliferation made it one of the most reproduced productions to that time. "The show became a giant university, in which a skilled team found the talent, trained it, and moved performers up from understudy to small role to larger role, and from tour to Broadway."[72] The *Line* became part university, part industry. While the mass production of the show had its downsides, it must be emphasized that the show employed a lot of dancers: as the *New York Times* reported, "In a period of worldwide unemployment, 'A Chorus Line' may soon be the world's biggest mass employer of dancers."[73] The musical was born of a desire to give dancers steady work, and it achieved that thousands of times over. Holtcamp argues that the show's onstage "audition isn't to determine the best actor or dancer. It's to find the best worker."[74] And, to an extent, that was true of casting *A Chorus Line* as well. But above all, *A Chorus Line*'s unprecedented success was born from love of dance and dancers. It was about giving dancers the chance to dance and bringing Broadway to audiences the world over.

Consensus does not exist among those who cast the show and those who performed in it when it comes to duplicating the original cast—and given the sheer number of personnel who worked on its multiple productions, consensus is indeed likely impossible. Co-choreographer Avian later said, "Casting always is the biggest challenge. Just finding those people and trying not to duplicate the original cast. The roles, however, are very specific. They corner you in terms of their age and ethnicity and it's difficult to

CASTING AND RECASTING *A CHORUS LINE* 49

veer too much."[75] The efforts not to simply duplicate the originals were met by the demands of reproducing the original continuously from 1975 to 1990 and then again in numerous tours and in twenty-first-century revivals on Broadway in 2006 and at New York City Center in 2018. While Avian felt he tried not to simply copy the originals, Lee describes her approach differently. She explains, "Michael Bennett handed me the torch to pass on. My job was to honor the original book and choreography and lighting. And so that was my job. And well, because I was one of the authors, it was . . . my honor to pass that on."[76] Lee notes that her job is to honor the dancers with whom she co-created the show and those whose life stories are portrayed. She made a promise to "honor everything that [they] have contributed to the show." Viewed in this light, casting is not about only adherence to a type or a mold but is also a way of paying tribute to the real people who bared their souls for this show.

The original cast, despite not becoming stars, became the standard against which critics and some audiences measured the show's replacements. The original cast became standard-bearers for the musical's original staging and meaning, too. Many, like Lee, went on to restage the show numerous times while others returned to the production as performers throughout its original run. When original cast members returned to the Broadway production, they found it changed. Procedures had been put in place to maintain the show and keep some semblance of what the original was. If Bennett's style of directing might best be described as "Method," years later the show was being run by dance captains and stage managers who took more of a paint-by-numbers approach. Laurie Gamache, Broadway's final Cassie, recalled, "Management was very specific. They said your hand goes up here, you go like this, you run over here, you do this. But they never told me how or why. They never gave me specific motivations. I had to do that myself."[77] McKechnie observed that when she returned to play Cassie in 1986, she "saw they weren't really doing Michael's choreography. They were doing a sort of half-assed version of it. And I couldn't really blame the dancers. It's just that over time, things got diffused."[78] Cilento rejoined the line, too, and noted, "They started telling me that my legs were too high, to put my legs down, and I said no. That's when the friction started happening. They were trying to clean the show and they were making everyone a machine."[79] The originals returned to find copies of their colleagues, facsimiles of what the show had been. For the originals, the show was their lives and their bodies

Figure 1.3 Chorus lined up on stage for 2nd New York call of the stage production *A Chorus Line*, medium shot. 1976. Credit: Martha Swope. © The New York Public Library for the Performing Arts.

its material, while for the replacements (pictured in Figure 1.3), it was a steady job and their bodies the machinery that kept it going.

Though they were not the parts they played in all cases, the original cast was imprinted on them, which was a sticking point for critics later on. Reviewing a replacement cast, critic Martin Gottfried in *New York Post* decried, "*A Chorus Line* is not what it was. . . . Instead of being selected for appropriateness to a part, replacements seem to be chosen in an effort to physically duplicate the original cast member."[80] In the *New York Times*, Clive Barnes also noted something similar about the first replacement cast, writing, "If I had one fault to find with the present production, it would simply be that the present performers and performances are possibly too closely modeled on the originals, often to actual physical types."[81] Some roles adhered more closely to this than others, while roles like Zach and Cassie could have more leeway.

Because *A Chorus Line* is about casting, the process of casting and recasting it attracted attention particularly since its origins determined recasting the show, as well as the meta-theatricality of casting the musical about casting a musical—a typical line from an article in the *New York Times* about this process proclaimed, "It was life imitating art imitating life."[82] The show depicts the pitiless reality of casting Broadway musicals and did not spare those cast on the line. *A Chorus Line*'s basis in heightened reality led to Lee's quip that "we were the first reality show because we played ourselves."[83] The show's 2006 Broadway revival inspired a behind-the-scenes documentary, *Every Little Step*, that captured the actual heartbreak and elation of dancers auditioning for, getting cut, and getting hired for that production. The documentary also captured a newly flexible approach to casting the white characters in the show; as noted earlier, the non-white characters had long been troublesomely cast with more flexibility.

When the show was revived in New York in 2006 [Clip 1.4] and 2018 (restaged by Avian and Lee), the casting breakdowns were more detailed in terms of character than in terms of body type than for the original production. This shift toward greater detail reflects more about how the industry had changed in response to social shifts than anything about casting *A Chorus Line*. Apart from the roles where race is specified (Connie, Diana, Paul, and Richie), the only nods to physical characteristics were for Connie ("must be no taller than 5'3"") and Judy ("tall and thin").[84] The types were set by this point, and if they veered from the original, it was to cast more inclusively and imaginatively so that the production wasn't just "a group of white dancers" onstage—in the 2006 revival, Deidre Goodwin played Sheila, the first Black dancer to do so on Broadway; in 2018, AAPI actor J. Elaine Marcos, who had played Connie several times in her career was cast as Val this time (making her the rare actor to play both roles). These instances are few, but they reflect the creative team's desire to keep the musical grounded in 1975 while also staying abreast of contemporary casting and social norms.

Dancers' Bodies on the Line

The dancers from *A Chorus Line*'s original workshops signed away the rights to their life stories for $1, and not all of them even ended up getting cast in the eventual show. Both of these facts caused hard feelings, especially when the show became enormously profitable for its authors. Cilento later said, "We were the authors of the show, and we should have been paid accordingly."[85] Bennett reached an agreement with the dancers to share 0.5% of the show's revenue between them, a share of his royalties and related income. In the end, it did not make any of the dancers rich. Even though the show came to exist in order to create work for and on a specific group of dancers, the original cast never received meaningful financial compensation considering how much profit their lives made for others. Their bodies *were* the line, literally and metaphorically. In addition to signing their life stories away for only $1, the original cast signed away their likenesses, too.

Their bodies were the show's logo, featured on merchandise from T-shirts to beach towels to posters. The dancers' bodies became quite literally iconic symbols of the musical. In this way, *A Chorus Line*'s logo and merchandise mirrored the show's finale by presenting an anonymous line made up of individuals. You could wear the dancers' bodies even if you didn't have a dancer's body. Theatre journalist Robert Viagas explained that the dancers' bodies stood out on Broadway because they were young—they were not the middle-aged bodies of typical Broadway protagonists like Dolly Levi and Tevye.[86] *A Chorus Line* capitalized on this in its "body-hugging outfits." "The audience came away thinking, I want to look like that. I want to get in shape," Viagas noted.[87]

As their bodies circled the world on the show's logo, the roles the original cast played continued to follow them to the point that, when given the chance, they took care to distance the characters from their selves. On *Donahue* in 1990, both McKechnie and Blair mentioned that the roles they originated were not wholly based on their respective lives, with Blair pointedly noting that she did not have plastic surgery like Val.[88] Even though the show nodded to body modification in the 1970s, it could not have predicted how prescient Val's story would go on to become, especially on Broadway. A sea change occurred between 1975 and the twenty-first century, especially when it comes to dancers' bodies, which have become increasingly toned and sculpted. Lean and lithe bodies were out, muscular ones were in. The original production helped, in part, to spark to 1970s and 1980s leotard-centric fashion and fitness trends in the United States—dancer bodies were aspirational bodies for mainstream culture. This was the era when the dance-based workout Jazzercise was popularized, setting the stage for later boutique fitness operations like SoulCycle and Barry's BootCamp.[89] Jazzercise, like later ballet barre-based workouts, was born from dance aesthetics and dance technique and further helped cement the entanglement of dance, fitness, and body culture. Even *A Chorus Line* replacement Reinking was part of the trend with her book *The Dancer's Workout*.

When *A Chorus Line* was revived in 2006 and 2018, dancers' bodies and their training were quite different from what they had been in 1975. In the 1970s, dance training was still mostly classically based with emphasis placed

CASTING AND RECASTING *A CHORUS LINE* 53

more on aesthetics and expression than virtuosity. Beginning in the 1980s, dancers often grew up participating in dance competitions as students; learning attention-getting tricks and striving for ideal bodies began to be important. Dance technique increasingly became more about who could do five pirouettes on both sides and kick their face rather than who could tell a story with their body—in order to be competitive, one had to be fierce. Avian viewed the changes positively, noting, "The quality of the dancing is much higher than it was when we made it. Also, then you had the singing chorus, or a dancing chorus; it was hard to get people who could do everything really well, and now that is the norm."[90]

To meet the demands of a brutally competitive labor market, dancers have to be more fit and toned, strong vocalists, and act well enough to understudy speaking roles. Many also enter the industry now with four years of conservatory training in musical theatre BFA programs under their belts. BFA programs were new in the 1970s, and their explosive growth paralleled the years of *A Chorus Line*'s record-breaking Broadway run. The physical demands of the industry changed in response to this training, and the bodies available to the industry have also changed in kind. If fitness culture produced a homogenized look, Broadway dancers have contributed to it. Lee notes that dancers of her generation "did not go to the gym to pump up, and we did not go to have abs. The costumes [for *A Chorus Line*] have had to be let out, expanded and . . . the bodies have totally changed because the requirements are different. Roles are more athletic."[91] Increasingly more skills need to be concentrated in one performer's body (sometimes even the ability to play an instrument) for that person to gain employment, and this has led to homogenization and loss of individuality from the dancers' bodies to their voices—compare the distinctively individual voices on the original cast album to the very polished but homogenous sounds of the 2006 revival cast album. The trend toward homogeneity may begin in BFA programs, but these programs respond to the demands of the industry as much as they precipitate them. *A Chorus Line* is in some respects both a cause and an effect of these trends in training and the bodies produced as a result.

A Chorus Line was built on the quirks of its original cast, not all of whom were polished singers or actors of great depth or even the most technically proficient dancers—it really *was* a collection of idiosyncratic individuals. Its success paradoxically created the conditions for the erasure of that very individuality, evinced by the dominance of the triple-threat. Would any of the dancers in the original cast make the cut today? Many probably would not, which is less a judgment of their talent than a reflection of how drastically industry casting norms have changed. In its way, the show predicted how the business would become more pitiless when it comes to bodies. As Michael Bennett said, "We very carefully considered who would get the job. It's not arbitrary at all. The tall people get the job. Good-looking people get the job. People who haven't been personality problems all evening get the job, if you notice."[92] Bennett's comments foreshadowed both the on- and off-stage conflict of his next Broadway hit, *Dreamgirls*. In the chapters that follow, I reframe Val's questions from "Dance: Ten; Looks: Three" to ask you, reader: Have you caught on? Have you seen what they were hiring?

PART II
SIZE

2

Dreamgirls, Size, and the Body Politics of Padding

A few times a generation, the meeting of an actor and a character in a musical creates something truly magical. Jennifer Holliday's legendary performance as Effie White in *Dreamgirls* (1981) was one such occasion. She won the Tony Award for her performance, but Effie was the first, and as of this writing, and *only* role that Holliday ever originated in a new Broadway musical. Since *Dreamgirls*, Holliday has only appeared as a replacement in supporting roles in Broadway revivals. What happened? Holliday's career serves as a touchstone for how Broadway casts fat women and the narrow range of representation the industry's gatekeepers permit Black women to embody in musicals.[1] Being a fat Black woman is less a kind of triple-threat than it is a triple whammy on Broadway, and each of these three facets of identity (size, race, and gender) over-determined Holliday's career to an extent along with her critical reception. For comparison, consider that Holliday's size led critics of *Dreamgirls* to de-emphasize her character's sexuality, while mere months later, they hailed white actor Kathi Moss in *Nine* (1982) as "the earthy fat lady" afforded a "tambourine-shaking tarantella" celebrating her sexuality.[2] Like Holliday, Moss stopped the show using her big voice, but unlike Holliday, Moss's body and voice did not become part of the show's legend and neither did they become open targets of scorn and derision from the press or the show's creatives.

It is always open season on fat people. Body shaming, fat phobia, and fat stigma run rampant in the United States. This chapter opens with a discussion of size in this country and how casting Broadway musicals reiterates dominant attitudes toward all fat women, and fat Black women in particular. I then trace the multiple and conflicting narratives around Holliday's casting and performance as Effie and how her presence continues to loom over the role even when it's played by another actor. *Dreamgirls* will never leave Holliday as much as Holliday can never leave *Dreamgirls*, but the show did go on after Holliday left, and the chapter's final sections highlight how

Broadway Bodies. Ryan Donovan, Oxford University Press. © Oxford University Press 2023.
DOI: 10.1093/oso/9780197551073.003.0003

casting and recasting Effie became the locus for a myriad of labor issues. Broadway musicals, even ostensibly fat-positive ones, are complicit in labor practices that prolong fat stigma at the same time they enforce gendered and racialized stereotypes of size—often including racist, sexist, and fat phobic representations. The onstage and offstage narratives of *Dreamgirls* demonstrate how Broadway musicals and US society reify the structural inequalities that regulate gender, race, and size. Broadway is a battleground for body politics, and it demands that fat ladies sing.

Dreamgirls examines the look and sound of the American dream and the costs of achieving it. It epitomizes the backstage musical as it tells the story of a 1960s girl group The Dreamettes (loosely based on real-life group The Supremes),[3] made up of lead singer Effie White and backup singers Deena Jones and Lorell Robinson (shown in Figure 2.1). The musical centers on the conflict wrought by a change in the group's lineup when the smaller-voiced and thinner-bodied Deena replaces Effie as lead singer. The Dreams' manager Curtis considered Deena more conventionally attractive and more in line with what he felt white mainstream audiences wanted. Effie protests,

Figure 2.1 *Dreamgirls* (Imperial Theatre, December 20, 1981–August 11, 1985). Music by Henry Krieger. Book by Tom Eyen. Lyrics by Tom Eyen. Shown: Jennifer Holliday, Sheryl Lee Ralph, Loretta Devine. Credit: Photofest.

"Nobody can see her on a record!"[4] Curtis also swaps his romantic allegiance from Effie to Deena shortly thereafter. After being replaced in the group (now called The Dreams), Effie expresses her pain in one of Broadway's most thrilling first act finales, "And I Am Telling You I'm Not Going." In the second act, Deena's star rises while Effie struggles to remain afloat. Curtis quashes Effie's comeback single and this, coupled with the revelation that Effie was pregnant with Curtis's child at the end of Act I (unbeknownst to him and Deena), drives the second act. The musical concludes at the farewell performance of The Dreams, which turns into a reunion performance when they invite Effie to sing with them one last time.

Dreamgirls explores themes tied to racial capitalism (defined by legal scholar Nancy Leong as "the process of deriving social and economic value from the racial identity of another person")[5] and the politics of "selling out" and "crossing over." Deena sold out and achieved crossover appeal while Effie was left nearly abject; the aesthetics of thinness and whiteness triumph over those of fatness and Blackness. *Dreamgirls'* onstage narrative resonates more than most musicals with its offstage body politics. Critic Bonnie Allen's stinging critique in *Essence* magazine lays bare a cruel irony of the economic consequences of the very racial capitalism the show itself sought to critique: "They done taken our blues and gone to a place where we can't afford to hear them. Maybe that's the ultimate form of crossover."[6] The show's conflicts center on gender and race in and beyond the music industry, and, crucially, body size—which became quite a vexing issue when it came to casting and recasting Effie White. Casting Effie represents a synecdoche for the spaces in which Broadway and the United States itself permit fat Black women's presence.

Recasting Size in the United States

People typically deploy *fat* as an insult, and using the word can initially be discomfiting. In order to neutralize the stigma associated with the word, activists and scholars have reclaimed and repurposed it, since "seemingly well-meaning euphemisms like 'heavy,' 'plump,' 'husky,' and so forth put a falsely positive spin on a negative view of fatness."[7] Casting notices and critics' reviews are littered with these euphemisms. *Hairspray* star Marissa Jaret Winokur even kept a record of how the media described her body when she was starring as Tracy Turnblad on Broadway; these included "'chubby,'

60 SIZE

'hefty,' 'dumpling-shaped,' 'dimple-kneed.'" She noted, "People don't want to say the word 'fat.'"[8] [Clip 2.1] The press's evasiveness admits the discomfort around discussing size, which in turn leads to further avoidance of acknowledging how US society marginalizes fat people. It remains common to hear fat pathologized in medical terminology like *morbidly obese*. The United States government itself has been responsible for the "war on obesity," along with funding medical research advancing the prospect of fat as pathological, all of which "has caused and reinforced the treatment of fat people as second class citizens."[9]

Whether in the latest fitness trends, news reports about the so-called obesity epidemic, or the plethora of fad diets, weight is one of the central ways US culture attends to bodies. Fatness has, in part, historically determined who fits where in society and what kind of labor one's body does or does not do.[10] Many of the roots of fat stigma can be traced to the nineteenth century and the growing industrialization and urbanization of America.[11] Fatness went from being a sign of wealth to a sign of excess, self-indulgence, laziness, and moral failure as its meaning underwent a class change: because "it became possible for people of modest means to become plump, being fat was no longer a sign of prestige."[12] Upper-class women in turn began to lose weight to avoid association with working-class bodies. The ties between class, gender, and size only became stronger as decades passed and fat stigma eventually materialized in twenty-first-century wage penalties: even just being perceived as overweight (a truly indeterminate term) meant a woman could earn $9,000 less per year than thinner women.[13] This is a vicious cycle: anti-fat attitudes lead to fat women who earn less being pressured to spend more to weigh less.

Anti-fat prejudice persists as a class issue intimately connected to race. It should be no surprise that fat stigma finds many of its roots in the pseudo-science of eugenics, popular at the turn of the twentieth century. Eugenicists equated the pursuit of a fit body with the dominance and survival of the white race.[14] The concept of the racialized fat body developed alongside the subjugation and enslavement of African people beginning in the seventeenth century and met its match in eugenics. Fear of fat and fear of Blackness became intermingled by the twentieth century. Sociologist Sabrina Strings argues that "fatness became stigmatized as both black and sinful" as a result of nineteenth- and twentieth-century moralistic attitudes that became the foundation for the treatment of Black Americans, regardless of body size, that continues unabated in the twenty-first century.[15] Strings concludes that "the fear of the black body was integral to the creation of the slender aesthetic among fashionable white Americans."[16] Fear of fatness was tied to anti-Blackness.

Thinness itself became another "form of American exceptionalism" imbricated in whiteness.[17] Stigmatization fed by racism and classism led to a vicious cycle of exclusion that economically penalizes Black Americans, further compounded by misogyny (or misogynoir—the hatred of Black women—in this case). The cost of being Black, fat, and a woman is material—the wage penalty just for being a Black woman in the United States means that for every dollar a white man earns, a Black woman earns just $0.64.[18] If Black women's labor is clearly devalued in this country, so then are their laboring bodies.

The notion that thin, conforming bodies are the most valued, economically speaking and otherwise, is tied to whiteness.[19] Sociologist Tressie McMillan Cottom explains, "Economic and political conditions produce a white hegemonic body as the ultimate expression of beauty."[20] Body aesthetics are always gendered and, in the United States, "most girls are taught—that we should be slender and small. We should not take up space. We should be seen and not heard, and if we are seen, we should be pleasing to men, acceptable to society."[21] The combination of the aesthetic and economic value placed on gender and race led to what theorist bell hooks terms "a devaluation of black womanhood that permeated the psyches of all Americans and shaped the social status of all black women once slavery ended."[22] This devaluation continues to inform how Black women and their bodies are treated in representation and in reality.

US American culture and media position fat as needing elimination. In response to what sociologists Samantha Kwan and Jennifer Graves call the "fashion-beauty complex," which proposes that "unwieldy, loose, and jiggly fat must be tamed," thin and toned bodies gain moral superiority over fat ones.[23] Advertising exhorts all women to purchase products that help achieve thinness, and this ties into whiteness as a determining factor. Fat women and girls learn that society considers their bodies unfeminine and undesirable. This stigma determines everything from how fat women are represented to how and where they work. Fat women experience more stigma and employment discrimination than fat men, due to purposefully unachievable (yet always able to be purchased) standards of beauty for women.[24] *New York Times* columnist Lindy West notes the material effects of being unvalued: "As a fat woman, my body is also lampooned, openly reviled, and associated with moral and intellectual failure. My body limits my job prospects, access

62 SIZE

to medical care and fair trials, and—the one thing Hollywood movies and Internet trolls most agree on—my ability to be loved."[25]

Fat is notable for its visibility, which raises the paradox among fat people of feeling invisible. Fat studies scholar Kathleen LeBesco explains how "fat, unlike gender, *is* written on the body for *all* to see."[26] Fat stigma, too, rests on a paradox of visibility, because it makes certain bodies invisible due to the very visible attributes that stigmatize them—fat people may be stared at and also ignored. Activists and scholars have banded together to combat fat stigma by naming the structures that enable it. Fat liberation never punctured mainstream consciousness quite like gay liberation or the civil rights movement, although it emerged in the same era. Like disability rights advocates, fat liberationists recognized that fat is an identity that cuts across all bodies and vectors of identity. Fat liberation is feminist and intersectional and recognizes that fat "is also a queer issue, and a racialized issue, and an issue of class."[27]

Fat liberation encourages people to come out as fat just like one can come out as lesbian. Coming out as fat harnesses language's inherent power and uses it to reclaim one's identity from stigma. Lack of representation most clearly articulates the devaluation of fat people, which underlines the systemic, structural nature of the value placed on the minority rule of thin, fit bodies. Fat becomes stigmatized because society perceives it as something that a person can put on or take off at will, something that one *can* control but does not; the social psychology of stigma indicates that " 'visibility' and 'controllability' are the most important dimensions of stigma."[28] In other words, fat people's perceived inability to control their appetites shirks the mandate of personal responsibility that undergirds neoliberal capitalism.[29] Sociologists Kwan and Graves explain that neoliberalism becomes enacted on and through the body because "the body is a domain of personal responsibility."[30] Society equates fat with personal failure, since, in this view, the fat person's inability to control their behaviors and appetites reveals their inability to conform to dominant body aesthetics, too.[31]

Fat studies emerged from the fat liberation movement and embraces its radical stance toward the mainstream.[32] The discipline of fat studies analyzes how fat stigma extends beyond moral judgments to how fat people, especially fat women, are denied full participation in US society. Scholars and fat liberation activists fight back against "how, in the United States, the bearer of a fat body is marked as a failed citizen, inasmuch as her powers as a worker, shopper, and racially 'desirable' subject are called into question."[33] Being a fat woman in the United States means having one's subjectivity itself questioned.

Broadway and Body Shame

Fat people experience oppression as a result of pervasive anti-fat attitudes, or fat stigma, that have profound effects on nearly all facets of their lives from uncomfortable seats at theatres and airplanes to receiving stares and slurs in public. Fat stigma's relationship to the labor practice of casting raises many questions as a result: How do fat female bodies fit into socioeconomic and representational systems that stigmatize them, especially the closed economy of Broadway musicals? How are fat bodies gendered, racialized, and sexualized in musicals? How do Broadway musicals paradoxically normalize *and* stigmatize these bodies in performance through the use of fat suits, and in reception via critical responses? Broadway's body issues reflect broader structural patterns of discrimination in the United States since in Broadway musicals themselves, "the defining issue is who counts as American, and how that matters."[34] In other words, *who* is represented onstage and *how* they are represented determines their status as an American onstage and off. One way of understanding musicals is as fundamentally about assimilation into US American values since "there are outsiders who need to be converted, assimilated, or accepted into the group."[35] Given how fat bodies are marked and how musicals attempt to define who counts as American, where does this leave fat bodies on Broadway, and especially fat Black women's bodies?

The casting of Broadway musicals demonstrates that *some* bodies are deemed superior to others. The language used to discuss casting reinforces the relationship between body type and visibility: we speak of "getting seen" for roles and whether or not one "is the right fit," which means that some bodies are *not* seen and do *not* fit. Broadway traffics in stereotypes, and actors are often bluntly told they aren't "the right fit" because of their appearance. While there are numerous subjective factors that go into casting, the fact remains that fat phobia is often a primary barrier to employment. Nearly all leading roles are typically cast with bodies that conform to social imperatives for thinness, even when the script or character description does not mention weight. Broadway has never cast a fat Cinderella, Nellie Forbush, or Eliza Doolittle even though nothing about these roles inherently requires thinness. To cast a fat woman in one of these leads would be to admit that fat women have been denied the full range of representations commonly available to thin people.[36]

Consider the fact that *Dreamgirls* and *Hairspray* are the *only* hit Broadway musicals of the past forty years in which fatness is *sometimes* a prerequisite for playing the female lead. These musicals center the tangled relationship between body size, gender, music, race, and representation; *Dreamgirls* is about which bodies get to make music on television and onstage, while *Hairspray* is about which bodies get to dance to that music on television—essentially, which bodies are considered thin and white enough to be seen on TV. *Dreamgirls* theatricalizes these body politics when the thinner, vocally lighter Deena Jones becomes a successful pop star but not the bigger bodied, bigger voiced Effie White. Audiences carry into the theatre with them the knowledge of who society deems beautiful and "the notion that fat and beauty are antithetical."[37] Broadway allows fat women to be powerful but rarely beautiful, let alone sexy.

Effie White and Tracy Turnblad have become iconic roles not only because they are star-making parts but also because their visibility as leading roles available to fat women underscores how the characters' narrative arcs are tied to fat visibility itself. These roles uniquely give a fat woman the chance to play a full range of emotions and emerge as something other than a victim. Marisha Wallace, who played Effie in the 2017 West End production of *Dreamgirls*, knows that Effie is a rarity. She observed, "As a Black woman ... you never get a full arc, you only get a caricature." She also noted that it was "kind of nice to do all of those things in one show," which prompted her to ask, "Why aren't there more roles like this?"[38] Broadway places Black women in double binds. Musical theatre scholar Stacy Wolf's observation that musicals punish women in their narratives but celebrate them in performance applies doubly here, since Black women often have agency in performance through their bodies that does not exist in the text or the narrative.[39] Performance scholar Daphne Brooks explains, "Black women's bodies continue to bear the gross insult and burden of spectacular (representational) exploitation."[40] Performance can shore up or destabilize this burden through the body of "the performer who, through gestures and speech ... is able to confound and disrupt conventional constructions of the racialized and gendered body."[41] Yet even a musical like *The Wiz* (1975)—as expressive of Black joy as Broadway gets—includes its own kind of fat phobia; its villain Evillene is fat. The Lion even refers to her as "your fatness" at one point, drawing a swift rejoinder out of Evillene just before Dorothy throws a bucket of water on her and sends her to an end, eradicating her fat, and thus villainous, body.

Musicals' narratives typically constrain Black women and confine them to proscribed roles—even the title role in *Caroline, or Change* is a domestic worker (the precise kind of role the industry has historically limited Black women to playing); yet Caroline is also a powerhouse of a role that sits right next to Effie and *Gypsy*'s Rose in terms of the virtuosity required: the body in performance permits momentary liberation from the confines of the character and her social status. But when a musical ends, audiences must consider what its song and dance are advancing or effacing. Who remains unseen in certain roles reveals the ones dominant culture excludes as a matter of course. In an industry where appearance matters for employability, Black women are held to bodily standards of beauty determined by whiteness. The aesthetic standards set by whiteness and imposed on all bodies invert how the very form of the Broadway musical itself depends on Black aesthetics of song and dance (especially jazz sounds and moves); since these too have been whitewashed for mainstream audiences, it makes a perverse sense that the bodies onstage are subjected to similar processes. For evidence that the casting of Broadway musicals reproduces aesthetic values from the dominant culture, one need look no further than *Hairspray*; since it opened in 2002, fewer than twenty musicals (excluding revues) have opened with Black women in the leading role; size and race compound the lack of available roles.[42] More than 250 musicals opened after *Hairspray* before the pandemic closed Broadway.

When a fat female actor walks into an audition, sociocultural expectations and stigmatizing structures accompany her. While all actors are often told they aren't the "right fit" because of their appearance, fat women confront assumptions about what counts as fat, too: a casting director told one actor I interviewed, "You're not fat enough to be our fat girl."[43] The language in casting breakdowns guides actors to self-select which roles appear appropriate for them. Gender, height, race, and weight requirements narrow the pool even further on top of vocal range and dancing ability. Casting notices for the 2016 City Center Encores! production of *The Golden Apple* repeatedly stated, "We are not looking for heavy character actresses."[44] When it comes to size and casting, Broadway continues to rely on outdated and narrow notions of body type. Casting necessarily remains an inherently fraught and subjective labor practice, the consequences of which extend beyond simply who gets the part. Being discriminating in casting falls under the umbrella of creative license, yet the lack of opportunities for fat actors reveals that weight-based discrimination is and has been so widespread on Broadway that the industry accepts it not just as natural but as neutral. Broadway has decided which bodies are allowed to play which roles. This series of decisions not only

66   SIZE

reveals failures in the casting process but also belies the Broadway musical's vision of itself as an even somewhat inclusive institution.

Yet fat women's increasing visibility in theatre combats structural inequality because representations inform not just how fat people feel about themselves but also their own sense of possibility. Considered in light of the fact that "more than two-thirds of American women [are] classified as overweight or obese," it becomes more galling that body type plays such an outsized role in casting.[45] Despite the vague and sometimes indeterminate meanings of "overweight" and "obese" and their pathologizing implications, the majority of women in the United States could claim fat as an identity. Fat bodies are statistically the most common American kind of body to inhabit and yet simultaneously the most un-American.

Broadway Number: "And I Am Telling You I'm Not Going"

Though it lost the Best Musical Tony Award to Tommy Tune's production of *Nine*, *Dreamgirls* had staying power. Michael Bennett's original Broadway production of *Dreamgirls* opened on December 20, 1981, and played 1,521 performances. Henry Krieger's score is a pastiche of 1960s and 1970s soul, pop, and disco sounds. Tom Eyen's book and lyrics support the nearly sung-through musical's rapid narrative development. Eyen was also originally directing the show before Bennett took the reins. Bennett, co-choreographer Michael Peters, Eyen, and Krieger ensured that the pace of the musical was fast and furious. *Dreamgirls* depends in large part on its casting: who plays Effie makes or breaks the production. Audiences and critics alike want to see whether her "And I Am Telling You . . ." lives up to Jennifer Holliday's iconic performance in the original cast.[a]

The first act of *Dreamgirls* culminates in one of the Broadway musical's most iconic songs: "And I Am Telling You I'm Not Going," Effie's *cri de coeur*. The song fits into the musical's mostly sung-through dramaturgy and grows out of the recitative-heavy "It's All Over," the confrontation between Effie, the Dreams, and Curtis. "Fat" is Curtis's ultimate insult to Effie as he swiftly dumps her and kicks her out of the group at once [Clip 2.2]:

CURTIS
EFFIE, PLEASE! STOP EXCUSING YOURSELF

YOU'VE BEEN LATE, YOU'VE BEEN MEAN
AND GETTING FATTER ALL THE TIME.[b]

Curtis and Effie are left alone in the dressing room when Effie launches into "And I Am Telling You . . ." In Bennett's staging (as seen on the production's Tony Awards performance), they stand about ten feet apart as Holliday begins to sing. Holliday's stillness emphasizes her vocal and facial expressiveness, with her face wearing the mask of tragedy. She takes a few halting steps toward Ben Harney as Curtis as she begins the next verse, raising her arms as if to embrace him, her voice becoming full-throated and accented with her signature gospel-inflected growls. She reaches Harney and begins to stroke his hair. He stands unmoving and rigid.

Holliday as Effie changes tactics as her emotions develop; she moves from caressing him to backing away in anger and hurt as she sings, "I'm not waking up tomorrow morning and finding that there's nobody there." She rocks side to side, spreading her arms wide as she approaches Curtis again. He starts to leave but she pleads with him, "Please don't go away from me/Stay with me." At this point, she presses her body closely in his as if to seduce him into staying while holding him in place. He frees himself and runs out as Holliday rages incandescently. Holliday's ability to keep topping herself vocally and emotionally ratchets up the already high intensity. She uses her entire body to evoke Effie's pain and fury—stomping, stepping, arms gesticulating, face grimacing, shoulders heaving. These movements lay Effie's claim to her subjectivity and her desirability as a fat Black woman.

As the song nears its conclusion, Holliday doubles over as if in physical pain and launches into the refrain once more. The notes become more sustained and seem to come from somewhere deep inside her. She uses the backs of the dressing table chairs for support standing and clutches at her stomach in a fit of desperation that also seems to steel her against the pain streaking down her face. Holliday haltingly makes her way back to her dressing table and sits, clutching at her body and then seemingly up to the heavens before extending her arms out to the audience. She takes her signature deeply gasped breath in between singing "You're gonna love" (GASP) "me," extending the song's musical drama into the space between the notes (this moment is captured in Figure 2.2). The dressing table and Effie are swept upstage during the final note as Deena and the new lineup

Figure 2.2 Jennifer Holliday singing "And I Am Telling You I'm Not Going" in a scene from the Broadway production of the musical *Dreamgirls*. (New York). 1981. Credit: Martha Swope. © The New York Public Library for the Performing Arts.

of the Dreams enter and sweep Effie into the background while singing a phrase of their new song. The curtain falls and, in the words of critic Frank Rich, "Broadway history was made."[c]

An unexpected assist, however, helped project Holliday's performance into the upper echelon of legendary performances. Gary Gunas, one of the general managers of the Broadway production, recalled a specific change that made this number pop. Gunas was sitting with Bennett and costume designer Theoni V. Aldredge during tech rehearsals when Bennett felt that Holliday looked "too powerful" and "successful" for that moment in the narrative. Bennett solved this by having the production carpenters come onstage and shorten the legs of Holliday's chair. He recalls, "And all of a sudden . . . the whole character for the song appeared" as a result of her shortened stature and position behind the table.[d] While Holliday's performance was magic, a little theatrical trickery of its own helped. The staging made Effie look smaller and thus, weaker, complicating the narrative's stance toward size since it admits that bigger was, if not better, more powerful.

When "And I Am Telling You . . ." took on its own life outside of *Dreamgirls*, it often became just another opportunity for big-voiced singers of all sizes to test their chops. Moving it outside the musical's context also removed some of the whiff of subjugation it carried in the narrative and allowed it to be refashioned as a celebration of Black excellence in talent shows at the Apollo and on televised singing competitions alike.[e] Holliday's performance imprinted the song so much that even her riffs became part of the song's ongoing life outside of the musical.

[a] This analysis is based on the 1982 Tony Award performance. runneryoshi105, "Jennifer Holliday 'And I Am Telling You.'"

[b] Eyen and Krieger, *Dreamgirls*, I-12-51.

[c] Rich, review of *Dreamgirls*, December 21, 1981.

[d] Playbill, "Old Show Queens—Episode 3—On Directors."

[e] See writer Mark Harris's September 30, 2021, Twitter thread about Holliday's reprise of the song on the 2021 Tony Awards for more detail: https://twitter.com/markharrisnyc/status/14436398 28394958851.

"What About Me?": Jennifer Holliday and Effie White

Dreamgirls made an overnight star of twenty-one-year-old Holliday in 1981. She had been in workshops of the show since she was nineteen. *Dreamgirls* producer and Michael Bennett associate Bob Avian recalls, "She was very young, heavy, and definitely did not fit the glamorous image of a leading lady. She did, however, possess a voice that was a gift from heaven."[46] Holliday famously left the production during the summer before its Broadway opening after a disagreement over her character's downward trajectory and absence from the second act. Recasting Effie proved difficult even before *Dreamgirls* left the workshop phase. Jenifer Lewis and Alaina Reed played Effie during

Holliday's absence. It turned out that nobody could sing "And I Am Telling You..." quite like Holliday, and Bennett realized the show needed her.

Holliday and Bennett reconciled, leading Eyen and Krieger to write Effie's character into the second act, and so Holliday rejoined the production. In the summer of 1981, they could not have foreseen how this period would come to mark Holliday's life and help to blur the lines between Jennifer and Effie. To a surprising degree, Holliday's career would eerily come to mirror Effie's. The parallels between them were striking: both were young, fat Black women with big voices perceived as difficult. Avian remembers, "Jennifer was always on the verge of being difficult; it seemed to be a form of self-protection for her."[47] While starring in the 1983 Los Angeles production of *Dreamgirls*, Holliday told an interviewer, "From the very beginning I've managed to maintain the separate identity from the show that I've always hoped for. When a performance of *Dreamgirls* ends at 11:20 pm, Effie stays on stage and Jennifer goes home. To be perfectly honest, I don't mind having that close identification with the character because, quite frankly, I do consider it my show."[48] And it remains hers to a degree perhaps only matched by Barbra Streisand's claim to Fanny Brice in *Funny Girl* (1964).

Over time Holliday herself came to see parallels, telling CBS *Sunday Morning* in 2006, "I am Effie, it's not, 'no I am not the essence of Effie,' I *am* Effie." She asserts that after starring in the film, Jennifer Hudson "got to take Effie off and I never got to take Effie off. I always had to be Effie...that destroys me more than anything else."[49] The link between Effie and Holliday became as much about size as anything; Holliday became known as much for the size of her body as the size of her voice. CBS correspondent Russ Mitchell confirmed this overlap, noting, "Offstage Jennifer Holliday and Effie White were becoming one and the same: struggling with weight problems and feelings of rejection. Holliday gained one hundred pounds in one year and became more and more isolated."[50] In a 2016 interview, Holliday remembered her body when she was starring in *Dreamgirls*: "It was such an awkward size for me, you know, so it's still sometimes very hard for me to look having lost two hundred pounds. And now and so to kind of look back at that time, sometimes I feel like I don't want to go back there."[51]

Being a fat Black woman and starring in a Broadway hit in 1981 meant Holliday was the target of scorn from mainstream critics, who openly denigrated her size, often in the same sentence in which they lauded her talent. Acknowledging her weight to some degree is understandable: it was (and remains) notable when Broadway casts a fat actress of any race in a

DREAMGIRLS, SIZE, AND BODY POLITICS 71

leading role, let alone a fat Black woman. Critics went out of their way to find metaphors and euphemisms to describe Holliday's body. Clive Barnes wrote, "Miss Holliday is just tremendous—something like a battleship should be named after her."[52] Walter Kerr explained, "Miss Holliday—in a rasp of rage called 'I Am Telling You I'm Not Going'—pumps enough blood and bile and reedy power into her song to make us suspect that once she's done she'll finish him off in two bites."[53] Stanley Kauffman wrote that Holliday "belts her songs like a fullback crossing for a touchdown,"[54] at once portraying Holliday's body as athletic and un-ladylike. The critics (all white men) and their repugnant ways of writing about body size reveal just how socially acceptable it was then to plainly denigrate fat people.

The Black press referred to Holliday's body quite differently when they mentioned it at all (Monique La Master's review in the *Los Angeles Sentinel*, for instance, discusses Holliday's performance in only superlatives). Ali Stanton, writing in the *New York Amsterdam News*, noted, "In a society where to be thin is almost like being Black was in the Sixties—beautiful— the talented Jennifer not only must accept the fact that she is a rather plump pigeon—although pretty—but she must also listen to a song admonishing 'You get so heavy on me.' What blatant torture!"[55] Stanton was among the few critics to note the social pressure to be thin as well as to ponder how performing the show itself might have felt to Holliday.

One thing was consistently clear: critics saw the conflict in *Dreamgirls* as about Effie's size, especially when embodied by Holliday. *Ebony* magazine noted, "Effie is dropped because she is overweight, not very glamorous, thought of as a troublemaker, and has a voice that is a bit 'too Black' for 'crossover' appeal to White audiences."[56] Rich wrote, "Effie no longer fits: she's fat, and her singing is anything but light. And Curtis's bad news does not end there. Not only does he have a brand-new, svelte Dream in costume, ready to replace Effie on stage, but he also has chosen another Dream to replace Effie in his bed."[57] Kerr noted that Curtis replaced Effie "partly because of a troublesome temperament but mainly because" he "wants to replace her with a slimmer look and a tamer sound."[58] A consensus of critics agreed that Curtis made Effie sing backup and then fired her because she was fat and getting fatter and less attractive to him.

Holliday gained a reputation for being difficult while playing Effie, as noted above. But not only was she still very young; the demands of performing Effie are extremely intense—so much so that it has since become common for its producers to cast one actor to play matinees and one to play evenings, though the original Broadway production did not adopt this practice. The difficulty of singing Effie eight performances per week on Broadway led the producers to contract Holliday for just six performances a week during the show's Los Angeles engagement following her Broadway run. Lillias White performed Effie at matinees in Los Angeles since the producers scheduled five-performance weekends and it would have been virtually impossible to sing the role five times in one weekend and remain vocally healthy. Holliday still began missing performances in Los Angeles, due in part to vocal strain. The missed performances took a toll on the box office, causing the production to close early because of lost revenue. Producer Bernard B. Jacobs explained that the production "was marketed as starring Jennifer Holliday. As you know, because of illness, Miss Holliday has had to miss many performances." He went on, "She just didn't appear with any degree of regularity." *Dreamgirls* refunded around $50,000 per week to disappointed ticket buyers in LA.[59] To combat the losses and attract audiences, the production began generating publicity featuring White, an unusual move for a matinee performer. Holliday was being openly pushed aside and derided. Remarks at the time by White, Bennett, and others on the production team commenced a trend in which they and the press denigrated Holliday, her weight, and her behavior and attempted to reframe Effie as *not* fat.

Is Effie Fat? Replacing Holliday and the Problems of Padding

Although Holliday eventually stopped playing Effie, she continues to be so associated with the role that most reviews of *Dreamgirls* written since 1981 mention her. She remains the standard against which audiences and critics measure every other Effie—even if they never saw Holliday in the role. The headline of *Newsweek*'s review of the 2017 West End production explicitly posed the comparison: "Is Amber Riley a Match for Jennifer Holliday?"[60] Holliday's success created a problem for the original creative team in casting her replacements. Not only did replacements need the specific talent and ability required to sing and act the role, but they also had to follow a legendary performance and somehow make the role their own. This wasn't necessarily a negative, as Sharon Brown, who played Effie on Broadway, observed, "Everybody is amazing [as Effie] because Jennifer Holliday set the bar so high."[61]

When asked whether it would be difficult to replace Holliday, Bennett replied, "Well, I have understudies right now who are very good in the role.... I think that I will find other people who will be very good in it. They will be different."[62] Kecia Lewis, an Effie understudy in the original production, recounted, "None of us sounded like Holliday.... We didn't all have to be like Holliday."[63] If the creative team allowed some flexibility, audiences and critics had different expectations. Holliday's first replacement on Broadway was Vanessa Townsell (pictured below in Figure 2.3), an unknown telephone operator cast at an open call in Los Angeles during a well-publicized nationwide talent search. An article in the *New York Times* covering Townsell's debut in the role notes, "Holliday is a larger woman than Miss Townsell, and because girth figured in the plot, Miss Townsell was aiming to be one of the other singers in the trio. Having gained weight eating out of boredom at her phone job, she recalled, 'I put on a black dress for the audition to slim myself.'"[64] Critics compared replacements not only to Holliday's performance but also to her body in ways not applied to other replacements in this production. Rich re-reviewed the production for the *Times* with its new star, contending that Townsell "scales down Effie in a way that serves the show. Both more

Figure 2.3 Vanessa Townsell, Loretta Devine, and Sheryl Lee Ralph in a scene from the replacement cast of the Broadway musical *Dreamgirls*. (New York). 1983. Credit: Martha Swope. © The New York Public Library for the Performing Arts.

74 SIZE

reserved and less hefty than her predecessor, this actress is more in balance with the other Dreams—and more credibly their victim."[65] Rich's review is typical of the way several critics described Holliday's body as haunting Effie as much as her voice did.

Yet the once-open acknowledgment of Effie's size disappeared once Holliday left the original production. The creative team took pains to disavow Effie as fat, and by extension, Holliday's body and her association with the role. Casting *Dreamgirls* mirrored its narrative as the producers and creative team replaced Holliday with noticeably thinner actors—just like Deena replaces Effie in the lineup of the Dreams. The producers and creatives surely felt the need to ensure that the show remained a viable property without Holliday, reasonable enough given the number of jobs and the amount of money involved. However, the lengths taken to achieve this end are striking. Violet Welles, a press agent for the California production, explicitly slammed Holliday, proclaiming to a reporter, "People who have worked with [Holliday] feel that at this point it works better without her. Essentially, it's an ensemble show, not a star show, and she was playing it like a star." She then zeroed in on Holliday's body: "The others who have played Effie have not been such big women. You could understand why a manager wouldn't want an ungainly looking woman in a group like the Dreams."[66] But before Holliday departed the West Coast engagement, critics and writers there went to town writing about her body.

Critics discussed fat, and specifically Holliday's body, as if it alone had the power to disrupt the narrative and the audience's reception of the musical. Critic Jack Viertel wrote a feature on White during the Los Angeles run encapsulating the production's turn against Holliday and revealing the new reception of Effie that the creators and production hoped to advocate.[67] Viertel echoed Rich's earlier comments about how the balance of the plot shifted without Holliday, noting that the casting change made the plot less obvious. He explained, "But something essential changes when White plays the role. She's not fat, and she's not especially ungainly either. She doesn't intimidate us the way Holliday does, and everything about "Dreamgirls" becomes a little less obvious, and a little more human than it was before."[68] Writing that the role seems more "human" with a thinner actor in the role implies that fat people are less human and less deserving than thin people, which only compounds multiple ways that fat Black women have already been dehumanized.[69] Viertel was far from alone in using this kind of rhetoric to describe the impact of Holliday's absence. Reviewing the 1983 San Francisco

DREAMGIRLS, SIZE, AND BODY POLITICS   75

production, Gerald Nachtman wrote that the original production "starred alleged blockbuster Jennifer Holliday, a two-ton shouter who smothered the musical, crushed all plot sense with her bulk and bent the show out of shape with her presence." He went on to call White "more subtle and lifelike" than Holliday.[70] While these kinds of conversations surely occurred behind closed doors, they were now out in the open in the press.

An article published in the San Rafael, California *Independent Journal* just before the tour opened in San Francisco invites readers to feel sympathy for White precisely because she was *thin,* and the production required her to wear a fat suit. White noted that the padding was uncomfortable, but she also told the interviewer she believed "obesity is a health hazard" and "I don't ever want to be overweight." Writer Steve Cassal posed the question that would haunt every production of *Dreamgirls:* "But does Effie really need to be fat?" White told him, "The way the show was put together, it was never designed to be about a girl who is replaced because she's fat. The show was not written about a fat girl. It's about a girl who can't change with the times, who can't conform like everybody else."[71] Yet it is Effie's body that is non-conforming as much as her unwillingness to conform vocally and make her voice smaller. The marked change in White's rhetoric from an earlier Los Angeles television appearance, wherein she addressed the numerous references to Effie's weight, foreshadowed what has become an ongoing disagreement. When the tour played Chicago, White even told a *Jet* magazine reporter that Bennett told her, "We don't want you to look or be like [Jennifer]."[72]

The question of whether Effie is fat or not has continued to vex and provoke both critics, fans, and those who have played the role. The unwillingness of some critics to see Holliday as fully human remains disturbing, and the debate over whether the plot makes more or less sense with a thinner actress returns each time *Dreamgirls* does. A thread on the BroadwayWorld. com message board entitled "Effie White—Does She Have to Be Heavy?'" generated over 170 responses when the film adaptation premiered in 2006.[73] User MargoChanning posted a detailed history of the casting of the role on Broadway and argued "that 'weight' was the LAST criterion [Bennett] was looking at as far as future Effies were concerned."[74] It may or may not have been the last criterion, but it was undeniably part of his consideration when recasting Effie. When Roz Ryan was playing the role in 1984, she noted, "The reason that they removed Effie to put in the new girl was for the look, it had nothing to do with Effie's talent," going on to note that she herself had "been a fairly large woman all my life."[75]

The fact that Bennett cast thinner actors like Sharon Brown as Effie complicates the question of whether Effie is fat. When Brown played Effie on tour in Los Angeles, a headline of the *Los Angeles Times* review of show noted her body size; it reads " 'Dreamgirls' Strikes New Svelte Chord." Critic Don Shirley noted how the meaning of the musical changed for him. He writes, "No longer is it possible to interpret the show as a plea on behalf of the overweight. Brown—unlike her celebrated predecessor, Jennifer Holliday—*looks* as if her Effie could actually fit the conventional notion of a 'dream girl' without too much strain." Shirley's review goes on to note that with Brown as Effie he feels the conflict is only about Effie's voice, not her size. He concludes, "Without the cosmetic issues raised by Holliday, the show may lose a little of its pathos. But its analysis of cultural history becomes clearer and more meaningful."[76] For Shirley, the fact that size was just a "cosmetic issue" that somehow obscures the show's meaning belies his ambivalence about the role size played in casting Effie. Size fundamentally matters to *Dreamgirls*' production and reception; it is not merely cosmetic.

One element of casting Effie that generates agreement is the need for a big voice. Musical theatre scholar Dan Dinero argues that "And I Am Telling You I'm Not Going" exemplifies what he calls the "*ultimate* big black lady song."[77] He explains, "There is the excessive body of the singer: she is often large, especially in comparison to the other bodies onstage. She also looks and sounds black, a blackness that appears as racial excess in contrast to everything else onstage."[78] Depending on its casting, *Dreamgirls* hinges on these kinds of excess: Holliday made a smash in the role because she was too fat and too Black, and her voice was too big to blend. These performances of bigness and Blackness draw on gospel vocal styles and musical theatre conventions; the combination of these elements proves irresistible and shows that no show is unstoppable. No matter the size of Effie's body, audiences familiar with the musical come to *Dreamgirls* anticipating the performance of "And I Am Telling You . . ." and hoping that it stops the show. A big voice may have been a primary factor, but the amount of energy devoted to Effie's size disproves claims that size did not matter.

Throughout the life of the original production on Broadway and on tour, Bennett and others from the creative team publicly disavowed notions that Effie had to be cast with a fat actor but nevertheless frequently cast fat actors in the role. Bennett told the San Jose *Mercury News* just before the San Francisco production opened, "I'm very happy that Lillias is here as Effie because the play is much more in proportion with her. As Jennifer put on weight, it became about how they throw the fat girl out. Well, that's not the story of the play. It's about how they needed a pop singer to make the white charts."[79] The surviving members of the creative team doubled down on this story when *Dreamgirls* came back to Broadway just a week before Bennett's death from AIDS in 1987. Co-choreographer Michael Peters told the *New York Times*, "There's a greater focus now on the human element that comes as a result of the change in scale and the fact that without Jennifer, the show becomes more of an ensemble piece."[80] Eyen was even more direct, telling the New York *Post*, "The essence of Effie is more human now."[81] He emphasized this line to the *Daily News*, saying, "Actually, I had never envisioned Effie as a heavy person. It worked out fine, but that wasn't the original intention. My idea was of a mentally heavy person, heavy attitudes, a lot of pressures on her."[82] Eyen's attempt to re-write the history of casting Effie runs into one major roadblock: evidence to the contrary.

The major problem with these post factum arguments is that, apart from the creators' willingness to disparage Holliday to the press, evidence exists that they did envision Effie as at the very least "chubby" if not "a real fat girl," as one casting notice indelicately stated. What they decided to be the distinction between "chubby" and "fat" remains unclear. While in development, *Dreamgirls* was called simply the "Tom Eyen Musical," and a casting notice for it in *Back Stage* in July 1980 demonstrates that Eyen had considered size important enough to be part of the description: "**Effie Melody White:** a short, semi-heavy, difficult black diva with a great voice trapped in a rock and roll world."[83] A 1981 casting breakdown from Johnson-Liff Casting for *Big Dreams* (then the show's title), lists the following requirements:

EFFIE WHITE
Age 18–30. Black. Battleship singing voice—has to do it all. Incredible range from low to very high. "Gospel" background is good. Must have great emotional as well as technical range. Great soul. Can be chubby but should not be a real fat girl. Should have character and must have strong dramatic facility and weight.[84]

This language went on to become the standard breakdown for the role; a 1982 memo sent to Los Angeles agents by Johnson-Liff used the exact same language. An earlier version sent to Actors' Equity in May 1981 is slightly longer and includes language cut from later versions with the most notable difference reading, "Can be chubby or chunky but should not be a real fat girl.

78   SIZE

Does not have to be a great beauty. Should have character as opposed to real sex appeal and glamour."[85] A hand-written draft of an earlier casting breakdown likely written during pre-production states, "Women should come in looking Really Foxy + attractive (for EFFIE'S This is not important)."[86] While these descriptions beg the question of what "a real fat girl" is, they also point out whose bodies the casting team considered foxy and attractive. The irony is that Holliday, a "real fat girl" according to critics and the creative team, won the role and a Tony Award for playing it.

The description of Effie in a 1982 casting notice for future replacements removed any description of her body. It reads, "**Effie White**: 18–30, Black, battleship singing voice. Must have remarkable star caliber voice with enormous emotional power and soul and with wide range. Gospel background."[87] Undoubtedly, the character of Effie changed and developed throughout the course of the show's multiple workshops, but the sustained disavowals of Effie as fat further ring false when one considers that Nell Carter played Effie in the first workshop in the late 1970s.[88] In one of the ultimate absurdities related to *Dreamgirls* and its plotline about Effie being too fat to be on television, Carter left the show's workshops because she was becoming a television star on shows like *Ryan's Hope* and *Gimme a Break*. By the time *Dreamgirls* cast its Bus and Truck tour in 1985, the language used to describe Effie had morphed again. The casting breakdown opens by stating, "Everyone in the cast must be between 18 and a young 35. It is important that everyone in the cast be very attractive and have great style and charisma. Women should be 5'4"–5'8"; must move well, and be sexy and feminine." Predictably, the description of Effie reads quite differently:

> **Effie White**: 18–30, battleship singing voice, sings "And I'm Telling You I'm Not Going." Must have remarkable star calibre voice with enormous emotional power and soul and wide range, gospel background is good for this role, the specific physical requirements for the women in the show do not pertain to Effie: she should be different, in some way, from the other girls.[89]

Once again, the description singles Effie out as unattractive and unfeminine even if size was now absent from the breakdown.

The shift in the narrative around *Dreamgirls*'s casting was partially achieved by sometimes hiring thinner actors, but crucially through the use of padding, or fat suits. Some, though not all, Effie replacements wore padding, "an ambiguous item—part costume and part prosthesis. It is generally made out of foam and latex, which are sculpted, sometimes weighted, and sewn into a swim suit worn underneath the actor's costume to represent the contours of a fat body."[90] *Dreamgirls* used padding to make replacement Effies resemble Holliday, especially if they were thin. Yvette Cason recalled that she was a size 6 when she auditioned for the show, hoping to be cast as Lorell. When she was cast as Effie, she said, "They put a fat suit on me, which I took off in the second act.... It looked like I had been to Weight Watchers."[91] White also auditioned with the role of Lorell in mind, later saying she "had no interest in being Effie" since she was "like a size 6/7" and was "not gonna gain 200 pounds."[92]

It is curious that Vanessa Townsell, Holliday's Broadway replacement, was evidently not padded while, at the same time, Lillias White wore padding as Effie in California (Figure 2.4 shows White in rehearsal for this production). In an interview on local Los Angeles television in 1983, White acknowledged that she wore the padding "because there are a lot of inferences made to Effie being overweight in the first act and it also makes more sense when she comes back in the second act and when she sings 'I Am Changing' to really have changed and lost the weight and to really have this wonderful look and be glamorous and different from the person that she was seven years before."[93] [Clip 2.3] Reframing "I Am Changing" as a song about having lost weight and becoming a new person reads as though Effie *had* to lose weight in order to return to the stage and gain back her voice, the prime instrument in musicals. And, realistically, maybe she did in the show's narrative and its historical context.

The archives of *Dreamgirls* costume designer Theoni V. Aldredge contain measurements and costume inventories with evidence contradicting the creative teams' disavowals of Effie's fatness. Aldredge's measurements for White entitled "LILLIAS WHITE WITH PADDING" were for costume shop Barbara Matera LTD to use to build her costumes. These measurements approximate Holliday's size when she played the role without padding, of course, and though both women were 5'4", White's padded costumes were still about 3" smaller than Holliday's. White later recalled that Matera and Aldredge "made the Effie's costumes fit the Effie's body" since everyone's body was different from Holliday's.[94] The inventory sheet for Brenda Pressley, who covered Effie and Deena, reads, "NOTE: Brenda wears a fat suit, therefore the Dreams outfits worn as Deena don't fit as EFFIE."[95] Ultimately, if Effie's

Figure 2.4 Lillias White in a rehearsal shot from the National Tour of the Broadway musical *Dreamgirls*. (Los Angeles). 1982. Credit: Martha Swope. © The New York Public Library for the Performing Arts.

weight is not supposed to matter and have no bearing on the plot, then why did the creative team approve of Holliday's replacements wearing fat suits at all?

What, then, of the fact that when Holliday returned to play Effie in a 1994 Atlanta production, *she* wore a fat suit? In the *Atlanta Journal and Constitution*, Dan Hulbert wrote, "We should all have the problem Jennifer Holliday faces in the revival of her Tony Award-winning role in 'Dreamgirls': she's too thin" (Note the echoes of the earlier feature on White). Holliday said, "I have to wear a 'fat suit' for the show! I'm a size 8 now, but Effie's got to be an 18. So I need some serious padding."[96] Holliday returned to the role again in Atlanta in 2007, this time without padding. Her attitude toward Effie's body was different this time around: "I am substantially smaller than I was back then. It didn't change the character, but it did make a change in terms of what I was going to try to do. Wear a fat suit? I opted not to just to see if I had enough acting chops to pull it off, to show the emotions of the woman in love, and her heartache. Heartache is heartache, and shouldn't be predicated on whether she's a big woman."[97] Whether or not Effie is fat changes the musical; if Effie is visibly thin, it makes little sense when Curtis accuses her of "getting fatter all the time" because no one knows she is pregnant yet. The audience is left to assume that she is merely a difficult diva rather than a fat girl with a big voice pushed aside for her slimmer counterpart. The most recent time Holliday played Effie was in a 2012 production at the MUNY in St. Louis. Holliday told a reporter then that "she and the director will have to decide whether she needs to play Effie wearing a 'fat suit.' "[98] The fact that the debate over Effie's size has been reframed to the point that thinness itself became the issue further highlights how much of a problem fatness is perceived to be.

The use of a fat suit represents a deliberate choice by production to ensure that a character looks a certain way, a decision not made lightly given the expense of creating custom-made costumes and padding. However, the use of fat suits is more complicated than simply falling under the category of artistic license. The fat suit itself reinforces stigma because it can be put on and taken off at will, an act unavailable to the fat person perceived as morally suspect for their inability to lose weight. The implicit message sent by fat suits is that fat is somehow performative, recalling the casting notice explaining that Effie "should not be a real fat girl." Though the debate over whether Effie is fat may never be settled, the fact remains that Effie is one of few leading roles available to fat Black women in Broadway musicals but also one whose casting is contested due in part to anti-fat attitudes.[99] Perhaps those uncomfortable with seeing Effie rejected because she is fat are more comfortable with seeing her "tossed out because she was unreliable, erratic, a bitch, unprofessional, and, most crucially, was unable to adapt to the demands placed on black musicians and singers who were trying to cross over to the white pop mainstream."[100] The meaning of *Dreamgirls* changes accordingly depending on whose body embodies Effie. Size matters.

82 SIZE

Dreamgirls Post-Bennett

Dreamgirls's 2016 West End premiere starred Amber Riley, who has been outspoken about her weight since rising to fame through television's *Glee*. [Clip 2.4] Eric Woodall at Tara Rubin Casting was responsible for the US casting of the West End production, including finding Marisha Wallace, and worked on casting its anticipated yet still not materialized Broadway transfer. He helped create the casting notices for the production's June 2017 auditions, which did not mention weight at all but focused instead on other aspects of Effie:

EFFIE WHITE
18– late 20's. Lead singer of "The Dreamettes." Later she gets fired from the group when Deena gets given the lead. Headstrong, sassy, temperamental, a diva. Powerful gospel singer required with brilliant belt. African American. Principal role.[101]

Woodall sidestepped the debate over Effie's weight as he discussed crafting casting breakdowns such as the one above: "As a casting director, we're dealing with what's written. . . . There are only a few lines in the script that really support that she's large, and you could argue that that's in the point of the story where she's pregnant."[102] Casting directors usually turn to the writer if the property is a new one, but if it is a revival, they "can pull from something that already exists." When it came time to cast this *Dreamgirls*, Woodall says the issue of fat suits never came up but that size shadowed the process nevertheless: "We actually explored some ladies for [Effie] that weren't that large, because . . . you really don't have to have someone who is obese, you know? It can just be a little bit curvy, and so we have been encouraged to explore ladies like that. . . . I had to walk a fine line, because [these actors] knew the role and they thought, 'Why are you calling me? I'm not fat.'"[103] Though this production's creative team decided not to mention Effie's size, in actors' minds she is fat. Wallace even remarked that the production team never made her appearance an issue, saying, "Nobody cares what size I am, nobody cares what I look like."[104] The surprise expressed by some actors invited to audition who do not consider themselves fat reveals that actors still perceive Effie as a role for a fat woman. Amber Riley's public body positivity adds layers to the debate about whether Effie is fat or not since the West End production did, after all, cast a fat Effie even though the casting breakdown did not include size- or weight-based criteria.

Riley revealed to MTV that casting directors told her to lose weight, noting how her opportunities are restricted because of her appearance. "Being the person I am, you know, the size I am, being a woman, being a black woman, there's not a lot of roles for us," she explained.[105] Riley has spoken out about deciding not to change her body to conform to the entertainment industry's unrealistic standards. On her Instagram, she posted a video where she asked her followers, "Why does me being fat offend so many people?"[106] She went on to list the various parts of her body that she appreciates and tells her followers she does not consider being called *fat* an insult: "My ass is fat and the fellas love it. And so do I!" Riley triumphed as Effie and won the 2017 Olivier Award for Best Actress.

Effie standby Wallace was one of two standbys for Riley and regularly performed the role, coming to the show's rescue when Riley and several company members were out with pneumonia in early 2017.[107] [Clip 2.5] Wallace keenly felt both the demands of playing Effie and the history of casting the role after Holliday: "I feel like it used to be bigger, back in the day when people would cast that show, it was a big Black girl. Then they also realized that the bigger Black girls can't do the dancing. They didn't have the stamina, so they need someone who's in the middle more."[108] She went on to remark that "you have to be big [to play Effie] but you have to be healthy and fit," while noting that these are not mutually exclusive.

The role of Effie is not only vocally demanding but also emotionally demanding. The pressure to measure up to memories of Holliday's and Hudson's award-winning performances exists whether you are the standby or the star. When Riley left the production, producer Sonia Friedman took the unusual step of casting three actors who shared the role. In a statement, Friedman explained, "The thrill of *Dreamgirls* is to experience the brilliance of the human voice. Effie White is arguably the biggest sing in musical theatre history, which is why we have cast three extraordinary vocalists to play this iconic role."[109] Given the role's historical toll on actors, Friedman's triple-casting of the role seems like a kind of insurance against Holliday's history repeating itself.

At the same time, Friedman's statement acknowledges that prospective audiences will see one of three "real" Effies and no understudies. This is canny marketing since the role itself became the draw rather than Riley once she departed. Wallace played the role for somewhere between four and six performances per week, while Karen Mav did one performance, and Moya Angela played between one and three. It is common for other vocally

84 SIZE

demanding roles like Eva Peron in *Evita* and Christine in *The Phantom of the Opera* to have one performer do the matinees and the other the evening shows, but that has not always been the case for Effie. Holliday's Broadway understudy Sheila Ellis asked, "Can you imagine an opera diva singing one of her roles that often during one week? In 'Evita' . . . Patti LuPone had to do the role only six times a week and it wasn't as strenuous as that of Effie."[110] The difference in how many performances per week Evitas did versus the number for Effies speaks volumes about Black women's labor on Broadway. One wonders how Holliday's career and reputation might have been different had she not been initially contracted to play Effie eight times a week on Broadway.

Dreamgirls remains one of a but handful of leading roles specifically written for Black women in Broadway musicals. None of the women who played and understudied Effie on Broadway or on tour ever again played a romantic leading role on Broadway. Even Lillias White, who has had arguably the most successful Broadway career of any Effie, winning a Best Supporting Actress Tony Award for *The Life* (1997), has appeared in most of her Broadway shows in featured roles. Suffice it to say, the other women who played Effie in Bennett's production (Sharon Brown, Vanessa Townsell, Brenda Pressley, Julia McGirt, Kecia Lewis, Edwina Lewis, Roz Ryan, Sheila Ellis, and Yvette Cason) stood little chance of repeating Holliday's success. Effie White became more famous than those who played her.

The practice of padding persists on Broadway. Fat women continue being denied chances to play the range of characters available to thin women. Black women are still routinely denied leading roles available to white women. Fat Black women face intersecting and compounding structural barriers to employment. All of this represents a sad state of affairs for an industry that attempts to deliver a convincing performance of inclusivity eight shows a week. While the US population itself grew increasingly fatter from the 1980s to today, Effie was the only fat female leading lady seen on Broadway—until Tracy Turnblad.

If fat suits represent a specific kind of straitjacket for performers, for Black women they also play into another representational trope: the demand that the "big Black lady" stop the show.[111] This cultural expectation emblematizes the paradox into which fat Black woman performers are thrust by the Broadway musical: remain peripheral to the narrative yet central to spectators' expectations of what musicals do. "Dazzle us with your voice, but know your place," Broadway seems to say. *Dreamgirls* continues to ring so true because Effie dazzles audiences before being put in her place—she is the "big Black lady" but she's also still a fat Black woman in the United States. And though the actor playing Effie may or may not be fat, the contradictions of casting and playing Effie reveal the role and, by extension, musicals themselves as sites of struggle over what it means to be a fat Black woman in the Broadway industry and in this country. Even when fat is fake and/or disavowed, the history of casting *Dreamgirls* and the mixed messages the original production sent in its casting breakdowns and costuming admit that, to quote songwriter Fats Waller, "thin may be in, but fat is where it's at."

3

"Must Be Heavyset"

Casting Fat Women in Broadway Musicals

Fat shaming on Broadway certainly did not start and end with *Dreamgirls*, though a notorious earlier incident also involved Michael Bennett. This musical featured the unfortunate but apt title *Seesaw*. The show was in trouble during its out-of-town tryout in Detroit in 1973, and it had more than its share of backstage drama on the way to Broadway: producers replaced the original director and choreographer with Bennett, then many in the cast came down with the flu, several chorus members were fired while the show was still out of town, and last, the producers replaced leading lady Lainie Kazan with Michele Lee.[1] Kazan's starring role as dancer Gittel Mosca was going to be her chance at Broadway stardom after being Barbra Streisand's standby in *Funny Girl* nearly a decade earlier. But, as Bennett's associate Bob Avian noted, "The first decision Michael made was to replace the talented but miscast" Kazan.[2] Despite being informed she would not be taking the show to New York, Kazan's contract still obligated her to play the role nightly in Detroit while Lee rehearsed the role for Broadway during the day. While none of these things are uncommon in out-of-town tryouts, what makes this situation notable is that Bennett openly and explicitly fired Kazan because of her size.

Kazan's firing became newsworthy as *Seesaw* teetered its way to Broadway. Patricia Bosworth covered the musical's trajectory from out-of-town disaster to Broadway hit for the *New York Times*. She referred to Kazan as a "zaftig nightclub singer," and noted that Kazan reportedly "had trouble learning her lines" and "quarreled violently" with the original director.[3] Critics were not kind to the musical or to Kazan in Detroit. Bosworth explains, "The consensus of opinion was that she didn't look like a dancer or move like a dancer. She was also some 40 pounds overweight." That Kazan's appearance played a role in her firing does not shock, nor does the fact that her weight was a contractual issue. *Seesaw* composer Cy Coleman recalled, "When we cast Lainie, she promised she'd lose those 40 pounds. She said she'd have it

Broadway Bodies. Ryan Donovan, Oxford University Press. © Oxford University Press 2023.
DOI: 10.1093/oso/9780197551073.003.0004

written into her contract that if she didn't lose the weight, we could fire her. Unfortunately, we never checked to see if that stipulation was in the contract." Avian corroborates this report, writing that Kazan "was a zaftig woman, and not believable as a dancer."[4] Bennett fired Kazan, reportedly causing "a tantrum that Bennett will not soon forget" when Kazan was "told her weight had proved the biggest problem."[5] Kazan lost the role but won an important battle: because the producers never wrote the weight clause into her contract, the production had to pay her salary (reportedly $3,000 a week) for the run of the show.[6]

Bosworth's article caused Kazan herself to write a letter to the *Times* decrying how *Seesaw*'s creatives discussed her firing in the press. Kazan defended herself against the claims that weight was the problem, explaining that she was "being massaged and 'wrapped,' to help me (along with a rigid diet) to successfully lose the weight I had gained during my pregnancy and recent illness."[7] She recounts, "The tantrum which Michael Bennett was witness to must have taken place in the 'twilight zone.' The only meeting we had—at my request—lasted approximately 10 minutes." What remains notable about Kazan's ouster from *Seesaw* is how eerily it presaged Effie's narrative arc in *Dreamgirls* ten years later—and Bennett's clear ambivalence toward nonconforming bodies. Kazan's very public firing trailed her for years. Body issues trailed her too. As she prepared to play Rose in *Gypsy* in summer stock in 1992, she told an interviewer, "I'm trying desperately to keep my weight down—my nemesis—and keeping myself real clear."[8] Kazan was far from alone in struggling to find work in a business obsessed with thinness and unwelcoming and often outright hostile to bigger bodies. This chapter first surveys the handful of supporting roles available to fat women in Broadway musicals and how the actors cast in these roles navigate the industry's fat phobia. I then take an extended look at the only hit musical of the new millennium so far to star a fat woman as the romantic lead: *Hairspray*. I detail *Hairspray*'s casting process, its narrative, the contradictory nature of its fat-positivity, and conclude by noting the long-term career impacts of playing roles like Effie White and Tracy Turnblad.

Narratives of Size Onstage and Off

Fat women so rarely get the chance to play leading roles on Broadway that Kazan's firing still seems an omen decades later. Much more common are

88   SIZE

secondary roles: fat best friends and comedic sidekicks there to support the thinner leading lady.[9] Tracy Turnblad was not Broadway's first role specifically for a fat white girl, but it was the first in a smash hit. Five months after *Dreamgirls* opened in 1981, *Do Black Patent Leather Shoes Really Reflect Up?* opened and ran for five performances. The show featured Maureen Moore as Becky, a Catholic school girl taunted by her elementary school classmates for her weight. Becky's first song, "Little Fat Girls," is her response to being bullied for her size. One of her classmates asks, "How do you spell Becky?" and the rest taunt her by replying, "F-A-T, Fat!"[10] Becky sardonically sings: "*We know Jesus loved little children/But I think that all the kids he knew were thin;/I can tell from the pictures in the Bible story book/That fasting and famine were 'in.'*"[11]

In 1983, *The Tap Dance Kid* (*Dreamgirls* composer Henry Krieger's follow-up to that show, intriguingly) opened on Broadway and featured the song "Four Strikes Against Me," sung by Martine Allard as the fourteen-year-old character Emma. She sings, "*Isn't it enough that I'm young/That I'm female/Black/and fat?*"[12] She lists the four strikes against her: age, color, gender, and size. While the show highlights Emma's interest in law, its final scene also reveals where its priorities lie, as Emma's final lines in the show reveal: "You know what you said about me stuffing my face? . . . I'm gonna try to cut that out." Allard won the prestigious Theatre World Award for her performance and received a Tony nomination but has never appeared on Broadway since.[13] *Tap Dance Kid* and *Do Black Patent Leather Shoes . . .* at least represented stigma's effects on young girls (to an extent), even if size was cast in stereotypical lights by associating these characters so strongly with food.

While *Black Patent Leather Shoes* and *The Tap Dance Kid* never became widely produced, other musicals with roles for fat girls did. What stands out is just how little has changed about musicals' representations of fat, and that what has is that the conforming bodies onstage have become even thinner. There was little outcry over the lack of fat representation until 2020 (as noted in the introduction to this book). Fat politics remain inconspicuous and fear of fat is still ubiquitous. Musicals typically associate fat characters with food. Roles from different eras—e.g., Hildy in *On the Town* (1944), Jan in *Grease* (1972), Madame Thénardier in *Les Misérables* (1987), Becky in *Waitress* (2016)—all display what theatre and fat studies scholar Jennifer-Scott Mobley calls "fat behaviors," exhibited in a character's "inability to control her mouth, which results not only in her large size but her outspokenness."[14] It should come as no surprise that these roles are all about eating and food.

Hildy's showstopper, "I Can Cook Too," is a string of comically sexual double entendres ostensibly about cooking. [Clip 3.1] Jan, described by the show's licensing company as a "funny, loud, compulsive eater," often appears with the rest of *Grease*'s Pink Ladies eating or with food in hand.[15] In *Waitress*, Becky serves food and pie all day long at the diner while having an extramarital affair—a side dish depicting the stereotypical insatiable sexual hunger of the fat woman.

Fat characters began to appear more regularly in musicals after 1970, often as the recipient of anti-fat stigma rather than necessarily as the butt of jokes, especially off-Broadway. William Finn's off-Broadway musical *A New Brain* (1998) features the song "Poor, Unsuccessful, and Fat," which is about exactly what its title suggests. The revue *Five Guys Named Moe* (1992) celebrated size in "I Like 'Em Fat Like That." *Gigantic*, previously called *Fat Camp*, opened off Broadway in 2015 and featured several performers who would go on to play roles where size mattered, including Bonnie Milligan (in *Head over Heels* on Broadway), Larry Owens (in *A Strange Loop* off-Broadway), and Ryann Redmond (in *Bring It On* on Broadway). In *Bring It On* (2012), Redmond's character did not make the cut for the school cheerleading team in part because of her size. She is on the receiving end of an empowerment anthem called "It Ain't No Thing," in which one of her classmates tells her, "So, you got a little baby fat/It ain't no thing."[16] Redmond made headlines in 2019 when she replaced Gregg Hildreth as the snowman Olaf in Broadway's *Frozen*. The role had previously only been associated with fat male performers (Josh Gad voiced the role onscreen), making Redmond's casting a coup.[17]

And then there's *Mean Girls* (2018), which depicts how fat oppression and gendered standards of beauty reinforce each other. Fat jokes are less the point here (though the show has a handful of them) than the fact that *Mean Girls'* narrative depicts fat as something to be feared—the plot hinges on queen bee mean girl Regina George gaining weight by getting duped into eating weight-gain bars rather than diet bars. The show references fat throughout, whether in throwaway moments like Cady's joke in "It Roars" about meeting an obese person when moving back to the United States from Africa, or in "Meet the Plastics," in which Regina sings that she never weighs "more than 115." This lyric in particular raised a red flag for Renée Rapp, the second actor to play Regina on Broadway. Rapp told *Teen Vogue*, "I think it's really important that I'm not a Regina who's 115 pounds. I don't even remember weighing 115 pounds." She concluded, "Every single body type, every single gender, race, everyone needs to be more represented in the arts, and we're inching

90 SIZE

closer to that."[18] Broadway inches toward inclusion when it could leap. Even when musicals do include fat characters and show harm caused by fat stigma onstage, the way the industry treats fat offstage is a different matter.

While musicals' narratives attended to size in various ways, the media focus on actors' non-conforming bodies remained constant. Reporters regularly query women of all sizes about their bodies. Perhaps because *Hairspray* was so explicit in its portrayal of fat positivity, journalists felt licensed to write numerous feature stories focusing on the body of the actor playing Tracy and her diet and exercise routine. The press resorted to metaphor to address *Hairspray*'s heroine, even when not addressing her specifically—such as *Variety* headline " 'Hairspray's' Full-Figured Tony Tally." The production itself encouraged this kind of winking treatment in its advertising tagline, "Broadway's Big Fat Musical Comedy Hit." A few years later, a *New York Times* reporter asked Broadway actor Lindsey Mendez if she had a healthy relationship with her body. Would this question be asked of thin actors? Or of men? Mendez's response noted how she worked to change her relationship to her body. She said, "I grew up being, I don't want to say a plus-size girl, but a girl of curves and substance. But you know, as time has gone on, I've developed a more healthy lifestyle, and now I feel like I'm in a normal body type. I don't know if they consider a size 6 or 8 normal, but to me it's normal."[19] Mendez was then playing the lead off-Broadway in *Dogfight*, a musical where she played a character considered a "dog" by others. Mendez's other notable Broadway roles include, of course, Jan in the 2007 revival of *Grease*, and also Elphaba in *Wicked* and a Tony Award winning turn as Carrie in the 2018 revival of *Carousel*. Mendez's career has challenged typecasting and also represents how actors with "normal body types" are still held to unrealistic body standards.

Broadway actor Lisa Howard has been told that her whole career would be different if only she would lose weight, and then she would magically get cast as the lead and not the featured player.[20] She finally did win a standout part in the ensemble musical *It Shoulda Been You*, in a role described in the casting breakdown as "overweight and not comfortable with that fact or anything else about herself."[21] Howard's *Shoulda* solo "Beautiful" is about being told she had a "pretty face" but needing to lose weight in order to find a man. Her character's showstopper, "Jenny's Blues," also was size-related, causing her mother to quip, "Why is she talking like a big black woman?," self-consciously calling attention to Broadway's big black lady trope.[22] [Clip 3.2] Howard again won a Broadway role associated with size in *Escape to Margaritaville*

(2018), where she portrayed a woman pressured to lose weight by her fiancé. As people in the industry pressured Howard herself to lose weight, she was playing roles that required her to reenact that onstage nightly.

Body shame exerts pressure on actors outside of narratives. Keala Settle played Tracy on tour in *Hairspray* for nearly three years and has had great success since, winning a Tony nomination and four featured Broadway roles, including Becky in *Waitress*. Settle dealt with overt fat phobia when she was Tony-nominated for *Hands on a Hard Body* in 2013: not a single fashion designer offered to dress her for the ceremony as they routinely do for acting nominees. Because the production had already closed, Settle used her unemployment checks to pay for awards season outfits. One of her former dressers from *Hairspray* sent her $1,000 in gift cards so that she could attend the Tony Awards in style like her fellow nominees.[23] Hawaii native Settle has broken barriers as a Maori woman on Broadway, but she relates feeling that she never fit in as a multi-racial actor, telling a reporter, "I couldn't fit in anywhere."[24] Settle's ethnic and racial identities intersected with her size in the industry, so her personal and professional success in the 2017 musical film *The Greatest Showman* with her anthem of self-acceptance "This Is Me," was that much more meaningful.

Fat actors are sometimes placed in the position of defending their bodies. Critics lauded Alysha Umphress's turn as Hildy in the 2014 revival of *On the Town* (a role previously played by Lea DeLaria in the 1998 Broadway revival), but Umphress made headlines of a different kind when she appeared off-Broadway in the 2018 revival of *Smokey Joe's Café*. In the *New York Times*, critic Laura Collins-Hughes, wrote "Ms. Umphress, by the way, is bigger than the other women onstage, and the costume designer, Alejo Vietti, doesn't seem to have known how to work with that, dressing her in an unnecessarily unflattering way."[25] Umphress responded on Twitter, maintaining, "While the overall point was to malign the costume designer, her phrasing made me the sacrificial 'fat' lamb."[26] While Collins-Hughes did not explicitly knock Umphress's body, the dig was implicit. Fat phobia thrives in the space between plausible deniability and glaring obviousness. When there are few roles explicitly designated for fat actors, it is easier to ignore the explicit and pervasive discrimination they face on a regular basis precisely because it is so ubiquitous. Body discrimination continued unchecked for decades on Broadway. But sometimes a musical celebrates body positivity in text and performance. In 1997, that musical was *The Life*.

92 SIZE

Broadway Number: "My Body"

A decade after playing Effie in the *Dreamgirls* revival, Lillias White won the Tony Award for Best Featured Actress in a Musical for her performance as Sonia in *The Life* (1997). *The Life* takes place in gritty 1980s New York in the world of hustlers, pimps, and sex workers; in other words, a world where the body is capital. White stopped the show cold with "The Oldest Profession," an ode to the aging body of a sex worker. But another number from the show directly confronted body shaming, as the show itself did in its casting. *The Life* was one of the first Broadway musicals to have a truly size-inclusive, multi-racial ensemble who owned their bodies' sensuality, though the narrative complicated the fact that the women's bodies were also for sale and under the control of pimps. *The Life's* female ensemble ran the gamut of body types from former Fosse dancer Lynn Sterling to future Tracy Turnblad understudy Katy Grenfell. The idea that *all* body types are desirable (these women are all sex workers, after all) was radical for Broadway.

In "My Body," the women sing out in response to being chided by a group of religious do-gooders, proclaiming, "My body is my business and nobody's business but my own."[a] As seen on the 1997 Tony Awards broadcast, Joey McKneely's staging is clearly indebted to Fosse's choreographic style and its kinesthetic focus. Fosse, however, would probably never have cast this ensemble, since he usually cast only thin dancers in his heyday. *The Life's* milieu itself represents a harder-edged update of Fosse's *Sweet Charity* (1966). Both shows feature scores by Cy Coleman, and "My Body" has "Big Spender"-like moments in the look if not exactly the sound. The working girls of *The Life* line up downstage like the dance-hall hostesses of *Charity* as they sing the opening lines (as shown in Figure 3.1). Each of the seven women wears form-fitting costumes displaying their bodies to potential johns: busts are pushed up and out of bodices, fleshy thighs are exposed, and everyone wears high heels.

"My Body" alternates between seductive and confrontational. The ladies celebrate their bodies as they implicate the audience: when Sharon Wilkins sings, "What if I'm a sinner? I ain't exactly alone," all of the women onstage lean toward the audience and open their eyes wide at them. To make the point that these women present a unified front against body shaming, much of the song is sung in unison, with only the occasional harmony. The ladies strut around the stage, circling toward spectators

Figure 3.1 Chorus of The Ladies in the stage production *The Life*. May 1997. Credit: Carol Rosegg. Billy Rose Theatre Division, The New York Public Library for the Performing Arts.

like each one is a potential john. Solo moments are accentuated with full-chested shimmies. During the number's dance break, the debt to Fosse becomes clear as they perform unison shoulder rolls and hip isolations and movements reminiscent of 1960s social dance the jerk.

One thrilling moment in "My Body" comes when Wilkins and Grenfell, the two biggest girls in the ensemble, take center stage, raise their arms overhead, and stand gloriously shaking their entire bodies, daring the audience to bask in their self-acceptance. [Clip 3.3] The dance break continues with some more Fosse-esque jazz hands and angular poses before culminating in a final repetition of the song's chorus, joyfully belted at full voice. If Fosse style came to stand in for sex itself, its appropriation here repurposes and repoliticizes whose bodies get to dance and be sexy on Broadway. "My Body" begins as a defense against sex-shaming, and it becomes a celebration of what it means to exert the agency of your own body and to take pleasure in how it moves and how it sounds at any size. *The Life* was not without its share of problems, but it sang and danced a kind of body positivity on Broadway before Tracy Turnblad made it there.

[a] This analysis is based on the Tony Awards performance. Blazian2006, "The Life—My Body."

"Must Be Heavyset": Casting Tracy Turnblad

Hairspray opened on Broadway on August 15, 2002. *Hairspray*'s creative team (music by Marc Shaiman, lyrics by Scott Wittman and Shaiman, book by Mark O'Donnell and Thomas Meehan, direction by Jack O'Brien, choreography by Jerry Mitchell) celebrated Tracy Turnblad's size in the narrative but not without complications. The creators explain, "Tenacious Tracy Turnblad, lovable as she is, is fat, and all of us, lovable as we are, are somehow, metaphorically, fat." They note how Tracy's size also serves as a metaphor for being "skinny, clumsy, new in town, female, foreign, black, Jewish, gay, naïve, brainy, too short, too tall, overeager, shy, poor, left-handed, over-freckled, pyrokinetic (like *Carrie*), scissor-handed (like *Edward*), or musical-comedy-loving."[27] *Hairspray*'s approach to difference prompts audiences to identify with Tracy since *Hairspray* makes her difference (and everyone else's) universal. Despite the seeming-universality, casting Tracy was very specific.

Casting director Craig Burns worked on *Hairspray* from the beginning, and for him it remains a favorite production even after two decades as a casting director. Burns enjoyed working with people who "just weren't normally considered for leads in a show, and now all of a sudden these girls are getting a chance because we need a fat girl. There was so much joy in that."[28] That fat girl was Tracy Turnblad, "a high-spirited, irrepressible, chubby teen girl; she loves to dance and is eager for her life to kick in."[29] The plot itself initially hinges on size and casting since Tracy dreams of dancing on "The Corny Collins Show," the after-school teenage dance television program on her local Baltimore station. When a spot on the show opens up, Tracy pleads with her mother Edna to let her audition, but Edna begs off, telling Tracy, "People like us . . . You know what I'm saying. They don't put people like us on TV—Except to be laughed at."[30] This moment is poignantly humorous since Edna is a comic drag role (immortalized on screen by Divine and on stage by Harvey Fierstein). Tracy auditions anyway and the show's producer fat-shames her, underlining how Tracy's empathy for other oppressed people is born of her own experience. When Tracy finds herself in detention because of her beehive hairdo, she meets fellow student Seaweed and he teaches her some of his dance moves. Seaweed is Black, Tracy is white, and while after-school detention might be integrated, "The Corny Collins Show" is not. Tracy's dream to dance on TV becomes a mission to integrate the show instead (and to win the love of its resident heartthrob, Link Larkin).

Tracy wins a spot on "Corny Collins," not from the audition, but when Collins himself spots her at the Sophomore Hop dancing moves she learned from Seaweed. After getting on TV, she becomes locally famous for being the big dancer with the even bigger hair. Tracy and Motormouth Maybelle, Seaweed's mother, organize a protest against the Collins show that culminates with everyone being arrested and jailed. Everyone is swiftly released except Tracy, the organizer of the protest. However, Link breaks her out of jail just in time for her to burst onto the set of "Corny Collins"—alongside Motormouth, Seaweed, and all of her Black friends from detention—to learn she's won the title of "Miss Teenage Hairspray." The musical crescendos in a feel-good, catchy finale, "You Can't Stop the Beat," in which "the beat" aurally and metaphorically signifies progress toward a more inclusive and integrated world.

Filmmaker John Waters explained that he hoped the Broadway adaptation of his 1987 film *Hairspray* would be a hit so that "there will be high school productions, and finally the fat girl and the drag queen will get the starring parts."[31] He understood that the enforcement of bodily conformity in casting is present even in high school. *Hairspray*, like *Dreamgirls*, resonates powerfully for the ways that its onstage narratives of the struggle between individuality and conformity intersect with its casting and staging. Casting Tracy required finding a specific look and sound and the star quality needed to carry the show.

The *New York Post* reported that an early open call for *Hairspray*'s 2002 Broadway production drew around 400 performers,[32] and the press documented that more than 1,000 actors lined West 43rd Street in Manhattan in April 2016 hoping for a chance to play Tracy in NBC's adaptation of *Hairspray*. Casting Tracy garnered headlines for several reasons: roles like Tracy are often cast through open calls attracting hundreds of aspirants. Because they tend to be cast with young performers often making their professional debuts, the press agent's job is to create a sense of excitement around the unknown discovery. On top of garnering publicity, casting through open calls actually works. Burns notes that he cast "six or seven" Tracys from open calls.[33] The scarcity of roles for fat young women reveals that the supply of performers willing to put themselves up for consideration far outstrips industry demand. Settle won the role of Tracy in the national tour at an open call, though she had to endure seven callbacks before being offered the standby position to Carly Jibson. Settle later recalled that she "had no idea" what she was doing through the process, recalling her relative inexperience

96 SIZE

at the time.[34] Casting *Hairspray* became something of a spectacle in and of itself, and between the film musical and the live TV version, there have been several high-profile searches to cast the new Tracy Turnblad. The fact that the original Tracy Turnblad, then-unknown Ricki Lake, went on to boffo success as a television personality after starring in the movie only enhances the property's sense of intermediality. Fierstein's casting as Edna in the Broadway and television versions further deepened the vortex of self-referentiality. And yet the attention paid to casting Tracy raises the question: Why does casting other leading roles not attract comparable amounts of attention? Where is the press at an open call for Julie Jordan in *Carousel* or Celie in *The Color Purple*? That there are rarely open calls for these roles admits the relative ease of casting them.

Waters has repeatedly spoken about the importance of Tracy's fatness to the property, telling *Newsday*, "I want to make sure that Tracy will be fat, not just plump. When was the last time you saw two fat girls as stars of a Broadway musical who also get the guy?"[35] As the show headed for Broadway, *Hairspray* presented casting directors with a few challenges. Choosing the language for the casting breakdowns was sensitive, especially when it described Tracy's body. Despite Waters's comfort with the word *fat*, the casting breakdown sent to agents and used in open calls for Tracy scrupulously avoided it. The casting team decided on *heavyset* instead:

[TRACY TURNBLAD] Female, Caucasian, 5'3" or shorter, to play high school age. Must be heavyset. Outgoing, unstoppable, goodhearted with a vibrant, lovable, spirited personality. Loves to dance. Becomes a teen heroine. Strong pop belt singer and great mover. LEAD.[36]

Burns explained, "We didn't use chubby or fat. I used heavyset because . . . you don't want to offend anybody in a breakdown." He went on to add that initially they knew "you need a fat girl. It's like, 'that's the role.' This is what it is. . . . But it was definitely set up at the beginning, that on the breakdown, that we would always use 'heavyset.' " In 2002, Burns felt that *fat* would have been too blunt and potentially insensitive to attract actors to play Tracy, though he contends, "Now it's different. Now it's like things are a lot freer," though he concedes that he probably still would not use *fat*.[37] Some actors who played Tracy also avoided describing her as fat; one said, "You need to be chubby but you have to be zaftig. . . . It's interesting because they're very picky in how they cast, 'cause they want chubby girls but they want them to be curvy."[38] The creative team sought a clear type: a short fat young woman who can dance and sing the moves and sounds of the 1960s with enough charisma to carry the show.

Size was just one factor in winning the role. Broadway actor Kathy Deitch auditioned for Tracy several times over a period of four years, ultimately not getting cast because O'Brien told her she was "too sophisticated" for the role. Yet she felt a lot of external pressure to get the part, observing, "Just because I'm chubby, everyone assumed that I would be Tracy." She remembered feeling disconsolate about the process before her manager finally told her, "There is an essence about you that isn't right according to the director. And so, it has to go beyond just you're chubby and you sing and you dance well."[39] Simply being the right "type" is not enough. Kathy Brier was the first replacement Tracy on Broadway, a role she won after eight auditions. She told an interviewer, "I was the shortest, thinnest girl in the [audition] room and so I thought, 'I'm way too thin for this. They're never going to cast me.' . . . I just didn't think I was physically the right type for it, and I know how [on] Broadway, that's such a big part of how people get cast—is their look, not necessarily their talent."[40] Brier and Deitch's different perceptions of what type the production sought show how type is crucial and also how casting depends on intangibles.

Untangling Gender, Race, and Size in *Hairspray*

If casting *Hairspray* was complex, it only echoed how the show's narrative handled the body politics of gender, race, and size. *Hairspray* takes a tongue-in-cheek tone even when addressing serious social issues: its opening moments feature Tracy singing about being "hungry for something that I can't eat," calling attention to her literal and metaphoric appetites.[41] *Hairspray*'s strategy of using humor sometimes subtly undermines its fat-positive stance, as it makes many fat jokes—often in the same breath that it asks for fat acceptance. Though *Hairspray* works hard to be in on the joke, it laughs at and with its characters, e.g., when Edna sings, "You can't stop my happiness/'Cause I like the way I am/And you just can't stop my knife and fork/When I see a Christmas ham."[42] *Hairspray*'s fat jokes land because they are delivered with a wink *by* fat people (and/or actors appearing fat due to padding). Realism isn't *Hairspray*'s point though; the show invests in creating its own myths where injustice gets resolved through song and dance, racial

98 SIZE

integration happens through dance, and women are linked through the consumption of beauty products.

Waters based his film on a local Baltimore television show called "The Buddy Deane Show," though he noted, "The one thing that was pure fiction in [*Hairspray*] was the idea that a fat girl could have gotten on that show. A fat girl never would have gotten on 'The Buddy Deane Show.' Even in segregated Baltimore, a black girl would have had more chance."[43] Waters imagined a more inclusive world in his film. He explained, "There was no real Tracy; she's totally in my imagination and stood for every misfit and underdog—hippies, blacks, gays, fat people—who came to see my movies. She dances on the show, gets the boy and wins the title. That doesn't often happen in real life."[44] For Waters, the fairy-tale aspect of the story was precisely the source of its empowerment: "It's about the teenage white girl who gets a black guy. The fat girl gets a straight guy, and her mother's a man who sings a love song to another man."[45] It wasn't an obvious candidate to be a hit, but it became one and then some.

Hairspray's notable use of Black aesthetics aligned it squarely with mainstream culture's adoption and appropriation of Black music and dance in particular. While *Hairspray* uses music as a racial signifier, dance too contains racialized meaning: the white and Black teens initially dance different dances until Tracy adopts the social dances of her Black schoolmates. *Hairspray* presents this move as appreciation rather than appropriation and ties it to Tracy's acceptance of her body.[46] Her dancing body found a welcoming community in one that has historically rejected whiteness's enforcement of body conformity. Tracy's fat dancing body ultimately integrates "Corny Collins," first with Black dances, then with Black people, challenging enforced racial segregation and the fat stigma that first prevented her from dancing on television. It is easy to read Tracy's actions as using Black aesthetics for her own fulfillment since this musical (by an all-white-male creative team) treads the line of Tracy's instrumentalization of Blackness. That this kind of appropriation is emblematic of the development of musicals themselves adds resonant dramaturgical and historical dimensions to the show's politics since it celebrates rather than critiques this process. To a large extent, Black people exist in *Hairspray* to make whites feel good about themselves and learn something.

An emblematic example of *Hairspray*'s use of Black aesthetics occurs during "Welcome to the 60's," when girl group The Dynamites suddenly appear as mannequins in a shop window before springing to life and joining in the song. [Clip 3.4] Though they never appear again in the musical, here they cue the audience into the sound of the 1960s while serving as a reminder of the kind of labor Black women often perform on Broadway. Their thrilling vocals make their brief appearance one of the show's more memorable musical moments, yet they remain accessories to the plot as animated props leading the white women to empowerment. This is so typical of what Broadway musicals command Black women to do that *Hairspray* songwriters Shaiman and Wittman later wrote a song about it: "A Big Black Lady Stops the Show" in *Martin Short: Fame Becomes Me* (2006).[47] While Broadway has produced musicals that challenge this formula in their narratives (*Caroline, or Change*) or in their casting (Audra McDonald in *110 in the Shade* [2007 revival]), these exceptions give the appearance of inclusion without addressing core issues of exclusion: the vast majority of musicals remain directed, designed, produced, and written by white men for audiences comprised of primarily white women. *Hairspray* was no different.

Even though *Hairspray* runs on stereotypes, it's not mean-spirited. Waters glibly summarized the plot as about "a fat white girl fighting for racial integration."[48] Tracy cannot achieve integration without Maybelle, whose role trades in stereotypes of fat Black femininity. Maybelle's dramaturgical function is to empower the white women through music, dance, body-positivity, and rhyme; she teaches the white women in the musical to accept their bodies during "Big, Blonde, and Beautiful." [Clip 3.5] It is acceptable for a Black woman to be fat in *Hairspray*, but Edna's discomfort with her own size demonstrates how fatness and whiteness together are not so easily accepted, gesturing toward the implicit anti-Blackness underlying fat phobia.

However, *Hairspray* complicates its treatment of race by disrupting conventional musical theatre dramaturgy in its distribution of musical numbers: Maybelle, a featured part, has the prime musical spots that would typically be assigned to the lead (Figure 3.2 depicts Mary Bond Davis as Maybelle in the original cast). Maybelle sings both the Act I finale, "Big, Blonde, and Beautiful," and the eleven o'clock number, "I Know Where I've Been." These songs require a show-stopping voice, furthering the association of the size of the voice with the size of the body and the race of the singer. Maybelle's songs stand out from the rest of the score in style and substance. Her songs transmit the dual messages that *Hairspray* works to put across: body positivity in the former and racial equality in the latter. Shaiman explains that "almost everybody involved with the show" told him and Wittman that "Tracy should sing the eleven o'clock number," but that they

Figure 3.2 *Hairspray* (Broadway, 2002), Music by Marc Shaiman. Lyrics by Scott Wittman and Marc Shaiman. Book by Mark O'Donnell and Thomas Meehan. Directed by Jack O'Brien. Shown *center*: Mary Bond Davis; at *right*: Dick Latessa. Credit: Photofest.

"simply didn't want our show to be yet another show-biz version of a civil rights story where the black characters are just background. And what could be more Tracy Turnblad–like than to give the 'eleven o'clock number' to the black family at the heart of the struggle?"[49] Assigning the marquee musical spots to Maybelle puts *Hairspray*'s money where its mouth is since the "big, blonde, and beautiful" Black lady has its most important voice. Yet what is

Maybelle's voice in service of if not teaching white women to accept their bodies and to feel good about the future promise of civil rights? Maybelle knows where she's been and where she's going, but where is she now?

Winning the Role and Weighing In

If Maybelle's voice defines *Hairspray*'s sound, Tracy's body defines its look and moves. Tracy's body thus became a kind of touchstone for a myriad of issues. Marissa Jaret Winokur was the first person to audition for the role and played Tracy in all of *Hairspray*'s pre-Broadway readings, which made the creative team wonder who else might be out there—could the first person they saw for the part actually be the one? Bernard Telsey Casting launched a national casting search in Baltimore to find unknowns to play Tracy while Winokur was rehearsing the role for the final reading in New York.[50] Burns notes that this was not about replacing Winokur before the opening but rather about a head start finding understudies and replacements: "We knew we were going to need to start finding these girls."[51] Winokur remembers this somewhat differently. In a diary entry published in *Hairspray*'s companion book, she writes of how producer Margo Lion "showed [director Jack O'Brien] a picture of a girl who auditioned for them in Baltimore . . . for my role . . . yesterday . . . THAT I AM PLAYING TODAY! . . . Wait, I can't believe they were auditioning people for my role yesterday."[52] This casting search was the correct timing for the production, even if it was awkward for Winokur. Playing Tracy had already become the stuff of dreams even before it opened on Broadway.

When the production held auditions in New York the month after its Broadway opening, hundreds came, including many who saw playing Tracy as their chance to break through. "The role is something that I can play, because I can never be Eponine in *Les Misérables*. I've struggled with this for a long time, because on stage it doesn't matter what you look like, but what you weigh," related Tracy-hopeful Lisette Valentine.[53] Casting director Bethany Berg noted, "These girls are real people; they're what most of America looks like, and we're looking for those people that are happy and confident."[54] The notable change in language acknowledging fat women as "real people" stands starkly opposed to how those casting *Dreamgirls* did not want "a real fat girl." The explicit acknowledgment of what bodies in the United States look like nods to the composition of the musical's audience. Yet even when

102 SIZE

acknowledging the positive elements of casting a fat female lead, the press was still unable to resist weight-related puns: the title of the article referenced above is "Sizing Them Up."

Despite starring fat women, *Hairspray* undermined its fat-positivity by not only using fat suits for its actors (including those who played Tracy, Edna, and Maybelle) but also including weight clauses in the contracts of some of the actors who played Tracy. At the same time the show promoted fat acceptance, it was having weigh-ins. Weigh-ins are more common in the concert dance world, especially in ballet companies, but they are not exactly uncommon in Broadway musicals though they are often used for child actors: for instance, the orphans in *Annie* (1977) all had height and weight clauses in their contracts. When she joined *Hairspray* as a standby Tracy, Katrina Rose Dideriksen discovered at her first weigh-in that she was not the only one being weighed; the actress regularly playing Tracy was also contractually obligated to maintain a certain weight, whereas Dideriksen was told to lose twenty pounds. She recalls the price of playing Tracy: "She is the ingénue, she wins the guy, she saves the day, and yes, she's funny and she's lovable and all those things, but in this very real-girl way.... It was really this underlying pinch to realize that subconsciously I was being told I was still wrong for it, that there was something I had to fix.... In the end, I don't think they realized how hurtful, and how anti-*Hairspray* it really was for them to be like, 'Lose twenty pounds.'"[55] Dideriksen's experience reveals the paradox Broadway expects fat women to navigate as well as how the industry ties size to employment by exploiting fear of fat. She notes that the "unrealistic" goal weight designated by the production caused anxiety over whether her contract would be terminated if the number on the scale was too high or too low.[56] A kindly wardrobe team member would round the number from the scale up or down accordingly if actors were slightly over or under their contractually obligated weight. The production undertook all of this effort despite the fact that actors wore fat suits.

Broadway's *Hairspray* put padding on people who were already fat. Waters himself later came out publicly against using fat suits, writing, "I'm also usually the lone holdout on the fat-suit debate, always against casting a skinny Tracy and putting her in one. Isn't a fat suit the blackface of insult to overweight girls? ... A skinny Tracy is like a white Li'l Inez or a female Edna. It's just not right."[57] Fat suits parallel (and differ from) Blackface since each form of wearing the "other" positions thinness and whiteness, respectively, as a "seemingly natural signifier for morality, propriety, and appeal."[58] *Hairspray*'s

"MUST BE HEAVYSET"   103

adoption of Black aesthetics was not only in its sounds but was mirrored in the body politics of padding. Waters was not so outspoken about the Broadway production's use of fat suits, though. Burns says that the fat suits were not an issue during casting: "It didn't really come up, because I think everybody just knew. You know, ultimately eventually [the creative team] wanted that shape . . . they just want a certain shape. A girl could be heavy, but they might need padding somewhere else to just give that Tracy-kind-of-shape that they wanted. So, it really wasn't something that we said, 'Oh, you're gonna need to be padded,' it just went with the territory, and girls just accepted that."[59] Whether or not those cast as Tracy knew about the padding before they signed the contract does not mitigate the complexity of feelings caused by wearing it while also having one's weight monitored. Size was part of being cast, but it also then kept actors in constant jeopardy.

Maintaining a certain size was perhaps less about fat phobia than it was in response to the sheer physicality of playing Tracy and the fear that actors would become *too thin*. Nevertheless, Tracy is essentially a dance lead and she does not even sing during crucial moments in the narrative. Tracy dances so intensely throughout the show that the creative team feared that actors who played Tracy would lose weight from all the dancing, which also nods toward why they used padding and mandated weigh-ins. The *New York Post* reported just before *Hairspray*'s opening that "Winokur has lost weight—enough to send a frantic theater crew bringing candy and chocolate shakes to her dressing room. As the chunky star of 'Hairspray' . . . the 29-year-old needs to stay plump to play the Ricki Lake role."[60] The article's headline, "Worth the Weight," raises the question of what or who is worth the weight—Winokur? The chocolate shakes and candy? Starring on Broadway? The seesaw of being told to maintain your fitness while being fed sweets? As the production tried to fatten up its leading lady, it also pressured her to exercise, a practice that would continue throughout the Broadway run and on the road. Anxiety over Tracy's weight began with its source film, though. Waters remembers: "Ricki [Lake, the film's Tracy] started to lose weight, and I remember we would feed her cupcakes and Dove Bars and stuff."[61] The weight clause placed those playing Tracy in a catch-22 where both fat and thin were enemies.

Brier told *Newsday*, "It's a weird kind of a thing. You're supposed to be this chubby girl, and yet the show is so active you have to train to be an athlete."[62] Because Tracy dances so much, the creative team was anxious about the stamina of bigger actors. Not surprisingly, stereotypes about fitness and body size played a part in casting. Employment law scholar and fat activist Sandra Solovay notes, "The stereotypes about what kind of work a fat person cannot or should not do are broad" and promote the idea that fat people "are not fit so they should not be in any position that requires strength, speed, stamina, or other significant physical demands."[63] According to the *New York Times*, "Jack O'Brien, the director of 'Hairspray,' said he never doubted that Ms. Winokur was right for the role, only whether she had the stamina for it. 'Did she have the chops to do eight shows a week?' Mr. O'Brien said. 'I don't think anybody knew. I don't think she knew.' "[64] But Winokur had previously appeared on Broadway as Jan, of course, in a revival of *Grease* and performed eight shows a week for nearly four years before *Hairspray*. Winokur sang and danced her heart out for a long run in *Hairspray* (Figure 3.3).

Concerns about fat people's stamina and ability reveal how deeply fat phobia reaches, even when, like O'Brien, those perpetuating these well-worn tropes are not necessarily ill-intentioned. *Hairspray* was the first time many

Figure 3.3 *Hairspray* (Broadway, 2002). Music by Marc Shaiman. Lyrics by Scott Wittman and Marc Shaiman. Book by Mark O'Donnell and Thomas Meehan. Directed by Jack O'Brien. Shown *center* stage: Marissa Jaret Winokur. Credit: Photofest.

"MUST BE HEAVYSET" 105

young actors playing Tracy carried a show as its leading lady, which came with a tremendous amount of pressure, and the creative team needed to be certain the actor could handle that burden. Producers told Winokur point blank during the show's Seattle tryout that she was "carrying a ten and a half million dollar show."[65] When she played Tracy, however, Winokur was older and more established in the business than many of her successors. Settle explained that playing Tracy at such a young age had taken a toll on her, saying, "Truth be told, every Tracy had that [pressure.] . . . You can interview every single one of them and they'll tell you the same thing. Each of us got shot out of a cannon, expected to become this torch for their company."[66] The contractual weigh-ins faced by the young women hired to play Tracy added stress to the already intense demands of playing the role while receiving decidedly mixed messages about diet and exercise.

The production sent some contenders for Tracy to something known as "Tracy Camp," a program for potential future Tracy Turnblads who needed more training according to the creative team. Burns explains that the impetus behind the practice was that "we show auditions to the creative team, and then they would say, like, 'oh, this girl is ready to go to the show so we'll just hire her, but this girl is a more "in-training" kind of a girl. So we need to put her in "Tracy Camp" . . . and then let's see if she's applicable in the future.' "[67] According to Burns, this was due to the relative inexperience and youth of the actors under consideration. Dideriksen explains how she "started actually learning [the Tracy track] with a Canadian company, just as a Tracy camper" before being hired to stand by for the role on the national tour. She remembered that she went to "Tracy Camp" with no promise of actually playing the role: "I got hired with no promise of any other position or any other contract. . . . We were there for those five weeks, learned everything, and then we were sent home. At that time, there was not a lot of talk about keeping the image or the shape or anything, or what would happen."[68] *Hairspray* was one of several musicals to find and train potential cast members this way. Shows with specific casting needs like *Billy Elliott, Jersey Boys*, and *Hamilton* also developed training programs to create a casting pipeline.[69] Before them, *Miss Saigon* set up training schools in London and Manila. Like the Tracy campers, the "*Saigonsistas*" (as they were known) were guaranteed auditions but not contracts.[70]

"Tracy Camp" was born out of practical considerations to keep the various productions up and running smoothly because it was a challenge to cast Tracy. Burns notes that Tracy hopefuls "had to be really special, so we found

106   SIZE

them all, but it wasn't like we had twenty people in our back pocket that we could go to, you know what I mean? We definitely had to go out there and train and find the really special ones."[71] Dideriksen recalled that at "Tracy Camp" the creative team seemed to be "worrying bigger girls weren't as co-ordinated. . . . We had this extra week of dance that was just dance rehearsal, and a lot of talk about getting our stamina up, and how to last. True, Tracy, for a non-big girl, is a heavy role. She's on stage most of the time, and most of that time is doing a lot of dancing. It's a lot of dancing and singing at the same time, it would be a lot for anyone, but they were especially concerned that this was supposed to be a bigger girl on top of it."[72]

Burns backs up Dideriksen's assessment of the particular demands of this role: "I remember Jerry Mitchell saying that the girls would have to . . . be really good at cardio to dance the show, and he was like, 'I need you to do 45 minutes on the bike and then you'll have a milkshake.' They had to keep their weight up, but then they also had to do their cardio."[73] If the creative team and producers were so invested in monitoring the weight of the actors playing Tracy, then why bother with fat suits at all?

Will *Dreamgirls* Ever Leave You?

Long after the padding has been removed for the last time, some roles continue to stay attached to an actor. Dideriksen, who eventually played Tracy on Broadway in *Hairspray* and opposite Fierstein in Las Vegas, explains that long after she left the show, "there was this stigma of still seeing me having Tracy on my resume. . . . It was a while ago. I look nothing like I did when I did it, but I can't take that off my resume because then it looks like I have no big credits. . . . You have to have those things on there, because that's what people take seriously, but then they see that and they go, 'But you're not Tracy, so I don't get it.' "[74] In one of the strongest indications of the stigma of being considered a Tracy Turnblad–type, despite the fact that Tracy is a lead, two actors who understudied the role do not list Tracy—a lead on Broadway— among their credits on their websites.[75]

Actors know that their size matters; many are unable to escape association with particularly iconic roles even after their body sized changed drastically. The two women most associated with *Dreamgirls*, Jennifer Holliday and Jennifer Hudson, are prime examples of actors who capitalized on weight loss while also remaining inextricably linked to Effie. Holliday has been public about her decision to have gastric bypass surgery, which she underwent to change both her body image and her career prospects. But the surgery didn't bring the desired career results. Holliday explained, "Nobody wanted me small. They only wanted the old Jennifer Holliday. They were uncomfortable with my new look, my new attitude—everything."[76] Ironically, the onstage demands of *Dreamgirls* reproduced its narrative conflicts offstage for Holliday, who thought thinness would translate into new opportunities. *Dreamgirls* clearly cost Holliday, but it also gave her a name and a legacy. The press routinely refers to Holliday as "Broadway's original dream girl" (even her Instagram handle, jenniferhollidaydreamgirl, seals the connection) and Effie remains the sole part she originated on Broadway. Her returns to Broadway have all been as a featured replacement in revivals: as the Teen Angel in the 1994 revival of *Grease*, a stint as Mama Morton in the 1996 revival of *Chicago*, and as Shug Avery in the 2015 revival of *The Color Purple* in the role originated in that production by Jennifer Hudson. Holliday succeeding her successor was a meta casting coup on the part of producers that further associated these actors with each other and with Effie. Her career as a recording artist took off after *Dreamgirls* in the 1980s and 1990s; its success sadly echoes Effie's line in *Dreamgirls*: nobody can see her on a record.

Hudson lost so much weight after starring in the *Dreamgirls* film that she became a spokesperson for Weight Watchers, and her weight has been tabloid fodder ever since. Hudson espoused body positivity when she played Motormouth Maybelle in the live television version of *Hairspray*. But a female actor's weight garners headlines, whether they make ads for Weight Watchers or not. Even *Hairspray*'s original Tracy Turnblad (on film) Ricki Lake's own cycle of weight gain and loss has attracted more media attention than almost anything she has done in her career. On Broadway, Winokur shot to fame for playing Tracy, and the role has marked her career. Winokur has maintained her celebrity status by becoming associated with weight loss; she was a contestant on ABC's *Dancing with the Stars* after hosting a cable television weight loss competition called *Dance Your Ass Off*. In 2009, she wrote a blog series for *People* magazine titled "Calling in Fat," aimed at taking readers along on her "weight loss journey."[77] Winokur's notion that one could "call in fat" to work underlines the challenges fat women face in the labor market. Winokur's weight was always considered fair game by the press when she was in *Hairspray*. A *New York Times* feature timed to coincide with her opening night as a lead on Broadway repeatedly made the point that Winokur was breaking the "conventional wisdom" about how fat women should act and

108 SIZE

what they should wear: "Heavyset women are expected to wear their clothes long and loose-fitting. Ms. Winokur likes her skirts short and her T-shirts tight."[78] Winokur noted her casting's significance but did not frame it around her size, saying, "Here I am, the young character actress. . . . I'm the lead this time." Though Holliday, Hudson, Lake, and Winokur may have shed weight, they may never fully shed the association with the roles that made them famous. Weight loss complicates and also perhaps extends the narratives of these actors' careers, but it has not translated into more leading roles.

Broadway musicals have made strides toward including bodies beyond a sample size in featured roles and ensembles in the twenty-first century. As with other kinds of diversity, however, this can look like tokenism when only one person exists onstage whose size stands apart from a sea of conforming bodies. Within the industry, some actors are beginning to speak out against pervasive body shaming. Broadway veteran Deitch started an internet talk show called *Plus This!* to turn her "outrage into action" after learning that 67 percent of US women wear a size fourteen or higher.[79] She told *Playbill*, "We're way in the majority. We're like *really* the majority of women, and yet we are invisible, and we aren't represented anywhere."[80] The Broadway League reports that the Broadway audience is also 67 percent female (and 77 percent Caucasian).[81] This means that the Broadway audience has seen very few musicals where their own body type has been represented in a leading role or otherwise. If some viewed *Hairspray* as a fantastical representation of being a fat woman, then we should conversely acknowledge that the majority of musicals themselves promote fantasies of all other types of bodies too. The lack of fat representation infects actors' senses of self, as they may not be able to see beyond the industry's dominant vision of type. Redmond recounts getting submitted for certain roles by her agent and discounting her chances before the audition; she says, "I automatically do it in my head because it's been so ingrained that there are these specific types in musical theatre, and you fit in this box."[82] Breaking out of the typecasting box remains challenging.

The Instagram account Humans of Broadway created a series called #BodyPositiveBroadway addressing typecasting. In her post, Katy Geraghty, an ensemble member in *Groundhog Day* on Broadway and Tracy in Oregon Shakespeare Festival's 2019 production of *Hairspray*, writes, "Don't forget that typecasting can also be your friend and the reason you have a job. . . . Your self-worth [sic] in life or in theatre is not dependent on if you can be a princess in a ballgown."[83] Geraghty is correct about the employment benefits of typecasting (namely, a job), but seeing a fat girl play a "princess in a ball-gown" would represent a powerful sea change on Broadway because of the messages it would send to audiences, creators, performers, and producers about whose bodies are valued and who gets to play whom. Playing a princess may or may not change an actor's self-worth, but being represented will undoubtedly change at least one audience member's life. Size matters, not just to actors but to audiences as well.

While the financial stakes of casting decisions are visceral to producers, for actors, casting is also a numbers game guiding them to find and shape their own niche—in essence, shoring up typecasting's persistence. West End *Dreamgirls* star Marisha Wallace explains, "Why do I want to compete with the 70 other skinny Black girls? . . . They can always find a big Black girl who can sing, but they can't find a big Black girl who can dance and sing, so I save people money."[84] After Effie, Wallace's next two West End roles were Becky in *Waitress* and Maybelle in the 2021 revival of *Hairspray*. Broadway's steep economic pressures impose material effects on the lives of fat actors, who will not be cast in leading roles—the highest-paying ones. Fat women already face an additional economic burden simply from being fat in a society that restricts their earning power; being just thirteen pounds "overweight" cuts a woman's earnings by $9,000 a year.[85] In Broadway's competitive labor market, roles are sparse and unevenly distributed even for those who possess the dominant Broadway Body. Broadway is far from being the only industry guilty of this discrimination; fat oppression is systemic. As fat acceptance activist Marilyn Wann argues, "When being thin or fat in our society confers privilege or oppression, the stakes are high."[86] The economic and political stakes of representation raise the bar even higher for those with non-conforming bodies, and overlapping facets of oppressed identities compound the inequity.

The lack of fat actors cast in leading roles belies Broadway's vision of itself as a fully inclusive institution. The use of fat suits perpetuates fat stigma. If you are fat, your opportunities for being cast in a Broadway musical are severely limited because of how you look. Deitch explains the direct effect that her size has had on her ability to be cast: "There were things that, if I had been thinner, I would have been asked in for. That definitely has happened. No one asked me to lose weight for something ever, but it was clear I wasn't even getting in the door because I wasn't thin."[87] While casting remains just one part of advancing toward fat acceptance, it is the one that can have an immediate, visible impact as actors and audiences await new musicals to be written, produced, and cast that will expand conceptions of which bodies *are* fit for Broadway—and not just as comic support or best friends. Even in musicals that *could* be cast with a fat actor as their lead, it doesn't happen. Deitch points out that *Waitress*'s leading lady "is pregnant for most of the show, and she is not allowed to be a fat girl."[88] Fat actors are de facto barred from playing the majority of leading roles.

It is poignant to view Winokur's Tony Award acceptance speech, where she proclaims, "If a 4'11" chubby New York girl can be a leading lady in a Broadway show and win a Tony then anything can happen."[89] Anything, except more Broadway roles, apparently. In fact, according to the Internet Broadway Database, no actor who played Tracy during *Hairspray*'s nearly eight-and-a-half year Broadway run has yet been cast in another leading role on Broadway. Why is this? Even though Tracy had a height limit of 5'3" or shorter, height must be ruled out when considering what factors are keeping past Tracys from playing other leading roles on Broadway: many of Broadway's most famous leading ladies are short: Patti LuPone is 5'2", Bette Midler is 5'1", Liza Minnelli is 5'4", and Bernadette Peters is 5'3". Winokur has a Best Actress Tony Award for playing Tracy, yet only one credit in a leading role on Broadway. When Burns was asked whether he had been able to cast anyone who played Tracy in another leading role, he demurred, "That's a good question. . . . There have been other opportunities, but I don't know. I still think it's definitely a type, and it's harder to find roles that are right for these girls."[90] In 2011, Winokur addressed the fact that she has not returned to Broadway and expressed her frustration at the lack of roles available to her, explaining that she thought she'd try Hollywood instead of "just waiting for the next chubby girl role on Broadway because they're few and far between."[91] She hoped she'd get to return to Broadway when she was forty and could be cast as a comedic lead, which is exactly the lie that young fat actors are told about what will happen once they age out of playing ingénues and juveniles.

Even as Broadway inches toward becoming more inclusive, barriers remain—mostly in the inability of Broadway producers and creative teams to imagine an actual world that, like *Hairspray*'s Baltimore, is "hot pink and filled with promises of romance, stardom and the righting of social inequalities."[92] When will a fat woman again be cast in a leading role on Broadway in a musical? Will that musical mention fat in the narrative or not? Will the press write about her body or her diet and exercise routine? Will she be replaced by an actor wearing padding? Will the gap between those bodies considered representable onstage and the majority of American bodies continue to grow? What if Broadway recognized fat women as deserving of the full range of representation given to women with conforming bodies?

It might look something like *Head over Heels* (2018), which featured Bonnie Milligan as Princess Pamela in a fairy-tale-esque take on the jukebox musical. During the show's brief run, Milligan tweeted, "We are serving amazing body positivity at @HOHmusical, where I get to play the most beautiful girl in the land, who has a love story, and nothing about my weight!!"[93] Pamela ended up getting the girl (and having her newly discovered sexuality immediately accepted by her family). Audience members would wait for Milligan at the stage door, and she recalls "meeting so many women who are moved and say, 'Thank you! You don't know what it means to have a big girl up there being joyful and pretty and dancing.' I understand how important and beautiful it is because *I* never saw that. . . . I don't think we talk enough about size diversity in casting."[94] *Head over Heels* won the Extraordinary Excellence in Diversity on Broadway Award from Actor's Equity in 2019.

The presence of a show like *Head over Heels* on Broadway could precipitate more inclusive casting practices, yet Broadway's history indicates otherwise. Unlike *Dreamgirls* and *Hairspray*, *Head over Heels* struggled to find an audience and closed after just 188 performances. The financial success of earlier musicals that were inclusively cast did not automatically beget more inclusivity. There is a twenty-one-year gap between *Dreamgirls* and *Hairspray* and a sixteen-year gap from *Hairspray* to *Head over Heels*: this strongly suggests that money surely is not the sole barrier to inclusive representation. After all, *Dreamgirls* and *Hairspray* were both long-running, award-winning, financially lucrative musicals that proved that stories about fat women starring fat women can be viable money-makers. Even though *Head over Heels* flopped, it nevertheless marked important progress in the politics of representation on Broadway by casting a fat woman in a role where the show's narrative (but not its publicity, which promoted Milligan's size) never mentioned size (and this inclusive casting extended to the show's casting of transgender performer Peppermint in a supporting role as I'll discuss in chapter 5).

Because size-inclusive casting intersects with so many facets of identity, I will close by noting that for as much as *Dreamgirls* and *Hairspray* both focus on television's power to mediate race and size through singing and dancing bodies, each presents the inverse adoption of aesthetic values: *Dreamgirls* dramatizes the strategic adoption of white aesthetics as a chance to accrue cultural and financial capital, whereas *Hairspray* stages the adoption of Black aesthetics as the path to self-acceptance and cultural capital. That these exchanges are crucially embodied by bodies marked by race and/or size shows that Broadway typically allows Black performers and fat performers limited ranges of representation. Fat bodies become the conduit through which Broadway works out the politics of cultural appropriation; the use of fat suits adds historical layers to this process because it recalls some elements of blackface performance, namely, the embodied performance of an other. Like Black performers who performed in blackface in and beyond the Gilded Age, "fat actors may also capitulate to caricaturing the lives of fat people many times because work is work."[95] These musicals stand out because they challenge Broadway's bias toward normativity even as they reinforce it. Casting is Broadway's process that enforces de jure size discrimination. When a non-conforming body breaks through this system, it remains notable, which alone should give pause. Structural inequalities and bias made it nearly impossible for this person to get there in the first place, which is why such casting is celebrated and rare.

The presence of Effie, Tracy, and Princess Pamela, along with the handful of supporting roles discussed, demonstrates how fat stigma operates on and off-stage on Broadway in the narratives of musicals and their casting practices. These practices reveal which bodies have capital on Broadway and how "the stigma attached to being fat is a control mechanism which supports a power structure of one group of people over another."[96] Race and gender inform how actors with non-conforming bodies are treated and whether Broadway permits their participation. By not casting fat women outside of certain roles, Broadway musicals do their part to enforce the system of gendered bodily norms policing how *all* women act, consume, and labor in the United States. For fat women, both their inclusion and exclusion on Broadway are contingent on their appearance.

A few months before *Dreamgirls* opened, Bennett described his view of that musical's central conflict in three questions summing up the lens through which Broadway continues to view who and what are viable subjects for representation: "It's about, are you marketable? Is it saleable? Will it make money?"[97] Despite the smash hit status of *Dreamgirls* and *Hairspray* and the advances made in *Head over Heels*, Broadway continues to say no to most fat women. While Lainie Kazan's firing from *Seesaw* in 1973 brought Broadway's body politics into the open—after all, Bennett did not tell her it was her voice that was too big—body shaming remained the open secret of Broadway's glass closet. Broadway loves for fat ladies to sing, especially fat Black ladies, but too often puts them back in their designated place once the song ends.

PART III
SEXUALITY

4

La Cage aux Folles and Playing Gay

Just before *La Cage aux Folles* opened on Broadway in 1983, journalist Ross Wetzsteon claimed, "Out-of-the-closet pathos has been acceptable to Broadway audiences at least since *A Chorus Line*, but in *La Cage* there's out-of-the-closet pride."[1] It may have seemed that Broadway was out of the closet at least since 1970, when Lauren Bacall memorably proclaimed she was "But Alive!" in *Applause*'s gay bar scene, but profound ambivalence and disagreement existed offstage over how gay representation could successfully attract straight audiences and avoid contemporary gay politics. When *La Cage* opened, critics faulted it for being too timid about its gayness. *La Cage* director Arthur Laurents summed up the controversy, saying, "I don't know what [critics] wanted. Perhaps they wanted the two men to have sex right on stage. That would have been more daring, and it would have lasted one night."[2] Was *La Cage* just a gay musical for straight audiences?

La Cage's appearance on Broadway at the moment when the gay rights movement shifted from ideologies of liberation to pride was auspicious. The musical's politics of assimilation were present in both its narrative and its casting. Its recalibration of family values marked a shift in gay representation on Broadway that mirrored the ideological split within contemporary gay politics, a rift brewing years before a 1979 *Time* magazine cover story reported on the rupture, explaining, "Among the gays, there is a basic split between those who flaunt a defiant lifestyle and the closeted, who grant that 'drag queens' and 'flaming fags' have called attention to the gays' plight by marching in the streets, yet would never dream of emulating them."[3] *La Cage* played both sides in the form of a farce, since it played the heterosexual world for laughs but took the world of drag queens seriously. This show remains remarkable for its presence on Broadway in 1983 because it was the first Broadway musical to feature a gay couple as its romantic leads and because it became a smash hit at a time of immense homophobia in the United States.[4] The burden of representation thus weighed more heavily on *La Cage*'s creators than on those of most musicals. The stakes were at once cultural, economic, personal, and political.

Broadway Bodies. Ryan Donovan, Oxford University Press. © Oxford University Press 2023.
DOI: 10.1093/oso/9780197551073.003.0005

116 SEXUALITY

As much as the institution of the Broadway musical was historically a haven for gays, it excluded them from its onstage narratives for decades—Broadway did not consider gays and lesbians representable even though they often created and performed in the musicals that could not include them because of rampant homophobia. This duality is most keenly felt in the form's plethora of normative heterosexual romance narratives, often written by gay men, and most visibly by casting straight actors in LGBTQ+ roles.[5] *Village Voice* critic Julius Novick noted the historical disparity in his review of *La Cage*: "After decades during which homosexuals wrote, composed, directed, choreographed, designed, performed, and paid good money to see musicals celebrating heterosexual love, at last there is a musical—a hit musical—celebrating homosexual love."[6] *La Cage* librettist Harvey Fierstein would explain the seeming contradiction, saying, "Why do gay writers write about heterosexuals? One [reason] is social, the other is financial."[7]

Playwright William M. Hoffman described the bind of being gay in the theatre in the years just before *La Cage*, writing, "There is a myth that gay people can lead openly gay lives in the theater, where everyone is supposed to be accepted on their merits. . . . [I]t is almost obligatory to appear straight in the public eye if you want to survive in the theater."[8] The paradoxes of gay representation in the early 1980s are the subject of this chapter. An overview of how Broadway musicals staged homosexuality before *La Cage* opens the chapter and is followed by a historicization of how changes in gay politics primed *La Cage* to meet its moment. The bulk of the chapter then explores how the original production of *La Cage* cast its gay and drag roles and what that meant for the musical's politics.

La Cage has been too easily dismissed as fluff; it is more compellingly viewed in light of what musical theatre scholar Stacy Wolf terms the musical's "ability to do double duty—to promote conservative values and to provide empowering representations . . . sometimes simultaneously."[9] That *La Cage* consistently performed this double duty is evidence of its need to navigate oppression. Nowhere was this duality more evident than in *La Cage*'s casting, and contradictions in casting extended from the leads down to the chorus (Figure 4.1 shows the company of *La Cage*, with its heterosexual stars front and center). It is through the politics of casting that Broadway musicals embody and perform identity itself, and the stakes are higher for the marginalized than the mainstream. Like all musicals, *La Cage*'s approach to casting reflected its historical context and the norms of its day. However, the show itself—and its creators—were busy creating the very conditions that

Figure 4.1 Gene Barry and George Hearn with drag performers in a scene from the Broadway production of the musical *La Cage Aux Folles*. August 1983. Credit: Martha Swope. © The New York Public Library for the Performing Arts.

made open homosexuality not only possible but celebrated in later Broadway musicals. *La Cage* attempted to make change while its casting recreated the status quo. These contradictory stances were then-unremarkable products of their time, and its casting was essential to both the show's success and its inevitable shortcomings.

Broadway Musicals and Homosexuality: "Do They Have to Flaunt It?"

Broadway musicals signified homosexuality for so long that it was common to see plays referred to as *gay plays* but rarer to see musicals labeled *gay musicals*, perhaps because to utter the phrase would have admitted its redundancy.[10] For open confirmation of the connection, one need look no further than the 2011 Tony Awards' opening number, which joked that

118 SEXUALITY

Broadway was "Not Just for Gays Anymore," delivered with a wink by out gay Broadway star Neil Patrick Harris. [Clip 4.1] Scholars note the connection between musicals and gay men in particular, as well as its dissonance: Wolf explains the symbiosis of this particular relationship, writing, "Gay male culture is produced in part through engagement with musicals";[11] theatre historian John Clum opines, "Broadway's version of a gay musical is always problematic—foregrounding a comforting, stereotypical version of gayness for the bridge-and-tunnel crowd";[12] queer theorist D. A. Miller claims, "No gay musical is apt to elucidate what makes any musical gay."[13] While it is no longer a secret that Broadway musicals carry this association, relatively few Broadway musicals feature LGTBQ+ characters as protagonists. The gay best friend, like the fat best friend, is there to support the hetero-normative lead's journey.

Lesbian activist and writer Sarah Schulman describes how a typical narrative might work: "Gay people are rarely allowed to be the heroes unless they are tragic heroes, rescued by straight people. Straight audiences must not be expected to universalize to a gay or lesbian protagonist."[14] According to musical theatre scholar Elizabeth L. Wollman, despite more gay characters appearing in musicals in the years following the 1969 Stonewall riots, "these characters were often secondary and more often than not they embraced age-old stereotypes—the evil, bitchy queen; the swishing, squealing sidekick."[15] This kind of representation persists—see Damian, the teenage show queen sidekick, in *Mean Girls* or Elder McKinley in *The Book of Mormon*, who sings and tap dances about "turning off" his sexuality. These and other gay characters in musicals reinforce the stereotypical connections between gay men and musicals even as they also poke fun at the stereotypes. Broadway musicals might have *gay* written all over them, but they are still overwhelmingly straight.

When Broadway musicals acknowledged LGBTQ+ identity at all, it was largely in the guise of white cisgender gay male characters. This makes sense considering that so many musicals have been created by white cisgender gay men, and yet, in this way, it also shows how Broadway mirrors the structural inequalities in the United States, from misogyny and transphobia to white supremacy. White cisgender gay men were the first group within the LGBTQ+ population to gain a lot of visibility. The increasing representation of LBTQ+ people (minus the G) since 2000 follows offstage gains in visibility for those communities. Yet the number of musicals with gay male characters still far outstrips those with lesbian characters, which itself surpasses the number of musicals with bisexual, trans, or queer characters. Musicals with characters who perform in drag are relatively small in number though large in cultural impact and length of run. Musicals that *do* include gay male characters almost always associate them with performance, usually either as performers or as performance obsessed—making performance either a career choice or a survival strategy in a homophobic world. When musicals acknowledge gayness, it is generally within narrow boundaries on a spectrum from *freak* to *fabulous*. Musicals often contain homosexuality within the frame of a backstage musical, sanctioning the theatre as the space where *it* and *they* belong, drawing a sharp line between onstage and off.

La Cage was far from the first Broadway play or musical to include gay characters, though its approach *was* different, which made director Laurents unsure. He explained, "Since it's always been next to impossible to find a happy homosexual on the Broadway stage who is still happy at the final curtain, the notion of a multi-million-dollar Broadway musical with two happy homosexuals on stage at the final curtain seemed completely impossible to me."[16] This seemed impossible due to the low social position of and outright discrimination and stigma against gays and lesbians in the early 1980s, coupled with Broadway's decades-long checkered history of gay representation. It was never truly a given that Broadway was safe for gays. Events that occurred five and half decades before *La Cage* set the stage.

In 1927, police raided theatres to stop sexual "perversions" from being represented onstage, partially in response to the threat of Mae West's play *The Drag* coming to Broadway.[17] Police arrested West during the raid and forced the offending plays to close as a result of the City Hall–sanctioned raid.[18] The raids "are significant because . . . they resulted in legislation known as the Wales Padlock Law, which explicitly prohibited plays 'depicting or dealing with the subject of sex degeneracy, or sex perversion.'"[19] However, Wales Padlock did not mean gay characters completely disappeared from the stage. "Effeminate men have long been burlesqued on the stage, but the first bona fide homosexual characters in a musical were probably the 'Green Carnation' Quartet in Noel Coward's 1929 *Bitter-Sweet*. The first major homosexual character in a musical appeared twelve years later as Russell, the fashion photographer in *Lady in the Dark*, and a screaming queen," notes journalist Terry Miller.[20] Wales Padlock was not always strictly enforced, and Broadway plays and musicals alike (e.g., *A Streetcar Named Desire* and *Lady in the Dark*) tested the boundaries of permissibility in the 1940s with coded references to

120 SEXUALITY

homosexuality. Coding became the strategy of choice (Cole Porter's musical theatre lyrics, in particular, excel at this).

While the odd gay character existed in musicals before the Stonewall riots, the confluence of stigma, homophobia, and the law meant that representations were often either veiled so that only gay spectators and those in the know picked up on them or they were "the occasional screaming queen" legible to heterosexuals.[21] There was the odd coded reference like the one in Jerry Herman's 1966 musical *Mame*, in which two platonic girlfriends nodded to a famous literary lesbian couple when they sang, "I'll always be Alice Toklas/if you'll be Gertrude Stein." The 1967 repeal of Wales Padlock coupled with the gay liberation movement's emergence allowed musicals to step out of the closet more fully. *La Cage* was not even "the first Broadway musical to focus on a gay male relationship"; two flops (*Sextet*, 1974; and *Dance a Little Closer*, which lasted one night in 1983) had already featured gay couples in their narratives.[22] *Dance a Little Closer's* "Why Can't the World Go and Leave Us Alone" was the first romantic duet for a gay male couple on Broadway—sung on ice skates no less! In the 1970s, off- and off-off-Broadway musicals included more gay representation than Broadway did. Wollman explains that these musicals "were intended to entertain and empower gay men, but also to educate and reassure straight audiences who were new to and unfamiliar with gay culture" while also downplaying gay male sexuality.[23] *La Cage* picked up this trend for 1980s Broadway audiences.

But Broadway featured a lesbian love song long before *La Cage's* middle-aged gay romance. A long-overlooked show at the vanguard of lesbian representation in musicals is Melvin Van Peebles's 1971 *Ain't Supposed to Die a Natural Death*. The show featured a lesbian love song, "10th and Greenwich," sung by a Black woman to her lover jailed inside the women's prison located at West 10th Street and Greenwich Avenue.[24] [Clip 4.2] This song and its historical importance have remained largely overlooked in musical theatre histories. Critics at the time noted the show's lesbian representation but ignored its historic nature—for instance, Clive Barnes's *New York Times* review simply noted a "lesbian calling to her girl friend in the Woman's house of Detention."[25] Lesbian representation has long been a quieter presence in Broadway musicals than that of gay men. *Ain't Supposed to Die . . .* had an openly lesbian character, but another coded representation was seen in Matron "Mama" Morton in *Chicago* (1975/1996 revival). These representations were so rare that musical theatre scholar Wolf was compelled to note that for lesbian spectators, "the challenge is to determine how lesbians appear where none officially exist."[26] Wolf's reparative readings offered a necessary corrective for all of the decades in which lesbian representation in musicals was negligible.[27]

Off-Broadway audiences, at least, had been primed for exactly the kind of representational politics they would find on Broadway in *La Cage*, since "between 1972 and 1975, homosexuality was featured in several off-Broadway musicals (*Dear Oscar, Sextet, Boy Meets Boy*) and revues (*The Faggot, In Gay Company, Lovers*)."[28] Broadway audiences had seen stereotypical gay characters in musicals such as *Coco* (1969) and *Applause* (1970), which were both financially successful in the Broadway season immediately post-Stonewall (1969–1970).[29] A revival of *Irene* (1973) featured a stereotypical gay character, "Madame Lucy," and *Seesaw* in the same year featured Tommy Tune as a gay character "at a time when gay characters were rarely depicted in a sympathetic light."[30] Tune received a Tony nomination, but Michael Bennett cautioned him against bringing his boyfriend, Michel Stuart, as his date to the ceremony. Tune recalled that, unlike fellow nominees, he was not shown on camera as the nominees were announced: "I had arrived, but there was still that odd thing about the TV camera not picking me up in my seat—was it because of Michel Stuart? I've thought about this a lot, and I've decided the answer is, *yes*, because of Michel Stuart."[31] *A Chorus Line* depicted gay characters who were recognizably human and featured gay actors in gay roles, inevitably outing those who were playing composite versions of themselves. In sum, there were numerous theatrical antecedents that primed Broadway for *La Cage*.

La Cage aux Folles opened on Broadway on August 21, 1983. The familiarity of its plot helped mainstream audiences assimilate to its gay content. Fierstein explained, "Basically it's the same plot as 'You Can't Take It with You,' 'The Munsters,' 'Mame'—a classic farce plot about a weird family with a normal kid."[32] The musical, like the immensely popular 1978 French film of the same name, is based on the 1973 stage farce by Jean Poiret. The setting is drag nightclub La Cage aux Folles in St. Tropez, France; the time, summer. Long-term couple Georges and Albin own, manage, and live upstairs from the club. Georges is the club's emcee while Albin is its headliner as Zaza, his drag persona. Georges and Albin's lives are going along smoothly until George's son (from a fling), Jean-Michel, arrives with unexpected news: he is getting married to the daughter of the Deputy General of the "Tradition, Family, and Morality Party," who has "pledged to close down all the transvestite clubs if elected."[33] Jean-Michel's next bit of news is more unpleasant as

122   SEXUALITY

his fiancée Anne and her parents, the Dindons (*dindon* is French for turkey), are coming to dinner the following night. Jean-Michel and Georges sing the show's paean to heterosexual romance, "With Anne on My Arm," which is then reprised by Georges and Albin in the gender-neutral "With You on My Arm." Jean-Michel wants to trick his in-laws-to-be into thinking he comes from a traditional family, and so he has invited his estranged birth mother to take the place of Albin, who actually raised him in her stead, thus setting up the musical's primary conflict. Jean-Michel serves as the character that straight spectators can identify with; his journey from homophobe to ally serves as a model for the audience, too.

When Jean-Michel's mother does not show up, Albin concocts a plan to save the dinner by appearing in drag as her. All is going well until the butler Jacob burns dinner, leading the party to dine out at Chez Jacqueline, where fellow diners recognize Albin/Zaza and coax him into singing for them. At the end of his song, Albin rips off his wig just as he customarily would have done onstage, unmasking his identity and setting up the plot's resolution in the revelation of mistaken identity. Deputy General Dindon and his wife then realize they need the help of Albin/Zaza and Georges to get out of Chez Jacqueline without being seen by the photographers waiting outside. The solution is to dress the Dindons in drag and have them join Zaza's performance at La Cage that night. Jean-Michel's marriage receives everyone's blessing and the musical ends on an uplifting note as the bigots are saved by the drag queens and the heterosexual romance proceeds unimpeded, of course. As in *Hairspray* and other musicals, in *La Cage* the marginalized characters teach the more mainstream ones something about how to live.

La Cage became a hit despite opening to mixed and contradictory notices. Mainstream critics faulted it—especially Fierstein's libretto—for not going far enough in its depiction of gays while the gay press found more to like. In his *New York Times* review, Frank Rich called Georges and Albin "homogenized homosexuals" and the show itself "the schmaltziest, most old-fashioned major musical Broadway has seen since *Annie*."[34] He cautioned audiences not to "go expecting an earthquake," noting that "in its eagerness to please all comers, this musical is sometimes as shamelessly calculating as a candidate for public office." Rich's stance was incongruous considering his employer, the *New York Times*, banned the word "gay" from appearing in print from 1975 to 1987.[35] Ironically, *La Cage* was not gay enough for the *Times* in 1983. Rich's critique echoed those of other critics, who contended that *La Cage* did not possess the courage of its convictions and was afraid of offending the largely heterosexual audience.

The responses of critics for alternative and gay newspapers were generally more supportive, and though not all loved the musical, they at least understood its historic nature. In the *Village Voice*, Novick recognized the balancing act the musical had to perform: "Homosexual theater characteristically rejects ordinary middle-class values; *La Cage aux Folles* embraces those values. That is what enables it to achieve its mission of making the idea of homosexuality acceptable to the ordinary middle-class audience."[36] Terry Miller's review in the downtown gay paper *New York Native* asks, "Is *La Cage aux Folles* as good as you have heard? No. It's better. A lot of talented people worked very hard to create a fun '50s musical with a contemporary gay sensibility. The finished product is cause for celebration."[37] Michael Grumley's *Native* review explicitly called attention to the affirmative representation of a gay relationship: "In the twoness of *La Cage* is its magic: to see two men walking off into the sunset together, beneath the gilded arches of the Palace Theatre, is extremely satisfying."[38] These reviews counter what the mainstream press viewed as *La Cage*'s central weakness: its stereotypical depiction of gays. Casting straight men in the roles largely went unremarked by most critics, who viewed it as perfectly normal at the time since that was who nearly always played leading roles. The decades-long work to question and denaturalize this practice was just getting under way, dependent on the ever-shifting tides of LGBTQ+ politics and identities.

La Cage, Liberation, and Pride

Before gay pride became the dominant ideology of gay rights, gay liberation was prevalent (and before that, there were the homophile movements of the 1950s). In the 1970s, gay liberation aimed to rethink traditional sex and gender roles for all of society—not only gays and lesbians—and sought to eradicate capitalist, heterosexist, patriarchal structures.[39] Paradoxically, despite its anti-capitalist stance, gay liberation would not have been possible without capitalism, which "made possible the emergence of a gay identity and the creation of urban gay communities."[40] Gay liberation's stance toward capitalism meant that it would necessarily stand in opposition to the commercial aims, and thus the politics too, of any Broadway musical. However, this did not mean that a Broadway musical couldn't try to have it

124 SEXUALITY

both ways. The "bigger, grander, glossier" aesthetic of gay culture as evinced in *La Cage* was ironically begat by anti-capitalist gay liberation.[41] *La Cage* thus represented the Broadway-ification of gay liberation's aesthetic of excess but minus its sexual liberation, anti-capitalism, or solidarity with other social movements. Those not seeking liberation or revolution sought assimilation primarily through legal protection and incorporation into the mainstream, and this shift occurred profoundly in the early 1980s. *La Cage* straddled the line between assimilation and liberation.

However, *La Cage* also reflected the stance of assimilationists, which made it seem "as if we have to claim 'sameness' in order to advocate for equality."[42] In 1983, Fierstein explained his approach to gay representation, saying, "We're showing that marriage, commitment, family, don't have to belong to heterosexuals. We decided early on that our greatest enemy would be the tendency to hide, to avoid being honest. If a gay show is a hit and doesn't make a statement, what's the point?"[43] *La Cage* instructed spectators to accept gays not despite their difference but because of their essential sameness. This move opened *La Cage* up to accusations of being too assimilationist, too universalizing, too comforting.

The timing of *La Cage*'s Broadway opening gave its politics additional resonance. In New York City, Christopher Street Liberation Day began in 1970 to mark the first anniversary of the Stonewall riots and was later known as Gay Pride starting in 1984—*La Cage*'s first summer on Broadway.[44] The replacement of *liberation* with *pride* marked a crucial inflection point in the shift to a more corporate gay *equality* movement as pride became commodified and liberation a relic of a hedonistic past. The anti-capitalist, sexually free ideologies of gay liberation faded into the background in the early 1980s as AIDS tore through the world. While gay liberationists saw economic issues and sociocultural issues as parts of the coalitional struggles with other movements like Black Power and Women's Liberation, the rise of neoliberalism in the 1970s and 1980s undid what solidarity there was and, as social movements splintered, the way for the politics of assimilation to take hold was set forth.[45] Conservative politicians and media used identity politics to divide the mainstream rather than unite the marginalized. Concurrently, the rise of the right wing "Moral Majority" and its emphasis on traditional American family values meant, not entirely ironically, that *La Cage*'s middle-aged and presumably monogamous Georges and Albin more than met the moment.

Laurents understood the cultural stakes of the show and directed it to prove that "most straight American men . . . could nevertheless be gotten to applaud gays. They and theirs were the target audience, not the converted. If the show was any good, gays and the gay-friendly would provide audible support with laughter and applause. It was the enemy I was after."[46] *La Cage* co-opted the traditional family values that were anathema to gay liberation and refocused them on a family headed by a drag queen, her lover, and their son. Fierstein explained, "Everyone says I'm old-fashioned, that I'm trying to turn homosexuals into heterosexuals, but I believe that love and marriage and family and commitment do not belong to heterosexuals. They belong to the human experience, and gays should have those options."[47] That Fierstein used drag as the medium to do so also spoke back loudly to drag's low status in gay liberation.

For all its freedoms, gay liberation left little doubt as to drag's place. Theatre historian Laurence Senelick explains, "Drag performers were held in low esteem as a disgrace to a newly conspicuous gay community: apolitical, anti-feminist, unmacho, carnival jesters districting from the serious concentration with which clones pursued sex on piers, in back-rooms and empty trucks."[48] Gay liberation's emphasis on sex ultimately led to the body conformity of urban-dwelling gay men in the 1970s, who were commonly referred to as *clones* because of their increasingly similar and homogenous muscular bodies. Gay liberation's heightened and joyfully hedonistic sexuality passed by the monogamous middle-aged gay couple of *La Cage*, making them perfectly safe for Broadway audiences. That Albin sings the musical's anthem, "I Am What I Am," about his identity as a drag queen and not as a homosexual sealed the ideological separation in the show.

Several members of the creative team were ambivalent about drag in *La Cage*. Arthur Laurents did not want to direct the show because, as he put it, "drag turned me off."[49] He never believed the producers would find enough investors to finance the show due to its subject matter, and he did not initially want to audition drag queens, preferring to cast theatre actors. Herman, too, was uncomfortable with drag. He later explained, "I certainly don't want to spend *my* life in drag. I am a homosexual man who has never made any bones about his sexuality, but I would be mortified if somebody put a dress on me. . . . I like masculine clothes and masculine homes and masculine furnishings."[50] Costume designer Theoni V. Aldredge explained her own hesitance to the *San Francisco Chronicle*, saying, "It just didn't appeal to me

126   SEXUALITY

to be doing a drag show. I have nothing against them. I just don't do drag."[51] They may have held their noses, but they still could smell a hit in the making.

But drag was no stranger to Broadway theatregoers in that era. The musical *Sugar* (1972), based on the 1959 film *Some Like It Hot*, was a hit that required its two male leads to spend much of the evening in drag for comedic effect. Theatre scholar David Román explains, "The success of drag on Broadway in the 1980s, in such commercial hits as *Torch Song Trilogy*, *La Cage aux Folles*, and even *M. Butterfly*, demonstrated the demand for this type of gay performance," even though this demand left some spectators "with impressions that see gay men as entertainments" divorced from history or humanity.[52] Unlike his collaborators, Fierstein saw *La Cage* as a chance to grant dignity to both drag queens and gay men. He recounts, "A few years ago those people were looked at as freaks. What makes me cry in 'La Cage Aux Folles' is the attitude those drag queens have. They are not making fun of themselves."[53] Fierstein fought the idea that drag was a retrograde gay cliché but selling this to audiences in a country largely disapproving of homosexuality presented a challenge. Laurents described how contemporary sociopolitical realities determined his approach: "Despite all the drag, it was a family show."[54] Drag in *La Cage* was sanitized and desexualized just like its representation of homosexuality; the show's camp approach to gender and sexuality aimed to appeal to mainstream audiences.

La Cage also reflected racism in the United States and the absence of coalitional identity politics: Jacob is the show's only featured role regularly cast with Black and Latino actors in major productions, and he is the live-in domestic help. Actors Robin DeJesus (2010 revival), *A Chorus Line*'s Ron Dennis (1980s tour), William Thomas Jr. (original production), and Michael Benjamin Washington (2004 revival) all memorably played the role. In this way, *La Cage* was representative of the exclusion and disenfranchisement of vast segments of LGTBQ+ Black and Latinx people from movements for equality and gay rights. None of the musical's three Broadway productions ever cast anyone but white actors in the leading and supporting roles (apart from Jacob), though the ensemble has since been more inclusively cast. If in 1983, the production's focus was less on the show's racial optics onstage than it was on attracting straight white audiences, that reflected the aftermath of both the civil rights movement and gay liberation and how both movements' advances went only so far.

Because it was then so pervasive, homophobia inevitably shaped nearly everything about *La Cage*. "It is crucial at this point to understand how overt and vulgar the oppression against gay people was at that time," observes Schulman. "There was not even a basic gay rights anti-discrimination bill in New York until 1986."[55] As a result, overt physical displays of physical affection between men were so stigmatized in 1983 that the creative team methodically excluded them from the show. Prior to the Broadway opening, Laurents said, "I think gays are at the lowest end of the scale. Everybody looks down on gays."[56] He felt that Georges and Albin couldn't kiss for "risk of losing the audience we had worked so carefully to get."[57] Fierstein disagreed. Laurents recalled, "The [note] from Harvey was, 'The men should kiss at the end'" while others felt "the two men shouldn't even touch."[58] Fear and internal and external homophobia drove many decisions about the show; homophobia extended beyond the auditorium when executive producer Allan Carr had to be talked out of painting the Palace Theatre's exterior completely pink.[59] A decade after its premiere, Laurents explained, "I was very careful to keep sexuality out of it because . . . I felt this was an entertainment and that if I could do it right, it would help people see gays and not get turned off. . . . [I]t ran almost five years, and if it had screamed and yelled like Larry Kramer, it wouldn't have. It's a musical. [Straights are] not going to go, and in those days, they wouldn't have."[60] No one then could have foreseen the mainstreaming of gay representation and drag that would occur beginning in the next decade.

Gays were a marginalized but increasingly vocal minority beginning to harness their political muscle in the 1980s. While *La Cage* aimed to disentangle itself from gay politics onstage, being gay *offstage* became inherently political and increasingly tied to visibility, as gay politicians like San Francisco's Harvey Milk began urging people to come out in the 1970s.[61] But just as with fatness, bigots view homosexuality as a choice that individuals can control but choose not to, and the rise of AIDS only solidified these homophobic views. Sociologist Gerhard Falk notes the performative dimension of anti-gay attitudes: "Homosexuals suffer discrimination and rejection because of something they do. It is only in their performance that their stigma becomes an issue."[62] The *doing* of homosexuality made it an issue, rather than *being* gay—which only echoed dictums from the evangelical family values crowd like "hate the sin, love the sinner." Associating homosexuality and performance presents its own kind of ontological conundrum—if homosexuals are always performing identity, what lies underneath the performance? Contradicting the message of *La Cage*, it was less "I Am Who I Am" than "I Do Who I Am." The show's casting, however, suggested "I'm Not Who I Am Playing."

128   SEXUALITY

"Try to Imitate My Walk": Casting and Playing Gay

"So, like I said, we ended up with two heterosexuals. But what are you going to do? They have to work too."—Harvey Fierstein[63]

The casting of straight actors as *La Cage*'s leading gay couple and the ensuing volume of publicity around their heterosexuality made financial sense in 1983—Carr and his partners produced the show to make money after all—even though it was at odds with the musical's message. Casting *La Cage* happened in a context where actors viewed playing gay roles as a major career risk. The show's casting director Stuart Howard noted, "Sometimes it was very difficult" to get actors to even audition for the show given the timing and the subject matter.[64] He explained, "Many stars weren't interested in auditioning and they weren't interested in auditioning for these roles in this show." There were no well-known gay actors who could carry a Broadway musical who were also publicly out in 1983; and so, *La Cage* could not have cast gay stars even if they had tried. When asked whether casting two heterosexuals as the stars of the original production was strategic given that it was 1983, *La Cage* producer Barry Brown responded, "No, the conscious choice that we made at the beginning was to be very careful so that an audience would understand that these two men loved each other deeply, but never saw them as going to bed together. Because it was 1983. And it had little to do with AIDS."[65]

Casting George Hearn as Albin and Gene Barry as Georges was, by some measure, a disavowal of musicals' inherent gayness even though casting straight men as gay characters (written by gay men) flaunted the open secret of musical theatre's homosexuality.[66] Laurents was thus very careful about how the roles were to be played. Howard recalled Laurents requiring even celebrities to audition because "Arthur had never seen these people play this kind of role and wants to make sure they are never winking at the audience saying 'I'm straight.'"[67] The media spotlight on the heterosexuality of the show's stars provided cover for Broadway's open secret to continue since Jerry Herman and Arthur Laurents remained publicly closeted at the time. While Fierstein was then publicly out, he was pretty much alone among high-profile theatre folks. Other actors who were publicly out and famous were nearly impossible to find on Broadway, whether playing gay characters or not. Fear of coming out coupled with a public code of silence kept many in the closet even though within the industry itself one could be openly gay. For instance, actor Larry Kert, who would later tour as Georges in *La Cage*, was out to colleagues but not to the theatregoing public or the press.[68] *La Cage* incrementally helped to break this barrier, but another decade had to pass before coming out was more common and thus safer to do.

Hearn, who won the role of Albin at his first audition, told the *New York Times* about his *La Cage*-related anxiety, including waking in the middle of the night in a panic. He said, "I'd bolt upright and think, 'I'm going to do what? I couldn't believe I was going to do that in front of God and everyone—in Times Square, no less.' "[69] However, his anxiety was not about playing gay; he explained, "I didn't have any trepidation about playing a homosexual. Major actors do, because major actors are image conscious but I'm not a major actor and I had no particular image to tarnish. But playing a transvestite—I didn't know if I could handle it. It's exposing yourself to the possibility of ridicule; you worry about looking foolish, and about exposing the female side of your nature."[70] Gender crossing was scarier than homosexuality for Hearn, even though he famously donned drag at his audition for *La Cage*. *People* magazine even featured a photo of Hearn captioned, "What identity crisis?" alongside photos of Hearn and his girlfriend, underscoring the perceived social threat of playing gay and doing drag.[71] Hearn was game, however, and he had to learn how to walk in heels and to develop different strides for Albin, Zaza, and Sybil with the coaching of cast member Linda Haberman (Figure 4.2 shows Hearn in full Zaza drag).[72] (Ironically, this was the inverse of the coaching Albin received in "Masculinity" within the musical.) *La Cage*'s casting and its use of drag shored up traditional gender roles as much as they subverted them.

Hearn's performance earned him a Tony Award and much critical praise, and critics also noted Barry's quieter turn as well. Few major actors had yet played gay roles by 1983, which would change in the coming decades.[73] Straight actors would go on to make a habit of winning awards for playing gay, which increasingly was "a reflection of how oppression operates, not the reverse as is sometimes claimed or thought."[74] The visibility of a straight actor winning a major award for playing gay made it more difficult for gay actors to be considered for the same role because this would deny an opportunity for straight actors to demonstrate their virtuosity and signal their liberalism. The degree of difference between an actor's self and his role indicates the perceived difficulty of playing the role in the minds of many critics, awards voters, and spectators. Despite the presence of many openly gay actors, playing gay remained catnip for straight actors well into the 2010s.

130 SEXUALITY

Figure 4.2 *La Cage Aux Folles* (Broadway, 1983–1987). Based on the play by Jean Poiret. Music and lyrics by Jerry Herman. Book by Harvey Fierstein. Directed by Arthur Laurents. Shown: George Hearn. Credit: Photofest.

Barry's discomfort with playing the gay "straight man" to Hearn's drag queen and "the possibility of being stigmatized" almost kept him from taking the role.[75] Barry's role was less showy than Hearn's and, though he did not appear in drag, he did have to sing Broadway's newest gay romantic duet, "Song on the Sand." Barry told an interviewer, "You really do become the part you play. In rehearsal, George and I didn't look at each other as a man or woman, but as someone we dearly loved. If I ever had a problem,

I'd just think of my own wife."[76] Barry's logic reveals the mental leap he had to make to play a gay man. More troubling was Barry's outright denial of the sexuality of the couple; he explains, "We determined in rehearsals that my role of Georges would be played pretty straight. It's not really a homosexual part in the sense that we are playing two people who love each other who are involved in a family relationship,"[77] which directly conflicted with Fierstein's insistence that family relationships and love be available to gays. However, the show's universalizing logic of love and family blunted Barry's discomfort with playing gay. Barry consistently made his feelings about gays quite clear, telling *People*, "I don't want to be part of [Fierstein's] platform. I'm just playing a role."[78] Barry was afraid that taking the part would embarrass his family.[79] This discomfort extended to outright denial that made it to the pages of the *New York Times*, wherein he reiterated, "I'm not playing a homosexual—I'm playing a person who cares deeply about another person." He continued, "The role is loving another person onstage. It doesn't matter whether it's a man, a woman or a giraffe; it has nothing to do with sexuality, as far as I'm concerned. I play the dignity of the man, his concern for his lover and his concern and love for his son."[80] The odious comparison to a giraffe notwithstanding, Barry's refusal to admit that he was playing a gay man reveals the depth of his fear. Where's the dignity in such denial?

Barry seemed compelled to explain his approach in numerous interviews before the Broadway opening, but not all actors who played Georges felt this way. Peter Marshall played Georges later in the Broadway run, and when asked if, like Barry, he sought his family's advice first, he said, "Oh God, no, not at all! I never thought twice about it. If I got my family together to ask them they would have laughed so hard, they'd say 'Get outta here, are you crazy? Grab it!'"[81] When the original production opened in the West End with Hearn, his new co-star Dennis Quilley's logic echoed Barry's. Quilley said, "Heterosexuals make the very best gays on stage. . . . If you're gay you must be tempted either to stand back and not commit yourself or to go too far and indulge yourself. But I could play it objectively, just as I would, say, a murderer."[82] That the first two actors to play Georges in major productions compared playing a gay character to a wild animal and a murderer admits that seeing Georges as merely human was a challenge, even in a musical that sought to humanize gays, that these actors were not yet fully equipped to meet. These attitudes toward gays were widespread and they were what counted as tolerant in the mainstream then.

132   SEXUALITY

Once *La Cage* opened, critics took notice of the publicity devoted to the stars' heterosexuality. In the *New Yorker*, Brendan Gill exclaimed, "How tiresome it must be for these admired actors to be praised in the press for the feat of successfully impersonating homosexuals!"[83] Critic Robert Brustein perceptively identified the casting as emblematic of the musical's approach to identity in the first place, writing, "It was a shrewd move to cast heterosexual actors in these central roles, because it was a way to help the audience more readily accept the homosexual characters they play. But this is precisely the kind of evasion that makes *La Cage aux Folles* often seem so crudely manipulative, so dishonest and so crass."[84] The common wisdom was that the show hedged its bets by casting heterosexual actors as its leads, and in many ways, it did precisely that. The betrayal of *La Cage*'s casting was not just that it cast two straight men but that it also did not cast a single drag queen in the show. Senelick notes, "The professional drag community was outraged: why hadn't any of the experienced cross-dressers who had auditioned (like Lynne Carter) been cast. . . . These complaints missed the point: if the musical were to lure the general public, it had to be sanitized of any whiff of deviance."[85] Casting provided ample publicity even as it revealed the limits of *La Cage*'s incremental approach to gay representation.

When the first national tour opened in gay-friendly San Francisco, its stars spoke candidly about their approach to acting gay. The tour's Albin, Walter Charles, told the *San Francisco Chronicle*, "I didn't study gays. . . . I try to play the situation. I let the music and the costumes do most of the work. I go for the emotion, I make that real, make it beautiful. . . . This is what Arthur [Laurents] harps on all the time, the humanity—don't lose that. Otherwise it gets into caricature, then it slips into camp."[86] Keith Michell played Georges and he "said he looks at his role in non-sexual terms, feeling he is playing a person who cares deeply about another person. . . . Certainly, neither mince on stage. In his role Michell does not dress in drag, nor is he effeminate. He is debonair."[87] Given the de-sexualized nature of the roles themselves, it remains striking that so many interviews focused on the actors' offstage sexuality. Convincing potential spectators that its stars were heterosexual became the show's publicity strategy of choice.

Producer Barry Brown was in the room for *La Cage*'s Broadway auditions and his experience counters the narrative that the straight actors were cast because of their heterosexuality. When I asked him about the casting, he replied, "There's a really perfectly simple answer: because they were the best ones to audition. They came in, they auditioned with lots of other people, and they were the two best ones. That's why."[88] The creative team and producers kept their focus on making the most successful musical they could and maintain that they did not focus on anything else. The "best actor for the role" reasoning is so common in casting discourse that theatre scholar Brian Eugenio Herrera terms it the "mythos of casting," which he argues "simultaneously provides ideological rationale for the acknowledged inequities in the allocation of the paid and unpaid labor of actors while also sustaining faith that the apparatus of casting can (and sometimes actually does) work to identify the 'best' actor for a given role."[89] *Best* is always a value judgment, dependent on who was brought in to audition in the first place. Brown insists, "We never thought about [casting] as a message." Whether its creators intended to send a message or not, audiences inevitably received one both before attending and once at the show itself.

Casting the Cagelles and the "Real" Girls

La Cage placed more emphasis on its chorus than most musicals. These ten dancing men and two women were central to *La Cage*'s appeal because the casting of their roles in the show openly invited scrutiny over their bodies, specifically about their gender and sexuality. The Cagelles were the show's Broadway Bodies, and the drag elements of the show had the dancers playing at being gendered subjects and sexual objects. Whether gay or not, the male dancer was assumed to be, especially in the 1980s United States and most especially if he was dancing in drag. Many forms of Western theatrical dance have been associated with homosexuality in this country at least since Vaslav Nijinksy's 1916 American tour with the Ballets Russes, and this set the stage for the later perception of Broadway chorus boys as gay, too.[90] The stigmatization of male dancing is a labor issue and a sociocultural one; dance's historic perception as "women's work" contributed to the stigma attached to male dancers since dance is "too strongly [associated] with the feminine ever to be considered man's work."[91] Despite Broadway's reputation as gay-friendly, homophobia has also delineated which spaces within the industry tolerated open homosexuality. This, too, shifts in accordance with social norms. Broadway musical ensembles began to be more gay-friendly onstage in the 1970s with the success of *Pippin* in 1972 and *A Chorus Line* in 1975. Bob Fosse recalled that when casting *Pippin*, "Always before, if I found a male dancer that I knew was homosexual, I would keep saying, no, you can't do that, don't be so minty there. This time, I used the kind of people they were to

134 SEXUALITY

give the show a kind of individuality, and they were so happy about it I think it helped the show."[92]

Casting is a primary site where Broadway disciplines homosexuality and thus reveals the workings of internalized oppression since many doing the casting are gay themselves. Original *La Cage* cast member David Engel remembers an interaction with a gay choreographer who asked him, "'Will you butch it up?' He goes, 'You are totally gay.'" Engel notes that this choreographer offered the comment in the spirit of helping him since one had to be able to act straight to get cast. He took the advice to heart, saying, "I saw exactly what he was talking about. . . . I appreciated it."[93] Despite the fact that dancers could be more open about their sexuality offstage, onstage they were typically required to play it straight. The industry expected this performance of heterosexuality, and it became the necessary strategy for career survival for decades, re-inscribing the terms of the closet step by step. *La Cage* thus embodied one of the paradoxes of gay identity and musicals at the time; John Clum noted that "the queerness of the chorus boy only became confused when it became acknowledged, for acknowledging the queerness of the chorus, which in a strange way also acknowledged the queerness of some of the audience, led to odd, futile attempts to keep the musical itself closeted so as not to scare the straights away."[94] *La Cage*, however, used the ensemble's bodies (pictured in Figure 4.3) and their genderfuck not just to avoid scaring straight audiences away but actually to entice them.

The twelve Cagelles in the original Broadway production were infamously cast with ten men and two women meant to keep the audience guessing their gender. [Clip 4.3] Casting two women was the result of quick thinking on Laurents's part during backer's auditions while raising money for the show. A potential investor inquired, "Why aren't there any girls in the chorus line?"[95] Taking the investor's money meant more compromise; Fierstein was against casting women as Cagelles, later noting, "It was a silly cop-out. They were so scared of the material. I was openly gay. I didn't ever consider making apologies for what we were doing."[96] This was yet another nod toward making Broadway audiences comfortable with the show's subject matter: "If the audience knew they were all men, it could relax. Yet, since the program indicates that two of them are women, the audiences is forced to make choices," according to *New York* magazine.[97] This guessing game meant that the Cagelles' bodies needed a certain kind of uniformity so that audiences could not immediately guess their gender. The Cagelles' bodies, onstage at least, were another central way that *La Cage* repudiated contemporary gay politics since

Figure 4.3 Drag performers in a scene from the Broadway production of the musical *La Cage Aux Folles*. August 1983. Credit: Martha Swope. © The New York Public Library for the Performing Arts.

these bodies were not merely the bodies of gay clones but were, by some measure, their opposite since several layers of drag hid their bodies after all. Casting two cis women and ten cis men who could pass as women onstage bought into dominant aesthetics of beauty determined by the straight male gaze. None of this was exactly like drag for gay audiences.

Original Cagelle Deborah Phelan noted that the Cagelles "play a key role in the play. Les Cagelles tie the whole play together. They're the show within the show. They get the energy going."[98] Because of the Cagelles' dramaturgical functions and the fact that they were drag roles, casting them had different demands from those involved in casting the chorus of a typical musical. A 1984 casting call for replacements lists some of the requirements:

> "La Cage aux Folles" (M). Starring Peter Marshall. Equity chorus auditions being held Sept. 24: femme dancers who sing well at 10 a.m. (last name A thru K), 5'7" or taller, strong jazz, tap and possible acrobatics; male dancers who sing well at 2 p.m. (last name A thru K), strong jazz, tap, and

136 SEXUALITY

possible acrobatics, since choreography requires use of high heels, suggest you bring a pair to audition, although not a requirement.[99]

It's not every audition where male dancers are instructed to bring high heels. Brown sat in on all of the original auditions for the show and remembers, "The casting of those twelve Cagelles was a monumental job. First of all, everybody in the city auditioned for it. Everybody you could think of auditioned for it. So, it took days of auditions to whittle it down."[100] More than 2,000 dancers auditioned for the twelve spots. Choreographer Scott Salmon explained that "no real drag queens were engaged" for the ensemble because "the demands are too great for any but professional dancers."[101] The demands of the casting process were unique to La Cage, too. Salmon observed:

> The hiring of the people was very interesting. The tension you see in Chorus Line in two hours, these kids undergo over a period of weeks—the men are very vulnerable. We have to see people who have some sense of an androgynous quality. At the same time they must be technically very good dancers, they need to have a freedom to express some individuality, and they have to look good, their legs must be great. When they get down to the very final day of the audition, they undergo a two-hour makeup. They are dressed in heels, hose and a leotard, and then they are asked to do the combinations they had done before. And that's where you would find those people who would want to show me "I'm not really a performer like this. I'm really very masculine." They'd come out in high heels and walk stomp, stomp, stomp. I could tell which people would make jokes by stumbling on purpose, and which people were very secure within themselves and would just do it.
>
> The men have bare legs quite often in the show but they wear three sets of support stockings, which not only firm the legs and lift them up, but also cover any need to shave. We thought, "If we have them shave their legs and do a lot of that stuff, it makes them feel in another world. We want them to feel like actors playing a role, not like people who live their entire lives from the androgynous aspect of being drag performers." Nor are we trying to put anyone down. They do a number called "Masculinity," so they have to be equally as masculine as they are feminine.[102]

Phelan notes that even the nine women at the final callback also had to show up in Cagelle drag, and casting director Howard asked each one whether she "minded performing in drag."[103] Engel's audition experience in Los Angeles

LA CAGE AUX FOLLES 137

was decidedly different; producer Carr asked him to perform a striptease during the audition. Engel was down to his underwear before someone finally told him he could stop. He booked the job.[104]

The casting process displayed the musical's complicated, often contradictory, approach to identity. Beginning with auditions, making men comfortable with drag was part of the process. *La Cage*'s drag stressed artifice, unlike drag queens who emphasize *realness*, or the ability to pass. That the production did not require the male Cagelles to shave their bodies was less about their onstage characters than it was about allowing them to feel masculine after the curtain call. *La Cage* was all about illusion down to the stockings. Salmon reiterated this in directing their gender performance, reportedly telling the male dancers, "You're not here because you're screaming faggots or because you look or move like women."[105] But why *couldn't* those be the exact reasons for being cast as a Cagelle—especially since the point was to keep audiences guessing?

When the show was up and running, its print ads and posters often featured a female Cagelle, effectively offering potential spectators a tease of the show's gender play. Selling the gender guessing game, however, was just another evasion of *La Cage*'s homosexuality. If the show was well cast, the two women in the chorus would assuage any potential discomfort straight men felt for desiring the Cagelles, and so even the male Cagelles needed to appeal to straight men. *La Cage* was more complicated than it seems because it can be convincingly received in contradictory ways. The Cagelles toyed with audiences by claiming they "are what they are," but they embodied the reality that identity is illusory. If *La Cage* perfected the art of the tease in its casting and recasting of gender identity and homosexuality, what did it mean for a straight man to sing gay anthem, "I Am What I Am?"

Broadway Number: "I Am What I Am"

"I Am What I Am" is one of those first act closers that, like *Gypsy*'s "Everything's Coming Up Roses" and *Dreamgirls*' "And I Am Telling You I'm Not Going," reliably stops the show. Unlike those songs, which are both about denial, "I Am What I Am" is an anthem of acceptance. In the show, the melody changes function from when first heard as the opening number, "We Are What We Are," sung by the Cagelles, as a tease about their gender identity, to first person singular for the first act finale.

Laurents explains, "The song had to be sung in drag; that would mean sung in the nightclub where the play took place, but not as a number, because then it would merely be a message sung by a performer, not a character; and not without motivation, because then it would merely be a number in a show. It had to be an emotional outburst, but what did it burst out of?"[a] When Albin tears off Zaza's wig at the climax, his identity underneath the wig is suddenly exposed not just to the audience but to himself.

"I Am What I Am" was the production's song of choice for awards show performances, which seems straightforward enough but ended up completely embodying the tensions inherent in the show's approach to performing identity. *La Cage*'s original cast recording received a Grammy nomination, and the cast was invited to perform on the February 28, 1984 televised broadcast of the 26th annual Grammy Awards. Hearn declined, not wanting to miss any Broadway performances to travel to Los Angeles, which meant that his understudy Walter Charles would perform "I Am What I Am" in his place on the broadcast.[b] Jamie Ross, Barry's standby, appeared as Georges alongside Charles.[c] Charles performed the number in full drag at the Grammys [Clip 4.4], which was quite a departure even for television audiences who had likely seen drag used for comic effects like Flip Wilson's famous drag character Geraldine in the late 1960s and 1970s. Taking a drag queen's feelings seriously wasn't exactly business as usual.

However, at the Tony Awards that June, the same song received quite a different performance. *La Cage* was nominated for nine Tony Awards, including two nominations for Best Actor. Hearn was slated to sing "I Am What I Am" on the telecast. The performance begins with Barry as Georges introducing the musical's opening number, "We Are What We Are." The Cagelles performed the number in full drag, finishing to applause and removing their wigs as the camera zooms in to clue home viewers into the musical's gender play. Then, a cutout of Al Hirschfeld's line-drawing of Hearn as Zaza floats onstage as Hearn walks onstage *wearing a tuxedo* instead of Zaza's drag to sing "I Am What I Am" as the announcer says, "And now Zaza, the leading lady of *La Cage aux Folles*, Mr. George Hearn." [Clip 4.5] Instead of the song as a declaration of Albin/Zaza's identity, it became another chance for Hearn to publicly claim his *heterosexuality*. Given that it powerfully stages a moment of self-acceptance in the show, "I Am What I Am" here represented yet another emblem of Broadway's ambivalence toward non-normativity.

Original Cagelle Engel felt "the words he's singing went against the fact that [Hearn] did have some kind of shame about appearing on national television in drag. He wanted to just be him."[d] There was no wig to remove at the song's conclusion, no identity to expose underneath the drag. To have the song performed as a celebration of Hearn's heterosexuality was a stunning betrayal of Albin's message but was also typical of the contradictions of producing a gay narrative for heterosexual audiences at the time. When Hearn won the Tony later that night, he opened his speech by jokingly stating, "What some people won't do!"[e] The juxtaposition of Charles performing in full Zaza drag on the higher-rated, higher-profile Grammy Awards and Hearn performing in male drag on the lower-rated, lower-profile Tony Awards is a whiplash-inducing example of the ways *La Cage* tried to have it both ways.

"I Am What I Am" found its own life outside of the musical, surprising Herman, who recalled, "I never thought it would take its place as an anthem; I wrote it for a character at a specific moment."[f] That the most famous versions were by Black women and gay icons only cemented its status as a gay anthem: disco diva Gloria Gaynor scored the first hit with the song in 1983 [Clip 4.6], followed a year later by Shirley Bassey's theatrically grandiose rendition. Removed from its musical theatre context, the song became a staple of gay clubs and gay pride parades the world over. Yet it is telling that the song became a hit when sung by women, seducing gay men into identifying with a strong female voice, much like Broadway musicals themselves do.[g] After all, in the show itself Zaza is the leading lady. She embodies D.A. Miller's theory that "the female performer will always enjoy the advantage of also being thought to *represent* the stage, as its sign, its celebrant, its essence, and its glory; while the male tends to be suffered on condition that, by the inferiority or subjection of his own talents, he assists the enhancement of hers."[h] And though Miller was not describing the relationship between Georges and Albin in that quote, he might as well have been. While "I Am What I Am" may be Zaza's at first, in the end it serves as Albin's reclamation of his whole self—which is bound to his male drag offstage and his female drag onstage. Perhaps the ultimate point of *La Cage* is that no one is who they proclaim to be, even when they are belting it out downstage center.

[a] Laurents, *On Directing*, 120.

[b] Hofler, *Party Animals*, 179.

[c] Theatergeek1122, "Walter Charles 'I Am What I Am.'"

[d] Engel, interview with author.

[e] MrPoochsmooch, "La Cage aux Folles 1984 Tony Awards."

[f] *La Cage aux Folles* program, Playhouse Theatre, 2008.

[g] Miller, *Place for Us*, 87–89.

[h] Miller, *Place for Us*, 71.

AIDS and *La Cage*'s Impact

The de-sexed couple in *La Cage* thus demonstrates perfectly the political and personal shift from ideologies of liberation to those of assimilation and pride in the age of AIDS. This move echoed the message of gay activists at the time: stop having sex. Along came *La Cage* where the gay couple barely touched each other, let alone kiss. Outside of the theatre, debates raged among gays. Writer Edmund White remembers, "We were incensed: Like most gays (and many straights), to us political liberation meant the freedom to be promiscuous."[106] But free love grudgingly gave way to safe sex in the age of AIDS.

AIDS informed *La Cage*'s presence and its reception. The show attracted occasional protestors despite its family-friendly politics. Brown remembers when one of the national tours played Buffalo in the 1980s, "there were people carrying placards in front of the theater saying, 'Homos go home, we don't want your filth in our city.' "[107] One actor who toured with the show recalled arriving in Atlanta and discovering that "the stage hands at the Fox were wearing latex surgical gloves in protest."[108] Public attitudes toward gays in the 1980s furthered homophobia; a majority of respondents to a Gallup poll felt that "homosexual relations between consenting adults" should be illegal. According to Gallup, it was only in 1985 that responses swung in that direction; when asked this question in 1982, 45 percent of respondents said that gay sex should be legal, versus 39 percent opposed.[109] While *La Cage* played on Broadway and toured the United States, public attitudes toward gays shifted for the worse as fear of AIDS grew. Gay liberation's sexual freedom evaporated as AIDS ravaged first gay men, and then the world. AIDS became inevitably linked to anything portraying gay men in the 1980s, whether it was part of the work or not. *La Cage*'s depiction of love in the time before AIDS suddenly seemed nostalgic.

The burden of gay representation was steep in this climate, making *La Cage* and the work it did more complex than it first seems—substance existed beneath the sequins. David Engel explained the juxtaposition, saying, "You couldn't really be out, certainly not professionally in most professions. Right as we're gaining a little ground, AIDS comes along, and it just undid so much of the progress. And at the same time, the show happened."[110] Ten years before *La Cage* opened, the American Psychiatric Association voted to remove homosexuality from its *Diagnostic and Statistical Manual* (*DSM*). Though homosexuality was no longer officially considered a mental illness after 1973, it would remain a crime until 2003 for men to have sex with other men because of sodomy laws still on the books. US voters overwhelmingly elected Ronald Reagan president in 1980 and his lack of action on AIDS—essentially state-sanctioned discrimination—contributed to mass death and increased the stigmatization of gays and people with HIV/AIDS. During *La Cage*'s original Broadway run in 1986, "The Supreme Court upheld a Georgia law by ruling that consenting adults do not have a constitutional right to engage in homosexual acts in private."[111] It's not hard to understand why Laurents would not let the leading men of *La Cage* kiss given the sociopolitical climate that would only get worse before it got better. Anti-gay attitudes permeated the highest levels of government; the Reagan administration openly joked about AIDS at press conferences.[112] By the time Reagan gave his first public speech on AIDS in 1987, a staggering six years into the epidemic, more than 20,000 Americans had died of AIDS-related causes.[113] AIDS hit Broadway especially hard.

When the creative team began working on *La Cage*, they couldn't have foreseen how what was then known as "gay cancer" would become AIDS. Brown remembered that during the time they were putting *La Cage* together, they "never thought about it, never talked about it. It was a non-issue."[114] Laurents explained his attitude at the time: "Just about the time we went into production, something called GRID infected the gay community. Even when GRID turned into AIDS, it was largely ignored, even by the population hardest hit."[115] As AIDS spread, so did ignorance and fear. Fierstein remembered how AIDS-stigma infected the original company of *La Cage*, recounting that "Gene [Barry] wouldn't get on an elevator with the chorus boys in *La Cage*. These are people he's been rehearsing with for months. . . . All of a sudden, he didn't want to get on the elevator with them. That kind of stupidity at the beginning of the AIDS crisis was everywhere, so if it was in our community and people that should have known better, why could it not have been in the general population?"[116] Barry's fears were not confined just to AIDS, and "the show's publicist, Shirley Herz felt that Barry's concern went beyond the disease. 'He kept asking me if people would think he was a homosexual because he was in *La Cage aux Folles*.' "[117] These attitudes grow out of the fear that gay men's *bodies* themselves were sites of contagion. As the clone look of the 1970s gave way to bodies ravaged by AIDS, gay men's bodies went from tight and toned to wasting away precipitously fast.

The incongruity of a Broadway musical in the 1980s daring to declare "the best of times is now" is unbearably poignant, especially as the theatre lost so

142   SEXUALITY

many to AIDS. Fierstein lamented, "We lost half the cast of the first production to AIDS."[118] Theatre owner James Nederlander Jr. said that he thought "it was a groundbreaking show" that "would have been more successful had there not been the AIDS scare at that time."[119] The show's co-producer, George W. "Fritz" Holt, died of AIDS-related pneumonia in 1987. As was typical, his obituary listed his cause of death as "complications from pneumonia" and included no mention of HIV/AIDS nor of his ex-partner and co-producer on *La Cage*, Barry Brown.[120] Conservatives blamed people with AIDS, especially gay men, both for spreading the virus and for contracting it in the first place as a result of their behavior, which conservatives viewed as immoral and uncontrollable. *La Cage* was not the only production to fall prey to AIDS stigma; Tommy Tune remembered how his *My One and Only* co-star on tour in the mid-1980s stopped kissing him onstage because her husband was worried that Tune "might have AIDS."[121]

The original production of *La Cage* closed on November 15, 1987, eight months after the birth of ACT UP (AIDS Coalition to Unleash Power). ACT UP's tactics of direct actions and radical performative protest contrasted with *La Cage*'s gentler-albeit-assimilationist politics. LGBTQ+ activists were fighting for their lives in a country that betrayed and demonized them, making *La Cage* newly at odds with the tenor of the times. *La Cage*'s casting seemed to have squandered a momentous political opportunity by casting two straight men as George and Albin, but *La Cage* also created the possibilities for gay actors to play gay roles even if it didn't realize these possibilities at first. Its very presence allowed new possibilities to emerge. A cast member of the 1987 tour noted that it was "a cast of all openly gay men. Okay, maybe not openly to the press, but you're not going to change people's minds with a piece of theater if you can't get them into the theater."[122] He also noted, "Gay is not universal. Drag is not universal. Love is universal, and that is what made the show work. It wasn't about shying away from homosexuality, it was about exposing the shared truth." In shying away from homosexuality, though, the show unintentionally exposed hard truths about the status of gays in the United States.

La Cage means something to audiences because of and despite its contradictions; it veers between progressive (for the time) and conservative, constantly trying to have it both ways. Even its most scathing critics admit an attachment to the difference between what it *might* have represented and what it *did*. Queer theorist D. A. Miller counted among those disappointed, yet he too found the musical hard to entirely dismiss as a gay man hungry to see himself represented: "We would gladly put this disappointing show behind us, but as it also happens to be the goal we thought we were seeking, we hardly know to where we must move on."[123] *La Cage* matters because it pierced homophobia's veil in the 1980s eight times a week on Broadway and around the country. Laurents recalls that when he was staging "Song on the Sand," "I looked around that rehearsal studio, with the company sitting around, I saw half of them crying. They were gay and never thought this would be done on a Broadway stage in their lifetime."[124] Herman ended up proud of the musical's impact, noting, "I didn't write [it] as a militant piece. . . . But the fact that it has changed some people's ideas about gays, some prejudices about homosexuality is a real plus."[125] In performance, the show could transcend concerns over its casting. Questioning the show's politics risks ignoring the very qualities that gave the show its resonance: its politics of joy and acceptance seemed apolitical and out of step with the tone gay activism was then expected to take. And yet experiencing joy was itself a radical act in the face of mass death.

Laurents noted, "I've been in the theater a long time but I have never seen an audience respond as they do with this show. It's not the greatest story, or the greatest music, or the greatest direction. But something, when all this is put together, is at work that can't be analyzed logically."[126] Fierstein explained whom he saw as the musical's center, saying, "Everyone thinks the heart of the show is about the drag queen. . . . But actually, it's Albin's partner Georges and his son that have to figure it all out. When it comes down to it, it's their story and their honesty that's at the core of it all."[127] The musical allowed straight audiences to identify with (and perhaps to desire) gay characters, for once. Fierstein later claimed, "Anybody who saw *La Cage* live on stage left the theatre as a different person."[128] Simply seeing a love song sung between two men in a Broadway musical from 1983 to 1987 was a small revolution—even in its banality and bathos—when the prevalent images of gays in the media at the time were either those dying of AIDS or protesting their dehumanization by the US government. Broadway demanded that audiences "Look over There" while the president refused to even say AIDS out loud. Audiences of all stripes could pretend for a few hours that "the best of times is now," knowing full well that it was a lie.

La Cage made visible in Broadway musicals what had been hiding in plain sight for decades: their inherent, if latent, gayness. Visibility was part of what gay liberationists had sought, but now that a Broadway musical achieved a new level of it, what did it mean to have gay representation become

144 SEXUALITY

commodified for Broadway producers' profit? Schulman counters that representation and queer visibility, though important, are not enough: "Most Americans now know that homosexuals exist. Simply representing us is falsely coded as 'progress.'"[129] Laurents was well aware of these kinds of sentiments but felt that representation was necessary to counter those who "did not want gays to be seen as having the same problems as all other human beings."[130] Even though it depended on stereotypes to achieve that end, *La Cage* used stereotypes as a kind of Trojan Horse to spread its message of family values and its own brand of gay politics.

Laurents and Herman eventually came around and openly acknowledged the show's politics—only after it was an established hit. Both appeared in a promotional video for *La Cage*'s national tour in the 1985. Laurents then said, "The material is very dangerous. It walks a fine line. I was determined not to have any camp. Not to have any stereotypes. Actually, I think it's a very political piece. And I think, patting all of us on the back, it's so entertaining that people don't realize it's that political." Herman observed, "It's nice—I hate this word—but when a message comes out of a musical without trying. We didn't force that. It came very natural."[131] The creative team, it seems, knew what they were doing all along. Given the sociopolitical context and place of gays in the United States in the 1980s, the enormous financial stakes, and the number of jobs involved, their strategy was not only shrewd artistically but fiscally, too.

Despite making profitable properties like *La Cage*, LGBTQ+ people were still not so easily assimilated into all walks of US American life. Broadway changed its tune, but in crucial ways the United States did not. While legislation alone cannot fully solve structural homophobia, LGBTQ+ people are still denied full and equal protection under the law. It is crucial to note that as of this writing, there remains no federal anti-discrimination law and it was entirely legal to fire someone for being gay or transgender in one-third of states until 2020.[132] *La Cage* powerfully cast gay men as part of America (even though the show was set in France, which also signified *gay* at the time, Broadway musicals are somehow always about America). As Fierstein notes, "America is about money. It's a capitalistic country. If you make money, *that* makes you American."[133] Perhaps Fierstein was right about money making you American. If being represented on Broadway made gays commodifiable—even as it used heterosexuals to represent them—then who did that really liberate?

5

"Keeping It Gay" on The Great White Way

Scene: The 2000 Tony Awards at Radio City Music Hall

Rosie O'Donnell: "How's my beard?"
Nathan Lane: "I'm fine. How are you?"
Rosie O'Donnell: "I'm OK. Thanks."

Sometimes Broadway openly joked about the closet, as in the above exchange between two of Broadway's biggest names—one out, one closeted—at the 2000 Tony Awards.[1] [Clip 5.1] Lane memorably came out a few years later, quipping to a reporter, "I'm 40, single and I work a lot in the musical theater. You do the math. What do you need—flash cards?"[2] Like other publicly closeted but privately out actors, both Lane and O'Donnell preferred to keep their private lives private. While their sexuality was an open secret to theatre insiders, the general public was kept from it—hence the joking. It would have been safe for both to be out in Broadway circles but much riskier if they wanted to continue working in television and film, where coming out could still mean career suicide. After both came out, Lane and O'Donnell's subsequent returns to Broadway demonstrated that it *was* possible for stars to be out and still have a career, in theatre at least—this possibility marked an important shift in Broadway's relationship to the closet.

Lane and O'Donnell also could come out because Broadway's body politics meant they did not risk losing chances to play romantic leads since they were usually cast in comedic roles, though as stars they were still subjected to the financial pressures of carrying a Broadway show. On top of this, the increasing overlap and interplay of mass culture (especially television and the internet) with Broadway and changing social mores from the 1980s onward meant that Broadway's onstage conservatism was often at odds with its offstage liberalism when it came to gay and lesbian issues. Broadway's

Broadway Bodies. Ryan Donovan, Oxford University Press. © Oxford University Press 2023.
DOI: 10.1093/oso/9780197551073.003.0006

146 SEXUALITY

orientation toward sexuality until the late 1990s was that it was OK to be gay offstage if the stage door was also the closet door.

As Broadway increasingly featured more LGBTQ+ characters during the 1990s and 2000s than ever before, it still initially centered white gay male characters, though sometimes musicals were more inclusive, like *Passing Strange* (2008) and its several queer characters. Since musicals' creators are disproportionately white gay men, the increased representation was a kind of self-representation after decades in which gay characters appeared mostly as coded, camp, or stereotype (as noted in chapter 4). While musicals had not yet represented many under the queer umbrella, gay men's growing representation in the 1990s marked definite progress. Homophobia was so common that theatre scholar Jill Dolan noted that then it was "remarkable that queers have managed to move into a public representational frame at all."[3] Broadway's increased LGBTQ+ representation responded in kind to the newfound visibility of LGBTQ+ people in politics and, especially, mainstream entertainments in the late 1980s and 1990s. Broadway's embrace of queerness was not without ambivalence. As much as Broadway purports to be LGBTQ+ friendly, homophobia often comes from within the industry itself, whether in the euphemistic ways that agents, casting directors, choreographers, and directors give notes to performers, or from the top of the industry, where theatre owners like the Nederlanders make donations to politicians who support anti-LGBTQ+ policies.[4] But money doesn't always talk. Though *La Cage* proved the commercial viability of openly gay Broadway musicals in 1983, nine years would elapse before another Broadway musical—*Falsettos* (1992)—would attempt a similar feat.

The 1990s could rightfully be called the *Queer Nineties* due to the reclamation of the word *queer* by activists and scholars, and this chapter delves into the 1990s and its afterlives on Broadway. The rapid explosion of theatre artists coming out paralleled the increase in queer representation and opened new frontiers of queerness on and beyond Broadway. This chapter first surveys LGBTQ+ representation's sudden expansion in Broadway musicals during and just after the 1990s in concert with the growing visibility of LGBTQ+ rights in the United States. I then examine how Broadway musicals finally began to grapple with AIDS, and how they later practiced a troubling way of addressing it. The chapter then homes in on the coming out of Broadway actors in the 1990s, when making this move still carried a profound risk due to AIDS stigma and still-rampant homophobia. The newfound ability of out actors to be cast at all, coupled with the sudden increase

"KEEPING IT GAY"   147

of more queer characters to play was a measure of how things had changed. Finally, I interrogate how Broadway's body issues complicated its newfound queer-friendliness. Casting musicals became less about assimilating difference than about enforcing a kind of body conformity drawn from gay male body culture. The entanglement of gay male body culture and Broadway musicals found its way onstage, recasting the aesthetics of Broadway bodies in a different light.[5]

If the '90s were queer, they were hard-fought to be defined as such. The country was torn by explosive political battles over gay rights—from right wing politicians suggesting the enforced quarantine of people with HIV/AIDS in the 1980s to debates over the exclusion of gays and lesbians in the military in the 1990s.[6] When Bill Clinton was elected president in 1992, he promised to be the most gay-friendly president the nation had yet seen, and thus his signing of two anti-gay bills into law was a deep betrayal. Clinton had pledged to end the US military's ban on gays and lesbians serving openly, but he compromised by signing the bill known as "Don't Ask, Don't Tell," which placed enlisted LGBTQ+ servicemembers in a bind: "Gay people who wanted to join the armed forces would no longer be forced to lie about their sexual orientation, but they were still not permitted to disclose their sexuality."[7] In practice, this meant coming out would cost your job, recalling the Cold War–era Lavender Scare, where the federal government ferreted out and then terminated employees discovered to be gay. Congress did not repeal the policy until 2011, once the military had discharged more than 14,000 LGBTQ+ service members. Of course, many LGBTQ+ people were against the very idea of the military itself and used their energy to wage battles in other arenas. Coming out was a labor issue. As in earlier decades, discrimination started at the highest levels of the government and trickled down; but the reverse is true, too—homophobic politicians can't be elected without a homophobic electorate.

The larger questions being considered in the United States sought to address the place of gays and lesbians in society. Inclusion in the military was not necessarily the goal of gay activists but being excluded from it laid bare all the other ways that the United States had institutionalized anti-gay discrimination. Clinton's second anti-gay bill was the Defense of Marriage Act, signed into law when he was up for reelection in 1996. This bill defined marriage as the union between one man and one woman and restricted who could marry accordingly. After Clinton, the second Bush administration was even worse than the first, and by the twenty-first century, battles over the civil

148   SEXUALITY

rights of LGBTQ+ Americans were increasingly waged on multiple fronts, especially by voters and in the justice system. As much as there was regress, progress toward legal equality also happened. First, the Supreme Court made gay sex legal when it struck down sodomy laws in 2003 in Lawrence v. Texas. The following year, however, voters in eleven states approved initiatives banning same-sex marriage (as it was then-called). The Supreme Court made equal marriage legal in 2015, but perhaps the most sweepingly consequential LGBTQ+ Supreme Court decision came in June 2020, when a majority of justices agreed that the 1964 Civil Rights Act applies to LGBTQ+ Americans and that they could not be fired from their jobs because of sexual orientation or gender identity. This decision represented a huge win, though its focus on *firing* does not address discriminatory *hiring* practices that have excluded many LGBTQ+ people from employment, including on Broadway.

LGBTQ+ Representation in Broadway Musicals after La Cage

As US culture and mainstream attitudes toward gays and lesbians gradually shifted in the years after *La Cage aux Folles*'s Broadway run (1983–1987), so did Broadway musicals. The changes can be seen in *La Cage*'s creative team: while Harvey Fierstein was the only member of the *La Cage* creative team to be publicly out in 1983, by the 1990s both Arthur Laurents and Jerry Herman also publicly came out. Herman even shared his HIV+ status in 1992—a nearly unthinkable act in 1983.[8] Straight plays with gay subjects on Broadway helped shape the new terrain for musicals and musical theatre artists.[9] Fierstein's *Torch Song Trilogy* (1982) paved the way for Tony Kushner's two-part opus *Angels in America* (1993–1994) and Terrence McNally's *Love! Valour! Compassion!* (1995). Queer representation in musicals and plays of the 1980s and 1990s marked a shift away from the gay and lesbian representation of earlier decades, where plays that portrayed homosexuality at all showed it as deviant and/or in need of a cure, and queer characters were often dead when the curtain rang down, in plays like Tennessee William's *A Streetcar Named Desire* (1947) and Lillian Hellman's *The Children's Hour* (1934).

After only three Broadway musicals with gay or lesbian characters in the 1980s (*Dance a Little Closer*, *La Cage*, and *Grand Hotel*), that number more than tripled in the 1990s (including flops like *Nick & Nora* and hits like *Rent* and *Kiss of the Spiderwoman*), which then tripled again in the first decade of the new millennium (including *The Full Monty, The Wild Party, The Producers, Passing Strange,* and *[title of show]*) and grew further in the next decade, which began with the second revival of *La Cage* and ended with *Jagged Little Pill*.[10] Sometimes these characters were secondary roles like the two couples in *The Wild Party* (2000) or the manager of the Four Seasons in *Jersey Boys* (2006).

On Broadway, one was likely to find LGBTQ+ characters as comic relief and sidekicks to heterosexual leads. This was true in new musicals like *The Producers* (2001) and in revisals of older musicals like David Henry Hwang's new libretto for *Flower Drum Song* (2002), which traded stereotypes of Asian Americans for stereotypes of gay men. Hwang's attempt at including a "gay confidante" fell short, with critic Michael Kuchwara observing, "Talk about stereotypes. If you are going to perpetuate one at least give him better jokes."[11] Gay characters became a fashionable add-on as writers inserted gay characters into revivals and revisals of musicals whose narratives did not initially include them—and most of these productions flopped; others include the 2008 revisal of *Pal Joey*, the 2011 revisal of *On a Clear Day You Can See Forever*, the 2014 revisal of *Side Show*. Swish sidekicks and "fabulous" gay stereotypes were mainstays in Broadway musicals like *Spamalot* (2005), which featured the disco-inflected coming-out song "His Name Is Lancelot," and *Billy Elliott* (2008), in which Billy and his best friend Michael tap dance in drag. Drag became Broadway's preferred version of pride. [Clip 5.2]

There was an increase in lesbian and bisexual representation, but stereotypes of gay representation never went away, as supporting roles in *The Producers* (2001) and *The Book of Mormon* (2011) attest; *The Producers* featured the song advising to "Keep It Gay,"[12] [Clip 5.3] while *The Book of Mormon's* big tap dance is called "Turn It Off." "Keep It Gay" is director Roger deBris's philosophy for staging musicals, while "Turn It Off" jokes about suppressing one's homosexuality as a Mormon. *Rock of Ages* (2005) also included a slew of gay jokes and a seemingly unwitting gay couple who realize they "can't fight this feeling anymore." In 2007, *Legally Blonde* featured a song, "There! Right There!," that repeatedly joked about guessing whether a man was "gay or European." Broadway musicals self-referentially reclaimed stereotypes about gay men and musicals in *Mean Girls* and *The Prom* (2018). There are more musicals that practice this brand of self-reflexivity than those that grapple with the AIDS crisis, and this speaks to how musicals and US culture more broadly viewed gay men: as camp figures of fun.

150   SEXUALITY

At other times, LGBTQ+ characters were protagonists in musicals like *Falsettos* and *The Color Purple*—Celie in the latter is arguably Broadway's first lesbian protagonist, though she never self-identifies as such. But before *Rent* and *The Color Purple* existed, *Grand Hotel* (1989) staged lesbian desire. *Grand Hotel* is emblematic of several ways Broadway musicals and LGBTQ+ identity intersected in the 1980s and 1990s: its supporting character Rafaella embodies the paradoxes of LGBTQ+ visibility, AIDS severely impacted the show, its casting highlighted the stakes of actors coming out as the '90s began, and its director-choreographer Tommy Tune was famously not straight. Personal assistant Rafaella expresses her unrequited love for her employer, the ballerina Elizaveta Grushinskaya, in two songs: "What You Need" and "Twenty-Two Years/Villa on a Hill." Critic Frank Rich noted Rafaella's butch appearance and the oblique textual references to her identity in his *New York Times* review, writing, "Were she not dressed as a man, even the love she feels for the ballerina would dare not speak its name."[13] *Grand Hotel*'s obliqueness regarding Rafaella's desire recalled the decades in which musicals coded their queer references—if you picked up on the musical's aural and visual clues, you understood her feelings were deeper than devotion to her job. Rafaella's songs were Broadway firsts for this decade, though they did not mark the first time Broadway had let "the love that dare not speak its name" sing out.

Musicals after 1990 included lesbian characters most often only in secondary roles. In *Falsettos*, the lesbian couple next door is never even given names onstage, only in the *Playbill* (and in the advertising for the 2016 revival).[14] *Rent* (1996) famously featured a lesbian couple in Joanne and Maureen, whose songs were as memorable as their combustible sexual chemistry—this was as far from the kind of de-sexed gay couple seen in *La Cage* as you could get. After *Rent*, *The Wild Party* (2000) and *If/Then* (2014) followed. Lesbians received comic but stereotypical depictions in musicals like *Nick & Nora* (1991) and *Legally Blonde* (2007). While lesbian representation has demonstrably increased, only a handful of musicals with lesbian protagonists remain, and they are all variations on coming out: *The Color Purple*, *Fun Home* (2015), *It Shoulda Been You*, *Head over Heels*, and *The Prom*.[15]

While drag, gay men, and gender-crossing had been visible on Broadway for decades, other identities under the LGBTQ+ umbrella received greater representation only after 2010. Bisexual characters had been hinted at on Broadway in moments like *Hair*'s "bisexual love triangle" in 1969,[16] the stories of dancers in *A Chorus Line* who practiced kissing with other girls, the kiss between two women in *Aspects of Love* (1990), Cliff's bisexuality in the 1998 revival of *Cabaret*, and Shug Avery's sexuality in *The Color Purple*. The 2010s saw bisexuality take center stage in *Jagged Little Pill* (2019) and in secondary plots in musicals like *If/Then* (2014), the 2015 revival of *Spring Awakening*, *Be More Chill* (2018), and *Tootsie* (2019).[17] Bisexuality has been paradoxically visible and overlooked, much like lesbian representation. There remain very few transgender, non-binary, or gender nonconforming characters in Broadway musicals—and this lack has translated into pressure to get the representation of these communities right when they have been included at all. The only Broadway musicals (through 2020) to include trans characters in their narratives are *Priscilla, Queen of the Desert* (2011) and *Bring It On* (2012).[18] *Head over Heels* (2018) included the non-binary character of the oracle, Pythio. Broadway's lack of progress on more inclusive gender representation is a notable absence since it cannot seem to quit producing musicals where gender crossing and drag are played for laughs.

If Broadway was out of the closet onstage, offstage it was not quite so simple. Even though some musicals appear to celebrate identity onstage, this was not the case behind the scenes. LGBTQ+ acceptance increased steadily since the 1980s, the marketing campaigns for nearly all of the musicals mentioned in this chapter largely eschewed revealing their subjects at all.[19] The lack of lesbian representation mirrors the lack of gender parity in the determination of whose work gets produced on Broadway and the fact that, as critic Elisabeth Vincentelli notes, "there is the common wisdom that Broadway . . . is the province of gay men" since "gay stories are assumed to have a relatable universality—and thus a commercial appeal—that is not as easily granted to lesbian stories."[20] Solely looking at the numbers, it is clear that plays and musicals by women are de facto barred from making it to Broadway; lesbian representation only intensifies the barriers unless these are written by a man or secondary to the plot. Broadway might love a diva, but it largely excludes women writers; most producers and theatre owners have historically been and remain straight white men. While it has been clear for decades that gay men were welcome on Broadway (especially as characters that die by the show's end), there remains much work to do in fully and accurately representing lesbians, bisexuals, trans people, and everyone else under the LGBTQ+ umbrella.

Broadway Number: "Ring of Keys"

Broadway's ever-evolving relationship to queerness is not and has never been only negative. Indeed, sometimes Broadway has created space for remarkable advances like *Fun Home*, which offers a deeply complex representation of human sexuality. Best Musical Tony Award Winner *Fun Home* took the theme of sexual discovery further than any previous musical in a context in which coded references were no longer necessary. *Fun Home*'s lesbianism was not ignorable, and you could not fully describe the show without discussing it. Its inclusion of a butch lesbian as the lead character and its casting of out lesbian Beth Malone in the part were truly remarkable and would have been nearly impossible to imagine in earlier decades. Due to the one-two punch of homophobia and misogyny, *Fun Home* is also the rare Broadway musical written by two women (book and lyrics by Lisa Kron and score by Jeanine Tesori). *Fun Home* shows the development of cartoonist Alison Bechdel's lesbian subjectivity situated alongside her father's closeted sexuality and, ultimately, his likely suicide.

On paper, *Fun Home* seemed a tough sell, but it became an artistic triumph and a commercial one, recouping its Broadway investment after eight months.[a] It embarked on a national tour and played across the world from Manila to London. Of course, *Fun Home*'s success did not mean the end of homophobia in the theatre; each of the three times I attended the show there were incidences of audience members walking out when Joan and Medium Allison began to get physically intimate. Some Broadway audiences were clearly more comfortable with non-normative gender identities and sexualities when drag was the medium. And yet *Fun Home* dared to sing lesbian desire and identification into existence for Broadway audiences in a way that had not been done before. One song in particular powerfully encapsulates what makes *Fun Home* so singular: "Ring of Keys." *Fun Home* eschews typical musical theatre dramaturgy and splits its protagonist, Alison, into three roles: Small Alison (nine years old), Medium Alison (nineteen years old), and forty-three-year-old Alison.

In *Fun Home*, multiple pasts and the present co-exist simultaneously since Alison usually exists outside the action, seated at her desk drawing cartoons that Small and Medium Alison enact as they are drawn (this dynamic is captured in Figure 5.1 as Alison stands back and observes Small Alison at the start of "Ring of Keys"). This is a memory musical. "Ring of Keys" takes place in a diner where Small Alison and her dad, Bruce, are

"KEEPING IT GAY" 153

Figure 5.1 Sydney Lucas (*left*) sings "Ring of Keys" while Beth Malone (*right*) observes in *Fun Home*. Credit: Joan Marcus.

dining. Alison sets the song up by speaking back in time to Bruce since she is not in the scene but stands outside of it, observing and commenting. Though spectators don't see anyone enter, they hear the jingle of the bells on the diner's door right before Alison says to Bruce, "You didn't notice her at first, but I saw her the moment she walked in. She was a delivery woman; came in with a handcart full of packages. She was an old-school butch."[b] Small Alison stops in her tracks at the sound and the sight of the delivery woman who has just entered. She launches into "Ring of Keys" just after Alison says "butch."

The paradox of this song inspired by visual recognition is that the old-school butch remains unseen by the audience while Small Alison sings most of the song's lyrics directly to her. The audience must conjure up their own vision of this butch woman through the sung details of her appearance, as described by Small Alison (short hair, dungarees, lace-up boots, and her ring of keys) as well as her affective qualities (swagger and bearing).[c] Small Alison stands transfixed in place throughout the song. Her body radiates intensity, especially in Sydney Lucas's performance.

154   SEXUALITY

Lucas transmits an openness and vulnerability as Small Alison rejects the gender conformity her father forced on her. Part of what made *Fun Home* so radical on Broadway was how it charted Alison's awakening of both her sexuality and her gender presentation beginning when she was nine years old. "Ring of Keys" marks Small Alison's nascent recognition of her impending adolescence and the end of childhood. The fact that the show did this by presenting society and the pressures of the nuclear family as problems rather than Alison's sexuality challenged decades of homophobia, anti-gay stigma, and misrepresentation. If *La Cage* was a leap forward for gay representation in the 1980s, *Fun Home* further shifted the paradigm in the 2010s.

Fun Home's producers chose "Ring of Keys" for its Tony Awards performance, which promised a powerful statement about lesbian visibility. To make the song legible outside of its narrative context, the production added additional dialogue highlighting the father-daughter relationship (like its marketing campaign had done, too) and describing Small Alison's sighting of the delivery woman in greater detail. On the broadcast, Beth Malone as Alison says, "You didn't notice her at first, dad, but I did. I saw her the minute she walked in. I'd never seen a woman who looked like her. It was like I was a traveler in a foreign country who runs into someone from home, someone they've never met before but somehow just recognizes."[d] [Clip 5.4] Lucas then launched into the song. Unsaid were the lines that actually revealed *who* she had seen: the old-school butch. This excision undercut the song's power and revealed what *Fun Home's* producers and TV executives deemed acceptable for presentation on national television in June 2015—mere weeks before the US Supreme Court decision made marriage equality legal. While the lyrics contain references to the delivery woman's butch appearance, they resonate differently when the audience is not told explicitly who Small Alison is singing about.

Despite the physical presence of soft-butch Alison onstage, the performance on the Tony Awards erases the specificity of the "old-school butch" and contributes to the ongoing problems of lesbian (in)visibility in Broadway musicals, and that this erasure happened to the song that is the most profound moment of lesbian recognition in the entire history of the form makes it sting that much more. This capitulation to normativity frustrates the recognition of lesbian identity because it reiterates Broadway's ambivalence toward non-conforming genders and sexualities. Mixed messages might be the only kind Broadway knows how to send, especially when the stakes are high, like on the Tony Awards broadcast—Broadway's biggest chance to reach the mainstream. Considering that there had been well-publicized lesbian kisses on network television since 1991, it is particularly galling that even saying "old school butch" was too risqué for prime time in 2015.[e] Though an earlier Broadway musical, *Avenue Q*, famously included puppets singing "If you were gay, that'd be okay" in 2003, twelve years later Broadway was still so afraid of turning off mainstream ticket buyers that it was all too openly willing to closet queerness once again.

[a] Paulson, "'Fun Home' Recoups on Broadway."

[b] Tesori and Kron, *Fun Home*, 56.

[c] Tesori and Kron, *Fun* Home, 56–57.

[d] Tony Awards, "Fun Home Performance Tony Awards 2015."

[e] Heffernan, "It's February. Pucker Up, TV Actresses."

Broadway Cares: AIDS and Beyond

AIDS was inescapable for queer communities in the 1980s and it touched all aspects of life from personal to professional to political. Before AIDS became a chronic disease for those with access to treatment, it was the leading cause of death for adults in the United States for a time in the 1990s.[21] AIDS was so stigmatized that the media sometimes categorized people with AIDS as "innocent" or "guilty" victims in the press, with children and blood transfusion recipients designated as "innocent" and homosexuals and hemophiliacs as "guilty." This climate reflected and created a culture of fear around AIDS that persists since AIDS is still ongoing.[22]

The lack of action by President Ronald Reagan's federal government in response to AIDS galvanized activists.[23] AIDS initially appeared at first to infect only gay men, and anti-gay attitudes became bound with AIDS stigma. Haitians were also among the first groups disproportionately impacted by AIDS, and much racism and xenophobia was directed toward them. Public debates over whether people with HIV-AIDS should be quarantined were part of the mainstream, and AIDS became criminalized in repressive laws that made its transmission a crime in many US states. AIDS activists Gregg Gonsalves and Peter Staley note, "People living with HIV-AIDS in the 1980s and 1990s also faced other kinds of discrimination, including the loss of employment and housing, as well as outright violence, including assault and

156　SEXUALITY

murder."[24] AIDS was effectively a death sentence until the 1995 introduction of the lifesaving "cocktail" of medications that did not cure HIV or AIDS but made it chronic. The fourteen years between the discovery of AIDS in 1981 and the 1995 introduction of "the cocktail" came at enormous human cost, one that profoundly hit Broadway harder than most industries.

AIDS plagued every Broadway musical in the 1980s and 1990s and swiftly took its toll. Broadway musicals lost people from all facets of the industry: composer Howard Ashman, director-choreographer Michael Bennett, *Song and Dance* star Gregg Burge, *A Chorus Line* co-writer Nicholas Dante, producer and stage manager Fritz Holt, *West Side Story* star Larry Kert, and far, far too many others, many of them not even forty years old. In what would prove to be an eerily prophetic statement, Bennett told the *New York Times* in 1983 as *A Chorus Line* became the longest-running Broadway show, "The Actors Fund wanted to give me their award for lifetime achievement, and I said don't give it to me, I don't want it. I'm only 40! This isn't my life's work yet."[25] He was dead less than four years later due to AIDS-related lymphoma. AIDS and AIDS stigma continue to kill even those with access to treatment decades after the introduction of life-saving drugs; Broadway composer Michael Friedman's 2017 death from AIDS underscored the reality that AIDS is not over.

Even though Broadway musicals did not address AIDS directly until 1992, AIDS added resonance to musicals like *Grand Hotel* and made the show's hotel setting a metaphor for life itself. Leading man David Carroll's stay in the show itself was cut short by AIDS. With his soaring tenor voice, Carroll was one of Broadway's most notable actors by the time he starred as the Baron in *Grand Hotel*. After originating the title role in *Joseph and the Amazing Technicolor Dreamcoat*'s US premiere in 1976, he went on to star in *Seven Brides for Seven Brothers* (1982) and *Chess* (1988). Carroll died of an AIDS-related pulmonary embolism while recording *Grand Hotel*'s cast album months before the show closed in 1992, becoming one of the biggest Broadway stars to date to succumb to AIDS. His *New York Times* obituary did not mention AIDS, as it was typical of the times (and the *Times*) to obscure the cause of death due to the immense stigma of AIDS. However, the *Times* did mention Carroll's companion, Robert Homma, in the obituary.[26] Carroll was far from the only *Grand Hotel* cast member affected by AIDS.

Carroll's Tony-winning *Grand Hotel* castmate Michael Jeter only discovered Carroll's HIV positive status "when he saw a bottle of [early AIDS treatment drug] AZT in Carroll's hotel room." He later recalled, "The irony was,

Figure 5.2 *Grand Hotel* (1989–1992 Broadway). Book by Luther Davis. Lyrics by George Forrest and Robert Wright. Music by George Forrest and Robert Wright. Directed by Tommy Tune. Shown from *left*: David Carroll and Michael Jeter. Credit: Photofest.

I was playing a man who was dying and the star of the show, David Carroll, really was dying" of AIDS.[27] Jeter and Carroll stopped *Grand Hotel* cold in their thrilling song and dance "We'll Take a Glass Together" (pictured in Figure 5.2). [Clip 5.5] Jeter opened up about his sobriety on the 1990 Tony Awards telecast but not his sexuality or HIV+ status. He felt the professional stakes of revealing his sexuality were low as a character actor; he told *POZ* magazine, "Who's going to care if Michael Jeter is gay? He never gets the girl anyway."[28] Coming out as gay and sober was different from sharing one's HIV+ status, though. When Jeter revealed his HIV+ status in 1997, it was a much bigger deal because by that point he was a television celebrity on the CBS-TV sitcom *Evening Shade,* and he had much more to lose. He clarified the reasons for remaining silent about his HIV+ status as an actor, saying they were misunderstood and telling *POZ*, "It isn't a question of 'image.' The gay press has it wrong. The question really isn't, 'Should I disclose my status?' but 'will the insurance company put up the bond?' "[29] Coming out, whether about one's sexuality or HIV+ status, is a labor issue as much as a personal choice, determined in part by fiscal policies of producers and insurers.[30]

158 SEXUALITY

Jeter's revelation was brave, risky, and above all, *necessary* in the context of gay rights' increasingly higher profile in the late 1990s.

Before AIDS become chronic, Broadway musicals avoided staging it until *Falsettos* (1992). *Falsettos* opened one year before *Angels in America* made waves in US theatres for its depiction of AIDS. And even though it was explicitly queer onstage, offstage *Falsettos* relied on the same universalizing logic used by *La Cage* nearly a decade earlier: *Falsettos* star Michael Rupert recalled that director James Lapine told the cast, "This is not a gay play. This is a play about family."[31] But, after *La Cage*, why couldn't it be both? *Falsettos* opened when AIDS was a leading cause of death in the United States, and seeing AIDS represented onstage at that time was crucial to destigmatizing it even if only one member of its leading couple Marvin and Whizzer's relationship made it to the end of the musical alive. Rupert noted that men who had come to New York for AIDS treatment would meet him and express how much the show meant to them. After *Falsettos*, only one other Broadway musical in the 1990s staged AIDS: *Rent*.[32] *Rent* made a dent in mainstream consciousness by representing (and, to some, appropriating) queerness.[33] *Rent*, like *Falsettos* before it, featured a gay male couple and a lesbian couple but made both couples secondary to the heterosexual love story and the homosocial relationship between its two male leads. It also, as theatre scholar David Savran argues, used ethnic, racial, and sexual differences as markers of authenticity in the show's appeal to capture the 1990s multiculturalist zeitgeist.[34] For all its advances, *Rent* presented a typical narrative where only the gay character dies of AIDS; despite also having AIDS, its straight leading couple survives. In reality, AIDS did not spare heterosexuals, while in representation, it often did—they were the ones seen "living with, not dying from disease."

Broadway's reticence to depict AIDS was likely due to a confluence of factors: perhaps AIDS was too close to home to write about, it was too intensely stigmatized, the subject matter was a tough sell for tourist-driven Broadway, AIDS was challenging to represent in dramas let alone to sing about in musicals, and, crucially, AIDS killed so many creators, performers, and spectators who would have otherwise been alive. Despite offstage efforts by members of the Broadway community to raise AIDS awareness (through fundraising events like Broadway Bares, service organizations like Broadway Cares/Equity Fights AIDS, and the then-ubiquitous red ribbons adorning celebrities at awards shows), musicals themselves rarely brought it up onstage.

"KEEPING IT GAY" 159

The following decade also saw only two Broadway musicals address HIV/AIDS, both set in the 1980s: *Taboo* and *The Boy from Oz*, which opened across West 45th Street from each other in 2003. All of the musicals that staged AIDS depicted gay male characters dying of it since it was a fatal syndrome for most. The absences AIDS caused paradoxically created more presence for gay men. Schulman explains, "Since dying homosexuals were more palatable than any other kind, AIDS mitigated homosexuality enough to allow gay men more visibility."[35] Harkening back to prior decades when the queer was dead or "cured" by the final curtain, in the 1990s, a "good" homosexual on Broadway was one dying of AIDS. Gay men could not always kiss in Broadway musicals without consternation, but they could die onstage eight times a week.

AIDS took center stage again in *The Book of Mormon*, which trivialized AIDS and perpetuated racist stereotypes of Africa, the continent most directly affected by AIDS. *Vulture* critic Helen Shaw later took *Mormon* to task for how "black actors are forced to sell jokes about curing AIDS by sodomizing babies."[36] That *Mormon*, and its stereotypical homophobic and racist representations, was the *only* new Broadway musical in the 2010s to engage with AIDS at length stands in stark contrast to Broadway's offstage AIDS advocacy, especially considering that Black Americans and the entire continent of Africa are still disproportionately affected by AIDS. How could the actors in *Mormon* stand to face audiences during the two annual post-performance fundraising drives for Broadway Cares/Equity Fights AIDS when they had just finished making a joke of it?

Mormon also represents what theatre scholar David Román calls the "banalization of AIDS," which he explains is based on "an indifference that is no longer confined to the government, but endemic to the culture at large. In this scenario, AIDS is no big deal."[37] No longer a big deal, AIDS became a punchline written by straight white men who made their fortunes in television; this is especially distasteful in light of the scores of theatre people lost to the plague. *Mormon* epitomized the process that AIDS theorist Douglas Crimp describes as "a change in the way we think about AIDS, or rather a change that consists in our inability to continue thinking about AIDS."[38] From 2011 through 2020, apart from some ham-fisted throwaway moments in 2018's *Summer: The Donna Summer Musical* (which at least glancingly acknowledged AIDS but glossed over Summer's own anti-gay comments that she later walked back), the only musical to include AIDS was the 2016 revival of *Falsettos*.[39] The 2019 bio musical *Fela!* tellingly did not include the

160   SEXUALITY

fact that its subject, musician Fela Kuti, died of AIDS. Offstage, the theatrical community does care and does fight AIDS, but what is encountered onstage in musicals is largely its absence. Broadway musicals were one of the institutions most affected by AIDS and yet also one of the least likely to grapple with it, which speaks to what producers considered viable and who they considered representable.

Casting and Coming Out

If the post–*La Cage* era saw Broadway musicals shift from taking AIDS seriously to making a joke of it, their relationship to casting out LGBTQ+ actors took an opposite trajectory. But then who could, should, and would play these LGBTQ+ roles? There have always been LGBTQ+ actors on Broadway, but they have not always been able to live openly let alone be out professionally. As more and more LGBTQ+ roles existed (again, mostly gay male characters), debates arose over who should play them since actors were coming out in ever-greater numbers by the 2000s. Despite the fact that most Broadway performers generally have a lower profile than film and TV stars, the stigma of being gay or perceived as gay (let alone any other identity under the LGBTQ+ umbrella) was such that most Broadway actors in the 1980s and 1990s did not come out for fear of reprisal or blacklisting. Coming out could impact your career and your earning ability: according to a 2012 analysis by the Center for American Progress, "significant disparities in earnings for gay and transgender workers" underlined the unequal treatment of LGBTQ+ Americans in the workforce, especially when compared to the earnings of straight white men.[40] Homophobia thus exacted professional costs. Broadway was different by degree if not in kind.

The industry effectively policed itself, with gay men behind the scenes like agents and publicists counseling actors to remain closeted. The closet was strong despite *and* because it held its open secret that many in the Broadway industry were gay and because it functioned on both individual and institutional levels. As harmful as it was, the closet also represented a form of protection, since staying in it could allow individuals to keep their job and their relationship with their family as well as their privacy.[41] Broadway enforced its own version of don't ask, don't tell long before the US military did. Director-choreographer Tommy Tune noted that there was a code of silence around sexuality when he was coming up in the industry in the 1970s, telling an interviewer, "They didn't ask me [about] that because I think they knew the answer."[42] Tune preferred to keep his private life off-limits and the press agreed to keep his closet door closed; Tune's strategy was a commonly accepted and sometimes necessary one. Coming out meant losing the closet's protections and claiming political power through group identification.

Harvey Fierstein was the rare exception in the Broadway community because he was never in the closet. Television talk show host Barbara Walters interviewed Fierstein in 1983 and the interview serves as a stark reminder of gay men's social position then: [Clip 5.6]

WALTERS. A few years ago, I wouldn't have been able to do an interview like this probably and put it on the air. It would have been, "This is not the subject one talks about."

FIERSTEIN. *You* could have done it, you would have had to fight your censors and all that, but you could have done it and you should have done it. You know I am not the first gay star of a Broadway show. You know I am not the first gay writer of a Broadway show. It is such a ridiculous position.

WALTERS. You're the first openly gay.

FIERSTEIN. Yeah, but isn't that ridiculous?[43]

While Fierstein lived his life openly, many others did not feel they could afford the same risks. In the 1980s and 1990s, too many gay men only publicly came out in their obituaries. Coming out was a political act, even in the gay-friendly theatre, where plays and musicals with any gay content were labeled *gay plays*. Out gay playwright and librettist Terrence McNally explained that this label marginalized the plays and their writers and ironically only led to more closeting, noting, "It must be remembered this was a time, even in the theatre, traditionally the most welcoming venue for gay men and women, when it was good to be married" to an opposite sex spouse for appearances.[44] It was risky for writers to create gay parts and for actors to play them.

And Fierstein's next show after *Torch Song Trilogy*, *La Cage* provided an object lesson in the stakes of playing gay. Fierstein "felt strongly that only a fellow homosexual could bring the required pathos to the roles of Georges and Albin," and he remembered that he "insisted on openly gay leads for the show, and Laurents called me a bigot."[45] Fierstein fought against the then-accepted casting practices where straight actors could play any role. As director, Laurents made the casting decisions and was not too concerned with the sexuality of the actors despite being gay himself. Fierstein countered,

162   SEXUALITY

"Most gay actors have been beaten all their lives on some level, economically, politically, emotionally," making them primed to understand the characters more than a straight actor could.[46] Fierstein initially lost that battle, though Laurents did cast gay actors as replacements, and according to Fierstein, Laurents's views changed after seeing the results: "He called me to say, 'You are so right. What a difference it makes!' "[47]

Staying quiet carried its own gambles, too, since activists increasingly framed coming out as political. It became more common for closeted public figures in fields from professional sports to politics and pop music to be "outed." Outing rarely if ever happened on Broadway, which society already presumed to be lousy with homosexuals, but it made waves in mainstream culture. Tennis players Billie Jean King and Martina Navratilova were the first pro athletes to come out in the United States in 1981 after first being outed by the press. The press outed film idol Rock Hudson in 1985, the year he was one of the first celebrities to die of AIDS. But many others came out on their own terms: politician Barney Frank came out in 1987, actor Ian McKellen and singer Elton John both came out as gay in 1988. Stand-up comedian and sitcom star Ellen DeGeneres came out in 1997 at the same time as her sitcom alter ego to much fanfare, only to have ABC cancel her show. DeGeneres's subsequent years without work served as a warning.

As more and more gay people came out, gay representation in main-stream media and mass culture increased alongside the marked increase on Broadway. Gay characters, played mostly by straight men and/or closeted gay men, were featured in television sitcoms like *Will and Grace* (1998–2006). Straight actors like Tom Hanks won Oscars for playing gay in films like *Philadelphia* (1993). It was still one thing to *play* gay; it was another to *be* gay. For gay actors, coming out risked their being typecast as able to play only gay or lesbian characters. In practice, this happened to some actors but not others. For instance, after coming out, Howard McGillin continued to be cast in leading roles on Broadway as straight characters (the title character of *The Phantom of the Opera* and Archibald in *The Secret Garden*), which he said was based on his appearance, noting, "I know I look how I look."[48] The risks associated with coming out were still contingent on appearance, which, as ever, determined the kinds of roles available to actors.

The financial stakes were higher for actors playing heterosexual romantic leads than supporting characters or comic roles because those roles pay more. Film and theatre star Rupert Everett's career as a leading man ended after coming out publicly. He became Hollywood's preferred gay best friend

"KEEPING IT GAY" 163

for a time–and also a cautionary tale. Everett later said, "I would not advise any actor necessarily, if he was really thinking of his career, to come out."[49] Everett's concerns informed the decisions Broadway actors made, too. John Benjamin Hickey starred as Cliff in the 1998 revival of *Cabaret*, which made the role explicitly bisexual. Even though Hickey played a lot of gay roles, he described the calculations with his agents that went into choosing parts and whether or not he had played a gay character too recently to take on another one, noting, "It was a concern because you wanted to work" and that "your agents told you to worry about it."[50] One could play gay parts, but not too often.

If many actors remained closeted in the 1990s, some Broadway actors were out and proud about their sexuality, including Lea DeLaria, John Cameron Mitchell, Billy Porter, and Anthony Rapp—all of whom were out to varying degrees when they achieved Broadway success. Indeed, a 1999 profile of Mitchell noted, "From the very beginning, he has always been out as a gay actor."[51] Mitchell's sexuality was first mentioned by the press in a *New York Times* profile in 1992 while he was starring in an off-Broadway play *The Destiny of Me*, after he had achieved Broadway musical success in *The Secret Garden* (1991). He would go on to co-create iconic queer off-Broadway musical *Hedwig and the Angry Inch* (1998). Mitchell explicitly confronted then-contemporary debates over casting and identity, arguing in 1992, "If you restrict gay roles to gay actors, then it can be argued that straight roles should be restricted to straight actors, a dangerous position."[52] Mitchell's stance on casting and who should play whom remains both urgent and complex, especially regarding gender and sexuality since cultural understandings of these have shifted profoundly and swiftly.

Producers canceled a 2021 Australian production of *Hedwig* in response to an uproar when a cisgender male was cast in the title role rather than a trans or non-binary actor, prompting Mitchell and co-writer Stephen Trask to issue a statement clarifying that Hedwig is not trans. They explained that Hedwig's "gender journey ... is sparked by a coerced, non-consensual surgery. A young fem gay boy is bullied into a gender assignment by his boyfriend and his government in order to preserve the sacred binary." The creators contend, "Anyone should be able to play Hedwig."[53] Yet when LGBTQ+ roles have been available to anyone, the fact is they are usually cast with heterosexuals (a similar dynamic is even more common for disabled characters, as I'll discuss in chapter 6) instead of someone with life experience closer to the character's. Drawing together Mitchell's 1992 thoughts on who should play whom with

164 SEXUALITY

contemporary concerns over equity and representation makes it clear that even if representation were equitable, any actor playing any part would still face scrutiny. In terms of this chapter's subject, the questions become more about whose sexuality is allowed to exist on a spectrum (and whose is not) and who gets to decide these things and for whom.

But back in 1996, *Rent* star Rapp was "the only openly queer cast member" of the original cast, and he was playing straight onstage. Rapp told an interviewer in the late 1990s, "I've never labeled myself except to say I'm queer" while arguing for fluidity, concluding, "the future's all about inclusiveness."[54] Though Alan Cumming famously came out as bisexual when starring as the Emcee in the 1998 revival of *Cabaret*, Rapp was the rare Broadway actor in the 1990s who was out but eschewed gay or bisexual in favor of the all-encompassing queer.

While Rapp resisted a specific label, stand-up comic Lea DeLaria (pictured in Figure 5.3) had long been out as a self-proclaimed "fat butch dyke" when she made her Broadway debut as Hildy in the 1998 revival of *On the Town*, playing opposite Jesse Tyler Ferguson (who would later come out as gay).[55] *On the Town* thus featured two LGBTQ+ actors each playing the other's heterosexual love interest, one publicly out, one closeted. DeLaria's casting was remarkable because openly gay director George C. Wolfe sought her precisely *because* of her sexuality. She recalled, "George said, 'We need a lesbian.' At that time, I was the only lesbian. None of the others were out yet."[56] Casting a lesbian allowed DeLaria to play against the text since Hildy is perhaps musical theatre's horniest straight female character.[57] [Clip 5.7] Critics noted DeLaria's presence. The *New York Times* review referred to DeLaria as "the show's center of gravity," noting that she was "a confrontational comic from the frontier land of lesbian stand-up comedy."[58] DeLaria herself observed the importance of her presence in *On the Town* on Broadway, saying, "The biggest thing is I've achieved this moment and haven't had to spend one second in the closet."[59] DeLaria's success as an out butch dyke was trailblazing. That she was "the only lesbian" demonstrates the closet's power and calls attention to the fact that there were and are so few lesbian roles in musicals. DeLaria stole the show, and she returned to Broadway in the revival of *The Rocky Horror Show* in 2000 as Dr. Scott/Eddie, allowing her the chance to push Broadway's gender norms even further.

Another performer challenging gender norms since the 1990s is Billy Porter. He also repeatedly confronted the industry's systemic racism and homophobia in addition to its narrow definitions of masculinity. He notes, "I

"KEEPING IT GAY" 165

Figure 5.3 *On the Town* (Broadway revival, 1998–1999). Music by Leonard Bernstein. Book and Lyrics by Betty Comden and Adolph Green. Directed by George C. Wolfe. Shown: Jesse Tyler Ferguson and Lea DeLaria. Credit: Photofest.

was always out," and "there were repercussions."[60] Even though Porter was out, he rarely saw a representation of anyone who looked like him: "Even when LGBTQ stories started being told in the independent space and then in the mainstream, it was all white boys pretty much."[61] After making a splash in the 1994 revival of *Grease* playing the Teen Angel as an over-the-top flamboyant Little Richard type, Porter found himself pigeonholed. [Clip 5.7] He

166 SEXUALITY

says, "I spent the next seventeen years trying to dig myself out . . . of that image." When he tried to break into the music business after Broadway, he recalled "secret meetings with my management team about how I would behave."[62] Porter decided to leave Broadway, noting that the industry expected him to repeat his earlier success and to play roles where his only function was to stop the show rather than express his humanity. He observed, "Whether because of my sexuality, my race, bad timing or whatever, access and opportunity remained elusive."[63] He stayed away from Broadway until *Kinky Boots* brought him back thirteen years later. But even in a show like *Kinky Boots*, Broadway's ambivalence toward identity reared its head again in an unlikely way: Porter and librettist Fierstein disagreed about his character's sexuality, with Porter claiming Lola was gay and Fierstein arguing that he had written only heterosexual characters.[64] In his memoir, Fierstein noted he made Lola "a heterosexual transvestite" in order to avoid making her just another gay male character denied a love interest.[65] In line with his feeling that only gay actors could fully grasp the leading roles in *La Cage*, Fierstein felt the same about *Kinky Boots's* Lola, writing, "It wasn't until Wayne Brady took over the role that audiences finally listened to the character say that he preferred women and accepted him as a cross-dressing heterosexual."[66] Identity-based casting goes both ways.

In some respects, Lola fell back into the stereotypical roles Porter had avoided, while in others, his casting represented progress: an out gay Black man playing the lead in a smash Broadway musical was huge. Lola ultimately led Porter to a Tony Award and then five years later to an Emmy-winning performance on the FX television series *Pose*. While Porter's success initially came at much expense, his career reached new heights as he aged and times changed, allowing him to express himself more fully. His earlier refusal to give into typecasting cost him countless jobs but prioritizing his humanity allowed Porter to keep his integrity—and to build a career that honored who he is.

In the twenty-first century, being out became something less of a career barrier yet the typecasting of queer performers persists. Outing had mostly fallen out of favor as LGBTQ+ people became increasingly visible. If coming out became less newsworthy than before, playing gay remained fêted. Hugh Jackman's widely lauded turn as Peter Allen in the otherwise badly reviewed *The Boy from Oz* (2003) made both homosexuality and AIDS palatable for audiences who thrilled at the sight of Jackman camping it up. Musical theatre scholar Bruce Kirle explains that Jackman was "able to mainstream gayness in a way that was impossible for the real Peter Allen."[67] Mainstreaming gayness was possible because of the public difference between the role and Jackman's offstage identity as well as the different eras in which Allen and Jackman lived.[68] Playing gay proved to be catnip for straight actors eager to prove their prowess, perform their liberal politics, and bait awards nominators.[69]

Not surprisingly, the history of casting La Cage repeated itself, with difference, when it came to playing gay. Given the great efforts made by La Cage's original stars to proclaim their heterosexuality, it was extraordinary that the press for the 2004 Broadway revival ignored the fact that its stars (Daniel Davis and Gary Beach) were gay. The press's silence about two gay men, who were silent themselves, playing these roles on Broadway for the first time effectively closeted the actors. This omission occurred at a time when gay visibility was particularly important, denying the production the opportunity to assert its relevance to the national debates going on at that time over the validity of same-sex relationships. Given librettist Fierstein's stated preference for directors to cast gay actors in these roles, the fact that gay men playing Albin and Georges was not a part of the production's publicity represented another missed opportunity for La Cage to make a statement at a time when it would have been especially relevant. However, Fierstein's casting as a heterosexual in another notable Broadway revival was not a missed opportunity.

When Fierstein and O'Donnell took over as Tevye and Golde in the 2004 revival of Fiddler on the Roof, their casting raised the press's eyebrows. Fierstein's gravelly voice made him an unlikely fit for musicals but also singular—in other words, perfect for musical comedy stardom. For someone whose career was built on being out at a time when that was career-ending, it is surprising to see that history erased when the New York Times referred to his casting as Tevye as "the biggest risk of his professional life."[70] Fierstein said that reporters kept asking him if it was "going to be a strain . . . to play a heterosexual." Interviewers pose this kind of question when an actor plays a different sexuality from their own; when Hugh Jackman was about to finish his run in The Boy From Oz in 2004, an interviewer asked him, "Did you at some point ask yourself whether you really wanted to take on what must be the most flamboyant role in the world?"[71] Gay New York Times critic Ben Brantley himself used innuendo to refer to how Fierstein's sexuality aligned with Tevye, writing, "Mr. Fierstein inflects every line with at least a touch of the grandeur of old Hollywood movies" before noting that "it is sometimes hard to credit this exotic spirit as that of a tradition-bound father."[72] Fame accompanies an actor's performance, adding scrutiny to their choices

168   SEXUALITY

but also giving actors the chance to make statements through their presence. Fierstein noted the importance of his casting, saying, "I didn't do *Fiddler on the Roof* for political reasons, but let's face it: I have kids come up to me on a daily basis saying, 'I'm a gay kid or lesbian, I want to be in show business . . . but I'm not going to come out because if I do I'll only get stuck in those roles.'" His response to these youths: "The Nederlanders have handed me a $10 million production of *Fiddler on the Roof*, the most openly gay man there ever was . . . and the audience has no problem."[73] Casting's resonance and its flexibility create ripples beyond the auditorium.

While Broadway *was* casting gays and lesbians as straight characters, the press was still casting doubt. O'Donnell joined Fierstein ten months into his run, and her celebrity coupled with his caused critics to review this production a third time. In *Variety*, David Rooney noted, "What's most significant about this latest cast overhaul is less her perf than her pairing with Fierstein, which underlines the uniqueness of commercial theater in America as a mainstream artistic area in which an actor's offscreen sexuality is irrelevant."[74] But evidently not so irrelevant that it prevented Rooney from devoting three paragraphs to discussing their casting and their sexuality, noting that "the Broadway community operates by different rules" from those of film and TV, where there were still not yet many openly gay actors. Rooney also called attention to how the stars' involvement in politics inflects the production, writing, "Only in such an environment could a ferociously out gay man and lesbian, both of whom have served as gay political spokespersons, be enlisted to embody the archetypal Jewish mama and papa. And guess what? Onstage, their sexuality is a nonissue." Celebrity seems to trump sexuality in Broadway casting only until it doesn't. While Fierstein and O'Donnell got something of a pass because they were playing a long-married couple, it was also due in part to body politics since neither was young or thin or conventionally sexy.

Will and Grace star Sean Hayes received a decidedly different reception when he was cast as a straight romantic lead in the 2010 revival of *Promises, Promises*. Hayes garnered attention due to his long-expected but belated coming out just before the show opened. Hayes's professed reasons for staying publicly quiet about being gay echo many others in that he wanted to keep the focus on his work and thus increase his ability to get cast. The fact that Hayes remained closeted while starring as Jack, the unabashedly over the top gay character, on *Will and Grace* from 1998 to 2006 dogged him for years after the show was off the air. A *Newsweek* article questioning Hayes's believability as a famous out gay actor playing straight caused an uproar, further

"KEEPING IT GAY"   169

inflamed with the discovery that the author of the article was gay himself.[75] Whether the controversy was due to Hayes's celebrity, his sexuality, or a combination of both, it serves as a marker of what being out on Broadway meant in 2010 and how much and when an actor's public disclosure of their sexuality mattered to casting.

The year 2010 brought a second revival of *La Cage* in which both leads were again played by heterosexuals whose sexuality *was* fair game for publicity. *New York* magazine writer Adam Sternberg asked stars "[Douglas] Hodge (who is straight) and [Kelsey] Grammer (also straight) whether there's anything problematic, artistically or otherwise, in playing a gay couple. 'Most people just say to me, "You are gay," says Hodge. And I say, "I'm not." And they say, "No, you are." [Sir Ian] McKellen said that to me. He came over and sat on my lap.'"[76] Hodge used McKellen's approval as a shield against the discomfort caused by playing gay as well as the disappointment of the role being played by a straight actor. Grammer and Hodge sidestepped kissing each other on the mouth, according to Fierstein, who explains, "I later found out that what appeared to be a kiss on the mouth was actually a kiss on the hand, as Kelsey would slip his hand between the two of them so their lips wouldn't actually touch. Why are straight men such cowards?"[77] Fierstein replaced Hodge as Albin on Broadway in 2011, making him at least the fourth gay actor to essay Albin on Broadway (following Keane Curtis, Lee Roy Reams, and Gary Beach) but the most publicly out since his predecessors did not speak of their sexuality to the press while playing the part. He held steadfast to his conviction that "I Am What I Am" meant more when sung by a gay actor, saying, "I fought to cast homosexuals in the roles—if you stand up and sing 'I Am What I Am' without feeling your sexuality and your persecution right down to your painted toenails it's never going to be quite the same thing."[78] He forgave the amount of publicity devoted to Barry and Hearn's sexuality, arguing, "even gay people did it back then."[79]

Like the actors who came out at great risk in the 1990s, many actors in the new millennium still waited until they had achieved a modicum of Broadway success before coming out. Actors did not stay in the closet because they were afraid audiences would discover their sexuality but because they were afraid industry gatekeepers would. Despite Rooney's assertion that Broadway operated differently, homophobia in society and the industry itself still kept many in the closet. Tony winner Gavin Creel was out to friends and family but as he recalls, "I came out to the press when I was 33 [in 2009]. I wish I had done it sooner. But it was a different time."[80] Looking back at his

170 SEXUALITY

Broadway debut in the 1996 revival of *The King and I*, Jose Llana recalled, "I never thought I would live my life as an openly gay actor."[81] Llana's big break came as one of the (straight) young lovers in that show. He noted, "It was very convenient for me, publicly, to say that I was single—as with any young actors who are cast in leading or ingénue roles, I was worried that if a casting director found out I was gay it would affect my ability to be cast."[82] After coming out, Llana not only continued to be cast but played the King in the 2015 production of *The King and I* on Broadway, on tour, and in the United Kingdom. Llana's casting in seven Broadway musicals marked progress for gay and Filipino representation, especially as he was not only cast as gay characters: his biggest splashes have come as heterosexual love interests.

Jenn Collela, like many other actors of her generation, was also warned against coming out, but she did so anyway in 2008. In 2013, she explained, "Some directors and casting directors' vision of you in a straight role can sometimes be skewed if they know somewhere in the back of their mind that you're gay. I had both directors and CDs (casting directors) say that to me. But that was ten years ago [in 2003] and I think the mindset has shifted quite a bit since then."[83] After coming out, she continued getting cast in Broadway musicals as both straight and gay characters, including featured roles in *Chaplin* (2012), *If/Then* (2014), and *Come from Away* (2017). After DeLaria, Collella was Broadway's most prominent out lesbian performer. Beth Malone's casting as Alison in *Fun Home* was the first time an out lesbian was cast as a lesbian lead in a Broadway musical—and Broadway had had to travel a long road to achieve this milestone. While starring in *Fun Home*, Malone said that many lesbian actresses sent her letters thanking her for being out and visible. This gave her pause because, despite some progress, it remains challenging to be an out lesbian in musical theatre. She told *Playbill*, "I think, 'Well, I'm so happy, but I'm not sure you're going to get work because there is a lot of fear and prejudice. I'm not sure this isn't going to hurt you, but all I can say is, I hope you live a happier life, but it may not make you a more working actor.'"[84] DeLaria may have been Broadway's first openly butch actor in 1998, and Malone played Broadway's first butch protagonist only in 2015. The space between these two milestones reveals a void of lesbian representation as well as how misogyny and homophobia impact representation and those performing it.

The 2010s also saw new barriers crossed in gender representation in Broadway musicals. Gender non-conforming actor Alex Newell was cast as Asaka in the 2017 revival of *Once on This Island*, where he belted out "Mama

Will Provide," and this casting broke new ground. [Clip 5.8] Unlike Edna in *Hairspray*, where the audience's awareness of the performer's gender is the point, Newell played Asaka without that kind of self-conscious commentary in performance. This decade also notably saw two transgender performers cast in Broadway musicals: Peppermint as the non-binary oracle Pythio in *Head over Heels* and Alexandra Billings as a replacement Madam Morrible in *Wicked* in 2020. Their casting reflects how Broadway follows social progress and how it helps advance it. In these instances, the door to gender fluidity in casting is cracking open role by role. Peppermint made history as Broadway's first out transgender woman performer to originate a role in a musical. But Peppermint's casting revealed how unprepared the Broadway critical ecosystem was to embrace gender non-conforming actors; critic Ben Brantley misgendered her in a failed attempt at humor in his review.[85] Billings spoke to *Playbill* about how her experience as a mixed-race trans person matters, saying, "I live in a world that continues to be a place for a specific kind of person. My whole life has been about survival and trying to be seen in a world that does not acknowledge my existence." Unlike the gay and lesbian actors from earlier decades who argued that their identity was separate from their characters, Billings contended that her identity is inseparable from the role: "Trans or not, if I'm playing the role, it's going to be trans, because I'm trans."[86] As the 2010s shifted toward greater consciousness of non-conforming identities in the mainstream, gender identity and sexuality no longer had to be left at the stage door in the same ways they once had.

Though missteps like Brantley's happened (and were perhaps inevitable given the speed at which paradigms of gender have shifted, driven by younger generations), Broadway publicly celebrated its LGBTQ+ community. LGBTQ+ Pride found its way to the eyes of theatregoers in honor of the fiftieth anniversary of the Stonewall riots, when *Playbill* featured a series of articles called "*Playbill* Pride" in June 2019 about out Broadway actors. That the series focused on identities beyond gay white men and celebrities and turned toward lesser-known performers is a measure of how Broadway had changed, even as many of the performers noted their rarity in the industry. *Tootsie* dancer Jenifer Foote observed, "There are very few gay women actors in the business so that is something that occurs to me, that I'm often the lone person."[87] *My Fair Lady* star Christian Dante White noted, "I'm out, loud, and proud. I can feel it when I bow—I'm the only gay principal of color. I'm the only one out there, so I feel that added pressure and that added responsibility."[88] The list of younger Broadway actors who came out as LGBTQ+

172 SEXUALITY

during this decade grew to include Ariana deBose, Beanie Feldstein, Caitlin Kinnunen, Lauren Patten, and Ali Stroker, among many others.

Broadway actors appear to be, one hopes, out for good. In what would have been unthinkable just two decades earlier, a Broadway star came out about being HIV+ and openly gay while starring in Broadway's biggest hit. The stakes were enormous, both personally and professionally. As the first replacement in the title role of *Hamilton* in 2016, Javier Muñoz used the platform of the show's enormous cultural cachet to raise awareness of living and working with HIV. In an interview with *POZ* magazine, he said that it "feels like a responsibility to me to be outspoken about it and to be a voice that breaks the HIV stigma, because we're in 2016 and there is still a stigma."[89] Muñoz understood stigma both from his experiences growing up and his experiences as a Latinx actor in a racist industry that limited the kinds of roles he played. He notes that as a kid, "I was called a fag, I was called fatty.... I was made fun of for being Puerto Rican."[90] Muñoz persevered through body shaming, homophobia, racism, and AIDS stigma—and survived cancer while starring in *Hamilton*. Muñoz's openness about all of these facets of his identity were made possible by those who came before him, but they were made necessary by Donald Trump's election as US president in 2016 using ableist, body shaming, homophobic, misogynist, and, above all, racist and xenophobic rhetoric. Muñoz's actions were nothing less than heroic in this context. Muñoz cracked open a door through which others followed him. Broadway legend André De Shields came out about living with HIV for three decades while starring on Broadway in *Hadestown* in early 2020.[91] Billy Porter, too, publicly shared his HIV+ status, proclaiming, "This is what HIV-positive looks like now."[92] The fact that queer Black and Latino actors could be out as gay and HIV+ marks remarkable changes in society and on Broadway.

If from the outside, Broadway appears full of LGBTQ+ performers, Actors' Equity's statistics debunk any assumed overrepresentation: just under 6 percent of AEA Production Contracts (those used for Broadway and some tours) from 2016 to 2019 were signed by members who self-identify as LGBTQ+.[93] This statistic is in line with Gallup's 2021 estimation that 5.6 percent of US Americans identify as LGBT.[94] Though Broadway has gradually become more inclusive of a range of identities since the 1980s, the fact that so few gender non-conforming and trans performers have been cast in musicals belies oversimplified progress narratives of Broadway's inclusivity.

"KEEPING IT GAY" 173

Broadway once again revealed its ambivalence toward non-conforming bodies when it comes to gender identity. Musicals like *Tootsie* and *Mrs. Doubtfire* (2021) have been received as trans-phobic by some. But *Jagged Little Pill* is more emblematic of how Broadway sometimes sings out with one foot in its mouth. Yes, it featured a bisexual leading role, but it also mucked it up when it came to the gender identity of Jo, a secondary character with a big song. Trouble arose when Jo went from being referred to as non-binary to saying Jo was exploring *her* (as opposed to *their*) gender identity. As the production prepared to reopen after the pandemic shutdown, its producers released a statement addressing what some saw as non-binary erasure. They explained "the character of Jo is on a gender journey" and that they would "prioritize auditioning actors for the role who are on gender journeys or understand that experience personally."[95] It makes sense that *Jagged* took heat for its handling of this situation since Jo is one of few gender non-conforming roles in musical theatre by contemporary definitions. The furor also recalls historic and ongoing debates about who should play whom, what role authenticity plays in casting, and whose identities are considered malleable enough to play any role. But because theatre's broader structures of production remain largely intact, the demand for authenticity means that those who do not share the identities represented onstage may become arbiters or judges of how well someone performs that identity before they enter the audition and during it. *Jagged*'s producers addressed this potential by hiring a director of Leadership & Culture, "who will be an ongoing source of support, training, and advocacy for the company and crew." That's a Broadway first, but it is one that attempts to work within Broadway's existing corporate structure.

In terms of casting, how can Broadway think beyond the gender binary in casting when auditions themselves reinforce it through auditions divided by gender? Casting calls still often stipulate stereotypical gender roles, i.e., "women must wear heels," in addition to vocal ranges and other gendered qualifications. In a return to the concerns over coming out that marked the 1980s and 1990s, gender identity is now a new space of outing while also marking a return to the closet and self-policing because of the labor concerns involved. Will actors find work if they're open about being trans or non-binary? Identifying one's gender pronouns had become an industry norm by 2020, yet some actors may wish to keep their gender identity separate from their professional identity to avoid being pigeonholed, much like gay and lesbian actors in the 1990s did even though sexuality never became an explicit

174 SEXUALITY

part of casting like gender. Broadway's body issues persist, transposed onto different identities.

Turn It Off, Keep It Gay, or Just Be?

The increase in actors coming out and representation in narratives were mutually constitutive practices. The stars who came out made it possible for lesser-known actors and everyday people to do so as well as. Though Broadway did cast more openly LGBTQ+ actors and did include more LGBTQ+ representation, its casting practices continue to sustain one of the most damaging aspects of gay male culture: its body politics. Though Alex Newell made a splash in *Once on This Island*, he ran headlong into Broadway's body issues when he auditioned—four times—to be a replacement Lola in *Kinky Boots*. He recalls, "They said my weight would inhibit me from playing the role, which is not true, but to each their own. I was like, 'This is a show where they're encouraging you to be who you want to be. Don't let them tell you who you should be.' They literally looked me in the face and told me I was too big to play a role."[96] There is no compelling reason Lola needs to have a gay clone-style body, especially considering that she is a drag queen and drag has been historically welcoming to bodies of all sizes.

A casting breakdown for the Broadway production reads:

Lola/Simon (Lead): Male, 30–33
a strong comedic cross-dresser who needs to feel comfortable wearing everything from full glamour drag to nothing but boxing trunks. Must have a killer voice with power blues and gospel chops. Must move well. Must have star presence for this very challenging role.
Ethnicity: Black/African Descent[97]

There is nothing in the description indicating that size matters, and yet Newell was told his body was the barrier. Broadway's body shaming is bound to other forms of oppression, from racism to homophobia and so on, mirroring the exclusionary rhetoric seen in some gay men's dating app profiles: "no fats, no femmes, no Asians/Blacks/Latins." Broadway would do well to examine the intersections of gender, race, size, and sexuality more closely in its casting practices and could use casting to undo the dominance of the sculpted white gay male body as an ideal. When *Kinky Boots* was casting its non-union tour in 2017, the casting breakdown for Lola said that the "emotionally and physically challenging role requires the body of a boxer, with the soul of a Diva."[98] Aside from the fact that boxers' bodies come in a myriad of sizes (after all, the sport is defined by weight classes) and that boxing's *heavyweight* class garners the most attention, the reasons Newell was not cast were low blows.

Lola's dramaturgical function in *Kinky Boots* demonstrates another instance of Broadway's ambivalent embrace of queerness and Blackness: like *Hairspray's* Motormouth Maybelle, she exists to teach white heterosexuals to love themselves and each other in the show's narrative; "others" are almost always pedagogical for the mainstream. *Kinky Boots* used many openly gay actors (and a few straight men) playing drag queens to make mainstream audiences comfortable with difference. *Kinky Boots* exists worlds away from the kinds of bodies (and the kind of queerness) represented in *Fun Home*. But, truthfully, even Lola and *Fun Home's* three Alisons did not stray far from the norms of Broadway bodies. Broadway's hyper-fit ideal body is at once a capitulation to patriarchal ideals, an effort to distance the body from effeminacy (and from homosexuality itself at times), and an attempt to gain mainstream acceptance. The fit body is a purportedly moral body; historian Christopher E. Forth quips, "It took a firm character to have a hard body."[99] Hard bodies conveyed moral superiority and self-control in a society where a body's surface is falsely thought to reveal something essential about its interiority. As far as LGBTQ+ bodies are concerned, the implied morality of a hard body mitigated the supposed moral stain caused by non-normative sexual acts.

Body conformity in theatre is not relegated solely to gay men because it regulates *all* bodies. Former actor Bree Coven described how this ideology affected her, writing, "By the time I was twelve . . . I had figured out that gay men—tight, toned, and seminaked—belonged onstage dancing and that lesbians—frumpy and gruff in ripped-sleeve flannel—belonged backstage as stage managers or light operators."[100] Coven's description admits the lesbian's assigned place: backstage. Inclusion on Broadway still exists within a system built on exclusivity grounded in aesthetic disqualification. Broadway's reputation as a queer-friendly space and its actors' advocacy for LGBTQ+ causes give cover to its ultimate containment and commodification of queerness. Broadway is big business, and Broadway producers require profits. Broadway cares, but it's not a charity. Casting, coming out, and representation matter all the more in this environment because of what they represent, even

176 SEXUALITY

contained and commodified, to someone who has yet to see someone like them represented onstage.

Questioning Broadway's body politics is a way of understanding "how bodies are shaped by relations of power, or the way(s) social structure shapes how we perceive our bodies."[101] The price of inclusion on Broadway is admission into a system in which individuals are expendable and replaceable, where queerness has been flexibly cast. According to disability theorist Robert McRuer, under "the flexible logic of neoliberalism, all varieties of queerness—and, for that matter, all disabilities—are essentially temporary, appearing only when, and as long as, they are necessary."[102] Broadway regulates difference. Broadway may claim diversity and inclusion by being more LGBTQ+ friendly than most US institutions, but that stops where body conformity begins.

Gay actors continue to confront a specific kind of body shame. In 2021, actor Ben Bogen recalled the time a Broadway creative told him they were glad he had "butched up since they cast" him.[103] Other actors added their experiences of being told they were "too light in the loafers" or being given a "butch" class in theatre training and auditions. While there has been change since *La Cage* burst onto Broadway in 1983, the complexity of who should play gay versus who is gay finds itself enmeshed in the tangle of Broadway's body politics writ large. One can come out about being gay, lesbian, bisexual, trans, and so on but then what roles are available to them? And what does it mean for these actors to play it straight or another identity under the queer umbrella that they don't share? Even as undeniable progress has been made in US society at large and on Broadway stages in terms of LGBTQ+ inclusion, actors still find themselves too often trapped in the limbo of often being told to "Turn It Off," sometimes to "Keep It Gay," and rarely to "Just Be."

PART IV
ABILITY

6

Deaf West's *Awakening* of Broadway

Decades before Deaf West Theatre brought two musical revivals to Broadway, actor Bruce Hlibok make Broadway history as "the first deaf actor to play a deaf character in a Broadway production."[1] The musical was Elizabeth Swados's *Runaways* (1978). Hlibok played a small role in the ensemble musical yet made a big impact by signing, in rhythm, the songs in ASL (American Sign Language) alongside his singing castmates—a Broadway musical first. Critic Richard Eder observed, "Mr. Hlibok's mute gestures remain one of the haunting visual underpinnings to many of the songs."[2] Despite Hlibok's success, nearly a quarter of a century would pass before another Broadway musical featured Deaf actors. In the interim, Hlibok died of complications from AIDS in 1995 and never had the chance to appear in another Broadway musical.

ASL created one of the most compelling *coups de théâtre* in a Broadway musical, occurring near the end of the 2003 Broadway revival of *Big River*, a co-production of Deaf West Theatre and Roundabout Theatre Company. During the final chorus of "Waitin' for the Light to Shine," the cast stopped singing but continued signing the final verse's lyrics to the now-silent beat. The silence only emphasized the presence of music in the absence of sound. Theatre scholar Stephanie Lim notes, "For those who can understand ASL, the scene and song continue in these moments, whether or not there is anything auditory happening. Silence thus contains action and is not 'silence' in the traditional sense, but rather should be understood as a powerful and central act in and of itself."[3] The silence gave hearing spectators a momentary, fleeting experience of what attending a musical might feel like for d/Deaf and hard-of-hearing audiences.

Musicals privilege the aural and the visual; they are as much about *hearing* the score as *seeing* the staging, which makes the form often inaccessible to audience members and actors alike denied access and accommodation. Musicologist Raymond Knapp points out that musical theatre's "mainstream has also always been understood to be *able*: 'sound' in body and mind, and especially proficient regarding vocality and movement."[4] Deaf West's 2015

Broadway Bodies. Ryan Donovan, Oxford University Press. © Oxford University Press 2023.
DOI: 10.1093/oso/9780197551073.003.0007

180 ABILITY

Broadway revival of *Spring Awakening* challenged musicals' audio-centric bias by (sometimes) privileging ASL above vocalized speech.[5] The perception of musical theatre performance as a style of hyper-ability, embodied by the triple-threat performer, contributes to the exclusion of Deaf and hard-of-hearing actors and spectators because it misrecognizes the ability of these actors and ASL to make music and dance.[6]

Deaf West Theatre's *Big River* and *Spring Awakening* offer a more capacious understanding of the kinds of abilities musicals can include as they redefine what *ability* means on Broadway. As disability studies scholar Lennard J. Davis explains, "The term 'ables' describes everyone—not just those with physical limitations—and the term 'ability' includes but does not stigmatize 'disability.'"[7] The casting and staging of Deaf West's revival of *Spring Awakening* (*DWSA* hereafter) provided a notable model of accessibility and inclusion for Broadway. The production staged d/Deaf and disability identities pedagogically for hearing audiences, effectively creating what literary theorist Mary Louise Pratt calls the *contact zone*: "social spaces where cultures meet, clash, and grapple with each other, often in contexts of highly asymmetrical relations of power."[8] *DWSA* centered Deafness and Deaf actors as it compellingly staged the conflict between signing and oralism without fundamentally altering the musical's text to suit this new layer of meaning.

DWSA's *Playbill* included a note from director Michael Arden, explaining how and why the musical had been adapted and re-contextualized but not rewritten. He drew parallels between the history of censorship of Frank Wedekind's *Frühlings Erwachen* (1891), the musical's source play, and its historical context: when, in 1880, "the Second International Congress on Education of the Deaf (known as the Milan Conference) passed a resolution banning sign language in schools across Europe and the United States, declaring Oralism (lip reading, speech and mimicking mouth shapes) superior. The term given to Deaf students unable to succeed with the abusive oral method was 'Failure.'" Residential schools where deaf students and Deaf culture could thrive were closed as a result and students were mainstreamed into schools where they could not sign. Arden went on to explain some of the abuse deaf people faced from stigmatization to sterilization and to connect that "dark time in Deaf history" to *Spring Awakening*.[9] Oralism was becoming a prevalent method when Wedekind was writing his play, which gave Arden's concept a soupçon of historical authenticity. Additionally, *DWSA*'s ASL masters also incorporated specific ASL signs from circa-1891 to further give a sense of historical accuracy to d/Deaf audiences (although the show, of course, is set in Germany where ASL would not have been in use).

Arden made *Spring Awakening* fundamentally about deafness in ways that, due to the nature of their narratives, Deaf West's previous musicals were not. *DWSA* artfully staged the violence done to the Deaf in the practice of oralism and the mainstreaming of deaf students, which "is seen [by the Deaf] as cultural genocide since residential schools are [its] breeding ground."[10] By making *DWSA* about and inclusive of deafness and Deaf history, Arden's production took a reparative approach. By showing how oralism ultimately contributed to the character Moritz's suicide, Arden raised the stakes of the classroom scenes and implicitly made the case for ASL in educational settings—including theatres, since this production itself was explicitly pedagogical.

Excluding deaf and hard-of-hearing people remains theatre's norm. But what about reframing deafness not as hearing *loss* but as Deaf *gain*?[11] Scholars of Deaf studies H-Dirksen L. Bauman and Joseph J. Murray propose that Deafness and/Deaf people offer unique ways of exploring what it means to be human and that a deaf person does not lose their hearing so much as they gain Deafness. *DWSA* demonstrates what musicals gain by including Deafness. This chapter examines *DWSA*'s casting, how Deaf West recasts musicals in ASL, the critical reception of the production, and implications for the future of whose bodies are Broadway bodies.

"Sometimes We Do Musicals"

Deaf West Artistic Director DJ Kurs invited d/Deaf and hard-of hearing performers to audition for *DWSA* by signing, "Sometimes we do musicals. . . . Our musicals are inspiring to deaf and hearing audiences alike."[12] Kurs explicitly countered assumptions that musicals were only the domain of the hearing. Since Deaf West's beginnings in 1991, Founding Director Ed Waterstreet consciously made the company a space for hearing and d/Deaf and hard-of-hearing communities by casting and staging their productions with actors from each of these communities and using both ASL and spoken English in their plays. The company's website explains its mission: "Deaf West Theatre engages artists and audiences in unparalleled theater experiences inspired by Deaf culture and the expressive power of sign

182 ABILITY

language. Committed to innovation, collaboration, and training, Deaf West Theatre is the artistic bridge between the deaf and hearing worlds."[13] Deaf West staged only plays during its first nine years of existence.

Broadway was never part of Deaf West Theatre's mission, which has always been about its local Los Angeles community. Waterstreet explains, "I found out that although there were 2 million deaf and hard-of-hearing people [in Los Angeles], there was no theatrical art form for them. I was shocked by that."[14] Waterstreet founded Deaf West Theatre as a result. He did not expect the composition of its audiences to be so full of hearing spectators, observing, "The deaf audience wasn't even very big: 95% of the audience were hearing." The company shifted its strategy in response. Rather than stage plays only with and for Deaf and hard-of-hearing people, Waterstreet began to focus on connecting Deaf and hearing cultures through ASL theatre.[15] Waterstreet relays that the idea to do a musical at Deaf West was born of simple curiosity and a question: why not?[16]

In 2000, Deaf West sought out Broadway director-choreographer Jeff Calhoun to stage its first musical, *Oliver!* Calhoun agreed to take on the assignment following a heavy amount of skepticism. He admitted asking himself, " 'This is what my career has come to? I'm being asked to direct musicals with deaf actors?' Now, I'm embarrassed by that statement because it feels so arrogant."[17] He earned only $500 for two months of work directing the musical and found himself changed by the experience, noting, "It was the hardest thing I've ever had to do, the most fun I've ever had, and probably the most fulfilled as an artist that I've ever been." He returned to direct *Big River* in 2002 and then the original musical *Sleeping Beauty Wakes* in 2007.

In addition to providing Broadway pros like Calhoun their first point of contact with ASL theatre, Deaf West's musicals are also many hearing spectators' first point of contact with Deaf culture. Theatre works as an effective contact zone because the proximity of spectators and actors encourages the meeting of cultures. The dynamics of ASL, spoken English, projected titles, and song and dance concurrently communicating further emphasizes the potential of Deaf West as a contact zone. ASL musicals are inherently bilingual musicals, and since ASL is an *embodied* language, ASL and musicals are not the odd couple spectators may assume them to be. Davis explains, "Sign language is far closer to writing than is speech. Speech is an oral production linked to the mouth. Sign language can be seen as a form of writing done in space rather than on paper."[18] If Davis's notion of writing in space holds, it makes sense that critics often frame ASL in musicals choreographically, and audiences not fluent in ASL may experience it as dance rather than speech.

While ASL is integrally part of the staging of an ASL musical, it is not in and of itself choreographic. Unlike ASL and other sign languages, choreography and gesture are visual modes of communication, and *not* codified languages; to conflate them risks masking language's inherent power dynamics. ASL gestures have specific meanings as opposed to choreography's often abstract nature. According to *DWSA* ASL master Shoshannah Stern, "The big challenge is that A.S.L. is not a very abstract language—it's more concrete, it's visual and spatial."[19] ASL musicals do invite the comparison to choreography because signing signifies as both dance and speech during musical numbers. Staging ASL musicals reorients the spatial nature of sign language; it is customary to face each other when signing, but musicals are typically oriented toward the audience. Signing is not just how Deaf actors move and speak in ASL musicals; it is also how they *sing* with their hands and their facial expressions. Signing advances the musical theatre adage that characters break into song when they can no longer speak their emotions, and they dance when they can no longer sing them because signing in ASL musicals proves an effective means of embodying music, lyrics, movement, and text all at once. *DWSA* choreographer Spencer Liff choreographed ASL into the show's musical numbers out of necessity since it had to be timed to music that many of the cast could not hear. He collaborated with Alexandria Wailes, a d/Deaf actor working as associate choreographer, on incorporating ASL. The interplay between choreography and ASL meant that the musical numbers needed to simultaneously reach hearing and d/Deaf spectators through several modes of communication.

Deaf West's ASL musicals also taught another impactful lesson: that musicals can be inclusive of abilities previously excluded from Broadway. Kurs explains how d/Deaf actors "realize, perhaps subconsciously, that appearing on stage is the repudiation of the advice that their hearing parents were given when their child was born, that they were deficient and needed to be fixed. Appearing on stage and signing in front of a paying audience is the personal affirmation of the Deaf identity over pathology."[20] Deaf West's Broadway productions propose intriguing questions of voice: What changes in a musical when the definition of triple-threat becomes a performer who signs, dances, and acts?

184   ABILITY

"Two Left Hands": Casting *Spring Awakening*

Staging an ASL musical requires rethinking most of the usual processes of producing a musical, especially casting. When Calhoun staged *Big River*, he resisted following one rule for casting the show and let the narrative determine how the show would be cast in terms of which roles were speaking and which were signing—a most crucial decision when staging an ASL musical. The roles that are double cast with a deaf/hard-of-hearing actor or a hearing actor and those that are not inform the narrative, determining both hearing and deafness's place and function within the show. Since Deaf West's musicals drew such big audiences, their casting choices carried a lot of weight.

Deaf West's Broadway productions were never conceived with Broadway in mind, and so their casting procedures were not those of typical Broadway productions. In March 2014, Deaf West Theatre posted a YouTube video inviting actors to submit self-taped auditions for its upcoming ninety-nine-seat black box Los Angeles production of *Spring Awakening*. Casting via YouTube was not a publicity stunt: it made auditions accessible to actors unable to travel to Los Angeles and effectively served as the show's open call. Kurs noted that doing this musical would "allow us to find a new generation of talents who will be able to perform in musicals." Explicit in this appeal to performers was an invitation to d/Deaf performers to consider performing in musicals an option. Because the cast had to play adolescents, Deaf West needed to find young, possibly inexperienced actors, and so the casting video explicitly instructed actors on how to audition for the production and the casting needs of this ASL musical. *DWSA* director Michael Arden explains, "We're not only looking for deaf, hard-of-hearing, and hearing actors who are comfortable with music and rhythm and folk and rock music, but also for musicians who can play the score while voicing for our deaf and hard-of-hearing actors. So, there are many opportunities for every kind of actor, no matter where you lie on the hearing spectrum."[21] There were opportunities to be cast yet the economics of a ninety-nine-seat black box production precluded anyone involved from earning much; there was the opportunity and then there was the cost. What there weren't were many other opportunities.

Working outside of commercial theatre's constraints and financial pressures meant the ability to experiment, especially the chance to rethink casting and staging. But it also meant low pay for actors, too especially in the notoriously low-paying small-theatre scene in Los Angeles where *DWSA* got its start. An early casting breakdown for the production even called attention to this; it reads: "This is an incredible experience. The pay is minimal. This is a labor of love project with a high caliber team dedicated to making an impact on the theatre community in Los Angeles. Note that their production of 'Big River' also transferred to The Mark Taper and Broadway."[22] The minimal pay was offset by the tantalizing prospect of a Broadway transfer.

The video instructed Deaf and hard-of-hearing actors to sign a two-minute song for their auditions, a daunting task for those who could not necessarily fully hear the music or feel its rhythm. The video ends with the following instructions:

> Deaf Actors: please include a 2-minute classical monologue and a 2-minute ASL Music Video in your video.
> Hearing Actors: please include a 2-minute classical monologue and a 2-minute Folk/Rock song in your video. If you play an instrument, please accompany yourself or demonstrate your abilities.
> Seeking piano, guitar, bass (upright and electric), percussion, viola, violin, cello.[23]

Each role's multiple requirements complicated casting the show. Casting director Beth Lipari worked on *DWSA* in Los Angeles, and she noted the particularities of the process: "It was a big, tall order. Like, a very large order.... [H]alf the cast was going to be hearing impaired, deaf, and the other half was not. Everyone had to play an instrument. Everyone had to be able to sing pop-rock kind of music. Everybody had to be able to act, and willing to work for like $25 a week."[24] The d/Deaf and hard-of-hearing actors learned to sign to music they did not hear, and the hearing actors learned a little ASL for the auditions. Kurs explains, "During auditions we looked at the hearing actors to see if they had an ability to sign. We would give them a line and see what they would do with it. Some people had two left hands.... [T]hat was an additional level that we were conscious of, and that might have been a little different."[25] Casting *DWSA* meant layering artistic, economic, and practical aspects into each decision—which actors could afford to accept the contract had to overlap with those who had the necessary skills.

Together, the d/Deaf actor and their voiced counterpart create one role; the role sharing extended only to principal roles and not the ensemble or supporting roles. Kurs explained, "We have two people that are creating one character and that's an important aspect in our company. Again, and first and foremost, I'm looking at talent of course, and does it match the role and

186   ABILITY

what I envision."[26] Lipari noted the calculations that the creative team had to perform to match performers with roles: "She's an amazing singer, amazing actor, great, she plays the violin, then we brought her to the signing portion, and it was like, 'Oh my god, she can't sign.' And so, like, a necessary thing would be cut. It was so specific that you just knew when you found the person you were like, 'That's the person.' "[27] In short, there were multiple competing considerations for each part, and while this is true of every musical, ASL musicals require more.

For the in-person auditions and callbacks, an ASL interpreter was in the audition room and a d/Deaf actor reader as the actors' scene partner. The d/Deaf actors auditioning also had to adapt/translate the audition material into ASL themselves, adding an additional layer to the process for them. Arden explained how he could "get insight into an actor from how they choose to translate English into the sign language."[28] Assuring d/Deaf and hard-of-hearing actors that they would not merely shadow the hearing performers onstage but would be central to the action was crucial to the casting process. When initially recruiting actors in 2014, Deaf West highlighted the fact that ASL Masters would be integral to the production. Highlighting the importance of ASL Masters began in the show's casting call video, in which Shoshanna Stern, one of the ASL Masters, noted, "It is my duty to make sure that spoken English and music become equal to the ASL in the production. No one language will take precedence in the production."[29] [Clip 6.1] These steps attempted to address potential hesitancies on the part of d/Deaf performers as well as to acknowledge the specific kind of labor ASL musicals necessitate.

The video submission process worked. *DWSA*'s young leads, Sandra Mae Frank and Austin Mackenzie, were cast from taped submissions. Mackenzie was studying education at college when he saw the casting call and decided to submit a video—he was not even planning to pursue a career as an actor.[30] Many of the d/Deaf actors in the cast had never considered performing in a musical. Daniel Durant (who was cast as Moritz) explained how far away from him a musical seemed, saying, "I'm not even interested in music. I'm profoundly deaf."[31] Durant was the only cast member who stayed with *DWSA* from its first workshop in Los Angeles all the way to Broadway. Trying to sign lyrics during auditions daunted him. "Before *Spring Awakening,* I really didn't have a sense of music." He felt that the show helped him to better understand why hearing people enjoy music.[32]

DEAF WEST'S *AWAKENING* 187

The cast assembled for *DWSA*'s first production at the ninety-nine-seat Rosenthal Theater at Inner City Arts in Downtown Los Angeles, co-produced with Arden's company Forest of Arden. Though the production largely retained its cast from its first production at Inner City Arts, a few original members were unable to join when its success prompted an encore run at the Wallis Annenberg in Beverly Hills. At the Annenberg, the show picked up Andy Mientus, Arden's husband and the person who first suggested *Spring Awakening* to Arden as a potential collaboration with Deaf West, and Alex Boniello, who sang and spoke Moritz and played guitar. This cast would be the one that traveled with the production to Broadway, with a few exceptions.

After the show proved a hit in Los Angeles, producer Ken Davenport optioned it for Broadway. The casting breakdown for the production's Broadway engagement, which did not change substantially from its first production in Los Angeles, shows the choices Arden and company made about which characters would be Deaf and which would be hearing:

Seeking-Melchior (Hearing Actor): male, 18–20, all ethnicities. Wendla (Deaf Actor): female, 18–20, all ethnicities. Voice of Wendla (Hearing Actor): female, 18–20, all ethnicities. Moritz (Deaf Actor): male, 18–20, all ethnicities. Voice of Moritz (Hearing Actor): male, 18–20, all ethnicities. Ilse (Hearing Actor): female, 18–20, all ethnicities. Adult Men (Deaf Actor): male, 40–59, all ethnicities. Adult Men (Hearing Actor): male, 40–59, all ethnicities. Adult Women (Deaf Actor): female, 36–50, all ethnicities. Adult Women (Hearing Actor): female, 36–50, all ethnicities. Adult Hearing Male Standby: male, 40–59, all ethnicities. Adult Hearing Female Standby: female, 36–50, all ethnicities.[33]

When the production moved to Broadway, it added a few new cast members, including swings and standbys. Laura Collins-Hughes wrote about casting the Broadway production for the *New York Times*, noting the rarity of Broadway's need for d/Deaf actors—not seen on the Great White Way since the Deaf West/Roundabout *Big River* in 2003. The article poignantly ends with a quote from actor Rita Corey, who describes what the opportunity meant to her at sixty-one years old: "All of a sudden here, after 40 years of waiting and waiting for a Broadway show, I'm now having this opportunity. I am just so happy. I want to show what I can do."[34] Simply auditioning for a Broadway production offered validation to d/Deaf actors, and even if

188   ABILITY

they weren't ultimately cast, the chance to be considered at all still meant something.

Unfortunately, Corey was not cast as one of the adults in the show. Neither were the actors who played the roles in the Los Angeles productions, who the production replaced with name actors for the Great White Way. Broadway casting agency Telsey + Company took over at this point to recast the adult roles. Broadway economics demand stars, who apparently did not have to audition; according to the *Playbill* headline, "All It Took Was a Text!"[35] Marlee Matlin and Russell Harvard, Deaf film stars, joined the production and made their Broadway debuts in it. Hearing stage and television stars Camryn Manheim and Patrick Page were cast as the other two adults in the production (all four played multiple roles). Apart from the historic nature of being Broadway's second ASL musical, *DWSA* broke another important barrier by casting Ali Stroker in her Broadway debut, making her Broadway's first actor who uses a wheelchair.

DWSA's presence on Broadway advanced industry awareness (if not action) around casting, labor, and inclusion. Brought to the foreground was the fact that musicals make deafness, difference, and disability into metaphors by casting non-disabled and/or hearing actors in roles calling for deafness or disability. Casting actors who do not share the character's difference reinforces the power imbalances of the world at large because playing a role onstage and shedding that identity at the curtain call is profoundly different from living in a world that stigmatizes one's embodied difference. Many d/Deaf activists and advocates have asked, "Shouldn't a d/Deaf person play a d/Deaf character?" Frank wrote an article for the *Washington Post* in which she explains, "Seeing hearing people in deaf roles frustrates me to no end. We can see through the falsehood the second they start signing—hearing actors tend to lack the facial expressions that play such a huge role in ASL grammar."[36] She concludes, "We will show how we can bring the beauty of deaf culture to a character, but more importantly, how we can bring our abilities as actors."

If full-time employment in professional theatre is difficult for almost all actors, stigma and normalized discriminatory casting practices compound the lack of opportunity for d/Deaf actors. Labor concerns paint a stark picture for d/Deaf people in the United States. According to employment statistics released by the National Deaf Center in 2016, the year after *DWSA*'s Broadway run, only 48 percent of deaf individuals were employed, and 47 percent were not in the labor force at all compared to 72 percent of hearing individuals who were then employed. A profound annual wage gap of $11,530 exists between hearing workers and d/Deaf and/or disabled workers.[37] If exclusion from the US labor force is clear, Broadway's numbers are worse. No Broadway musical since *DWSA* has yet cast a d/Deaf actor.[38] *DWSA*'s inclusion of d/Deaf, hard-of-hearing, and disabled performers in all kinds of roles awakened Broadway to possibilities of inclusion it has yet to truly act on. Though it originally contained no d/Deaf characters as written, *DWSA*'s recasting of *Spring Awakening* with d/Deaf actors allowed Broadway to profoundly gain deafness.

Recasting *Spring Awakening* in ASL

Since *DWSA* was not Deaf West's first musical, its creatives relied on prior experiences to shape it. Producing director Bill O'Brien explained how the creative team had approached casting *Big River*, saying: "The question was, what happens when deaf people in their own language are forced to break into song? Translating *Big River* into American Sign Language was all about why these emotions need to be expressed in a poetic way. So the real trick is finding pieces that are actually enhanced by translating [them] into American Sign Language."[39] *Big River* worked in translation, but how would *Spring Awakening* play, being a tragic paean to adolescent angst set to poetic lyrics? The themes of Sater and Sheik's musical mapped onto Arden's concept, which depicted "a group of schoolchildren in 1890's Germany all coming of age in a time and place when they're not given all the information about what's going on with their bodies. It's really about two groups of people trying to communicate."[40]

Arden first staged a workshop production for Deaf West that reiterated the challenges of getting this material right, but it wasn't until after the workshop that his concept came together more clearly. Arden learned about the Milan conference while in rehearsals for the 2014 production at Inner City Arts, and it became the production's raison d'être. He said, "It's sort of been my fight in directing it to be able to tell that story that isn't on the page of *Spring Awakening*. . . . Trying to bring light to this huge event and the fallout and aftermath of this awful, awful series of decisions that were made by people who had no right to make them. Which is exactly what's happening in the play."[41] Arden quickly found novel ways to apply his new concept to the existing musical without changing the narrative or spoken text, such as staging the classroom scenes and showing how the teacher forbade Moritz

190   ABILITY

from signing there.[42] The creative team was always focused on trying to ensure that the staging placed equal value on ASL and English. Arden detailed his thinking: "If there are two deaf characters in a scene together it's silent. Because in the minds of those two characters, there wouldn't be an audible language. And if there are two hearing characters speaking to each other, we don't sign those scenes. Those are projected in the same way that the silent scenes are projected."[43]

The challenges of staging an ASL musical were evident from the very first workshop, where Arden and Liff intended to stage five or six songs but completed only two due to everyone's learning curve.[44] ASL musicals change the nature of the theatrical space on and off stage, and everyone working on the production—both the hearing people and the deaf—must reorient themselves as a result. That initial workshop experience led Deaf West to commit to staging a full production. *DWSA* choreographer Spencer Liff detailed how demanding rehearsals were for him—a hearing person trying to figure out how to stage an ASL musical: "It was the longest rehearsal process ever. . . . You can't use counts. You can't rely on musicality. Everything had to be visual. And how do you make two and a half hours out of sign language not look like two and a half hours of standing there signing?"[45] In addition to this, sharing roles meant that the d/Deaf actor and the hearing actor had to find a common tempo for their movements both during songs and spoken/signed dialogue. This was on top of the necessarily elaborate system of cueing used for the d/Deaf actors throughout the show. Manheim explains, "Many of the actors are singing, dancing, signing, acting, and cueing Deaf actors simultaneously."[46] The system of cues ranged from the visual and spatial to the physical: a lighting change, a look from one actor to another, or a tap on the shoulder.[47] The cues made staging and performing the musical much more complex, but they also point toward "the political possibility that staging commercial musical blockbusters need no longer depend on the sound of music," as performance scholar Sarah Wilbur theorizes.[48]

The hyper-detailed nature of the process took its toll on the cast and creative team during technical rehearsals. The fact that many cast members could not hear when the director told them to hold in place while the show was lit added to the safety concerns. The large number of different kinds of cues involved complicated the typical cue-to-cue tech rehearsal. "It just requires every single person involved, from the prop person to the dresser to every single actor to have 100% concentration at all times. Which is kind of exhausting mentally," recalled Arden.[49] However, the exhaustion was in service of telling the story and layering Deaf history onto the narrative. Kurs noted how Arden's concept shined a light on the present and the past, saying, "It takes place during a dark time in deaf history . . . in which hearing educators of the deaf got together and decided that deaf students should be taught orally and that sign language should be banned. It is the desire to normalize deaf people that proved destructive to the deaf individual then and still does today."[50] To explain how deep the fear of deafness was at the time, Arden cites the regular sterilization of deaf women as a way of eradicating deafness.[51]

Casting was the most visible embodiment of Arden's staging concept, and developing and refining it was a process. Katie Boeck, who provided the vocals for Frank's Wendla, explains that casting Moritz and Wendla with d/Deaf actors amplified the "theme of the difficulty in communicating."[52] The fact that Wendla and Moritz are both dead at the end of the musical while Melchior survives placed the treatment of deaf children and adolescents into sharp relief with how their hearing peers fared. Arden's casting of the show's adult roles with two deaf adults and two hearing adults who all played multiple roles allowed for Moritz and his father to be played by deaf actors, depicting the relationship of a deaf father and son for the first time on Broadway. Sharing roles between voice and sign shed new light on the narrative, as Mackenzie explains: "The voice actors aren't just voice actors, [they] are [their] own characters. People have equated them to the subconscious of the Deaf characters. . . . I see them as guardian angels."[53] Boeck described moments between her and Frank as guardian angel-like, noting how "honoring her choices, allowing her to be free within the moment" influenced her voicing of Wendla (pictured in Figure 6.1).[54] She observed that many of Wendla's lyrics are written in the past tense, which influenced how she sang and spoke the part of Wendla while Frank signed.

Years before Deaf West's production came into being, *Spring Awakening* lyricist and librettist Steven Sater presciently explained, "Throughout the show, one character cannot 'hear' what another is singing,"[55] which only intensified *DWSA*'s thematic conceit and revealed how apt it was. Sater's lyrics and Duncan Sheik's score comment on the dramatic action but are not necessarily part of it, making *Spring Awakening* ideal for an ASL staging. Sater and Sheik's musical adaptation of Frank Wedekind's 1891 German expressionist play *Spring Awakening* was selectively faithful to Wedekind in spirit if not always to the letter. They changed much of the plot and added a classroom scene, which, they explained, "allows us to see the repressive nineteenth-century German school system in operation: force-feeding young minds

192 ABILITY

Figure 6.1 Katie Boeck (*left*) and Sandra Mae Frank (*right*) in Deaf West Theatre's *Spring Awakening*. Credit: Joan Marcus.

a 'proper education,' while quelling all the life in them."[56] Arden made this scene central to his concept for the show since it could vividly demonstrate the experience of deaf students forced into mainstream education, forbidden from communicating in sign language. This scene allowed the musical to show the audience how deeply the adults failed the adolescents rather than how deaf students failed to assimilate. Staging the oppressive effects of mainstreaming only highlighted how mainstreaming cuts deaf people off from each other, which validated Deaf West's actors' experiences. *Big River* star Tyrone Giordano explains, "We're being isolated from one another in mainstreamed environments within our educational system."[57] *DWSA* star Durant reported that he attended, "a general education school, where I was the only Deaf person. It was hard to socialize. We're such different cultures."[58]

Spring Awakening centers on culture clashes between adults and adolescents, parents and children, young men and young women, and in *DWSA*, between Deaf culture and the hearing. The musical opens with Wendla's plaintive song "Mama Who Bore Me." Wendla unsuccessfully implores her mother to tell her how babies are conceived, illustrating the failure of the adults to be honest with their children. The scene shifts to the classroom, where the boys recite Virgil's *Aeneid* in Latin by rote for their cruel teacher. These two scenes set up the power imbalance between the adults and the teens. The classroom scenes in *DWSA* in particular demonstrated how oralism produced tragic outcomes—in this case, Moritz's suicide after he does not pass the school's advancement exam. The classroom scenes are juxtaposed with those depicting Melchior and Wendla's budding romance. Their sexual exploration tragically culminates in Melchior raping and impregnating Wendla. Since Wendla's mother has never explained sex to her, Wendla does not realize that sex leads to pregnancy and she does not even know she is pregnant until her mother tells her so after a doctor's visit. Melchior's parents send him to a reformatory as punishment for his actions. Unbeknownst to Wendla, her mother procures a clandestine abortion for her, and she dies as a result of the procedure. Melchior had planned to meet Wendla in the town graveyard after escaping the reformatory; but instead, he meets her fresh tombstone. The ghosts of Moritz and Wendla join Melchior in the cemetery and the musical ends with the cast reassembling onstage to sing "The Song of Purple Summer."

Sater notes that in "The Song of Purple Summer," the actors appear not as their characters but as themselves as they "tell us of the promise ahead."[59] This moment and this song are indicative of the kinds of issues that would be raised by translating *Spring Awakening* into ASL. "Purple Summer" gives the tragic plot a hopeful ending but also leaves some audience members wondering exactly what a purple summer is; as an article in *Playbill* claims, "Steven Sater may have written a song called 'Purple Summer,' but that phrase doesn't mean anything to the Deaf community."[60] Arden says, "We had to actually translate, like, what does 'purple summer' mean.... How do we express that to a Deaf audience?"[61] Beyond "Purple Summer," even the songs with more straightforward lyrics required some rethinking in ASL.

194   ABILITY

The ASL lyrics were completely different from their English counterparts; the spoken scenes could be translated in a more or less straightforward manner, though still not on a one-to-one basis. *DWSA* used three ASL Masters due to this complexity. Frank explained, "Instead of following exactly what the English words are, we go for more of the concepts and so once people see what the signs are and they're hearing the words, even if they don't understand each one right away, it all comes together and I feel like the ASL adds a whole strong layer that makes it oh so very visual."[62] Manheim described the mental shift she had to make even as an actor fluent in ASL and English, saying, "I know I'm saying one thing in English, and I'm watching Marlee sign something entirely different in sign language. It's a similar story. I mean, the audience is getting the same understanding of the story, but the words are all inverted and turned around."[63] Manheim aptly describes the benefits and pitfalls of Simultaneous Communication (SimCom), in which a person signs and speaks simultaneously even though they aren't expressing exactly correspondent modes or words. In theory, it does not privilege one language over the other, but in practice this is not always the case. Shannon Bradford, Deaf theatre scholar, explains that SimCom "may also engender a different misperception by hearing nonsigners: ASL may be read as an aesthetic stage language, akin to costuming or lighting rather than as a legitimate linguistic system."[64] Bradford also notes that SimCom also risks giving hearing spectators the impression that ASL is "merely a gestural representation of English," which is also not the case. *DWSA*'s use of SimCom highlighted the power dynamics intrinsic to bilingual musicals. It should be noted that many d/Deaf people do not consider SimCom effective, in part because it privileges voiced language due to the fact that talking renders the speaker's face unavailable for the nonverbal cues that are an integral part of ASL. Nevertheless, *DWSA*'s SimCom staging and its emphasis on the characters' inability to communicate became entwined.[65]

Awakening Broadway Audiences and Critics

DWSA was not only trying to attract hearing audiences but also aiming to educate them. In the *Playbill*, "A Note about the ASL Translation" explained how Arden et al. created this production:

Deaf West Theatre employs American Sign Language (ASL) Masters, who facilitate the adaptation and translation process from written English to American Sign Language. This process requires careful attention to preserving the integrity of ASL while adhering to the script as written. In addition to executing the translation, the ASL Masters must see that it appropriately reflects the actor and the character portrayed. The ASL Masters then work with each actor to ensure that the playwright's intentions, tone, rhythm, poetry, idiomatic expressions and humor are all reflected in each actor's signing.[66]

Big River's Playbill included no such statement for the audience, since Calhoun's concept for that show did not explicitly relate to d/Deafness in the way that Arden's concept did for *DWSA*. The note about the ASL translation informed audiences of several important facts: that ASL is not the same as written/spoken English, that this production requires different labor, that they are not seeing a literal translation, but an adaptation into ASL by an ASL Master, and that the ASL Master works with the actors much like a director in addition to creating the ASL translation.

An insert in the *Playbill* for *DWSA* encouraged Broadway spectators to "keep the conversation going" by following and interacting with the production's social media pages, presumably also providing word-of-mouth marketing for the show, while also inviting audiences to "join the guilty ones," its official online fan community. Finally, the insert suggested that audiences "Learn ASL" by taking local classes or downloading the app "Marlee Signs," featuring the production's star Marlee Matlin. The other side of the insert featured six pictures of cast members signing keywords related to the production: ASL, theatre, schools, dance, love, and applause. The *Playbill* included even more information about ASL in order to educate hearing audiences (pictured in Figure 6.2):

Thus, the *Playbill* explicitly frames *DWSA* as a contact zone and situates ASL next to choreography to further that connection despite the risk of equating them. It took a herculean effort to bring *DWSA* to Broadway and then to sell the show to hearing audiences and critics—hence the didactic approaches. Once on Broadway, though, *DWSA* had the misfortune of opening the month after *Hamilton*, which drew most of the media's attention as a once-in-a-generation monster hit.

Spring Awakening's mixed-to-positive reviews betrayed the fact that they were mostly written with hearing audiences in mind. Charles Isherwood's

Figure 6.2 Deaf West Theatre's *Spring Awakening* featured this insert in its *Playbill* instructing audiences in ASL. Credit: author.

review in the *New York Times* sought to assuage readers' anxieties about the production, writing, "Deaf actors in a musical? The prospect sounds challenging, to performers and audiences alike. But you will be surprised at how readily you can assimilate the novelties involved, and soon find yourself pleasurably immersed not in a worthy, let's-pat-ourselves-on-the-back experience, but simply in a first-rate production of a transporting musical."[67] Isherwood's framing of assimilation as something that happens to the audience is noteworthy since the production itself staged mainstreaming's forced assimilation of d/Deaf students. Other critics were not as taken. David Rooney of the *Hollywood Reporter* noted, "There's beauty in the descriptive power of ASL translations . . . and delicacy in the way the visual language conveys such things as tactile sensation or heartbeats. But more often, sad to say, it proves a distraction here, and the double casting dilutes the characters' emotional intensity, creating a disconnect."[68] In a more positive review, *New York* magazine critic Jesse Green detailed the staging's social impact in his review, calling it "a vision of community" and noting that the presence of "Deaf theatergoers" was felt "immediately evident after every number, when their hands rise and vibrate, like a grove of aspens."[69]

Like mainstream critics, Deaf and hard-of-hearing spectators also had mixed-to-positive reactions to the musical (there are few Deaf theatre critics, if any). Though many noted the power of seeing themselves represented in a Broadway musical, not all thought that the production was entirely successful. On the plus side, Rachel Kolb wrote in the *Atlantic* of the production's significance: "*Spring Awakening* prompts audiences to consider fundamental questions about the nature of full inclusion and communication. Without being remotely voyeuristic, it invites viewers to engage with the signs and choreography of its deaf and hearing actors, without any further explanation."[70] Kolb described how the sharing of the roles between Deaf and hearing actors created an inclusive space as a result of the staging and its lack of mediation though an ASL interpreter (as was the norm).

On the other hand, the *Guardian* brought five d/Deaf New Yorkers and an ASL interpreter to see the production and gauge their reaction. Several pointed out how the production's use of SimCom was actually a failure of accessibility. Spectator Max Graham-Putter explained, "I definitely struggled to understand some of the sim-com and found myself wishing that the hearing actors had Deaf shadows the same way the Deaf actors had hearing shadows. In this way, it was very clear that the play was designed for a hearing audience with a secondary intention of being accessible to the Deaf."[71] The use of SimCom ultimately reinforced the privileging of hearing audience members, seemingly at the expense of Deaf spectators' experience.

Despite reservations about the musical's realization for d/Deaf spectators, the spectators gathered by the *Guardian* concluded that seeing *DWSA*'s attempts at inclusion was meaningful. Seeing *DWSA* was the first time many

198   ABILITY

d/Deaf audience members had attended a show on Broadway other than an ASL-interpreted performance. A Deaf spectator Aleksandr Rozentsvit sent a letter to *Playbill* describing his experience: "I saw a mix of Deaf and hearing patrons that night, which was cool to see. Usually, I'm surrounded by hearing people in shows, or Deaf people at interpreted plays."[72] A blogger at *DeafDigest* noted, "The buzzword on Broadway right now is diversity. As part of the diversity theme, Deaf West's Spring Awakening play has been mentioned. The question behind this diversity buzzword is—will it attract new audiences? *DeafDigest* hopes it will."[73] However, the lack of sustained attention paid by the few d/Deaf media outlets combined with the dearth of Deaf theatre critics demonstrated a fair amount of indifference to an ASL musical.

DWSA's producer Ken Davenport always planned it for a limited Broadway run from September 2015 through January 2016, but it would likely have benefited from rave reviews that might have helped at the box office, which is where it ultimately fell short. Despite Davenport's insistence that the show would not extend—he wrote on his website, "I'm doing something that hasn't been done since the Angela Lansbury *Gypsy* in the 70s. I'm producing a limited run commercial revival of a musical"[74]—if it *had* been a huge box office hit, money is the language commercial theatre speaks best and Davenport surely would have extended the run. Broadway is rarely the space for transformative change, yet for a little over three months at the end of 2015, between *Hamilton*'s casting and *DWSA*'s presence, it seemed that Broadway might be on its way to just that. *DWSA* remains the last Broadway musical to include Deaf performers. The people onstage performing the representation might look, move, and sound different from Broadway's norm, but Broadway's offstage powers-that-be went unchanged: Deaf actors in a Broadway musical were yet again another kind of Brigadoon, only reappearing every few decades.

The Price of Broadway Inclusion

Even though Deaf West's *Big River* was a critical success during its limited run at the non-profit Roundabout Theatre Company in 2003, bringing *Spring Awakening* to the stage at all was a financial risk at every turn from its first ninety-nine-seat black box production in Los Angeles all the way to Broadway's Brooks Atkinson Theatre. Despite some very positive reviews, including in the seemingly all-important *New York Times*, *Spring Awakening* never really found its footing at the box office and did not return its $4.5 million investment to investors. According to financial figures reported by *Playbill*, the production's gross potential was $1,003,600 per week, and the box office receipts never cleared the $700,000 mark, with most weeks bringing in less than $500,000—meaning the production was hovering below 50 percent of its potential income.[75] An announced national tour never materialized, a likely casualty of the show's poor financial performance on Broadway. Financing *DWSA* had always been scrappy, though.

DWSA used the internet to find not only its cast but also its financing. It initially relied on crowdfunding to get it off the ground in Los Angeles and, later, to secure a spot on the Tony Awards broadcast, reflecting the overall underinvestment in ASL theatre in the United States. The production made it as far as it did only by crowdfunding. Its first Kickstarter campaign exceeded its goal, raising $30,706 from 285 backers.[76] The campaign's webpage explains why it sought crowdsourced funds, saying, "We're committed to making this show a sensory and visual experience," and the funds would enhance "the visual qualities of the production."[77] To add some luster, Jonathan Groff and Skylar Astin—original Broadway cast members of *Spring Awakening*—appeared in the Kickstarter video alongside Arden. In the video, ASL Master Stern explains that the production is "about what we don't talk about when we're talking," while Kurs promises "this production is going to be the perfect marriage of form and content." Arden offered access to tickets to those who "help out" since only ninety-nine seats were available per performance.

Producer Davenport saw *DWSA* during its run at the Wallis, where he fell in love with the production and then "had to raise $4.5 million in 86 days" to produce the show on Broadway.[78] Though it closed before the announcement of the Tony Award nominations, *DWSA*'s nomination for Best Revival of a Musical guaranteed it a coveted spot on the Tony telecast—if the production could cover the associated costs. Since Kickstarter had worked previously, Deaf West turned to it again, hoping to raise $200,000 this time to bring the cast, now scattered across the country, back to New York for rehearsal and the telecast, as well as to "get the costumes and instruments and props out of storage."[79] Davenport and the other Broadway producers stood to lose money by putting the production on the Tony telecast, because there was no national tour to recoup its Broadway losses, and with no tickets to sell, there was no longer a financial need to perform on the telecast. But those

200   ABILITY

at Deaf West knew that a performance on the Tony Awards would matter more than money, and so did Broadway personality Seth Rudetsky, who told Arden in an interview, "This is the kind of thing where I know Deaf people for years will go, 'Oh my God, I remember seeing it on the Tony Awards and it changed my whole life.'"[80] A few of the d/Deaf cast members appear in the new Kickstarter campaign signing together, "There's only one night a year that theater gets this major worldwide platform. Our performance will be an undeniable statement to the world that theater is for everyone, no matter who you are, and is inclusive."[81] Signing on the Tony Awards would say a lot. The Tony performance made a statement, but not without a complication or two.

Broadway Number: "The Bitch of Living"

The *DWSA* cast performed on the 2016 Tony telecast after raising $211,634 from 1,769 backers (for perspective, the production's Broadway home, the Brooks Atkinson Theatre, only holds 1,069 audience members). In a move that few expected, CBS censored the ASL translation but not the sung lyrics of "The Bitch of Living." This marked quite a shift from the original production's Tony performance in 2007, when network censors bleeped out the song's lyrics, which had already been altered for television (choosing "Totally Fucked" as part of their medley invited the bleeping to a large degree).[a] *DWSA* actor Mientus told *Playbill* that "the signs were a little too hot for TV, so we had to change some of the sign language."[b] That CBS censored the ASL was yet more evidence that the kind of paternalism toward d/Deaf people the production railed against was still alive and thriving, in addition to revealing an oralist bias—the censoring of the signing gave cover for the previously censored lyrics, while also censoring the very bodies signing.

Comparing *Spring Awakening*'s two Tony performances reveals intriguing similarities. Both open with a fragment of "Mama Who Bore Me" and segue into "The Bitch of Living." *DWSA*'s Tony medley stopped there while the original then went into "Totally Fucked." Critics lauded Bill T. Jones's choreography for the original production, especially his use of gesture. Lea Michele's performance of "Mama Who Bore Me" on the Tony Awards shows what Jones's choreographic language looked like, and it is immediately clear how Jones's contemporary dance background made Broadway dance differently. [Clip 6.2] By contrast, the *DWSA* performance opens with Sandra Mae Frank and Katie Boeck facing each across a broken mirror. Boeck strums a guitar slung over her shoulder and she sings the lyrics while Frank signs them to her. [Clip 6.3] Because ASL is a gestural language, these moments seemed to almost cite Jones's work. Whereas Michele looks at the camera as she sings, Boeck and Frank face each other because ASL requires seeing your conversation partner. The striking image of one character in two bodies separated on either side of a mirror cracked open a new window into the musical itself.

The two Tony Awards performances further diverted in "The Bitch of Living," one of the songs set in the classroom. In the original production, the actors all used handheld microphones that gave the show the feel of a rock concert, which was not possible for Deaf West given that this would have precluded signing. Jones's staging of this number simply on wooden chairs was much more stationary than Liff's for the revival. Liff's choreography featured the cast dancing with and on the scenery, moving the desks and chairs around the stage to different formations, allowing the performers to move in canon and to take advantage of different levels to make the ASL more visible, as well as allowing the musicians the chance to be incorporated into the staging. There is a lot of visual stimulation to be sure, though the choreography is all pedestrian movement (walking, jumping, running) that the ASL only enhances. If the visual cacophony made it harder to make out the ASL at times, it visually reflected the throbbing intensity of the sound of the rock music. *DWSA* necessarily featured a more maximal staging than Jones's original since the cast signed all the spoken and sung words, and many were captioned in the theatre; however, these were not captioned on the Tony broadcast, which was a missed opportunity (though home viewers could have used their television's closed captioning feature). Additionally, due to the complicated staging and abbreviated rehearsal time, the camera sometimes does not show which performer is singing, so it is unclear where the sound is coming from, and also the camera is late to show who is signing along. And since many d/Deaf or hard-of-hearing actors were in the cast, not everyone was singing even though

Figure 6.3 The ensemble of Deaf West's *Spring Awakening*. Credit: Joan Marcus.

everyone performed the choreography and the ASL (Figure 6.3 depicts a moment when the show's female ensemble signs together).

Above all, the performance gives viewers a sense of the inventiveness and detail that went into every moment of this production and how Arden, Liff, and company made ASL musical and choreographic. On top of this, seeing Ali Stroker dance across the stage in a wheelchair was another historic moment. *DWSA*'s musical numbers were complex to stage and to watch, but they made musical theatre accessible to audiences often excluded from the form. In order to work successfully, the musical numbers had to reach both d/Deaf and hearing audience members, and so, in this sense, there were two musical numbers happening onstage at once. This simultaneity made *DWSA* especially powerful because it did not just speak to multiple audiences, but it also sang, signed, and danced for them. The bodies onstage were extra-kinetically endowing Broadway with a new definition of triple-threat.

[a] Gioia, "ASL for *Spring Awakening* Tony Performance Was Censored by CBS."
[b] Gioia, "ASL for *Spring Awakening* Tony Performance Was Censored by CBS."

Toward a More Inclusive Broadway

DWSA lost the Tony for Best Revival, but the visibility of the Tony Awards broadcast allowed *DWSA* to reach more people in one night than it did during all of its previous runs combined. This performance undoubtedly mattered to so many because, as theatre scholar Amy Cook notes, "how we tell stories changes how we see ourselves."[82] Durant recalls, "My dream was to become an actor and to tour but I never thought of Broadway. I never thought that was even possible."[83] Thanks to Durant and *DWSA*, now others could dream of new possibilities. Liff recalled seeing a woman in a wheelchair in line waiting for an audition at Pearl Studios who told him, "I saw *Spring Awakening* and for obvious reasons I was incredibly inspired . . . and I'm able to come to these auditions now and put myself in positions [where the casting breakdown] doesn't specify an actress in a chair."[84] As Cook observes, "Casting might provide a way of refusing the roles we are given, the stories we are told. Can casting counter our way of thinking?"[85] Deaf West suggests that casting absolutely can.

For some d/Deaf and hard-of-hearing members of the *DWSA* company, Deaf West's casting translated into more work: Sandra Mae Frank has since played major musical roles like Joan in *Fun Home* and Hodel in *Fiddler on the Roof* at the Lyric Theatre of Oklahoma as well as other roles in non-musical plays; Treshelle Edmond, who played Martha in *Spring Awakening*, returned to Broadway in the 2018 revival of *Children of a Lesser God*; and Russell Harvard played the title role in *The Who's Tommy* at Maryland's Open Circle Theatre in 2016, appeared off-Broadway in Craig Lucas's *I Was Most Alive with You* in 2018, and on Broadway in Sam Gold's *King Lear* (2019). *DWSA*'s actors continue to build their careers, but the roles they do get cast in are not always enough to earn a living, and they are often few and far between.

Though Deaf West's two productions played short runs on Broadway (just 253 performances, including previews, for both *DWSA* and *Big River* combined), their impact reached far beyond New York City, even as Broadway and other institutional theatres across the country largely continue to pay lip service to d/Deaf and disabled actors, playwrights, and other theatre-makers. Through their inclusion on Broadway, *DWSA* and *Big River* raised awareness of the exclusion of d/Deaf, hard-of-hearing, and disabled people from the professional theatre. Deaf West's musicals also vibrantly demonstrate not only the political but also the emotional and theatrical power of ASL musicals. When the Obama administration invited the cast

204   ABILITY

to perform at the White House on November 18, 2015, as part of an event called "Americans with Disabilities and the Arts: A Celebration of Diversity and Inclusion," the invitation was in some ways even more profound than the Tony Awards performance because it showed that d/Deaf and disabled people belong not just on Broadway but in the White House. [Clip 6.4]

DWSA successfully raised awareness of the lack of work for d/Deaf people in theatre such that the National Endowment for the Arts held a roundtable entitled "Creating Opportunities for Deaf Theater Artists" in January 2016, which focused on inclusive ways to build upon *DWSA*'s visibility. The ensuing report included the striking fact that "in the decade since *Big River*, no Deaf actors had appeared on Broadway until the *Spring Awakening* production."[86] Unsurprisingly, the roundtable revealed that finances determine most decisions in theatres of all sizes, from a regional theatre like Deaf West up to commercial Broadway productions. Davenport chastised his fellow producers about their fear of producing ASL theatre, noting that it was less expensive than the common practice of importing British actors and productions. He argued, "It's about attitudes within the hearing culture and my fellow producers."[87] As of this writing, Davenport has not since produced another ASL musical. The onus for the inclusion of d/Deaf artists and artists with disabilities should not fall solely on companies with missions specific to those constituencies; ASL and d/Deaf theatre do not begin and end with Deaf West. Jim Nicola, artistic director of New York Theatre Workshop, notes, "We have to remove the sense that this is an extra burden. This is actually capital that we need to invest in to have a fairer art form."[88] Investing in this capital within the theatre begins with including d/Deaf artists at all stages of production from literary management to writing to casting and related staff positions. La Jolla Playhouse's resident dramaturg Shirley Fishman explains, "It's as simple as going to your casting director and saying: I would like to have disabled or Deaf artists come in for every show in the season."[89] Of course, inviting people into the audition spaces is one thing; actually casting them is another.

It's not only actors whom Broadway excludes and does not accommodate; d/Deaf audiences too often do not feel welcome in the theatre. Even after producing *Big River*, Roundabout Theatre has not fundamentally changed its own programming. Sign-language interpreted performances (SLIPs) remain the norm on Broadway and at most US regional theatres. SLIPs ultimately fail "on three levels: failure to appropriately capitalize the theatrical space; failure to conceptualize the interpreter as performer; and failure to create a

DEAF WEST'S *AWAKENING* 205

meaningful translation," according to theatre director Michael Richardson.[90] SLIPs fall short for spectators in terms of performance and adaptation/translation, as the interpreters are typically themselves responsible for translating the spoken dialogue into ASL. Richardson reveals that these failures are tied to casting: "In practice, rarely is there any kind of casting process; one interpreter is typically expected to represent the multiple characters onstage, and the determination of who will work on a particular show is often made only on the basis of interpreter availability."[91] He posits that the predominance of SLIPs is "easily seen as merely a symbolic fulfillment of the access and diversity agenda."[92] SLIPs are an after-thought of accessibility, constrained by finances and lack of imagination; they contribute to a less-than-satisfying experience for d/Deaf spectators.

Despite the artistic success and impact of *DWSA*, not much changed on Broadway afterward for d/Deaf and hard-of-hearing actors and audiences. Arden hoped that *DWSA* would challenge the prevalent ideology of American theatre:

> I hope that our production gave both audiences and theatre makers and producers an opportunity to see how exciting performers with different abilities can be. I think there's so many ways to tell stories and having deaf actors and hard-of-hearing actors and actors in wheelchairs, these things just don't happen. . . . I hope it served as an enlightening experience, to think, "Hey, why can't I hire a Deaf actor for this role? Maybe there's something, maybe I'll get something more out of it because of that." And an opportunity for audiences to come and enjoy theatre in their own language and to not feel like they had to come to just the one signed performance where they get to look to the side of the stage but miss what's happening on the stage.[93]

Lipari suggested that the barriers to more d/Deaf and disabled actors begin when hearing people let their good intentions remain intentions rather than actions, saying, "I find that was I very disappointed with myself that I didn't learn sign while I was with these actors. . . . I'm so mad that I didn't do it, because you get in this room with these brilliant people, and you want to converse. . . . I think people are scared . . . to work with deaf actors."[94] Lipari's candid admission explains why d/Deafness continues to function as it does in the theatre: because the majority of the population has not learned sign language, nor do they regularly encounter d/Deaf culture or people;

206 ABILITY

most crucially, d/Deaf people are rarely the ones in power making creative decisions. Lipari still feels *Spring Awakening* "will be probably the highlight of my career. I'm sure I could even work another 25 years, and nothing will touch *Spring Awakening*."[95] Other members of the production echoed Lipari's feelings. Kurs looked back with pride on the production a year after it closed: "The achievement of our production feels even more exceptional in the age of Trump. It is magical when deaf and hearing artists cross cultural and linguistic boundaries to work together in the purpose of creating art and even more so when hearing and deaf audience members sit together to enjoy the same show."[96]

Broadway's practices of inclusion and exclusion are tied, as ever, to money. If inclusion sells tickets, then it will be more likely to be replicated—and since neither of Deaf West's revivals was a money-maker, the situation for ASL musicals on Broadway remains precarious at best. Davenport noted, "A Broadway producer specifically cares about what's great, and then what's going to sell tickets, to be perfectly honest. The more we inspire Deaf artists to become playwrights, or Deaf playwrights to produce more work, the more we increase the chance of this culture being more exposed to mainstream America."[97] It remains less the case that the d/Deaf culture needs mainstreaming than that mainstream culture has much to gain from d/Deaf cultures. While Deaf West's *Spring Awakening* aroused Broadway to the possibilities of d/Deaf and disability inclusion, the casting of every Broadway musical (save one) since 2015 shows that Broadway's awakening itself might have been only a limited engagement.

7

Musicals, Physical Difference, and Disability

Broadway's nicknames unintentionally call attention to its structural inequities, perhaps most famously in "The Great White Way." Another nickname, "The Fabulous Invalid," takes its name from a 1938 play by Kaufman and Hart and refers to the perennial lament among theatre people that Broadway is in perpetual decline. If the former nickname, at least when used ironically, admits Broadway's white supremacy (it's actually a reference to the bright lights of theatre marquees), the latter points to the ableism endemic in the industry. But there's nothing fabulous about Broadway's employment of disability and difference primarily as metaphors used to explain difference.[1] Musicals use physical difference and disability to make meaning, everywhere from Elphaba's green skin in *Wicked* (2003) to Porgy and his goat cart in *Porgy and Bess* (1935). Disabled *characters* may be ubiquitous in musical theatre, but disabled *actors* are not; as disability studies scholar Samuel Yates observes, "An able body is at the center of musical theatre performance."[2] This tension underlines Broadway's long-standing preference for the kind of hyper-ability evinced by the triple-threat performer and the Broadway Body. Musicals treat disability like a costume that can be removed once the curtain falls.

Like homosexuality, disability and musical theatre's relationship has been complicated and involved closeting. Disability and homosexuality met in composer-lyricist Cole Porter, whose Broadway career and personal life speak to the social status of both homosexuality and disability in mid-twentieth century United States. Porter's songs are full of double entendres alluding to homosexuality (e.g., "You're the Top"), and his sexuality was an open secret in his upper-crust social circle from the 1920s on.[3] Porter wrote Broadway hits like *Fifty Million Frenchmen* (1929) and *Anything Goes* (1934) before breaking both of his legs in a horseback riding accident in 1937, which led to the amputation of his right leg in 1958. As was then the custom, the press corps-maintained its silence about Porter's sexuality but his disability

Broadway Bodies. Ryan Donovan, Oxford University Press. © Oxford University Press 2023.
DOI: 10.1093/oso/9780197551073.003.0008

208 ABILITY

inevitably became part of his public narrative since it could be openly written about; to have written about his homosexuality would have ended Porter's career. Porter alternately used a wheelchair, leg braces, and canes, and the press sometimes photographed him being carried into the theatre. While sex was prominent in Porter's lyrics, disability and physical difference were never major themes, even though some of his biggest Broadway hits came after his injury: *Leave It to Me* (1938), *DuBarry Was a Lady* (1939), *Kiss Me, Kate* (1948), and *Can-Can* (1952). After the amputation, Porter ceased writing and retreated from public life, reportedly telling friends, "I am only half a man now."[4]

While Porter kept disability offstage, fellow composer-lyricist Meredith Willson thought a great deal about how to depict disability onstage. As he was writing *The Music Man* (1957) in the early 1950s, Willson had a novel idea: "a subplot . . . involv[ing] a spastic boy—helpless in a wheel chair— not exactly a character you would normally select for a musical comedy."[5] Willson kept this character in multiple drafts of the musical despite trepidation from its producer. He explained, "You don't know how glued I was to the spastic-boy subplot—how badly I wanted to tell on a stage that spastics are muscularly retarded not mentally."[6] Morton DaCosta, the show's director, was among those against including the character, saying, "I would think the spastic boy should go."[7] Willson notes that he, too, eventually decided to give up the subplot, yet he wanted to "see him replaced if I could find any kind of related element to replace him with."[8] Willson's solution replaced the motor impairment with a speech impediment: a lisp for the character now named Winthrop: "A lisping kid instead of a spastic boy!"[9] Musicologist Raymond Knapp describes the implications of substituting the speech impediment for "spasticity, noting that it gave Winthrop's impairment a musical dimension and allowed his lisp to function as a metaphor."[10] The "spastic boy" was out, and Winthrop Paroo was in, rendered fixable and musical.

Broadway musicals employed disability and difference only in their narratives for decades. An actor who uses a wheelchair offstage and on, Ali Stroker, did not appear on Broadway until Deaf West Theatre's 2015 revival of *Spring Awakening*—nearly sixty-five years after Willson's aborted plan for the "spastic boy." However, in the intervening years, musicals did not ignore disability or physical difference: many of Broadway's most popular musicals relied on them as constitutive elements of their narratives. While disability is a capacious and sometimes vague descriptor in the world offstage, in the world of musicals it is treated very similarly to physical differences like ugliness and

MUSICALS, PHYSICAL DIFFERENCE, AND DISABILITY 209

mutilated bodies. The chapter opens with a discussion of the role disability plays in performance and the labor concerns that result. I then survey how musicals cast disability and physical difference as metaphors in narratives and I take an extended look at how these converge in *Shrek* (2008) and other shows that use fairy tales as their basis for explaining difference. These kinds of representations contributed to the onstage exclusion of disabled actors for decades, even as non-disabled actors *cripped up* to play disabled characters. Various manifestations of disability and physical difference made meaning in performance in Broadway musical revivals after 2010, including *The Color Purple*, *Hedwig and the Angry Inch*, *Porgy and Bess*, and *Violet*, which I cover next. I conclude by noting Tony Award winner Stroker's historic series of Broadway firsts. Broadway prefers disability when it stays metaphorical, difference when it's assimilated into the mainstream by the finale, and both absent by the curtain call. Yet, as theater scholar Carrie Sandahl argues, "it is difficult to turn disability into a metaphor when it is literally embodied."[11] The fact that there are so few examples of embodied disability in the casting of Broadway musicals reveals how disability is a device employed in musicals that enhances the domination of able-bodiedness itself.

Disability and Performance

Understanding how musical theatre employs difference and disability necessarily means using theoretical lenses from disability studies; this approach addresses physical, political, and social realms and "how they relate to enforced systems of exclusion and oppression."[12] Language is often a primary way of signaling exclusion or inclusion. Ability. Able-bodied. Accessible. Accommodation. Crip. Crippled. Disabled. Disability. Freak. Handicapped. Impaired. Non-normative. Normal. Universal. These terms, like most related to identity, are all contested and contain the possibility of stigmatization. Terminology constantly shifts and accumulates new meaning—for example, *crip*, like *queer*, has been reclaimed as a political statement of identity. All of these are also umbrella terms; their meanings are hard to pin down or agree on, particularly since context matters so much. Disability, for example, carries broad meanings because it is purposefully applicable to many different things. Yet as disability scholar Lennard J. Davis explains, even broadly drawn identity categories are bound to fail: "The categories 'disabled,' 'handicapped,' 'impaired' are products of a society invested in denying the variability of the body. The category 'disability' begins to break down when one scrutinizes who make up the disabled."[13] Even though the terms remain contested and inadequate, they invite consideration of how and why they apply only to certain individuals and groups of people with variable bodies. The broadness of disability potentially makes it one of the most inclusive identities since many people will experience some form of disability at some point in their lives.

Sociologist Erving Goffman details how "the stigmatized individual is likely to feel that he is 'on,' having to be self-conscious and calculating about the impression he is making."[14] If disability is viewed as a social construct rather than a biological reality, then "disability (like gender) can be understood as a performance: something you do rather than something you are."[15] Understanding disability as performance acknowledges that unaccommodating and inaccessible societies produce disability stigma; viewing disability through the lens of performance also implicitly acknowledges the presence of an audience.[16] If indeed there is a "sense that disability in daily life is already performance," then daily life turns people with disabilities into something able-bodied people are encouraged to gaze upon and stare at.[17] This process makes representations of disability and physical difference almost meta-theatrical and also reiterates the sense that disability is never permitted to simply exist without meaning. It is not surprising, then, that performances of disability and difference became central to Broadway musicals, where bodies bear extra-theatrical meanings.

Disability is socially constructed. Disabled people find themselves disqualified from many forms of labor and gainful employment because of a society that excludes them and a medical system that routinely pathologizes them. The medical model of disability supports the narrative that disability needs a diagnosis followed by a remedy or demise: the cure or kill false binary. This ideology and its resulting terminology result from nineteenth-century pseudo-scientific eugenicist thought and language, as evinced in "words like 'fit,' 'normal,' 'degenerate,' 'feeble,' 'defect,' and 'defective.'"[18] Eugenics, the pseudoscience of human improvement, was fundamentally about aesthetic-based disqualification so as to propagate the bodies eugenicists deemed a good fit for their ideal race. Eugenics introduced the idea of the norm against which deviance, whether statistical or embodied, would be measured. In other words, there could be no deviance without a norm: a heterosexual, white, able-bodied male.[19] Eugenicists sought to eliminate the identities they deemed defective, which all then fell under the umbrella of disability. These

MUSICALS, PHYSICAL DIFFERENCE, AND DISABILITY   211

categories were capacious, and "these peoples were clearly delineated under the rubric of feeble-mindedness and degeneration as women, people of color, homosexuals, the working classes, and so on."[20] Eugenics can thus be directly tied to white supremacy, homophobia, misogyny, and ableism.

The rise of eugenics happened concurrently with the industrialization of the US workforce and economy, and both led to the exclusion of non-conforming and non-normative bodies. Disability rights movements formed to address labor issues resulting from industrialization in the nineteenth century. Industry's need for standardization disqualified those whose bodies did not conform. Historian Sarah F. Rose explains, "As mechanized factory labor became increasingly central to the economy, employers in nearly all sectors began to demand workers [with] intact, interchangeable bodies."[21] Disabled workers found themselves excluded from many employment opportunities, and thus from society as a result. Broadway, too, would eventually discover the utility of intact, interchangeable bodies.

Disability studies challenges the ideologies that, like eugenics and ableism, shore up the norm's power over *all* bodies, not only those labeled disabled. It is telling (and essential) to consider how disability stigma operates in relation to power and how it is tied to US national identity itself. In the first half of the twentieth century, two American presidents hid their disabilities from the public: the extent of Woodrow Wilson's 1919 stroke and his resulting partial blindness and paralysis only fully came to light after his death, while Franklin D. Roosevelt's disability and his wheelchair use were so successfully hidden from the public as he campaigned for the presidency that he won the election and governed from 1933 to 1945 largely without having his wheelchair use revealed.[22] FDR's performance of ability helped him win the White House. But when he became a theatrical character decades later in *Annie* (1977), a dash of reality interrupted the real FDR's self-constructed narrative since the musical depicted him using a wheelchair. Unlike the photographs of Porter using braces or being carried, FDR and the Secret Service went to great lengths to ensure that photographs of him using a wheelchair were either not taken or destroyed. His disability may have been kept secret, but in accomplishing this FDR inadvertently revealed that able-bodiedness itself requires performance. FDR theatricalized able-bodiedness as a form of impression management.

Despite the highest office in the nation having been occupied by a disabled person (albeit one who went to great lengths to perform being nondisabled), exclusion and oppression remain the norm. Congress has passed

212   ABILITY

laws attempting to right these wrongs, but they have proven largely toothless and in many situations, impossible to enforce.[23] Exclusion from the labor
force later resulted in governmental assistance programs, which further
stigmatized disability and marked its recipients as unproductive workers and
failed citizens.[24] Historian Sarah Rose argues that it is attitudes toward disability that have hindered attempts at legal protection, explaining, "Unlike in
the case of other civil rights legislation, disabled people who wish to sue over
employment discrimination must first prove that they are qualified to do the
job and that their accommodation requests are reasonable; in other words,
lawmakers presumed that people with disabilities were by and large unqualified."[25] Disability must always prove itself, even to the body charged with
protecting disabled people.

The major achievement of the disability rights movement was the passage of the Americans with Disabilities Act of 1990. According to the US
Department of Justice, "the Americans with Disabilities Act of 1990 (ADA)
prohibits discrimination and ensures equal opportunity for persons with
disabilities in employment, State and local government services, public
accommodations, commercial facilities, and transportation."[26] The law
clearly states that persons with disabilities should have equal opportunity in
employment. But equal opportunity never materialized since no plan was
ever put in place to enforce the ADA, ensuring that the burden of enforcement rested on those seemingly "protected" by its passage.

The lack of enforcement of policies meant to protect disabled people
has made it possible for rampant discrimination to continue unabated
in nearly every field. Broadway musicals are not alone here—the vast majority of all entertainment, including professional theatre, shares this shame.
Casting remains inherently tied to disqualification based on aesthetics.
Actors with disabilities are rarely offered the opportunity to play any role,
let alone characters with disabilities. Though employment statistics reveal low employment for all union actors, they are especially dire for actors
with disabilities. In 2017, Actors' Equity Association (AEA) reported, "We
are aware that many members choose not to self-identify for any number
of reasons. Currently only 219 members self-identify as having a disability
of some kind, and we know those numbers are not representative of the actual population of our membership."[27] This means that just 219 out of over
50,000 members of the union were willing to self-identify as having a disability, which certainly reflects disability stigma. For comparison, note that
"12.6% of the civilian non-institutionalized population," or almost 40 million

people, self-identified as having a disability in 2015.[28] AEA's sister union the Screen Actors Guild reported that one-third of its "disabled members were able to find film or television work in 2003, and that they worked on average four days a year."[29] Buried in the data of AEA's 2020 Diversity and Inclusion Report is this fact: only seventeen out of the 3,182 Production Contracts issued from 2016 to 2019 went to members who self-identify as having a disability, representing just 0.53% of these contracts—AEA's most lucrative.[30] AEA's statistics are far worse than those for disabled people in the broader workforce. The US Department of Labor released a report in 2018 on people with disabilities showing that 18.7% of people with disabilities were employed and that most of the remaining disabled people were not in the labor market and therefore not counted as employed or unemployed.[31] Disabled people face structural barriers at every turn, and wanting to make it as a performer only compounds these since less than 1% of Broadway production contracts go to those who self-identify to AEA as disabled.[32]

AEA has tried to ensure that its language at least is correct when it comes to disability, even if they cannot always control what producers do or who they cast. AEA's policy document "Creating Equal Opportunity" states the following: "Equity has always been in the forefront of struggles against discrimination and has led the way for decades in the fight for non-traditional and inclusive casting. Casting policies designed to expand opportunities for women, seniors, actors of color and performers with disabilities are provided in all agreements."[33] But like the ADA and other pro-disability laws, these policies are largely unenforceable without a lawsuit. The power of producers prevents AEA from actually ensuring that casting becomes more inclusive. AEA can only make sure that auditions, rehearsals, and the run of the show follow certain procedures but it holds little sway over casting itself.

Difference, Disability, and Ugliness in Musicals

Disability, disfigurement, and physical difference in musicals further reflect how social norms enforce distinctions between the normative and the different. Think of how the pairing of Beauty and the Beast's external differences constitute each another. Since song and dance make musicals musicals, who sings and dances communicates a character's importance and value to audiences. Singing remains musicals' preferred mode of communication for

214 ABILITY

characters, and a character's inability to sing generally speaks to their status as outsider or other (there are plenty of non-singing outsiders peppered throughout musicals from Doc in *West Side Story* to Zach in *A Chorus Line*). Some musicals take speech away entirely and use muteness as a metaphor. Mute (or nearly mute) characters often use dance to communicate: *Finian's Rainbow's* (1947) Susan the Silent is a prime example; *South Pacific's* (1949) Liat has a brief danced interlude during "Happy Talk," but does not sing and speaks little dialogue. Musicals often sexualize mute female characters, too—for instance, both Susan the Silent and Liat's innocence is erotic to other characters, which contrasts with mute male characters like the comically horny King Sextimus in *Once upon a Mattress* (1959), who is mute until the show's end and who, until then, speaks less with his hands than by being handsy. *Grand Hotel* featured two non-speaking, all-dancing roles, the Countess and the Gigolo, who were silent if not explicitly mute. On top of that, the Countess is supposedly blind, making her ballroom dance ability seem that much more of a virtuosic *super-crip* performance, especially since Yvonne Marceau originated the role, and she was not blind.[34] Because they have no bearing on the narrative or the plot of *Grand Hotel* and only appear near its conclusion, the Countess and the Gigolo are prime examples of how musicals use what literary scholars David Mitchell and Sharon Snyder call narrative prosthesis: something added to a narrative that makes disability simultaneously literal and metaphoric.[35]

While mute and silent characters represent an important but relatively little-used trope, disability and physical difference appear with frequency throughout the musical theatre repertoire. Narrative disabilities create and reinforce tropes about disability itself, since they often reveal the disabled character in possession of a compensatory talent, often an essential goodness or inner beauty. A typical approach is what happens when, as in *The Who's Tommy* (1993), the triple-threat is disability: Tommy is famously "that deaf, dumb, and blind kid."[36] Tommy is a "supercrip," or a character whose disabilities are offset by some special talent: the musical suggests that despite his disabilities (as opposed to because of his actual abilities) he can beat anyone who challenges him to a game of pinball, his near-superhuman talent.[37] *Newsies* (2012) features a character named Crutchie after his mobility aid. He's the best friend to the lead and is depicted as an essentially good person there to help set the hero's journey in motion. *The Light in the Piazza* (2005) features the developmentally disabled, essentially wholesome, pure-voiced character Clara. *Piazza* depicts the closeting and stigmatization of disability and demonstrates how whiteness and class privilege allow disabled characters to pass as normative. Clara's singing ability as embodied by the actor portraying her compensates for her narrative disability, allowing her to remain marriageable and her difference invisible. Difference and disability prove central to Broadway's longest-running show all the way down to its iconic logo. Musicologist Jessica Sternfeld points that *The Phantom of the Opera* (1987) "is, at base, a modern version of a circus freak show."[38] *Phantom*'s logo is the mask used to hide the phantom's facial disfigurement, and the musical creates tension building up to the phantom's un-masking and, ultimately, his punishment.

Other Broadway musicals actually restaged the early twentieth-century circus freak show, albeit with very different intentions. The bio-musical *Barnum* (1980), about the showman famous for promoting the freak show, deftly avoided the seedier side of Barnum's history to focus on rosier aspects of the circus.[39] However, the musical does feature two of Barnum's "freaks," both of whom get to sing: Tom Thumb performs the number "Bigger Isn't Better," and Joice Heth sings "Thank God I'm Old." Both numbers call attention to the characters' differences of height and age, respectively. Tom Thumb was never cast with an actor who had dwarfism. The Broadway production used exaggeratedly large scenery to make Thumb appear small, and audiences were expected to suspend their disbelief to accept Heth as ancient—even though an actress in her twenties played the part. Though *Barnum* engaged with real historical figures, it was not alone in how it staged difference and disability for Broadway audiences.

Like the twentieth-century freak shows, musicals are often explicit about their invitation to stare. Musicals use non-normative bodies and freakishness to produce fictions of normativity for spectators. Without stigma, there is no freak.[40] *Side Show* (1997, revisal 2014) openly invited audiences to "come look at the freaks!" in its depiction of conjoined twins Daisy and Violet Hilton. It flopped twice on Broadway, suggesting that Broadway audiences might prefer that disability be kept metaphorical or less *freakish*, even when it was obvious that costuming and staging created the illusion of conjoinment. It is also possible that the show did not connect with audiences for a myriad of other reasons—from marketing to mixed reviews. *Carrie* (1988) was another infamous flop about a social outcast considered a freak in the world of the musical, and the audience was asked to root for her even as she sought revenge for her social exclusion.

216   ABILITY

Sometimes musicals also utilize the concept of the freak to include those whose queerness is enfreaked. *Taboo*'s (2002) first words are "give me a freak any day of the week," as it invites spectators into the queer subculture of London's gay clubs in the 1980s. *Hedwig and the Angry Inch*'s genderfuck made a spectacle of bodily difference; its earlier film adaptation (2001) even added a song called "Freaks." In *A Chorus Line*, Paul memorably relates, "Nobody at the Jewel Box had any dignity and most of them were ashamed of themselves and considered themselves freaks."[41] These musicals represent both the reach and the dilution of the term *freak*, applied to a range of people, whether those with congenital difference or those with queer sexualities and gender identities—like *disability* and *queer*, *freak* is a flexible concept.

The most common disability trope of all on Broadway remains casting non-disabled actors as characters with disabilities. Non-disabled actors performing disability is considered an opportunity to display virtuosity and empathy (just like performing queerness is for straight actors or a thin actor playing a fat character while wearing a fat suit). Since it "is considered a skill by nondisabled actors and not an identity, actual disabled actors are accused of not being 'real' actors when they play disabled characters."[42] Examples of this practice are legion and what follows are but a few.

The Rocky Horror Show (1975) featured the wheelchair-using Dr. Scott, played by Meat Loaf in the original cast and Lea DeLaria in the 2000 Broadway revival. Wheelchair user Nessarose in *Wicked* has been played by numerous non-disabled actors in its long Broadway run. *Playbill* spoke to seven former Nessaroses about what made the role special; two joked that wheeling Nessarose's wheelchair on a raked stage is where her strength came from.[43] *Bloody Bloody Andrew Jackson* (2010) featured Kristine Nielsen as a character in a wheelchair named "The Storyteller." The wheelchair was part sight-gag given that musical's penchant for irony and the fact that Nielsen is not mobility impaired. Elderly characters like Madame Armfeldt in *A Little Night Music* (1973) and Marie in *Sunday in the Park with George* (1984) appear in wheelchairs and sometimes use canes. While it would not have been impossible or perhaps even that challenging to find wheelchair users for the aforementioned roles, other musicals are so specific about a character's impairment that casting the role authentically would be a challenge—yet, even matching *some* characteristics of the actor and the role is a step rarely taken. One case in point: *Grand Hotel*'s Colonel-Doctor Otternschlag, described in a casting breakdown as having "only one eye, and one leg is missing/paralyzed" as a result of wounds suffered in World War I.[44] Production photos from

MUSICALS, PHYSICAL DIFFERENCE, AND DISABILITY 217

Grand Hotel's Broadway run show actor John Wylie wearing an eye patch and using a cane. Wylie's casting in a role that a disabled actor could have played represents Broadway's standard practice, but the role also presents the dilemma posed by casting roles written with multiple impairments: which one takes precedence? And who should decide?

Sometimes the point of casting a non-disabled actor is that the narrative hinges on the trope of overcoming disability. The 2012 flop *Leap of Faith*, for instance, was about a sham faith healer who attempts to make a boy who has lost the use of his legs walk again. *The Secret Garden* (1991) relies on several disability tropes from closeting to overcoming. Ten-year-old sometimes wheelchair-using, bed-bound Colin, tells his cousin Mary, "If I live, I may be a hunchback" before noting that he stays shut in because people stare at him when he goes anywhere.[45] Colin then sings "Round-Shouldered Man" about his father Archibald's stooped posture. The musical squarely sets up Colin to *transcend* his disability (especially since audiences learn that it is less a real disability than the malevolent work of his uncle in making Colin believe he's impaired), and indeed he stands up from his chair and walks in the second act, miraculously cured by the garden, proclaiming, "I'm not crippled!"[46] Archibald, originally played by Mandy Patinkin, is terrified of passing his hunched spine onto his son Colin. Archibald's sister-in-law refers to him as "a gloomy miserable cripple who hides himself away in that horrible house."[47] The Broadway production did not use prostheses or padding to show Craven's difference, but as *New York Times* critic Frank Rich pointed out, Patinkin took "every opportunity to display the tortured psyche of the lonely, hunchbacked uncle" by employing a "contorted posture (loping walk, dangled left hand)."[48] Not helping Patinkin's disability shtick was the fact that his character's overdetermined name foregrounds his outer condition (arched) and in his inner life (craven). Even as disability metaphors go, nuanced it is not, and Patinkin's performance was representative of how cripping up presents actors with the chance to ham it up. *The Secret Garden* is far from the only example of a Broadway musical using children's stories as a basis: Broadway loves fairy tales something *Wicked*, one might say. And by using fairy tales, musicals revive archetypes and stereotypes of disability and difference that shape how disabled people are treated in the real world.

On Broadway, "Once upon a time" opens Stephen Sondheim and James Lapine's fairy tale mash-up *Into the Woods* (1987), which dared to ask what happens *after* happily ever after. Familiar fairy-tale characters, archetypes, and disability tropes abound: Little Red Riding Hood, Jack (of beanstalk

218 ABILITY

fame), Cinderella, Rapunzel, a Wolf, a Baker, his Wife, and a Witch. In *Into the Woods*, the Witch embodies a classic fairy tale transformation trope. Her ugliness, a form of punishment handed down by her mother when the Witch lost magic beans as a child, comes with magic that serves as a form of compensation for her disfigured appearance. In the original production, star Bernadette Peters wore facial prostheses that gave her an exaggerated nose, a face covered with moles, fleshy folds of skin on her face and neck, and a gray fright wig to top it all off. Peters used a wooden staff as a cane that tellingly was not just a mobility aid but also the source of the Witch's powers. The staff made the connection between magical compensation, disability, and ugliness explicit by displacing their connection onto an object. The Witch sheds her ugliness only after drinking a magical potion and transforming into a conventional beauty–but in doing so, she loses her powers. [Clip 7.1] This substitution represents the common narrative trope of special powers or talents compensating for disability and/or physical difference, which comes in part from fairy tales but in theatre goes all the way back at least to Sophocles's *Oedipus Rex*, in which the blind seer Tiresias's blindness is mitigated by his ability to foresee the future. Blindness is wielded as punishment throughout *Into the Woods*: Cinderella's stepsisters, Rapunzel's Prince, and the Giant are all blinded during the course of the show. That none of these characters are nice or good underscores the negative tropes of disability at play.

Fairy tales act as barometers of who counts as beautiful or ugly, and ugliness is often connected to some form of disability or physical difference and amorality. Contemporary notions of bodily aesthetics and their ties to morality, gender, and physical difference are bound to the narrative tropes present in musicals, which instruct us from a young age about "that which is different; whether that difference is disfigurement or social exclusion."[49] Ugliness in musicals is as much about the character's ability to find love and be loved as it is about the audience's ability to read ugliness as metaphor.[50] But ugliness has another purpose in representation, which is to ask where our own bodies fit in the aesthetic hierarchy.[51] Offstage, ugliness has material effects. Like every other community covered in this book, there is a wage penalty associated with the stigmatized identity that is unevenly distributed and gendered. Economist Daniel S. Hamermesh studied the economic effects of beauty and reports that "the bottom 15 percent of women . . . received 4 percent lower pay than average-looking women. The top one-third of women by looks . . . received 8 percent more than average-lookers. For men, the comparable figures are a 13 percent penalty and a 4 percent premium."[52] If musicals demonstrate whose bodies are worth more than others, this worth translates to fiscal worth offstage. Ugliness, quite literally, doesn't pay.

Musicals based on fairy tales utilize aesthetics to perpetuate the conflation of physical differences and disability with ugliness and, usually, evil. The pleasure of musical theatre performance masks how musicals treat ugliness and physical difference alike.[53] Musicals employ ugliness and physical difference akin to how they use disability; the aesthetic work of non-normativity in musicals is analogous if not exact. Ugliness in musicals hinges on the myth of inner beauty leading to outward transformation. The inner beauty trope is common on Broadway, where it finds analogues in similar myths of the "inner thin person" inside a fat body and the non-disabled person inside the disabled character.

Disney musicals thrive on the dramatic transformation of a central character. The title character of *The Little Mermaid* (2008) trades her mermaid tail and her voice for the ability to walk on land even though each step feels like daggers stabbing her feet. The moral is not merely that beauty comes with a price tag, but that the cost of inclusion into mainstream society is shedding difference itself. Musicals and fairy tales use difference in service of shoring up notions of universality. When *The Little Mermaid* was about to open on Broadway, producer Thomas Schumacher said, "The reality is there are two minorities on the planet that are born into families: disabled people and gay people. Every other minority is born of a family. . . . That Ariel is an outsider in her own family connects with lots of places."[54]

Beauty and the Beast (1994) is another Disney musical that uses a theatrical reveal to show spectators the physical attractiveness of the performer hidden beneath the prosthetics. The Beast's outer beastly appearance is meant to reflect his inner ugliness, which "perpetuates the idea that people who look different from the 'norm' are manifesting in their outward appearance some inner flaw of character."[55] Belle tames the Beast and makes him worthy of love. The fairy tales Disney brought to screens and then Broadway stages in *Beauty and the Beast, The Lion King* (1997), and *The Little Mermaid* all contain archetypal ugly characters as their villains— think of *The Lion King*'s Scar, named after his physical difference, after all. But there is another Broadway musical adapted from a children's film that reinscribed fairy tale narratives of difference and made the monster the lovable hero—also propagating some pernicious connections between deviance, disability, and sexuality.

220 ABILITY

Shrek the Musical (2008) tackled ugliness head-on and attempted to capitalize on it—its marketing slogan was "Bringing Ugly Back." Ugliness is central to *Shrek*. In the opening number, Shrek's mother sings, "We're ugly son, which means that life is harder."[56] Shrek's fat, green, ogre-ish appearance terrifies everyone he encounters. Shrek is not the only character in this show who is different, though. The musical's chorus of fairy-tale creatures (the three little pigs, Pinocchio, the big bad wolf, and the ugly duckling, among others) sings about their otherness, which "turns the fairytale creatures into a victimized minority whose difference is an open secret."[57] Disability is never far from song and dance in *Shrek*; the three blind mice show up dancing with bedazzled white canes. In "Let Your Freak Flag Fly," the fairy tale characters point out that society has the problem, not them, echoing the social model of disability. *Shrek's* fairy tale creatures discover that their power actually lies in their difference. "Letting their freak flags fly" becomes a mantra of acceptance. [Clip 7.2] Difference itself is *Shrek's* norm.

The fairy-tale creatures had been forced into exile by Lord Farquaad, whose short stature marks his own difference: he's only four feet tall. *Shrek's* narrative is built on fairy-tale conventions. Farquaad cannot become king without marrying a princess. Like Rapunzel before her, the show's heroine, Princess Fiona, has been exiled to a tower where she awaits a prince to rescue her. Shrek agrees to rescue Fiona for Farquaad in exchange for the return of his swamp. Once Shrek rescues Fiona, she awaits his kiss since convention dictates that princesses must be kissed by their rescuer. When Shrek takes off his helmet and shows her his face, she is taken aback. He describes the position his appearance puts him in, saying, "I'm not the one with the problem, okay? It's the world who seems to have a problem with me." However, Princess Fiona has her own secret, revealed in the second act: she becomes an ogre after sunset as the result of a witch's curse in her childhood. Ugliness is a punishment here like it is in *Into the Woods* and *Phantom* but with its own unique twist meant to empower rather than enfreak. As in most fairy tales, the narrative untwists its complications and reaches a happy ending.

Shrek becomes a parable of self-acceptance while also unwittingly sending a troubling message that Fiona and Shrek could only fully find love with each other when their aesthetic differences were equalized. Though the show ostensibly promotes the notion that inner beauty is true beauty, it is actually ugliness that triumphs since Fiona and Shrek can only be compatible when both are ogres. *Shrek* implies that difference is ultimately sameness since "everyone turns out to be a freak, so everyone is the same after all."[58] While its narrative cleverly wrestled with difference, *Shrek*'s production had issues of its own.

The green prosthetics worn by stars Brian D'Arcy James and Sutton Foster hid their bodies but unwittingly mirrored how what scholars called "the ontology of Shrek—ugly-on-the-outside, beautiful-on-the-inside—is replicated exactly in the process that turned James from handsome actor to ogre. Difference is cosmetic."[59] The process for James involved not just prosthetics but a fat suit that made him monster-sized. Thin people can be villains, but only fat people are represented as monsters. But *Shrek* ultimately said more about Broadway's treatment of difference through its villain than its hero and heroine. The casting and staging of Farquaad make *Shrek* a prototypical demonstration of which differences are permissible as the butt of jokes on Broadway.

Farquaad's characterization in the Broadway production leaned heavily into stereotypes conflating physical difference with disability, amorality, and homosexuality. He is the evil queen of this fairy tale even though he is out for marriage to Princess Fiona because he needs a wife to satisfy his thirst for power. Broadway's original Farquaad, Christopher Sieber, is an out gay actor, and he used his tall body playing Farquaad's short one to contain Farquaad's difference and make it humorous onstage. Sieber's turn as Farquaad bears further exploration because it is emblematic of how Broadway musicals employ bodies to make meaning of difference.

The production primed audiences to laugh at Farquaad because of his height above all, as if shortness is automatically a sight gag (one is reminded of the lyrics of *Les Misérables'* "Little People"). *Shrek* links Farquaad's height with his villainy—is he evil because he is short or is he short because he is evil? *Shrek* achieved Farquaad's height onstage by having Sieber walk on his knees with his lower legs shrouded in a cape and by affixing a small pair of prosthetic legs from Sieber's hips to his knees. Sieber's performance thus had him on his knees for nearly the entire show. Kneeling for so long was physically fatiguing and ultimately damaging to Sieber, but it made his performance virtuosic for audiences, who were explicitly made aware of the fiction of Sieber's short stature in the curtain call, when he walked onstage at his full height. If *Shrek*'s employment of difference relied on the audience's familiarity with fairy tales' aesthetic norms, the musical ultimately sang out of both sides of its mouth since it appeared to celebrate difference in Shrek and Fiona's coupling. Farquaad's death, though, suggested that some differences deserve punishment. Disability appeared again in the show's finale, when

222 ABILITY

the gingerbread man shouts out the disabled character Tiny Tim's line from Charles Dickens' *A Christmas Carol*, "God Bless Us, Everyone!" just before the final blackout.

Broadway Number: "What's Up, Duloc?"

Farquaad's big song and dance number "What's Up, Duloc?" shows how *Shrek* attempts to speak to but also ultimately makes a joke out of difference.[a] This song and its staging evoke moments from other familiar musicals for young audiences like *The Wizard of Oz* and *Charlie and the Chocolate Factory*. The song establishes Duloc's rules and regulations and sets up Farquaad as a despot concerned with appearance above all. He sings about erasing difference and espousing conformity, instructing the identically dressed ensemble to "embrace the cookie cutter in Duloc." The look of the ensemble makes clear that they are dressed in Farquaad's image and color palette. "What's Up, Duloc?" draws its comedy from the contrast between difference and conformity and the irony of Farquaad's seeming obliviousness to his own very visible difference. The ensemble's uniform appearance comes across as the sort of self-referential joke about the conformity imposed on most Broadway ensembles. The number serves the narrative purpose of showing how Duloc's citizens contrast with the fairy-tale creatures cast out by Farquaad, and that they are played by the same performers only enhances the sense of duality in the production.

"What's Up, Duloc?" gives Farquaad a star entrance. Sieber vamps it up, sitting atop Farquaad's castle, crossing his tiny prosthetic legs with a wink, playing up the campiness of the role—even singing with a lisp for a phrase, linking disability and effeminacy. Farquaad sings of his demand for conformity: "We all have our standards, but I will have perfection." As the song's chorus begins, Farquaad comes down from the castle to dance with the ensemble, all of whom are taller than he is. Sieber dances jauntily on his knees as the ensemble moves around him. At one point, he calls two chorus boys over to him and they lift him and carry him, allowing Sieber the chance to skitter across the stage on his feet and not his knees and also allowing audiences to see him skitter along briefly on his own two feet. This fleetingly destroys the fiction of Farquaad's physical difference for a laugh since Farquaad is the comic villain-cum-evil queen. The pleasure of the song is meant to come in seeing Sieber dance on his knees, which he performs with aplomb and virtuosity (as pictured in Figure 7.1). Another sight gag concludes the number: the set pieces appear to shrink to make Farquaad seem like he's growing. The ensemble members fall to their knees to complete the illusion and land the punch line. The number builds to a standard Broadway razzle dazzle finish with unison ensemble choreography and lots of jazz hands. The song climaxes with Farquaad appearing to step on the backs of the ensemble, achieved by having Sieber walk across the stage behind them. *Shrek* makes it possible to be simultaneously charmed by Sieber's performance and disturbed by what the narrative mocks.

The reveal of Sieber's actual height worked to reassure audiences that his physical difference existed only in the narrative. [Clip 7.3] Sieber's performance was so notable that *Broadway.com* asked him to write about it. In his essay he describes the lengths taken to accommodate his height in the role, since the difference between his height and Farquaad's was remarkable. The experiences he describes in his essay are striking for how they resonate as disabling. He describes re-learning to walk and run on his knees "without worrying about being hobbled for the rest of my life," before going on to detail his physical regimen of preparation, including physical therapy, yoga, Pilates, and stretching.[b] Underneath Farquaad's

Figure 7.1 Christopher Sieber (*center*) leads the ensemble of *Shrek* in "What's Up, Duloc?" Credit: Joan Marcus.

224 ABILITY

short prosthetic legs, Sieber wore specially made prosthetics that fit his own legs from above the knee to his ankles. Because his costume was so cumbersome that he frequently needed to be loaded into set pieces, Sieber was often physically and socially isolated backstage, while the rest of the cast sang and danced onstage. On top of the isolation, Sieber's body was at constant risk of injury. He recalled, "I called out about six times because I'd wake up and I couldn't walk."[c] Broadway's demand for repetition causes wear and tear to its machinery—the bodies charged with representation.

At the risk of making Sieber's experience just another disability metaphor, it is worth noting that Sieber's description of his experience echoes various facets of disabled people's experiences from social isolation to the need for accommodations and to re-learn motor skills. Actor Christopher Marriner played Farquaad on tour and he too framed playing Farquaad in disability terms, joking with a reporter from the *Connecticut Post* "about being ready for a walker by the time the tour ends."[d] In *Shrek* and other musicals, "it's possible to see how both fairy tales and the ideology of able-bodiedness have combined to impose a very particular structure on the world in which we live. It is a structure that begins in a story but then stretches outward to encompass all aspects of disabled life—political, social, economic."[e] All of these roles have been cast with non-disabled actors, driving home the truth that *happily ever after* bumps into the reality of Broadway's exclusion of disabled performers.

[a] This analysis is based on the filmed stage production available on Netflix. Warren, *Shrek the Musical.*

[b] Sieber, " 'Yes, My Knees Are Fine.' "

[c] Shapiro, *Wonderful Guy*, 229.

[d] Meyers, "How 'Lord Farquaar' Stops the Show on His Knees."

[e] Leduc, *Disfigured*, 209–210.

Reviving Difference in the 2010s

Musicals often stage disability and physical difference as portals to personal growth (e.g., *The Color Purple* and *Hedwig and the Angry Inch*) and sometimes physical difference is there to serve as a contrast with everyone else onstage (e.g., *Porgy and Bess* and *Violet*). That the four musical revivals discussed in this section all cast actors who did not share the character's physical differences or disabilities was a given, yet taken together, these four

MUSICALS, PHYSICAL DIFFERENCE, AND DISABILITY   225

examples show how musicals in performance can subvert their text's often negative presentation of disability and difference—and also how they risk embodying stigma itself. One example in particular addresses how impairment brought new depth to a familiar role. All of these examples embody to varying degrees what Sandahl has termed "representational conundrums," which "describe challenging, puzzling, or paradoxical issues that are unique to or complicated by disability's presence" both in the text and in the flesh, especially in casting.[60] The star casting of the productions discussed in this section further complicated the conundrums at play.

Celebrity's symbolic capital works to assuage any potential discomfort audiences may feel over disability representation.[61] In the 2010s, revivals foregrounded the intersection of celebrity, disability, and physical difference. Celebrity's symbolic capital is never far from the "fetishized forces of capitalism" on Broadway since stars sell tickets.[62] When a dearth of disability representation meets Broadway's star system, audiences willingly suspend disbelief. Playwright Christopher Shinn argues, "This is not incidental but central to the success of these representations. They provide us with the comforting assurance that we are not witnessing the actual pain and struggle of real disabled human beings; it is all make believe."[63] This section covers four Broadway stars, the meeting of their celebrity bodies with some of musical theatre's most celebrated parts, and representations of disability, difference, and ugliness.

Ugliness in *The Color Purple* is not just a metaphor; it is also meant to be physical though standard casting practices preclude this. *Purple* tells the story of protagonist Celie's decades-long path to self-actualization centered in her body. The community deems Celie's body ruined from the start of the musical because, at the age of fourteen, she birthed two children after her father raped her. One of the church ladies of the show's ensemble describes Celie as "already ruint."[64] Celie's Pa puts her babies up for adoption and then attempts to marry her off to the local mean guy, simply named Mister. He rejects her, saying, "I don't want Celie. She ugly."[65] Only after Pa includes a cow as Celie's dowry, does Mister agree to marry her. It is an unhappy and abusive relationship, and when Celie becomes attracted to and eventually falls in love with Mister's mistress, Shug Avery, she begins to blossom. Shug is the first person to really see Celie, and she sings "Too Beautiful for Words" to her, describing her inner and outer beauty. Celie expresses her hard-won sense of self-worth in the eleven-o'clock number "I'm Here," which ends with her declaration: "I'm beautiful and I'm here."[66] [Clip 7.4] Celie's transformation from

226 ABILITY

ugly to beautiful mirrors her path from self-effacing daughter and housewife to self-actualized independent business owner.

Because *Purple* is a Broadway musical, the same aesthetics that produce what the narrative deems beautiful also informed its casting. Casting Celie is challenging since she ages from fourteen to forty-eight over the course of the musical, and the actor playing her needs to have a dynamite voice, acting chops, and star presence. On Broadway, Celie has only been played by conventionally attractive actors. The original production starred LaChanze, and then recording star Fantasia Barrino in 2007. The 2015 revival made a Broadway star of Cynthia Erivo. *The Color Purple* continued the long-standing trend of casting attractive actors to play ugly characters. Yet the narrative hinges on Celie's recognition that she is *not* ugly (on the inside, at least)—that, in fact, she is beautiful. Nevertheless, playing Celie came with a price. Erivo recalls, "I had to live inside a character that was shoved around onstage and called ugly for about two hours. . . . After time 350, 360, 400, it starts to wear at the skin a bit, so the person inside the character starts to hear it for real. So, imagine eight shows a week hearing the word ugly. And the only way I could get to this point to sing ["I'm Here"] is to go through that."[67]

Sutton Foster is no stranger to playing roles in which physical difference matters—notably, in composer Jeanine Tesori's musicals: she originated Princess Fiona in *Shrek* and played the title role of *Violet* in its 2014 Broadway debut (it premiered off-Broadway in 1997). Violet has a facial disfigurement as the result of a childhood accident, prompting her adult search for a miracle cure (a take on the familiar kill-or-cure disability narrative). Like Celie, Violet learns self-acceptance by the musical's end. Playing Violet was casting against type for Foster, who is known for her sunny disposition, tap-dancing skills, and wholesome girl-next-door good looks. Foster explained to the *Los Angeles Times* that the role was a deliberate choice to shake up her image, saying, "I want to be seen as someone who can do many things."[68] Foster garnered headlines during the Broadway production because she went without makeup as Violet. [Clip 7.5] As is usually the case in productions of *Violet*, there was no visible scar on her face despite the fact that the musical itself is about her quest to remove her facial scar. Audiences are meant to gauge the severity of the character's scar through the reactions of the other characters on encountering her. The star's presence coupled with the scar's absence made her difference an irresistible metaphor as well as an emblematic example of how musicals universalize difference.

MUSICALS, PHYSICAL DIFFERENCE, AND DISABILITY   227

Foster told *Vanity Fair*, "How the audience sees the scar is how Violet feels about the scar. . . . And then it becomes more of a universal idea as opposed to a completely specific deformity."[69] But instead of being about Violet's difference, the narrative around the production became about Foster forgoing makeup: instead of cripping up, she pared down. Staging musicals like *Violet* requires making the better of two difficult choices when it comes to how to represent difference. Making physical difference invisible has unintended effects; writer Amanda Leduc explains, "If a disability is not a disability so much as a symbol of something else, then once that symbol is realized, the disability can go away."[70] Though there would have been different risks if Foster had worn a prosthetic scar, the choice to depict Violet without a scar allows facial disfigurement to seem imaginary; both choices prompt consideration of the representational conundrum of how to best address Violet's disfigurement. *Violet* offers a kind of narrative prosthesis absent the prosthetic.

The 2014 revival of *Hedwig and the Angry Inch* opened with television star Neil Patrick Harris in the title role; a succession of other television stars replaced him, including Darren Criss, Taye Diggs, and Michael C. Hall. *Hedwig* is not a typical disability narrative, though even its title addresses the fact that Hedwig's botched sex-change surgery left her disfigured. When star replacement and *Hedwig* co-creator John Cameron Mitchell injured his knee mid-performance on February 7, 2015, the injury required him to wear a leg brace for the remainder of his run. Since Hedwig's physical difference is central to the musical itself, the injury made Mitchell's Broadway turn as Hedwig especially vital because of how deeply his temporary mobility impairment became woven into the show, amplifying the narrative's approach to difference. The presence of Mitchell's temporary mobility impairment underscored Broadway's predilection for able-bodiedness.[71] And Mitchell (pictured in Figure 7.2 before his injury), ever the trouper, did not let the brace hold him back.

The injury added new complexity to Mitchell's performance. Mitchell explains that he "took a wrong move and ripped a meniscus so I had an operation and took a week off, now back in a knee brace which makes that show kind of rawer and more spontaneous despite the lack of movement. . . . I can't do certain things but I keep the brace on because I actually like the show much better with it."[72] Mitchell's torn meniscus called attention to the tenuous fragility of ability itself. To a degree, this was already part of his performance in this production since he was reprising (now in his fifties) a role

Figure 7.2 John Cameron Mitchell as Hedwig during his Broadway run in *Hedwig and the Angry Inch*. Credit: Joan Marcus.

he first created in 1999. Mitchell's injury was the rare visible impairment to appear on Broadway and because his name was above the title, the economic pressures of Broadway necessitated his not missing performances.

The brace proved fodder for Mitchell as Hedwig to poke fun at himself, adding pithy ad-libs throughout calling attention to his injury: "You may have noticed that I'm working on my last leg here," for instance.[73] Mitchell's age and his use of a crutch and knee brace prompted critics to comment with regularity on his physical ability. *The Hollywood Reporter* critic noted

Mitchell's "limited mobility," while also explaining how this itself became a metaphor, writing, "It's somehow appropriate that Hedwig should have visible war wounds to match [her] emotional carnage."[74] *New York Times* critic Ben Brantley opined, "Mitchell's Hedwig appears more bruised and battered by life, and on the verge of all-out exhaustion" as a result of the combination of age and injury before going on to detail "a deeper sense of mortal shadows and ruefulness about this hobbling Hedwig."[75] Critics felt Mitchell's injury coupled with his age added depth and authenticity to his performance. Though far from being remotely similar to Hedwig's botched gender surgery, Mitchell's injury kept Hedwig's difference at once in and out of the realm of metaphor.[76] For critics, Mitchell's turn became yet another narrative of overcoming, situating the physically impaired and/or disabled body as a hurdle over which the virtuosic performer must jump.

Though "overcoming" became part of the show's reception when Mitchell tore his meniscus, *Hedwig's* narrative also relies on the kill or cure trope. Born Hansel in East Berlin during the Cold War, Hedwig is coerced by his mother and boyfriend into a "sex change operation" that will be his ticket to the United States.[77] Hansel must undergo this operation in order to emigrate with his American sugar daddy boyfriend Luther. Hansel became Hedwig after the unsuccessful operation, which left her disfigured—hence the "the angry inch" of the show's title. Because the surgery was non-consensual, Hedwig's identity remains in flux: while she identifies as female following the operation, she claims neither trans nor cisgender as gender identity. Playwright and *Hedwig* superfan Caridad Svich notes, "Hedwig's physical trauma serves as the psychological core of the show. Risen like Lazarus, she is resurrected into a body that has been mutilated and is physically rendered by its inability to be neither one thing nor another."[78] If the surgery itself allowed the show to riff on the kill or cure narrative, so did *Hedwig's* staging when it came to Mitchell's brace.

Hedwig's narrative culminates in another act of gender crossing, when the actor playing Hedwig becomes her young lover Tommy Gnosis. If Mitchell as Hedwig complicated easy understandings of queerness and disability throughout the musical, what are audiences to make of her transformation into an able-bodied straight white cisgender male rock star? In the revival, the transformation also served as a moment for the actor playing Hedwig to display his toned body on an actual pedestal. [Clip 7.6] As Hedwig, Mitchell wore elaborately theatrical costumes, but as Tommy, he stripped to only a pair of black leather trunks. The trunks were memorable but most striking

230   ABILITY

was what he was no longer wearing: his leg brace. After the transformation into Tommy, the brace was gone, making Mitchell's (and Hedwig's) body read as *able* again. Though the staging didn't require him to move very much at this point, his movement did not betray the injury. The transformation realized the effect of producing the ostensibly straight, white male body as the norm incarnate, even in the body of an openly gay actor like Mitchell. In a sense, this final transformation subversively reinstated the norms that the rest of *Hedwig* seems to challenge so powerfully.

If Mitchell's temporary mobility impairment added to *Hedwig*, two years earlier it was disability's displacement in another earlier revival prominently featuring its lead actor hoping for a leg brace that proved quite controversial. As producers steered *Porgy and Bess* to a Broadway revival, director Diane Paulus recruited playwright Suzan-Lori Parks to revise the libretto with an eye toward making Bess a more fully fleshed-out heroine and redressing the opera's racist caricatures. Parks and Paulus's version, newly christened *The Gershwins' Porgy and Bess*, opened on Broadway in 2012. Their changes attempted to update *Porgy*'s outdated racial politics for contemporary audiences, though the media's focus on race initially obscured what was at stake in the production's disability politics. Though Porgy still sings movingly (if in outdated language) about the social exclusion he experiences in the opening scene: "When Gawd made cripple, he mean him to be lonely,"[79] the new libretto rendered Porgy's body in a new form.

The original libretto refers to the "crippled" Porgy as getting around in a cart pulled by a goat; in subsequent productions, he also sometimes crawls on his hands and knees or uses a cane when not on the cart. Paulus and Parks cut the goat cart, and star Norm Lewis as Porgy used a cane and leg brace while also employing a highly affected performance of disability in his walk, ambling about with bent legs and turned in knees (pictured in Figure 7.3). [Clip 7.7] He told the *New York Times*, "Some people might miss the goat cart but what we've kept—and deepened, I think—is Porgy's acceptance of his lot in life as a cripple."[80] Lewis himself felt the cane endowed Porgy with a new strength "while the cart rendered him weak."[81] However, the goat cart served as a symbol of Porgy's agency and status in the social world of the play since the cart elevated Porgy and made him appear heroic. The show employs another disability trope since Porgy's status as its romantic hero "compensates" for his mobility impairment. The cart was an expression of Porgy's dignity and was a kind of disability representation not often seen onstage—not only

Figure 7.3 Norm Lewis (*left*) as Porgy and Audra MacDonald (*right*) as Bess in *The Gershwins' Porgy and Bess*. Credit: Michael J. Lutch.

is Porgy the rare disabled character who is also the romantic lead, but he also possesses enough brute strength to murder his rival with his bare hands.

One person who missed the goat cart was Stephen Sondheim, who sent a furious letter to the *New York Times* after reading of the proposed changes to the show during its out-of-town tryout at the American Repertory Theater in Cambridge, Massachusetts. As Parks and Paulus worked to update the opera and remove its regressively stereotypical depictions of Black people, they also aimed to give audiences the backstory of Porgy's disability, which suggests the desire to explain disability to audiences rather than simply allow it to exist. Parks went back to the novel that the opera is based on and found a line explaining that Porgy was "crippled from birth," which she included in her adaptation.[82] Sondheim scathingly decried the decision to substitute a cane and leg brace for a goat cart, writing,

> It's reassuring that Ms. Parks has a direct pipeline to Gershwin and is just carrying out his work for him, and that she thinks he would have taken one of the most moving moments in musical theater history—Porgy's demand, "Bring my goat!"—and thrown it out. Ms. Parks (or Ms. Paulus) has taken away Porgy's goat cart in favor of a cane. So now he can demand, "Bring my

cane!" Perhaps someone will bring him a straw hat too, so he can buck-and-wing his way to New York.[83]

Though the cane gave Porgy *stage* mobility not available to him with the goat cart, the change was apparently profound enough to make Porgy and Bess's doomed love affair *too* plausible to many critics.[84] Placing the crux of believability on Porgy's specific disability openly exhibits ableism, though. Because Porgy uses a cane and can get around on his own two feet, critics felt the production deemed him more worthy of love than when he used a goat cart. In her review in *Newsday*, Linda Winer noted that the "adaptation hobbles Porgy's poignancy by changing him from a hopeless cripple in a goat cart to a disabled man with a cane and a new leg brace. This makes Bess' love for him feel less radical and . . . a big Broadway hint of feel-good future remains."[85] It's clear that Winer and others felt the cart and the degree of Porgy's mobility impairment precluded a feel-good future for Porgy.

While the decision to cut the cart raised eyebrows, Lewis's cripping up did not, and this alone reveals more about what the Broadway industry—from creatives to critics and audiences—was willing to view as neutral at the time. Critics commented more on the changes to Porgy's backstory than they did on Lewis's walk. *New York* magazine critic Scott Brown referred to Lewis's casting as "the most felicitous case of miscasting I've ever seen" because he was too likeable, but he otherwise ignored Lewis's embodiment of Porgy.[86] *Hollywood Reporter* critic David Rooney described how Porgy "literally grows in stature and strength before our eyes."[87] Chris Jones of the *Chicago Tribune* noted that Lewis "does not seem like a radical departure for Bess. With his physical handicap dialed back and his handsome body matched by the most gorgeous voice, Lewis's magnetic and transfixing Porgy now feels like the most normative and sexy guy."[88] Only *New York Post* critic Elisabeth Vincentelli noted his cripping up at all, writing that Lewis "plays Porgy—lurching around with a cane instead of rolling on a goat cart—like the clichéd saintly cripple."[89] Not a single critic argued against casting a non-disabled Porgy. This is not just a failure of critics, though; the failure is Broadway's, too, as esteemed artists like Lewis, Parks, and Paulus made the misguided choice to trade on disability's differences of degree if not of kind.

Musicologist Stephanie Jensen-Moulton offered a dissenting voice about the changes made in this production and its casting. She noted that Parks's updates to the libretto included giving Porgy lines indicating that he's been "saving up for a leg brace and a new cane," which will allow him to appear

MUSICALS, PHYSICAL DIFFERENCE, AND DISABILITY   233

more able-bodied and thus more masculine. These updates were realized in Lewis's casting and performance, who, Jensen-Moulton argues, played "a Porgy who dreams of being cured." Lewis's performance coupled with Parks's alterations meant "a Porgy whose limp turns to a swagger by the end of the piece."[90] Ableism makes itself as visible as ever.

That the impetus behind the revisions was financial and not artistic was widely reported: the heirs to the Gershwin estate wanted a more licensable property that would be more lucrative. It is not much of a leap to see how disability could figure into the accounting: a cane costs producers a lot less than a goat cart and live goat. The cane was also a practical choice; the goat cart would have been hard to make work on the production's raked stage, according to Lewis.[91] If the goal of this revisal was to recast the opera itself from an opera into a musical that could be produced more regularly, then recasting Porgy's disability was simply capital saved. Rebranding *Porgy and Bess* as a musical changed its economic and aesthetic relationship to disability and to Broadway itself, since its rebranding frustrated those whose generic predispositions and attachments could not tolerate the ambiguity of being unable to definitively claim the show as an opera or a musical. Broadway shows are performed eight times a week versus opera's rotating repertory, and this too is tied to labor: Broadway performers must sing the role eight times a week, while opera singers might only perform two or three times a week. Reframing *Porgy* as a musical meant refashioning its representation of disability to conform with contemporary Broadway norms. That the 2012 Broadway production could still be seen as a regressive representation of disability is an indictment. When Broadway stages disability and physical difference, it is too often in service of the same old song and dance.

Ali Stroker Breaks Type

Given decades of Broadway's misrepresentation of disability and its exclusion of disabled performers, Ali Stroker's 2015 debut as Anna in Deaf West's *Spring Awakening* was nothing short of revolutionary. Stroker's *Playbill* bio explained that she was "the first person in a wheelchair to appear on Broadway," and noted that "Ali believes any limitation can be an opportunity."[92] Stroker cannily uses her platform to advocate acceptance of all abilities. She told *Howlround*, "I sometimes meet people who are not educated about how to handle certain situations and that is an opportunity for

234 ABILITY

me to explain and share with them how something could be handled."[93] If Stroker's presence forced conversations about Broadway's ableism, ableism itself almost prevented her from receiving the conservatory training that prepared her for Broadway. A few college musical theatre programs rejected Stroker because they were unable to conceive of how someone in a wheelchair could dance and unwilling to conceive of how someone in a wheelchair could become a triple-threat.

However, Stroker's casting in *Spring Awakening* almost did not happen because of concerns about the conflation of d/Deafness and disability. Casting director Beth Lipari remembers vividly "a discussion between the artistic director and us about how [casting Stroker] might not be a possibility . . . because he didn't want people thinking that deaf people were disabled."[94] That this was a conversation among *Spring Awakening*'s creatives reveals the extent to which debates over the terms of identity materialize the effects of disability stigma. Because the Deaf community views "themselves as a linguistic subgroup" who "see their state of being as defined not medically but rather socially and politically," they have largely resisted the label of disabled.[95] Deafness's difference from disability distances the Deaf from partaking in some of the political utility of disability identification. This separation does not necessarily mean that the Deaf think ill of disabled people and it can be understood as an attempt to honor the very different embodied experiences and identities that fall under these umbrella categories. Even if casting Stroker carried the risk that some spectators might associate deafness and disability, those charged with casting the show decided the rewards of casting her outweighed any potential risk. If anything, Stroker's casting redefined what makes a triple-threat in the twenty-first century.

When Stroker and *Spring Awakening* reached Broadway, the company discovered that backstage at the Brooks Atkinson Theatre was not wheelchair-accessible, so a dressing room was renovated for her on the stage level.[96] Broadway theatres were not conceived with accessibility in mind when they were built in the early twentieth century. And when Stroker won the 2019 Tony Award for her performance as Ado Annie in Daniel Fish's revival of *Oklahoma!*, it was a shock but not a surprise that there was no ramp from the auditorium to the stage of Radio City Music Hall that would have made the stage accessible for her. Stroker, who pundits widely expected to win for her joyous redefinition of the role and Ado Annie's signature song "I Cain't Say No" [Clip 7.8], had to wait backstage rather than in the auditorium with the other nominees as their names were announced. On Broadway's most important night, the message was clear: you might be nominated for a Tony, but if you're disabled, you'll still find yourself waiting alone in the wings. Luckily, Stroker won and wheeled herself center stage to collect her award (Figure 7.4).

Stroker has had a remarkably successful career, appearing on several television shows and in two Broadway revivals, on top of a flourishing career in regional theatre. She works regularly despite the barriers the industry places in her way. Stroker argues that her disability, rather than being a limitation, is in fact what has taught her to handle the ups and downs of the industry: "Having a disability is perfect training to getting into this industry because you're used to somebody saying 'you can't do that.'"[97] She explained to an interviewer how she deals with typecasting, saying, "Type has been a tough one for me because I just never really felt like I fit into one."[98] She learned to type herself because "very rarely in a breakdown does it say they are looking for someone with a disability. . . . I always feel like it's my job to actually break the idea of type." Due to her success and ensuing visibility,

Figure 7.4 Ali Stroker accepts the Tony Award for best featured actress for her role as Ado Annie in the Broadway revival of the musical "Oklahoma!" at the 73rd Annual Tony Awards in New York on Sunday night, June 9, 2019. Credit: Sara Krulwich/The New York Times/Redux.

236 ABILITY

Stroker is a name in the industry. It is not hard to imagine seeing a casting breakdown looking for an "Ali Stroker type" in the future.

Stroker is rarely mentioned apart from her wheelchair (this book included) or from explanations about how she came to use one. She notes that she performs a special kind of labor as a disabled actor that involves going out of her way to accommodate others, saying, "I have to be really solid and comfortable in how I'm moving. It also puts everyone else at ease if there's any fear or discomfort around what I do. I have to be the first person who's on board."[99] Stroker's advocacy and visibility have led her to become a role model. As she told *Teen Vogue*, "I remember young kids with disabilities coming to see the show and being like, 'I didn't know this was possible, and now I've seen it done, and I know it is.'"[100]

Stroker's Broadway successes have come in playing roles not written as disabled, a sure measure of progress and inclusion, especially at a time when the disabled characters that are written are still regularly played by non-disabled actors. Stroker explained her stance on authentic casting, noting that "having a disability is a full life experience, and somebody with a disability would represent that authentically." She clarified, "I always want to be hired because I'm the best actor, not because I'm disabled."[101] Can producers, audiences, and critics see Stroker's success not as either because of or despite her wheelchair, but as the result of the singular combination of talent and determination that it takes to make it as an actor? Stroker knows the impact that her very presence on Broadway can have to "help younger people realize that . . . your disability is not a disability. . . . You're just differently abled. So use what you've got."[102] If Broadway addresses its lack of accessibility and accommodation, and practices inclusive casting, Stroker will not be the last visibly disabled Tony winner. But luck or goodwill will not be what makes Broadway more accessible; it will be concentrated and conscious work to break type and transform the industry.

Disability's Presence

Stroker is only one person; her success cannot undo an entire system built on ableism. While her achievements are rightfully celebrated, they also must call attention to the fact that they took so long to happen at all. Stroker's casting only underlines just how normalized exclusionary practices were

MUSICALS, PHYSICAL DIFFERENCE, AND DISABILITY   237

for decades. It also speaks to whose identities casting directors and artistic teams considered neutral enough to play any role and also to those never even given chances. Sandahl observes that since there are so few disabled performers who break into mainstream professional theatre, one can actually name them and "the fact that it is even possible to do so is a testament to the practice's rarity."[103]

Every single role discussed in this chapter was originated by a non-disabled actor. Disability exclusion remains a structural problem with present-day problems bearing the effects of prior eras—performing marginalized identities has been used by the normative to put on full display Broadway's hierarchy of bodily aesthetics. In 2018, *The Guardian* asked whether the industry can start to conceptualize cripping up as offensive as it considers blackface.[104] Sandahl makes the case that though crip face and blackface "are not precisely analogous," they both identify "the violent erasure and displacement of oppressed people by such casting practices."[105] And the dynamic of erasure extends to fat roles played with actors in padding and queer roles inhabited by straight actors, too—and historical context is a key to unlocking how and why this changes and why it matters. And yet there is also the reality that "authentic casting" is not a one-size fits all solution to the conundrums casting creates. Sandahl's work challenges us to think beyond right or wrong, good or bad casting and instead to consider how representational conundrums related to disability produce material effects.[106] Casting each musical discussed in this book presents a conundrum that invites audiences and creatives alike to consider the inevitability of "authenticity" breaking down under scrutiny, especially concerning disability and physical difference. Despite the risks, Sandahl concludes, "Sometimes, when we are forced to make choices . . . we may choose to ditch the representational conundrum and take a stand. Context matters."[107] And context is always changing.

Appearance continues to count above all. British playwright and actor Athena Stevens argues that "ensembles, by definition, are meant to be everyone, so they should be inclusive. There is no reason why an ensemble for a musical can't include a performer with a disability. These shows have the money and they should have the imagination."[108] Maybe calling Broadway "The Fabulous Invalid" is apt: it is infected with ableism, but song and dance's fabulosity mask the severity. Difference is just metaphoric in most musicals because Broadway's preference for able-bodiedness is physical. There should

238   ABILITY

be dozens of Ali Strokers on Broadway, not just one. Despite disability's pervasive *presence* in narrative metaphors in Broadway musicals, its *absence* matters more: without the inclusion of disabled performers, producers, writers, directors, casting directors, agents, and designers, disability will continue to not really exist on Broadway at all.[109]

Epilogue: Recasting Broadway

Body politics have reliably—and visibly—played their role on US theatre's biggest stages and its economic seat: Broadway. If the histories presented in this book demonstrate Broadway's ambivalent embrace of non-conforming bodies, then moving forward Broadway must reevaluate how it approaches *all* bodies—not only those that do not conform. As I have argued in this book, aesthetic decisions on Broadway are always economic and political ones. In the epilogue, I turn not to Broadway itself but to those who are helping reshape a more inclusive industry often from the outside in.

Meaningful, lasting changes have not yet been made by industry gatekeepers and powerbrokers. The capacity of Actors' Equity Association remains administrative and essentially symbolic; its members are still inevitably at the mercy of producers. And yet change *is* coming—from the ground up rather than the top down. Broadway has been governed for more than a century by what writers Jeremy Heimans and Henry Timms call *old power*, which "is held by few" and "jealously guarded . . . closed, inaccessible, and leader-driven." Broadway will only meaningfully evolve through what Heimans and Timms term *new power*, "which is made by many. It is open, participatory, and peer-driven."[1] New power is clashing with old power on Broadway, most visibly rising from social movements like Black Lives Matter and other advocacy groups, many of which draw inspiration from the liberation movements associated with the identities covered in each of this book's sections.

I focus here on four that connect with this book's sections either because of their founder or their mission: National Asian Artists Project, Broadway Body Positivity Project, Ring of Keys, and Deaf Broadway. Each of these mission-driven groups formed in response to labor concerns and/or exclusion from participation in Broadway musicals, and each aims to reach under-served and under-represented communities. For as much as there is a so-called Broadway community, it is based more on where you work than who you are—and working on a Broadway show is the prerequisite for admission into that select club. These groups hope to shape a more inclusive Broadway onstage, behind the scenes, and in the audience.

Broadway Bodies. Ryan Donovan, Oxford University Press. © Oxford University Press 2023.
DOI: 10.1093/oso/9780197551073.003.0009

240 EPILOGUE

On Broadway, it is nearly possible to trace all paths back to Baayork Lee one way or another. Lee co-founded the National Asian Artists Project (NAAP), which began as a summer program for children in Manhattan's Chinatown in 2005. It makes sense that Lee should be the person to lead this organization, since her career began as a child performer in the original Broadway cast of *The King and I* in 1951 and that show itself later led to NAAP's inception. Lee's subsequent Broadway career paved the way for many to follow in her footsteps, especially her role in *A Chorus Line*'s creation and legacy, which ensured that generations of Asian and Asian American female dancers would at least have the chance to work. Lee was initially reluctant to share her story in *A Chorus Line* and Michael Bennett had to coax her into being in both the narrative and the production of the show. She initially told him, "'Nobody wants to listen to a short Asian who wanted to be a ballerina. Why do you want to put that in the show?' And he said, "Oh, no, no, no. Baayork. You know, I think a lot of people would be interested."[2] Lee's historic achievement as the first Asian-American woman to tell her own story in her own words in a Broadway musical—one that was decidedly not an Orientalist fantasia like *The King and I*—has been under-played in most accounts of the show.

The impact of even *A Chorus Line* went only so far, as Lee notes. "It's not until [2017] that we had Telly Leung playing Aladdin on Broadway and we had Ann Harada in *Avenue Q*. So, it took a long while, but at least, I could say that in, in forty-five years short Asian dancers have worked if they're not doing *King and I*. And at least one of them can do *A Chorus Line*."[3] Though *Aladdin*, *Avenue Q*, and *The King and I* give Asian and Asian American actors opportunities to work, they also promote, to varying degrees, stereotypes about Asia as an Orientalized place and about Asians and Asian Americans. However, Lee's work and focus at NAAP are not about finding the next Leung or Harada but are about providing access to the arts, engagement, and affirmation for under-served schoolchildren.[4] If Lee's career charted a path for professionals, her work at NAAP focuses on theatre's power to enrich everyone's lives, amateur and pro alike.

NAAP began when Lee had just finished directing a production of *The King and I* and she became concerned about the children in the cast after it closed. She asked her assistants Nina Zoie Lam and Stephen Eng what would happen to all of the performers, and they told her, "Well, they have to wait until the next *King and I* comes along, until there's a *Saigon*, because there's no work for Asians, you know?" Eng, Lam, and Lee co-founded NAAP as a result. They work to advance equity for Asian artists, including actors, directors, and writers in addition to their primary mission of education. NAAP partners with P.S. 124 in New York City's Chinatown to expose elementary schoolchildren to Broadway musicals. Lee explains, "It was very, very important for me to be able to give those kids in Chinatown an opportunity to open their mind to another world." NAAP's focus on education is not tied to labor at all and is holistic in its approach; Lee says, "I'm asking them to be our future ticket holders, to support theatre, and to understand what it takes to be in theatre." NAAP is a model of community engagement and in 2017, Lee received the Isabelle Stevenson Tony Award to honor her work with NAAP.

While NAAP represents a model of in-person community advocacy, other advocates are creating communities online. Performer Stephanie Lexis founded Broadway Body Positivity Project (BBPP) in 2019 as a response to the body shaming that typecasting perpetuates. Frustrated by the disjunction between her lyric soprano voice and the kinds of roles casting personnel told her she was right for left Lexis in a bind. She wanted to work but she did not want to risk vocal injury playing parts that her *voice* was wrong for but that industry standards deemed her *body* was right for. Broadway theatre's inability to conceptualize more inclusive casting led to the founding of BBPP.

BBPP is not just about size inclusivity; it aims to foster body positivity for *all* bodies. Lexis observes, "The only qualification for body shame is just having a body" and "those who are marginalized are going to experience it the worst."[5] In 2019, BBPP's Instagram featured a series of statements submitted by followers detailing their experiences being body shamed, ranging from being told by gatekeepers like casting directors and well-meaning college professors that they were too thin, too fat, too tall, too disabled, or too high-voiced to be in musicals. BBPP produces its own digital content with cabarets and holiday spectaculars reaching followers ready for more inclusive representation. Lexis explains that her role is "to soothe the inflammation wherever I can," and to that end, she regularly speaks at colleges and works with casting directors to dispel outdated notions of whose bodies are Broadway Bodies.[6] She notes the importance of addressing body shame both to college students about to enter the industry and those already working in it.

Like BBPP, Ring of Keys speaks to Broadway as a seemingly accepting industry that hasn't always been so welcoming in practice. Andrea Prestinario and Royer Bockus co-founded advocacy group Ring of Keys in 2018 to raise visibility for queer women, transgender, and gender non-conforming artists, because, as they explain, "queer identities have a history of being whispered

242 EPILOGUE

in our industry."[7] The two met while doing a reading of a musical at the behest of its musical director, who had separately told each that the other was lesbian. Prestinario noted in an interview that there were deeper implications, saying, "The fact is [musical theatre] is so gay but it's not queer."[8] They felt the industry was still sidelining lesbians and other queer performers while cisgender gay men received all of the spotlight. Prestinario and Bockus decided they needed to change that and to form a queer theatre community that looked beyond cis gay men, who largely had existing industry networks already.

The group takes its name from *Fun Home*'s song "Ring of Keys" and each member represents a *key* on the group's metaphorical ring.[9] With over 500 members in major cities in the United States, United Kingdom, and Canada, Ring of Keys has created a digital and in-person community focused on building inclusive networks. Through monthly workshops and newsletters, Ring of Keys makes its impact ripple beyond digital spaces. The group's website prominently features a directory of people who work in all facets of theatre from acting to production design and, like many other groups, their mission focuses on changing the entire ecosystem of theatre rather than simply addressing onstage representation.

Another group has also taken to the internet to reach a specific community and it, too, came about as a necessary solution to Broadway's lack of inclusion and accessibility: Deaf Broadway's mission involves providing "unprecedented visual language access for the Deaf community."[10] Once the group was up and running in 2020, demand for their ASL productions quickly grew. Large numbers of d/Deaf and hard-of-hearing people are curious about and hungry for musicals, and access has always been the barrier, whether due to lack of ASL inclusion, geography, exorbitant ticket prices, and/or involvement in the creative process. Deaf Broadway sought to address all of these barriers. As Deaf Broadway's website notes, "It's incredibly rare for Deaf people to be able to tell a popular story entirely on their own, in their own language, without influence from or control by hearing people or the mainstream theatre community."[11]

In their first year alone, Deaf Broadway produced ASL readings of *Company*, *Into the Woods*, *Legally Blonde*, *Les Misérables*, *The Rocky Horror Picture Show*, and *Sweeney Todd*. Their readings featured entirely Deaf casts performing in ASL simultaneously alongside filmed versions of the stage productions of each musical. Deaf Broadway's readings have brought together d/Deaf performers from around the United States, including many who have performed on and off Broadway, on television, and in film. Because these readings were staged on YouTube, they are accessible everywhere YouTube is—and so is auditioning for them. In the YouTube audition instruction video for *Rocky Horror*, Deaf Broadway director Garrett Zuercher invites actors to audition for any role they want to play regardless of whether their gender or skin color aligns with the way the show has been typically cast.[12] The only rule, "All characters must be played by Deaf or Hard of Hearing actors," applied to every part expect for Rocky (for whom they sought a hard-of-hearing or hearing performer fluent in ASL). Zuercher explained, "It doesn't matter what your body type is or how you identify." The internet has proven something of an equalizer for casting; Deaf Broadway makes its audition materials available on its website and its casting process more transparent than most. Staging these readings on Zoom in 2020 and 2021 also meant that performers could be located anywhere.

Deaf Broadway's audiences, creatives, and performers have made musicals their own, with their own hands. As performer Pamela Wright told an interviewer, "For Deaf theater or Deaf representation, we don't need to wait for people to give us the opportunity. Deaf Broadway did not wait. They went ahead."[13] Zuercher noted, "We already have Deaf folks on Broadway, but I would love to see a fully Deaf group on Broadway with Deaf directors, Deaf producers—Deaf everything. That's something that we still haven't really seen at any level."[14]

Not waiting for permission from above is how change starts. The work of all of these advocacy groups faces an uphill battle since they are usually small, lower-budget organizations fighting against a comparatively massive industry set in its ways—these groups are metaphoric Davids to Broadway's Goliath. All of the groups mentioned here have fought to redefine whose bodies belong in Broadway musicals whether by casting schoolchildren in Chinatown in after-school productions or taking to the internet to build inclusive networks. They are seeking not only to change Broadway's body politics from within the industry but also to revise them from without.

The persistence of the ideal Broadway Body has held sway inside the industry and in the media for far too long. A prime example is a long-running celebration of the physiques of chorus dancers encapsulates the politics of which bodies Broadway desires. For nine years, the weekly magazine *Time Out New York* annually published a photo series featuring Broadway's "hottest chorus boys" and "hottest chorus girls," usually prominently displaying their sculpted abs and bulging biceps. While those featured in the

244 EPILOGUE

photo spreads represented some ethnic and racial diversity, that's where the diversity started and stopped. These annual photo essays circulated decidedly narrow yet dominant definitions of the Broadway Body. These unrealistic bodily standards inform how those hoping to enter the business feel about their own bodies, too. I once asked students what was the most urgent conversation we could have about musical theatre. One responded, "Musical theatre has a long way to go before it can really be considered 'inclusive' and 'diverse.'" She went on to describe how "the overall 'Broadway body,' or the typical look you are supposed to have in order to make it" impacts her: "I am constantly being shoved into a mold by other people, despite that mold not staying true to who I am."[15] Broadway's body politics don't cease to exist outside of midtown Manhattan; they create barriers before many performers can even get started.

Recasting Broadway means recasting ideas of whose bodies matter. Typecasting can no longer remain an unexamined norm; Broadway gatekeepers should follow Ali Stroker's goal and break the idea of type itself. Casting's stake in the performance of identity makes it an ideal site to undertake the work of making theatre more equitable, inclusive, and representative of an infinitely vaster range of embodied differences. As the industry moves toward what is being called (as of this writing) *authentic casting* for the kinds of roles and identities covered in this book, it is worth considering how inclusive casting might extend beyond overly simplified and increasingly rigid notions of authenticity. For instance, in some musicals there cannot be such a thing as authentic casting, which presents quite an opportunity to make a statement. A production that did just so while embodying the intersections of identity covered in each section of this book is director Marcia Milgrom Dodge's 2021 production of *Disney's Beauty and the Beast* at Maryland's Olney Theatre Center. [Clip 8.1] Jade Jones, "a self-described queer, plussized Black woman" was cast as Belle and disabled actor and noted tap dancer Evan Ruggiero, whose leg was amputated as a teenager, was cast as the Beast (pictured in Figure E.1).[16] This casting represents how professional theatre's paradigm is incrementally shifting production by production.

This casting was so notable that *People* magazine took note of it, which almost never happens to a regional theatre production. Jones and Ruggiero told *People* that they both "assumed they'd be seen for other characters—Jones for Mrs. Potts or even Cogsworth, and Ruggiero for Lumière." Ruggiero said, "I could do a candlestick tap dance on my peg leg, and isn't that what everybody wants to see?"[17] (Ruggiero is well known for his tap dancing.) Jones said, "I've

Figure E.1 Jade Jones as Belle and Evan Ruggiero as the Beast in Olney Theatre Center's 2021 production of *Disney's Beauty and the Beast*. Credit: Teresa Castracane Photography.

never seen anyone like me on stage in a role like this, in an ingénue role, in a desired role. And I just think it's important because it's not like we don't exist."[18] Dodge told the *Washington Post* how the show's casting interrogated beauty itself: "Our production really challenges each of us to look around the room with an equitable lens in which all races, ethnicities, body shapes and abilities can be identified and celebrated as the most beautiful person inside and out."[19]

Critics lauded Dodge's casting and how the inclusion of a disabled Beast and a fat queer Black Belle made a show with retro gender politics into something more. In *DC Metro Theater Arts*, Darby DeJarnette observed, "With Ruggiero's Beast, you're immediately engaged in the exercise of considering how a disabled prince turns into such a hideous monster. It confronts, head-on, the ideas that we have about marginalized people being more empathetic and instead emphasizes the reality that shame about a disability (or a sexual orientation or gender identity) can be internalized and become poisonous."[20] Casting actors like Jones and Ruggiero in roles that they would not normally even be considered for because of how their bodies look and move shows the industry at large that it is possible and desirable to do so. [Clip 8.2] A next

246   EPILOGUE

step for inclusive casting would be to cast Jones and Ruggiero not just in a fairy tale musical but as leads in other musicals previously unavailable to actors like them.

Casting's profound power to challenge deeply embedded aesthetic norms is evinced simply by recasting familiar narratives with bodies heretofore unseen in them. Confronting Broadway's history of ambivalence toward nonconforming bodies is a critical step toward ensuring that it does not keep repeating itself eight times a week. Awareness without action only permits old norms to hold sway; actions like Dodge's casting of a fat queer Black woman and a disabled actor as romantic leads challenge the old norms and pave the way to a more inclusive industry, starting 200 miles or so from Broadway. Though the theatre industry itself is slowly beginning to change outside of New York, a crucial question remains: will Broadway change for good?

Notes

Introduction

1. Zahifito, "Donna Mckechnie sings 'Broadway Boogie Woogie Blues.'" Ed Kleban's draft notes for the song are in his papers at the New York Public Library. Billy Rose Theatre Division, New York Public Library. "Broadway boogie woogie / Edward Kleban," New York Public Library Digital Collections. Accessed November 19, 2020. https://digitalcollections.nypl.org/items/734ccc00-8358-0134-4f1c-00505686a51c. The song's title comes from a 1942–1943 painting by Piet Mondrian that evokes the energy of New York City and carries a strong sense of regimented movement patterns—like those of any well-drilled dance ensemble.
2. Genius.com, "If a Girl Isn't Pretty" lyrics.
3. Wolf, *A Problem Like Maria*, ix.
4. Davis, *Enforcing Normalcy*, 25.
5. Paulson, "Broadway Is Reopening."
6. See Lee, "'I Have to Be Thin.'"
7. Wolf, *A Problem Like Maria*, 33.
8. Foulkes, *A Place for Us*, 94.
9. Herrera, "Looking at *Hamilton* from Inside the Broadway Bubble," 230.
10. Pogrebin, "Lisa Howard on Her Latest Broadway Show, 'It Shoulda Been You.'"
11. Pao, *No Safe Spaces*, 14.
12. For further reading on casting and race, see Brandi Wilkins Catanese, *The Problem of the Color[Blind]: Racial Transgression and the Politics of Black Performance* (Ann Arbor: University of Michigan Press, 2011).
13. See Herrera, "Looking at Hamilton from Inside the Broadway Bubble," and Pao, *No Safe Spaces*, 4.
14. See Gallela, "Racializing the American Revolution," review of *Hamilton* GC *Advocate*, November 16, 2015, http://gcadvocate.com/2015/11/16/racializing-the-american-revolution-review-of-the-broadway-musical-hamilton/.
15. See Pao, *No More Safe Spaces*, for a history of the debates around race and ethnicity.
16. Cook, *Building Character*, 90.
17. Actors' Equity Association, "Auditions and Job Interviews." Emphasis in original.
18. Actors' Equity Association, "Equity Chorus Call Audition Procedures." Emphasis removed.
19. Madison, *Critical Ethnography*, 4.
20. Cook, *Building Character*, 2.
21. Actors' Equity Association, "2007–110 in the Shade and Les Misérables."
22. Actors' Equity Association, "2009–Billy Elliott."

248 NOTES

23. Actors' Equity Association, "Diversity Report: 2016–2019 in Review."

24. Actors' Equity Association, "Actors' Equity Association Releases Second-Ever Diversity and Inclusion Report."

25. Paulson, " 'Hamilton' Producers Will Change Job Posting, but Not Commitment to Diverse Casting."

26. Davis, *The End of Normal*, 42.

27. Sandahl, "Why Disability Identity Matters," 465.

28. Black Theatre United created an excellent guide: "A New Deal for Broadway: Equity, Diversity, Inclusion, Accessibility & Belonging for the Theatrical Industry," updated May 2022, http://www.blacktheatreunited.com/wp-content/uploads/2022/05/BTU-New-Deal-For-Broadway.pdf.

29. Reimers, "Making an Appearance."

30. *Statistical Abstract of the United States*; The Broadway League, "2018–2019 Broadway End-of-Season Statistics."

31. Jerry Mitchell is quoted in a promotional email from Tom Burke Vocal Studio to author, November 30, 2015.

32. Smart, "The Broadway Body Revolution of Mark Fisher Fitness."

33. Patterson, "The Secrets to Broadway Bodies."

34. Liff, "Follow Choreographer Spencer Liff's Workout Routine for a Broadway Body."

35. Gioia, "Thanksgiving for a Broadway Body!"

36. Mark Fisher Fitness is also a notably body positive organization working in the Broadway fitness space, though the Broadway fitness sector was somewhat slow to pivot away from Broadway Bodies to body positivity.

37. Patterson, "The Secrets to Broadway Bodies."

38. Patterson, "The Secrets to Broadway Bodies."

39. Gioia, "Is Weight Just a Number?"

40. Gioia, "Is Weight Just a Number?"

41. Kwan and Graves, *Framing Fat*.

42. Kwan and Graves *Framing Fat*, 142.

43. Garland-Thomson, *Extraordinary Bodies*, 6.

44. Johnson, "Building the Broadway Voice," 487.

45. Here, I draw from cultural studies scholar Brian Pronger's definition of body fascism: "the desire to order, organ-ize, control, repress, direct, impose limits." Pronger, *Body Fascism*, 110.

46. Jordan, "Sheryl Lee Ralph Is Glowing."

47. Iovannone, "Why Is There No Gay Men's Body Liberation Movement?"

48. Iovannone, "Why Is There No Gay Men's Body Liberation Movement?"

49. theaidsmemorial, Instagram post, August 8, 2020, https://www.instagram.com/p/CDoU0q-jSKu/.

50. Whitesel, *Fat Gay Men*, 37.

51. Bérubé, foreword to McRuer, *Crip Theory*, viii.

52. Goffman, *Stigma*, 128.

53. McRuer, *Crip Theory*, 2.

NOTES   249

54. Davis, *Bending over Backwards*, 39.
55. Centers for Disease Control and Prevention, "Adult Obesity Facts,"; "CDC: 1 in 4 Adults Live with a Disability."
56. Howe et al., introduction to *The Oxford Handbook of Music and Disability*, 2.
57. McKenzie, *Getting Physical*, 2.
58. Garland-Thomson, *Extraordinary Bodies*, 47.
59. Davis, *Enforcing Normalcy*, 86.
60. Rose, *No Right to Be Idle*, 227.
61. Rose, *No Right to Be Idle*, 2.
62. Rose, *No Right to Be Idle*, 36.
63. Monbiot, "Neoliberalism—The Ideology at the Root of All Our Problems." For a book-length study, see David Harvey, *A Brief History of Neoliberalism* (New York: Oxford University Press, 2005).
64. Guthman, "Neoliberalism and the Constitution of Contemporary Bodies," 193.
65. Kwan and Graves, *Framing Fat*, 6.
66. Duggan, *The Twilight of Equality*, 45.
67. Oleksinski, "When Did Celebs Become No-Talent Hotties?"
68. Davis, *Bending over Backwards*, 14. See also Hugh Ryan, "How Eugenics Gave Rise to Modern Homophobia," *Washington Post*, May 28, 2019.
69. Siebers, *Disability Theory*, 10.
70. In addition to eugenics, defining some people as sub- or non-human is deeply in-debted to colonialism, and these legacies both continue to produce harmful effects today.
71. Goldberg, "Study: Bias Drops Dramatically for Sexual Orientation and Race—But not Weight."
72. Garland-Thomson, *Extraordinary Bodies*, 32.
73. Goffman, *Stigma*, 1. Stigma translates from Ancient Greek to *mark* or *brand*, usually made by a stick.
74. Rather than attempt to fix an impossible definition of LGBTQ+ bodies, I want instead to draw attention to the "doing" of these bodies rather than their "being." In doing so, I am inspired by Jill Dolan's reading of bell hooks's formulation of feminist identity, which explicates the differences between "I advocate feminism" and "I am a feminist" as an action rather than an ontology. See Dolan "Practicing Cultural Disruptions," 342–343; hooks, *Feminist Theory*, 31.
75. For three different writer's experiences of coming out as disabled, see "How I Came Out about My Disability," *New York Times*, July 13, 2020 (updated July 20, 2020), https://www.nytimes.com/2020/07/13/us/disability-reveal.html.
76. Garland-Thomson, "Preface and Acknowledgments," *Freakery*, xvii; Sedgwick and Moon, "Divinity," 230.
77. While race and ethnicity certainly carry their own specific relations to visibility and power, they are not quite tied to coming out in corresponding ways (and of course there are exceptions to this, especially for multi-racial and multi-ethnic persons).
78. LeBesco, "Quest for a Cause," 65.

250 NOTES

79. Goffman, *Stigma*, 5.
80. An excellent body of work exists on Broadway, race, and ethnicity. See, for instance, the following on Latinx identity and Broadway: Brian Eugenio Herrera, *Latin Numbers*; David Román's chapter, "Latino Genealogies: Broadway and Beyond—the Case of John Leguizamo," in *Performance in America*: Alberto Sandoval Sánchez, *José, Can You See*.
81. Wolf, *A Problem Like Maria*, 38.
82. Sandahl, "Why Disability Identity Matters," 464.
83. Davis, *Bending over Backwards*, 4.
84. McNulty, "Playwrights Are Calling Out Racism in Theater."

Chapter 1

1. Del Deo and Stern, *Every Little Step*.
2. Barnes, review of *A Chorus Line*, May 22, 1975.
3. mitchellivers, "A Chorus Line on Donahue 2."
4. Gelb, "Producing—and reproducing—'A Chorus Line.'"
5. SaveLiveMusic, "I ♥ New York 70s Broadway Ad."
6. Samuel Yates notes that the term "triple-threat" comes to theatre from sports, specifically US football, and was coined circa 1939. Yates, "Disability and the American Stage Musical," 267.
7. Baayork Lee, interview with author.
8. Gennaro, "Evolution of Dance in the Golden Age of the American 'Book Musical,'" 51.
9. Gardner, *Agnes de Mille*, 40.
10. Brian Eugenio Herrera notes that *West Side Story*'s success "ultimately compelled a rising generation of young performers to train to be what would later come to be called a 'triple threat.'" In *Latin Numbers*, 114.
11. Yates, "Disability and the American Stage Musical," 268.
12. Winkler, *Big Deal*, 166.
13. Dunning, "High-Stepping into Stardom."
14. Mandelbaum notes that by 1970 there was often only one chorus comprising singer-dancers rather than separate singing and dancing ensembles. In *A Chorus Line*, 93–94.
15. Mandelbaum, *A Chorus Line*, 119.
16. Much has been written about the creation of *A Chorus Line*, and rather than repeat that here, I point readers to the following: Denny Martin Flinn, *What They Did for Love: The Untold Story Behind the Making of* A Chorus Line (New York: Bantam, 1989); Tom Rowan, A Chorus Line *FAQ: All That's Left to Know About Broadway's Singular Sensation* (New York: Applause, 2015); Gary Stevens, *The Longest Line: Broadway's Most Singular Sensation:* A Chorus Line (New York: Applause, 2000); Robert Viagas, Baayork Lee, and Thommie Walsh, *On the Line: The Creation of* A Chorus Line (New York: Limelight Editions, 1990).
17. Flinn, *What They Did for Love*, 8.

NOTES 251

18. The success of these off-Broadway workshops set new trends for developing and producing musicals off-Broadway with an eye toward Broadway, especially at the Public Theater, which later produced such notable transfers as *Caroline, or Change*; *Fun Home*; and *Hamilton*.
19. Bennett, Kirkwood, et al., *A Chorus Line*, 87.
20. mitchellivers, "A Chorus Line on Donahue 4."
21. Baayork Lee, interview with author.
22. Del Deo and Stern, *Every Little Step*.
23. mitchellivers, "A Chorus Line on Donahue 2."
24. Viagas, Lee, and Walsh, *On the Line*, 156.
25. Stevens and George, *The Longest Line*, 2.
26. mitchellivers, "A Chorus Line on Donahue 3."
27. mitchellivers, "A Chorus Line on Donahue 5."
28. Sandoval-Sánchez, *José, Can You See*, 85.
29. Sandoval-Sánchez, *José, Can You See*, 85
30. Román, *Performance in America*, 127.
31. Hoffman, *The Great White Way*, 148.
32. Hoffman, *The Great White Way*, 157.
33. Sandoval-Sánchez, *José, Can You See*, 88.
34. Mandelbaum, *A Chorus Line*, 334.
35. Papp and Turan, *Free for All*, 372.
36. Mandelbaum, *A Chorus Line*, 128.
37. Roberts, "Sammy Williams, Tony Winner in 'A Chorus Line,' Dies at 69."
38. Roberts, "Sammy Williams, Tony Winner in 'A Chorus Line,' Dies at 69."
39. Sandoval-Sánchez, *José, Can You See*, 98.
40. Goldfarb, "'A Chorus Line' Retains Its Kick to the End."
41. Baayork Lee, interview with author.
42. Mandelbaum, *A Chorus Line*, 170–171.
43. Taylor, "Singing and Dancing Ourselves," 290.
44. Mandelbaum, *A Chorus Line*, 172.
45. Kirle, *Unfinished Show Business*, 151.
46. Kelly, *One Singular Sensation*, 150.
47. *A Chorus Line* has eschewed casting stars save for a few notable exceptions: Tony Award winner Elizabeth Seal's ill-fated turn as Cassie in the original 1976 West End production, television actor Mario Lopez as Zach in the 2006 revival, and Antonio Banderas as Zach in the 2019 Malaga production. Stars disrupt the power of spectators' identification with the ultimately anonymous dancers.
48. Taylor, "Singing and Dancing Ourselves," 290.
49. Goldfarb, "'A Chorus Line' Retains Its Kick to the End."
50. Kirle, *Unfinished Show Business*, 151.
51. Baayork Lee, interview with author.
52. mitchellivers, "A Chorus Line on Donahue 3."
53. Flinn, *What They Did for Love*, 190.
54. Dembart, "22 Leap at Chance to Join 'A Chorus Line.'"

252 NOTES

55. *Backstage*, "A Chorus Line," June 27, 1975.
56. Flinn, *What They Did for Love*, 159.
57. Gelb, "Producing—and reproducing—'A Chorus Line.'"
58. *Variety*, "Legitimate: Shubert-CLO Share Subscribers for 'Chorus' & 'Wiz,' on Coast; Original 'Chorus' Cast to Tour."
59. Rowan, A Chorus Line *FAQ*, 235.
60. Holtcamp, *Interchangeable Parts*, 310.
61. Holtcamp, *Interchangeable Parts*, 310.
62. Stevens and George, *The Longest Line*, 25.
63. Baayork Lee, interview with author.
64. Stevens and George, *The Longest Line*, 21.
65. Stevens and George, *The Longest Line*, 22.
66. Stevens and George, *The Longest Line*, 167.
67. Shapiro, *Nothing Like a Dame*, 66.
68. Mandelbaum, *A Chorus Line*, 299. Co-choreographer Bob Avian also described the exhaustion of keeping the show going in his memoir, *Dancing Man*, 102.
69. Stevens and George, *The Longest Line*, 175.
70. Johnson, "Building the Broadway Voice," 477.
71. mitchellivers, "A Chorus Line on Donahue 2."
72. Mandelbaum, *A Chorus Line*, 322.
73. Gelb, "Producing—and Reproducing—'A Chorus Line.'"
74. Holtcamp, *Interchangeable Parts*, 309.
75. Del Deo and Stern, *Every Little Step*.
76. Baayork Lee, interview with author.
77. Stevens and George, *The Longest Line*, 16.
78. Shapiro, *Nothing Like a Dame*, 66.
79. Flinn, *What They Did for Love*, 184.
80. Quoted in Mandelbaum, *A Chorus Line*, 301.
81. Barnes, review of *A Chorus Line*, December 18, 1976.
82. Dembart, "22 Leap at Chance to Join 'A Chorus Line.'" The temptation to write about casting and staging the show in terms of its meta-theatricality was revived in Joshua Barone's article about the 2018 City Center production; Barone, "How 'A Chorus Line' Veterans Pass It on to a New Generation."
83. Baayork Lee, interview with author.
84. *Backstage*, "A Chorus Line" expires August 9, 2018.
85. Robertson, "'Chorus Line' Returns, as Do Regrets over Life Stories Signed Away."
86. Viagas et al., *On the Line*, 15.
87. Viagas et al., *On the Line*, 16.
88. mitchellivers, "A Chorus Line on Donahue 3."
89. Petrzela, "The Fitness Craze That Changed the Way Women Exercise."
90. Avian, interview with Roslyn Sulcas.
91. Baayork Lee, interview with author.
92. Stamberg, "Backstage of 'A Chorus Line' with Its Least Known Creator."

Chapter 2

1. Since Broadway has not cast a fat trans woman as of this writing, *woman* in this chapter refers to a cisgender woman.
2. Rich, review of *Nine*, May 10, 1982.
3. The plot is widely considered a loose re-telling of Diana Ross's replacement of Florence Ballard as the lead singer of the Supremes, something the musical's creators both denied and admitted at various times. Mary Wilson, the third member of the Supremes capitalized on the connection, calling her memoir *Dreamgirl: My Life as a Supreme.*
4. Eyen and Krieger, *Dreamgirls* Final Draft.
5. Leong, "Racial Capitalism."
6. Allen, "Dreamgirls Lights Up Broadway," 158.
7. Wann, *The Fat Studies Reader*, xii.
8. Dziemianowicz, "Baby, You're a Big Curl Now."
9. Solovay, *Tipping the Scales of Justice: Fighting Weight-Based Discrimination*, 150–151.
10. Farrell, *Fat Shame*, 18.
11. See Mobley, *Female Bodies on the American Stage*, chapter 1, for a detailed description of this process.
12. Fraser, "The Inner Corset: A Brief History of Fat in the United States," 12.
13. Shinall, "Occupational Characteristics and the Obesity Wage Penalty."
14. Forth, *Fat*, 261-62.
15. Strings, *Fearing the Black Body*, 6.
16. Strings, *Fearing the Black Body*, 212.
17. Strings, *Fearing the Black Body*, 147.
18. Paul, Hamilton, and Darity, "Discriminatory Penalties at the Intersection of Race and Gender in the United States."
19. The framing of bodies as either conforming or non-conforming is drawn from LeBesco, *Revolting Bodies*, and Kwan and Graves, *Framing Fat*.
20. Cottom, *Thick*, 47.
21. Gay, *Hunger*, 13.
22. hooks, "Continued Devaluation of Black Womanhood," 52.
23. Kwan and Graves, *Framing Fat*, 28–29.
24. King and Puhl, "Weight Bias: Does It Affect Men and Women Differently."
25. West, *Shrill*, 67–68.
26. LeBesco, *Revolting Bodies*, 6.
27. Simon, "The Feminist History of Fat Liberation."
28. Dovidio, Major, and Crocker, "Stigma: Introduction and Overview."
29. See also Crocker and M. Quinn, "Social Stigma and the Self: Meanings, Situations, and Self-esteem." Crocker and Quinn explain how the Protestant ethic of individual responsibility also affects anti-fat attitudes.
30. Kwan and Graves, *Framing Fat*, 6.

254 NOTES

31. Jennifer-Scott Mobley argues that the fat person's perceived failures are a violation of American ideals of "individual freedom and responsibility." Mobley, *Female Bodies on the American Stage*, 24.

32. Wann, *The Fat Studies Reader*, ix.

33. LeBesco, *Revolting Bodies*, 8.

34. Knapp, *The American Musical and the Formation of National Identity*, 104.

35. Most, *Making Americans*, 3.

36. Film star Rebel Wilson, best known for playing a character named "Fat Amy" in the *Pitch Perfect* film franchise, played Miss Adelaide in a 2016 West End production of *Guys and Dolls*, marking a notable departure from standard casting for the role.

37. Cottom, *Thick*, 46.

38. Marisha Wallace, interview with author.

39. Wolf, *Changed for Good*, 55.

40. Brooks, *Bodies in Dissent*, 7.

41. Brooks, *Bodies in Dissent*, 8.

42. These musicals include *Caroline, or Change, The Color Purple* (twice), *Hot Feet, 110 in the Shade* (2007 revival), *Memphis, Sister Act, The Gershwin's Porgy and Bess, Pippin* (2013 revival), *Shuffle Along . . . , Natasha, Pierre & the Great Comet of 1812, Once on This Island* (2017 revival), *Summer, King Kong, Oklahoma!* (2019 revival), *Tootsie, Tina, Jagged Little Pill*. Black women also replaced leads in Broadway musicals including *Cinderella* (KeKe Palmer), *Waitress* (Nicolette Robinson, Jordin Sparks), and *Wicked* (Brittney Johnson was the first Black woman to play Glinda on Broadway and other Black women have gone on as covers or understudies for both leading roles on Broadway and/or have played them full-time on tour).

43. Katrina Rose Dideriksen, interview with author.

44. Gioia, "Heavy Character Actress Need Not Apply?"

45. Christel and Dunn, "Average American women's clothing size."

46. Avian with Santopietro, *Dancing Man*, 117. Avian details how the role of Effie developed during the workshops alongside the tenuous relationship of Bennett and Holliday.

47. Avian with Santopietro, *Dancing Man*, 123.

48. Shapiro, "Jennifer Holliday: The Lady Does Things Her Way."

49. Holliday, interview by Mitchell.

50. Holliday, interview by Mitchell.

51. cunytv75, "Theater Talk: Jennifer Holliday."

52. Barnes, review of *Dreamgirls*, December 21, 1981.

53. Kerr, review of *Dreamgirls*, January 3, 1982.

54. Kauffman, review of *Dreamgirls*, February 1982.

55. Stanton, review of *Dreamgirls*, January 23, 1982.

56. Bailey, "Dreams Come True."

57. Rich, review of *Dreamgirls*, December 21, 1981.

58. Kerr, review of *Dreamgirls*, January 3, 1982.

59. Talcove, "'Dreamgirls' Turns into Financial Nightmare, Closes."

60. Ahmed, "'Dreamgirls' West End Review."

NOTES   255

61. Stars in the House, "Everything Effie."
62. Damien Slattery, "Dreamgirls—Audition in LA 1983—Michael Bennet & Michael Peters."
63. Stars in the House, "Everything Effie."
64. Blow, "Broadway."
65. Rich, review of *Dreamgirls*, September 23, 1983.
66. Taylor, "A Hot Roadshow Sells Its Sizzle."
67. According to those who were there, there was little love lost between Holliday and the Los Angeles company as she began missing shows and becoming difficult to work with. See Stars in the House, "Everything Effie."
68. Viertel, "Waiting in the Wings."
69. Rhetoric about who gets to count as human finds grounding in the pseudo-science of eugenics and the historic and ongoing violence of white supremacy and structural inequalities built into the United States.
70. Nachman, review of *Dreamgirls*, December 21, 1983.
71. Cassal, "Dreamgirl Lands a Hefty Role."
72. Moore, "'Dreamgirls' Tour Cast Loaded with New Talent," 55.
73. MargoChanning, "Effie White—Does She Have to Be Heavy?'"
74. MargoChanning, "Effie White—Does She Have to Be Heavy?'"
75. Rian Keating, "Roz Ryan."
76. Shirley, review of *Dreamgirls*, January 22, 1987.
77. Dinero, "A Big Black Lady Stops the Show," 39.
78. Dinero, "A Big Black Lady Stops the Show," 33.
79. Rosenthal, "Visions Dance Out of Dreamboy's Mind."
80. Gerard, "'Dreamgirls,' Revamped for Tour, Is Returning to Broadway."
81. Stephen M. Silverman, "Broadway's Dream Boy."
82. O'Haire, "Dreamgirls II."
83. *Back Stage*, "Stage Casting."
84. Johnson-Liff Casting, memorandum, 1981, Michael Bennett Papers.
85. Johnson-Liff Casting, memorandum, 1981, Michael Bennett Papers.
86. Unknown, n.d., Michael Bennett Papers. Punctuation in original.
87. "Open Call, 'Dreamgirls,'" *Backstage*, September 17, 1982.
88. Nell Carter became a Broadway star in *Ain't Misbehavin'* (1978), for which she won a Tony Award. She returned to Broadway in a 1997 revival of *Annie* as the spinster villain Miss Hannigan, making her the rare former Effie to play a lead on Broadway again.
89. *Back Stage*, "CASTING-EQUITY STAGE."
90. Reimers, "'She's too Big I Hope for Me to Compass.'"
91. Stars in the House, "Everything Effie."
92. Stars in the House, "Everything Effie."
93. Damien Slattery, "Lillias White—Dreamgirls—1983."
94. Stars in the House, "Everything Effie."
95. Aldredge, *Dreamgirls* designs and script.
96. Hulbert, "Tony Winner Returns in 'Dreamgirls.'"
97. Holliday, interview with Hughes.

256 NOTES

98. Newmark, "Holliday to Reprise 'Dreamgirls' Role at Muny."
99. Fat Black Women Have Fared Better Landing Leading or Featured Parts in Revues including *Ain't Misbehavin'*, *Black and Blue*, and *Smokey Joe's Café*.
100. MargoChanning, "Effie White—Does She Have to Be Heavy?'"
101. Broadway World, "DREAMGIRLS—Broadway Theatre TBA Auditions."
102. Eric Woodall, interview with author.
103. Eric Woodall, interview with author. These actors' concerns echoed those who eventually played Effie in the original production, too, but had hoped to play Lorell.
104. Marisha Wallace, interview with author.
105. Gajewski, "Glee's Amber Riley: Casting Directors Told Me to Lose Weight."
106. msamberpriley, Instagram, May 21, 2016, https://www.instagram.com/p/BFqH ejcM_8J/.
107. Snow, "Amber Riley Misses Dreamgirls Performances after Being Diagnosed with Pneumonia."
108. Marisha Wallace, interview with author.
109. BWW News Desk, "Marisha Wallace, Moya Angela, Karen Mav, and More Join DREAMGIRLS."
110. Ellis, interview with Bailey.
111. Dinero, "A Big Black Lady Stops the Show."

Chapter 3

1. Bosworth, "The Fight to Save 'Seesaw.'"
2. Avian with Santopietro, *Dancing Man*, 77.
3. Bosworth, "The Fight to Save 'Seesaw.'"
4. Avian with Santopietro, *Dancing Man*, 76.
5. Bosworth, "The Fight to Save 'Seesaw.'"
6. Avian with Santopietro, *Dancing Man*, 77.
7. Kazan, letter to the editor.
8. Klein, "Lainie Kazan Goes Back to Her Roots."
9. In the early twentieth century, fat actor Marie Dressler starred on Broadway in musical comedies like *Tillie's Nightmare* (1910) and in variety performances where her size transgressed the era's bodily norms. See Maya Cantu, "From the 1870s through World War I: The Spectre and Spectacle of the Human Body," in *The Routledge Companion to Musical Theatre*, edited by Ryan Donovan and Laura MacDonald (London: Routledge, forthcoming).
10. Powers et al., *Do Black Patent Leather Shoes Really Reflect Up?*, 23.
11. Powers et al., *Do Black Patent Leather Shoes Really Reflect Up?*, 23–24.
12. Blackwell et al., *The Tap Dance Kid*, 17.
13. Allard became a television producer as an adult but she did perform in the Westchester Broadway Theatre's 2019 production of *Ain't Misbehavin'* in Nell Carter's track—one of the only other few roles available to fat Black women. When

NOTES 257

City Center Encores revived the musical in 2022, they inexplicably revised Allard's role and cast it with a thin actress, omitting the word "fat" from the song.

14. Mobley, "Staging Fat," 156.
15. "Grease," Samuel French, https://www.samuelfrench.com/p/2155/grease, accessed August 12, 2019.
16. Original Broadway Cast, "It Ain't No Thing," 2012, track 13 on *Bring It On: The Musical.*
17. Beresford, "Olaf Gets Gender Swap in Disney's 'Frozen' on Broadway."
18. Dodson, "'Mean Girls' Musical Has a New Regina George in 19-Year-Old Renee Rapp."
19. McElroy, "A Vulnerable Center-Stage Moment."
20. Pogrebin, "Lisa Howard on Her Latest Broadway Show."
21. Broadway World, "IT SHOULDA BEEN YOU—Broadway Theatre TBA Auditions."
22. Quoted in Brantley, review of *It Shoulda Been You*, April 14, 2015. See also Dinero, "Big Black Lady."
23. "Keala Settle," *Theater People* podcast.
24. Yates, "How Maori Actress Keala Settle Became the Heart of a Hollywood Blockbuster."
25. Collins-Hughes, review of *Smokey Joe's Café*, July 22, 2018.
26. Alysha Umphress, Twitter post, July 23, 2018, 11:35 A.M., https://twitter.com/Crist alzheat/status/1021418512219344902.
27. O'Donnell et al., *Hairspray: The Roots*, 5.
28. Craig Burns, interview with author.
29. O'Donnell et al., *Hairspray: The Complete Book and Lyrics of the Hit Broadway Musical*, xv.
30. O'Donnell et al., *Hairspray: The Complete Book and Lyrics of the Hit Broadway Musical*, 14.
31. Waters, "Finally, Footlights on the Fat Girls." *Hairspray* was a known commodity before it became a musical; Waters's source film was a surprise hit and his biggest mainstream success. The film used casting to attract film audiences by using not just television stars Jerry Stiller and Sonny Bono but popular musicians Debbie Harry and Ruth Brown alongside Waters regulars Divine and Mink Stole.
32. Malykhina, "Sizing Them Up."
33. Craig Burns, interview with author.
34. "Keala Settle," *Theater People* podcast.
35. Pacheco, "Water's 'Hairspray' Is Beginning to Gel."
36. Craig Burns, email to author, September 29, 2017.
37. Craig Burns, interview with author.
38. Celebrity Radio by Alex Belfield, "Hairspray The Musical on Broadway—Tracy Turnblad Kathy Brier."
39. Kathy Deitch, interview with author.
40. Celebrity Radio by Alex Belfield, "Hairspray The Musical on Broadway—Tracy Turnblad Kathy Brier."

258   NOTES

41. O'Donnell et al., *Hairspray: The Complete Book and Lyrics of the Hit Broadway Musical*, 3; Mobley, *Female Bodies on the American Stage*, 107.
42. O'Donnell et al., *Hairspray: The Complete Book and Lyrics of the Hit Broadway Musical*, 123.
43. Jones, "Welcome to the '60s."
44. Green, "Good Hair Days."
45. O'Donnell et al., *Hairspray: The Roots*, 12.
46. Gottschild, *The Black Dancing Body*, 21.
47. Dinero, "A Big Black Lady Stops the Show." The song also references "And I Am Telling You . . ." as it calls attention to the convention.
48. Waters, *Mr. Know-It-All*, 31.
49. O'Donnell et al., *Hairspray: The Roots*, 142.
50. *Variety*, "Spotlight: *Hairspray*."
51. Craig Burns, interview with author.
52. O'Donnell et al., *Hairspray: The Roots*, 38.
53. Malykhina, "Sizing Them Up."
54. Malykhina, "Sizing Them Up."
55. Katrina Rose Dideriksen, interview with author.
56. Katrina Rose Dideriksen, interview with author.
57. Waters, *Mr. Know-It-All*, 41.
58. LeBesco, "Situating Fat Suits," 237.
59. Craig Burns, interview with author.
60. Weinstein, "Worth the Weight."
61. O'Donnell et al., *Hairspray: The Roots*, 9.
62. Brier, interview with Cox.
63. Solovay, *Tipping the Scales of Justice*, 160–161.
64. Pogrebin, "Big Hair and Personality to Match."
65. O'Donnell et al., *Hairspray: The Roots*, 39.
66. "Keala Settle," *Theater People* podcast.
67. Katrina Rose Dideriksen, interview with author.
68. Katrina Rose Dideriksen, interview with author.
69. Burns notes that *Jersey Boys* needed to be sure they had on hand enough actors to play Frankie Valli, while *Hamilton*'s choreography requires dancers fluent in the show's multiple styles. *Billy Elliott* needed to train its young dancers to suit the dance demands of the show.
70. San Pablo Burns, " 'How in the Light of One Night Did We Come So Far?,'" 126–131.
71. Craig Burns, interview with author.
72. Katrina Rose Dideriksen, interview with author.
73. Craig Burns, interview with author.
74. Katrina Rose Dideriksen, interview with author.
75. The two exceptions were actors who played and/or understudied Elphaba in *Wicked*: Shoshana Bean and Donna Vivino. Vivino understudied several other roles in addition to Tracy. "About," ShoshanaBean.com, accessed September 4, 2019, https://

www.shoshanabean.com/#about; "Home," DonnaVivino.com, accessed October 16, 2017, http://www.donnavivino.com/.

76. Quinn, "How Broadway Icon Jennifer Holliday Overcame Depression, Body Issues and Temporary Blindness to Stage a Comeback in *The Color Purple*."

77. *People*, "Marissa Jaret Winokur: I Had to Call in Fat."

78. Pogrebin, "Big Hair and Personality to Match."

79. According to a 2016 study, the average size is higher than 14 and is 16 to 18. See Christel and Dunn, "Average American Women's Clothing Size."

80. Gioia, "'Heavy Character Actresses' Need Not Apply?"

81. This data is for the 2015–2016 season. *The Broadway League*, "Research Reports."

82. Gioia, "Is Weight Just a Number?"

83. Humansofbroadway, *Instagram*, May 26, 2017, https://www.instagram.com/p/BUkp lHyhoVg/?taken-by=humansofbroadway&hl=en.

84. Marisha Wallace, interview with author.

85. Shinall, "Occupational Characteristics and the Obesity Wage Penalty."

86. Wann, *The Fat Studies Reader*, xiv.

87. Kathy Deitch, interview with author.

88. Kathy Deitch, interview with author.

89. awardscrazy, "Marissa Jaret Winokur Wins 2003 Tony Award for Best Actress in a Musical."

90. Craig Burns, interview with author.

91. Broadwaycom, "Show People with Paul Wontorek Interview: Tony Winner Marissa Jaret Winokur of 'Hairspray.'"

92. Brantley, review of *Hairspray*, August 16, 2002.

93. Bonnie Milligan, Twitter Post, September 6, 2018, 1:18 P.M., https://twitter.com/beltin gbonnie/status/1037752011335376896?s=11.

94. Snook, "Big, Blonde and Beautiful in Her Broadway Debut."

95. LeBesco, "Situating Fat Suits," 238.

96. LeBesco, *Revolting Bodies*, 63.

97. Bennett, interview with Gruen, *After Dark*.

Chapter 4

1. Wetzsteon, "'La Cage aux Folles' Comes to Broadway."

2. Laurents, interview with Behrens.

3. *Time*, "How Gay Is Gay? Homosexual Men and Women Are Making Progress Toward Equality."

4. Harvey Fierstein's *Torch Song Trilogy* made the improbable leap from off-off-Broadway to off-Broadway and finally to the Main Stem in 1982; it won the Tony Award for Best Play and ran for 1,222 performances, making it the first long-running "gay play."

260 NOTES

5. Michael Bronksi notes, "Who can come out and who remains closeted raises the important issues of what and how society allows gay artists to create, how this informs the creations, and how this affects gay sensibility. An interesting measure of social tolerance is the ratio of actual homosexuality portrayed on the stage to the number of gay people involved in the theater, and the appearance of covert aspects of gay sensibility in popular plays." *Culture Clash*, 111.

6. Novick, review of *La Cage aux Folles*, September 6, 1983.

7. Hofler, "What's in a Kiss?"

8. Hoffman, introduction to *Gay Plays: The First Collection*, xix.

9. Wolf, *A Problem Like Maria*, viii.

10. In this chapter, I deliberately use "gay" and "homosexual" rather than "queer" in order to reflect the terminology used during the time of *La Cage*'s initial Broadway run.

11. Wolf, *A Problem Like Maria*, 12.

12. Clum, *Something for the Boys*, 10. "Bridge and tunnel crowd" of course is its own stereotype.

13. Miller, *Place for Us*, 132.

14. Schulman, *Stage Struck*, 147.

15. Wollman, *Hard Times*, 72.

16. Laurents, *On Directing*, 115.

17. Schildcrout, "Drama and the New Sexualities," 456. Three other plays also precipitated the raid: Parisian import *The Captive*, West's *Sex*, and *The Virgin Man*, an import from London, all of which dealt with subjects that were risqué if not outright taboo.

18. Curtin, "Stopping the Captive's Pale Brethren in Their Tracks: The 1927 Broadway Show Raid," in *"We Can Always Call Them Bulgarians.*

19. Schildcrout, "Drama and the New Sexualities," 456.

20. Miller, " 'Sing Me a Song with Social Significance.' "

21. Kirle, *Unfinished Show Business*, 178.

22. Wollman, *A Critical Companion to the American Stage Musical*, 166.

23. Wollman, *Hard Times*, 52.

24. Hugh Ryan, Twitter post, June 28, 2020, 10:56 A.M., https://twitter.com/Hugh_Ryan/status/1277254491851698184.

25. Barnes, review of *Ain't Supposed to Die a Natural Death*, October 21, 1971.

26. Wolf, *A Problem like Maria*, 4.

27. While there was no lesbian representation in narratives, there were lesbian performers; notably, Ethel Waters was a Black lesbian blues singer and high-paid Broadway star in the 1930s and 1940s, but because of the era when she lived, she remained publicly closeted since coming out would have been career suicide.

28. Miller, " 'Sing Me a Song with Social Significance.' "

29. Kirle, *Unfinished Show Business*, 179.

30. Avian with Santopietro, *Dancing Man*, 79.

31. Tune, *Footnotes*, 51.

32. Bennetts, "Harvey Fierstein's Long Journey to the Tony and Beyond."

33. Herman and Fierstein, *La Cage aux Folles*, 28–29.

NOTES 261

34. Rich, review of *La Cage Aux Folles*, August 22, 1983.
35. Chomsky and Barclay, "The Editor, the Publisher, and His Mother," 1392. The owners of the *Times* suppressed LGBTQ+ content until 1987.
36. Novick, review of *La Cage aux Folles*, September 6, 1983.
37. Miller, review of *La Cage aux Folles*, September 12, 1983.
38. Grumley, review of *La Cage aux Folles*, September 26, 1983.
39. Bronski, *Culture Clash*, 197.
40. D'Emilio, *Rewriting History*, 11.
41. D'Emilio, *The World Turned*, 69.
42. Walters, *All the Rage*, 37.
43. Clarke, "Broadway."
44. "Our Timeline," NYC Pride.
45. Duggan, *The Twilight of Equality*, xvii.
46. Laurents, *Mainly on Directing*, 121.
47. Bennetts, "Here Comes the Musical 'La Cage.'"
48. Senelick, *The Changing Room*, 433. Senelick's description appears to apply to those who benefited from gay liberation without actually participating in the movement itself.
49. Laurents, *Mainly on Directing*, 115.
50. Herman with Stasio, *Showtune*, 233.
51. Stein, "Tony Winner Aldredge Talks Tricks of the Trade."
52. Román, *Acts of Intervention*, 99–100.
53. Bennetts, "Harvey Fierstein's Long Journey."
54. Laurents, *The Rest of the Story*, 91.
55. Schulman, *The Gentrification of the Mind*, 40.
56. Bennetts, "Here Comes the Musical 'La Cage.'"
57. Laurents, *Mainly on Directing*, 121.
58. Hofler, "What's in a Kiss?"
59. *The Fabulous Allan Carr*.
60. Laurents, interview with Sandler.
61. Walters, *All the Rage*, 54.
62. Falk, *Stigma*, 68.
63. Joe Windish, "Harvey Fierstein 1983: Torch Song, Letterman & La Cage."
64. Howard, interview with Thomas and Schneider.
65. Barry Brown, interview with author.
66. D. A. Miller theorizes that the closet hides the open secret that everyone already knows more than it closets homosexuality. Miller, *The Novel and the Police*.
67. Howard, interview with Thomas and Schneider.
68. See Laurents, *Original Story By*, 358, for a description of how Jerome Robbins taunted Kert for being openly gay during rehearsals of *West Side Story*.
69. Bennetts, "How Stars of 'La Cage' Grew into Their Roles."
70. Bennetts, "How Stars of 'La Cage' Grew into Their Roles."
71. Quoted in Hart, "The Selling of La Cage aux Folles," 15.
72. Stern, "The Real Gals in 'La Cage aux Folles' Admit That It Ain't Such a Drag!"

262 NOTES

73. This problem persists with greater frequency in film and on television. There are at least ten straight actors who have won Academy Awards for playing LGBTQ characters.
74. Schulman, *Ties That Bind*, 22.
75. Bennetts, "How Stars of 'La Cage' Grew into Their Roles."
76. Clarke, "Broadway Out of the Closet," 64-65.
77. Nelsen, "A First Peek Inside 'La Cage aux Folles.'"
78. Chambers, "Gene Barry Sings His Love Songs to a Man."
79. Burden, "Gene Barry Takes Roles in Good Stride."
80. Bennetts, "How Stars of 'La Cage' Grew into Their Roles."
81. Burden, "Marshall's No Square."
82. Quoted in Senelick, *The Changing Room*, 502.
83. Gill, review of *La Cage aux Folles*, September 5, 1983.
84. Brustein, review of *La Cage aux Folles*, September 19, 1983.
85. Senelick, *The Changing Room*, 502.
86. Zailan, "'La Cage' Stars Play It Straight."
87. Zailan, "'La Cage' Stars Play It Straight."
88. Barry Brown, interview with author.
89. Herrera, "The Best Actor for the Role."
90. For more on the history of the stigmatization of male dancers in Western Europe and its spread to the United States, see Burt, *The Male Dancer*.
91. Foster, "Closets Full of Dances," 169, 160.
92. Quoted in Winkler, *Big Deal*, 176.
93. David Engel, interview with author.
94. Clum, *Something for the Boys*, 201.
95. Hofler, *Party Animals*, 149-150.
96. Hofler, *Party Animals*, 150.
97. Wetzsteon, "'La Cage aux Folles.'"
98. Stern, "Real Gals."
99. *Variety*, "La Cage aux Folles."
100. Barry Brown, interview with author.
101. Shirley Herz & Associates, Press Release for national tour of *La Cage Aux Folles*, n.d., Theatre Collection, New York Public Library.
102. Newman, "Speaking of Dance: Scott Salmon," 703.
103. Stern, "Real Gals."
104. David Engel, interview with author.
105. Senelick, *The Changing Room*, 502.
106. White, "Four Geniuses, Gone to AIDS, as They Might Be Today."
107. Barry Brown, interview with author.
108. TimesSquared, "La Cage Aux Folles 1987 Tour."
109. Gallup, "Gay and Lesbian Rights."
110. David Engel, interview with author.
111. Deschamps and Singer, *LGBTQ Stats*, 44. This case referred to here is Bowers v. Hardwick.

NOTES 263

112. Lopez, "The Reagan Administration's Unbelievable Response to the HIV/AIDS Epidemic."
113. Gross, *Up from Invisibility*, 101.
114. Barry Brown, interview with author.
115. Laurents, *The Rest of the Story*, 91.
116. Kantor, *Broadway*.
117. Hofler, *Party Animals*, 175.
118. *La Cage aux Folles* program, Playhouse Theatre, 2008.
119. Kantor, *Broadway*.
120. *New York Times*, "George W. Holt 3d, Producer."
121. Tune, *Footnotes*, 46.
122. TimesSquared, "La Cage Aux Folles 1987 Tour."
123. Miller, *Place for Us*, 131.
124. Laurents, interview with Nesmith, 7–16.
125. Herman, interview with *Playbill*.
126. Kroll, "Broadway Glitters."
127. Connolly, "The Sex Is in the Heel." Punctuation in original.
128. Fierstein, interview, August 8, 2003.
129. Schulman, *Ties That Bind*, 5.
130. Laurents, interview with David Behrens.
131. John Clonts Scottsdale Arizona Real Estate Agent, "The Making of La Cage."
132. Zara, "It's 2019."
133. Hofler, *Party Animals*, 164.

Chapter 5

1. MissPoochSmooch, "2000 Tony Awards ~ COMPLETE."
2. Quoted in Abramovitch, "Nathan Lane Recalls 'Terrifying' Moment Oprah Tried to Out Him."
3. Dolan, "Practicing Cultural Disruptions," 337.
4. Eden Espinosa, Instagram post, June 7, 2020, https://www.instagram.com/p/CBJMx0Cnkc9/?igshid=hqfy1pbmbk3q. Espinosa's post features a screenshot of Broadway theatre owner James M. Nederlander's contributions totaling over $150,000 to Donald Trump's 2016 campaign.
5. For more on gay male culture and musicals, see Clum, *Something for the Boys*, and Miller, *Place for Us*.
6. For an overview, see Faderman, *The Gay Revolution*.
7. De la Garza, " 'Don't Ask, Don't Tell.' "
8. Straube, "R.I.P. Broadway Legend Jerry Herman."
9. Gay topics had been seen more regularly off-Broadway since the late 1960s, in plays like Mart Crowley's *The Boys in the Band* (1968) and Larry Kramer's *The Normal Heart* (1985) and at off-off-Broadway venues that produced queer work like Caffe

264 NOTES

Cino and LaMaMa Experimental Theatre Club. Lesbian characters were seen in notable off-Broadway plays like Maria Irene Fornés's *Fefu and Her Friends* (1977) and Jane Chambers's *Last Summer at Bluefish Clove* (1980).

10. There were many more off-Broadway musicals with gay and lesbian characters, especially in the 1970s. See Wollman, *Hard Times*.

11. Kuchwara, review of *Flower Drum Song*, October 16, 2002.

12. Rodgers and Hammerstein's 1953 musical *Me and Juliet* also featured a song titled "Keep It Gay," whose verse is clearly a double entendre about a "Don Juan" who refuses to marry. The chorus follows in which he implores, "Keep it gay."

13. Rich, review of *Grand Hotel*, November 13, 1989.

14. Anderson, "'Something Bad [Was] Happening.'"

15. For more, see Kregloe, "The Problematic History of Lesbians in Musical Theater."

16. Rado, interview with Lambert.

17. Whitfield, "A Space Has Been Made."

18. *Hedwig* creators John Cameron Mitchell and Stephen Trask have explicitly said that Hedwig is not trans, so I do not include Hedwig here.

19. Donovan, "If You Were Gay, That'd Be Okay."

20. Vincentelli, "The Boys in the Band Get to Broadway."

21. Altman, "AIDS Is Now the Leading Killer of Americans from 25 to 44."

22. According to the UN, more than 32,000,000 people have died of AIDS. UNAIDS, "Global HIV & AIDS statistics—2020 fact sheet."

23. See Lopez, "The Reagan Administration's Unbelievable Response to the HIV/AIDS Epidemic."

24. Gonsalves and Staley, "Panic, Paranoia, and Public Health," 2348–2349.

25. Shewey, "The Musical According to Bennett."

26. *New York Times*. "David Carroll Is Dead; A Broadway Actor, 41."

27. Kurth, "Michael Jeter Takes on Hollywood."

28. Kurth, "Michael Jeter Takes on Hollywood."

29. Kurth, "Michael Jeter Takes on Hollywood."

30. Actors' Equity Association, too, requires every Broadway production to post a bond for the actors' salaries in case the production suddenly folds, and insuring a production becomes more expensive depending upon the level of risk determined by the insurer. However, there is no evidence that producers would not hire gay men because of AIDS stigma.

31. Shapiro, *Wonderful Guy*, 75.

32. Several Broadway plays addressed AIDS: *Prelude to a Kiss* (1988), *Eastern Standard* (1989), *Angels in America* (1993), and *Love! Valour! Compassion!* (1995). Off-Broadway featured many plays and musicals dealing with AIDS during the era, and both of these musicals began off-Broadway themselves. On Broadway, the musical *The Life* (1997) also hinted at AIDS without directly addressing it.

33. See Schulman's *Stage Struck* for more on *Rent*'s appropriation of queer cultures (and her own writing).

34. Savran, "*Rent*'s Due."

35. Schulman, *Stage Struck*, 134.

NOTES 265

36. Shaw, "*The Book of Mormon* and *Hamilton* Already Feel Like They're from Another Time."
37. Román, *Acts of Intervention*, 275.
38. Crimp, *Melancholia and Moralism*, 17.
39. The 2021 biomusical *Diana* featured a scene where the Princess of Wales visited gay men in an AIDS ward of a London hospital, but the less said about it, the better.
40. Burns, "The Gay and Transgender Wage Gap."
41. Sedgwick, *Epistemology of the Closet*, 68.
42. Broadwaycom, "Broadway Legend Tommy Tune on 55 Years in the Biz."
43. Clippety, "Harvey Fierstein with Barbara Walters on 20/20 (1983)."
44. McNally, *Selected Works*, 359–360.
45. Hofler, *Party Animals*, 157.
46. Hofler, *Party Animals*, 158.
47. Hofler, *Party Animals*, 158.
48. Shapiro, *Wonderful Guy*, 110.
49. Everett, interview with Cadwalladr.
50. Hickey, interview by Wontorek.
51. Shewey, "The It Boy."
52. Weber, "A Minimalist Actor Now Warns to Excess."
53. Quoted in Cooper, " 'Anyone Should Be Able to Play Hedwig.' "
54. Rapp, interview with Walsh.
55. DeLaria, interview with Gushue.
56. DeLaria, interview with Gushue.
57. See Haplology Kloof, " 'Come Up to My Place'—On the Town (Broadway Revival, 1998)."
58. Brantley, review of *On the Town*, August 18, 1997.
59. Nassour, "Here Comes Lea DeLaria in *On the Town*."
60. Broadwaycom, "Show People with Paul Wontorek: 'Kinky Boots' Star Billy Porter on Life as a Diva."
61. Kirkland, "Billy Porter Arrived a Long Time Ago."
62. Broadwaycom, "Show People with Paul Wontorek: 'Kinky Boots' Star Billy Porter on Life as a Diva."
63. Porter, "The First Time I Refused to Keep Playing a Stereotype."
64. Musto, "Drag Queens and Gay Sex Back on Broadway Where They Belong!"
65. Fierstein, *I Was Better Last Night*, 288.
66. Fierstein, *I Was Better Last Night*, 317.
67. Kirle, *Unfinished Show Business*, 198.
68. Kirle, *Unfinished Show Business*, 199–200.
69. This is why the 2018 Broadway revival/premiere of *The Boys in the Band* was notable—because it cast all openly gay actors as the show's gay characters.
70. Fierstein, interview with McKinley.
71. Jackman, interview with Green.
72. Brantley, review of *Fiddler on the Roof*, January 21, 2005.
73. Fierstein, interview with Haskins and Riedel.

266 NOTES

74. Rooney, review of *Fiddler on the Roof*, October 13, 2005.
75. For more, see Thomas, "The Pink Elephant in the Room."
76. Sternbergh, "Ladies and Gentlemen."
77. Fierstein, *I Was Better Last Night*, 294.
78. *La Cage aux Folles* program, Playhouse Theatre, 2008.
79. theatertalk, "Harvey Fierstein Discusses 'La Cage aux Folles.'"
80. Creel, interview with Sturner.
81. Llana, interview with Thirsty.
82. Llana, interview with Hicklin.
83. Collela, interview with Piccoli.
84. Malone, interview with Hetrick.
85. Carley, "Peppermint Is Turning Broadway on Its Head."
86. Billings, interview with McPhee.
87. Peikert, "With Her 12th Broadway Show."
88. Peikert, "Broadway's Christian Dante White."
89. Muñoz, interview with Gutierrez.
90. Muñoz, interview with Brodesser-Akner.
91. Padgett, "André De Shields."
92. Porter, "Billy Porter Breaks a 14-Year Silence."
93. Actors' Equity Association, "Diversity Report: 2016–2019 in Review." Nationally, the figure was 7.92 percent. The actual numbers may be lower since the study reported the number of contracts rather than the number of individuals; an individual may have received several contracts during the years of the survey.
94. Jones, "LGBT Identification."
95. Tiwary, David, and Price, "Impact and Action."
96. Newell, interview by Pham.
97. *Backstage* "'Kinky Boots,' B'way."
98. *Backstage*, "'Kinky Boots' Nonunion National Tour."
99. Forth, *Fat*, 268.
100. Coven, "There's a Place for Us . . . Somewhere," 140.
101. Whitesel, *Fat Gay Men*, 146.
102. McRuer, *Crip Theory*, 29.
103. Ben Bogen, Twitter post, March 8, 2021, 8:59 P.M., https://twitter.com/BogenBen/status/1369105622898270211.

Chapter 6

1. "Bruce Hlibok," deafpeople.com. Before Hlibok, Nannette Fabray.
2. Eder, review of *Runaways*, May 15, 1978.
3. Lim, "At the Intersection of Deaf and Asian American Performativity," 26.
4. Knapp, "Waitin' for the Light to Shine," 815.

NOTES 267

5. Lim, "Silence, Gesture, and Deaf Identity in Deaf West Theatre's *Spring Awakening*." Lim explains that the show's use of ASL challenged "how audiences *hear* and *listen*."

6. A note on terminology: throughout the chapter I use Deaf (with a capitalized D) to refer to people/communities who identify as Deaf or hard-of-hearing; deaf (lower-case d) refers to the physical condition of deafness. I use d/Deaf to be inclusive of both.

7. Davis, *Enforcing Normalcy*, xiii.

8. Pratt, "Arts of the Contact Zone," 4.

9. Arden, "Director's Note," 18.

10. Davis, *Bending over Backward*, 37.

11. Bauman and Murray, "Deaf Studies in the 21st Century," 234.

12. Deaf West Theatre, "Deaf West's Spring Awakening: Casting Call."

13. Deaf West Theatre, "Deaf West Theatre."

14. Roundabout Theatre Company *Upstage*, "Waiting for the Light," 1.

15. Stephanie Lim theorizes that DWSA crosses what scholar Christopher Krentz calls the "hearing line," since it "exposes, challenges, and reconsiders the hierarchical positions of the Deaf/hearing worlds at the hearing line" as it aims to "bridge the gap between the two worlds." In "Silence, Gesture, and Deaf Identity in Deaf West Theatre's *Spring Awakening*."

16. Roundabout Theatre Company *Upstage*, "Waiting for the Light."

17. Cramer, *Creating Musical Theatre*, 55.

18. Davis, *Enforcing Normalcy*, 20.

19. Paulson, "Lights, Gestures, Action!"

20. Kurs, "American Sign Language."

21. Deaf West Theatre, "Deaf West's Spring Awakening: Casting Call."

22. *Backstage*, "Spring Awakening," 2014.

23. *Backstage*, "Spring Awakening," 2015.

24. Beth Lipari, interview with author.

25. HuffPost Live, "'Spring Awakening' Interview: Daniel Durant, Alex Boniello and D.J. Kurs."

26. HuffPost Live, "'Spring Awakening' Interview: Daniel Durant, Alex Boniello and D.J. Kurs."

27. Beth Lipari, interview with author.

28. DWSA [CC] Videos, "DWSA's 'Broadway Backstory' Episode."

29. Deaf West Theatre, "Deaf West's Spring Awakening: Casting Call."

30. Talks at Google, "Spring Awakening (Broadway revival cast) | Talks at Google."

31. HuffPost Live, "'Spring Awakening' Interview: Daniel Durant, Alex Boniello and DJ Kurs."

32. DWSA [CC] Videos, "DWSA's 'Broadway Backstory' Episode."

33. *Backstage*, "Spring Awakening," 2015.

34. Collins-Hughes, "'Spring Awakening' Revival Requires Signing."

35. Fox, "All It Took Was a Text!"

36. Frank, "Deafness."

268 NOTES

37. Garberoglio, Cawthon, and Bond, "Deaf People and Employment in the United States: 2016."

38. Mark Medoff's 1980 play *Children of a Lesser God* has played Broadway twice and did cast d/Deaf actors as d/Deaf characters. *DWSA* star Marlee Matlin made her name starring in the 1986 film version, winning an Academy Award in the process. Sam Gold's 2019 *King Lear* featured Russell Harvard as the Duke of Cornwall and Michael Arden as his interpreter.

39. Roundabout Theatre Company *Upstage*, "Waiting for the Light."

40. Deaf West Theatre, "Deaf West's Spring Awakening: Casting Call."

41. Arden, interview with Davenport.

42. DWSA [CC] Videos, "DWSA's 'Broadway Backstory' Episode."

43. Arden, interview with Davenport.

44. Liff, interview with Davenport.

45. Liff, interview with Davenport.

46. Seth Rudetsky, "Camryn Manheim Talks Career & Spring Awakening on Seth Speaks."

47. Liff, interview with Davenport.

48. Wilbur, "Gestural Economies and Production Pedagogies in Deaf West's Spring Awakening," 152.

49. Arden, interview with Davenport.

50. DWSA [CC] Videos, "DWSA's 'Broadway Backstory' Episode."

51. Arden, "Director's Note," 18.

52. Talks at Google, "Spring Awakening (Broadway revival cast) | Talks at Google."

53. Talks at Google, "Spring Awakening (Broadway revival cast) | Talks at Google."

54. Talks at Google, "Spring Awakening (Broadway revival cast) | Talks at Google."

55. Sater, *A Purple Summer*, 16.

56. Sater, *A Purple Summer*, 9.

57. Steketee, NEA Roundtable Report, 20.

58. HuffPost Live, "'Spring Awakening' Interview: Daniel Durant, Alex Boniello and D.J. Kurs."

59. Sater, *A Purple Summer*, 85.

60. Fierberg, "After Endless Hours, Spencer Liff Formed a New Language."

61. Seth Rudetsky, "Tony Nominated Director Michael Arden on Seth Speaks."

62. Talks at Google, "Spring Awakening (Broadway revival cast) | Talks at Google."

63. Seth Rudetsky, "Camryn Manheim Talks Career & Spring Awakening on Seth Speaks."

64. Bradford, "The National Theatre of the Deaf," 90.

65. See Lim, "Silence, Gesture, and Deaf Identity in Deaf West Theatre's *Spring Awakening*" for an in-depth close reading of how Arden and Liff staged the production foregrounding multiple failures of communication between the characters.

66. *Spring Awakening, Playbill*, "A Note about the ASL Translation," 18.

67. Isherwood, review of *Spring Awakening*, September 27, 2015.

68. Rooney, review of *Spring Awakening*, September 27, 2015.

69. Green, review of *Spring Awakening*, September 27, 2015.

70. Kolb, "*Spring Awakening* and the Power of Inclusive Art."

NOTES 269

71. Epstein and Needham, "Spring Awakening on Broadway: Deaf Viewers Give Their Verdict."
72. Rozentsvit, "How Broadway's New *Spring Awakening* Is Resonating for a Deaf Theatre Lover."
73. *DeafDigest* (blog), "DeafDigest Mid-Week edition, October 23, 2015."
74. Davenport, "Why I'm Producing Deaf West's Spring Awakening on Broadway. (Updated 2018.)"
75. *Spring Awakening* Grosses, *Playbill*.
76. Deaf West Theatre, "Deaf West Theatre Presents Spring Awakening," Kickstarter.
77. Deaf West Theatre, "Deaf West Theatre Presents Spring Awakening," Kickstarter.
78. DWSA [CC] Videos, "DWSA's 'Broadway Backstory' Episode."
79. Deaf West Theatre, "Deaf West Theatre's Spring Awakening Tony Performance," Kickstarter.
80. Seth Rudetsky, "Tony Nominated Director Michael Arden on Seth Speaks."
81. Deaf West Theatre, "Deaf West Theatre's Spring Awakening Tony Performance," Kickstarter. In return for donating, one could receive a mention on social media or, for $1,000, "an Interpreting/Translation Mentoring Session OR Learn Part of the Spring Awakening Translation Session with one of our ASL Masters and swing Elizabeth Greene (in person in LA or via Skype)!" $8,500 would buy lunch with star Marlee Matlin, while $10,000 would grant access to *DWSA*'s Tony Awards party in New York.
82. Cook, *Building Character*, 136.
83. HuffPost Live, "'Spring Awakening' Interview: Daniel Durant, Alex Boniello and D.J. Kurs."
84. DWSA, [CC] Videos, "DWSA's 'Broadway Backstory' Episode."
85. Cook, *Building Character*, 135.
86. Steketee, NEA Roundtable Report, 7.
87. Steketee, NEA Roundtable Report, 12.
88. Steketee, NEA Roundtable Report, 13.
89. Steketee, NEA Roundtable Report, 13.
90. Richardson, "The Sign Language Interpreted Performance," 63.
91. Richardson, "The Sign Language Interpreted Performance," 67.
92. Richardson, "The Sign Language Interpreted Performance," 70.
93. DWSA [CC] Videos, "DWSA's 'Broadway Backstory' Episode."
94. Beth Lipari, interview with author.
95. Beth Lipari, interview with author.
96. DWSA [CC] Videos, "DWSA's 'Broadway Backstory' Episode."
97. Steketee, NEA Roundtable Report, 28.

Chapter 7

1. *The Fabulous Invalid* is the name of a 1938 play by George S. Kaufman and Moss Hart. Though disabilities can be both visible and invisible, in this chapter I use the term *disability* to refer to visible disabilities. Lennard J. Davis explains in *The End of Normal*, 37, "In an ableist culture disability can't just *be*—it has to *mean* something."

270 NOTES

2. Yates, "Disability and the American Stage Musical," 265.
3. See Savran, "You've Got That Thing."
4. Markel, "The Painful Life of Cole Porter," 47.
5. Willson, *"But He Doesn't Know the Territory,"* 28. *Spastic,* as used by Willson, likely refers to cerebral palsy.
6. Willson, *"But He Doesn't Know the Territory,"* 58. *Retarded* was the word commonly used to describe intellectual disabilities at the time.
7. Willson, *"But He Doesn't Know the Territory,"* 90.
8. Willson, *"But He Doesn't Know the Territory,"* 99.
9. Willson, *"But He Doesn't Know the Territory,"* 101.
10. Knapp, "Waitin' for the Light to Shine," 818.
11. Sandahl. "The Difference Disability Makes," 89.
12. Siebers, *Disability Theory,* 3.
13. Davis, *Enforcing Normalcy,* xv.
14. Goffman, *Stigma,* 14.
15. Howe et al., *Oxford Handbook of Music and Disability Studies,* 5.
16. Howe et al., *The Oxford Handbook of Music and Disability Studies,* 5.
17. Sandahl and Auslander, *Bodies in Commotion,* 1–2.
18. Davis, *Bending over Backwards,* 20.
19. Davis, *Enforcing Normalcy,* 34.
20. Davis, *Bending over Backwards,* 14. Children born with physical difference and/or disabilities were sometimes excluded from society by parents and states who committed them to institutions and left them there to live out their lives.
21. Rose, *No Right to Be Idle,* 2.
22. Markel, "When A Secret President Ran the Country"; Porter, "How FDR Kept His Partial Paralysis a Secret."
23. The Rehabilitation Act of 1973 was the first law prohibiting employment discrimination against people with disabilities, and although it applied only to federal employment, it set the stage for the broader rights granted to disabled people passed under the 1990 Americans with Disabilities Act (ADA).
24. Rose, *No Right to Be Idle,* 2–3.
25. Rose, *No Right to Be Idle,* 227.
26. ADA.gov, "The Americans with Disabilities Act of 1990 and Revised ADA Regulations Implementing Title II and Title III."
27. Actors' Equity Association, "Looking at Hiring Biases by the Numbers."
28. Bialik, "7 Facts about Americans with Disabilities."
29. Ventura, "Working Miracles with Disabled Actors."
30. Actors' Equity Association, "Diversity Report: 2016–2019 in Review." The seventeen contracts do not mean that there were seventeen actors with disabilities, but that there were that many contracts—in theory, the same actor could be responsible for a number of those contracts.
31. US Department of Labor, "PERSONS WITH A DISABILITY: LABOR FORCE CHARACTERISTICS—2017."

NOTES 271

32. The statistics are somewhat better beyond Broadway: 4.77 percent of all AEA contracts went to members who self-identify as having a disability, yet the data show that their average salary was lower than that of members who did not identify as disabled. The figures account for only the 13.5 percent of members who responded to AEA's questions about disability: 86.5 percent opted out, which speaks to the ongoing stigma of disability in relation to employment. Actors' Equity Association, "Diversity Report: 2016–2019 in Review."

33. Actors' Equity Association, "Equity at a Glance."

34. The *New York Times* referred to Marceau's character as "the Blind Countess," though the libretto does not mention her disability and she does not speak. Gilford, "DANCE; Ballroom Style Glides onto Concert Stage."

35. Mitchell and Snyder, *Narrative Prosthesis*.

36. Original Broadway Cast, "Pinball Wizard," by Pete Townshend, in *The Who's Tommy*.

37. Knapp, "Waitin' for the Light to Shine," 820.

38. Sternfeld, " 'Pitiful Creature of Darkness,' " 796.

39. See Jackie Manksy, "P. T. Barnum Isn't the Hero the 'Greatest Showman' Wants You to Think," *Smithsonian*, December 22, 2017, https://www.smithsonianmag.com/history/true-story-pt-barnum-greatest-humbug-them-all-180967634/.

40. Chemers, introduction to "Staging Stigma: A Freak Studies Manifesto."

41. Bennett et al., *A Chorus Line*, 102.

42. Sandahl, "The Difference Disability Makes," 92.

43. Artavia, "Think You Know *Wicked*'s Nessarose?"

44. *Backstage*, " 'Falsettos,' 'Billy Elliot,' and 'Grand Hotel.' "

45. Norman and Simon, *The Secret Garden*, 53.

46. Norman and Simon, *The Secret Garden*, 89.

47. Norman and Simon, *The Secret Garden*, 66.

48. Rich, review of *The Secret Garden*, April 26, 1991.

49. Leduc, *Disfigured*, 20.

50. Musicals aimed at children are hardly the only productions that circulate representations of difference. Several of Stephen Sondheim's very grown-up musicals participate in this process with both physical and mental differences. In addition to *Into the Woods*' Witch, the musical includes three characters blinded as punishment for desire: Rapunzel's Prince and Cinderella's two stepsisters. *Anyone Can Whistle* (1964) and *Sweeney Todd* (1979) both have mad characters; *Follies* (1971) plays on the physical differences between old and young bodies; *Sunday in the Park with George* (1984) features the Boatman, othered by his class difference and his limp, a few characters who use canes, and the very old Marie, who uses a wheelchair in the show's second act. However, none of Sondheim's characters sing out physical difference quite like Fosca in *Passion* (1994), whose physical maladies are realized in her ugliness and compensated for in the narrative with a superior intellect made evident in her passion for reading. The original production created Fosca's ugliness by star Donna Murphy's use of a cane and makeup, including a large prosthetic mole prominently placed on her left cheek, to both metaphorically and

272 NOTES

literally represent Fosca's epilepsy. *Passion* culminates in Fosca's death, her difference finally extinguishing her intensity and her life.

51. Henderson, *Ugliness*, 13.
52. Hamermesh, *Beauty Pays*, 45.
53. Musicals that stage ugliness include *The Little Mermaid*, whose villainess Ursula is ugly *and* fat; *Wicked*, which others its heroine Elphaba because her skin is green; and *Cinderella*, probably the ür-text for gendered notions of aesthetic beauty in the opposition between Cinderella and her ugly stepsisters. In *Damn Yankees*, the temptress Lola has sold her soul in a Faustian exchange for youth and beauty. Even *Cats* offers a variation on this theme in Grizabella the Glamour Cat's fall from glamor into decrepitude and, ultimately, her salvation as she ascends to the Heaviside Layer.
54. Mead, "Under the Sea."
55. Leduc, interview with Disability Visibility Project.
56. Warren, *Shrek the Musical*. All further quotes from *Shrek* are from this filmed version.
57. Brater et al., " 'Let Our Freak Flags Fly,' " 171.
58. Brater et al., " 'Let Our Freak Flags Fly,' " 167.
59. Brater et al., " 'Let Our Freak Flags Fly,' " 167.
60. Sandahl, "Using Our Words," 130–131.
61. See Zazzali, "Star Struck!" for more on celebrity's symbolic capital.
62. Zazzali, "Star Struck!"
63. Shinn, "Disability Is Not Just a Metaphor."
64. Norman, *The Color Purple*, 114.
65. Norman, *The Color Purple*, 119.
66. Norman, *The Color Purple*, 173.
67. MAKERS, "Cynthia Erivo Performs 'I'm Here' from 'The Color Purple.' "
68. Foster, interview with Horn.
69. Foster, interview with Gaffney.
70. Leduc, *Disfigured*, 215.
71. Mitchell was far from the first Broadway actor with a temporary disability caused by injury. Danny Kaye temporarily used a wheelchair during the run of *Two by Two* in 1971. Tommy Tune broke his foot in *Busker Alley*'s out-of-town tryout, forestalling its Broadway run. Injuries are common occurrences on Broadway.
72. Mitchell, interview with Sale.
73. Rooney, review of *Hedwig and the Angry Inch*, March 13, 2015.
74. Rooney, review of *Hedwig and the Angry Inch*, March 13, 2015.
75. Brantley, review of *Hedwig and the Angry Inch*, March 13, 2015.
76. Petra Kuppers describes disability's "complex status—on the one hand, it references lived experience and its alignment with a bodily 'real.' On the other, it is used in much popular and high culture as a metaphor-generator." *Disability and Contemporary Performance*, 88.
77. *Sex change operation* was the terminology prevalent at the time of *Hedwig*'s creation, which came to be called *gender confirmation surgery* by the time of this writing.
78. Svich, *Mitchell and Trask's* Hedwig and the Angry Inch, 44.
79. Gershwin et al., *Porgy and Bess*, 36.

NOTES 273

80. Healy, "It Ain't Necessarily 'Porgy.'" James Robinson's 2018 production of the opera also had Porgy using a cane and a leg brace.
81. Jensen-Moulton, "Porgy's Cane"
82. Shea, "'Porgy and Bess.'"
83. Sondheim, letter to the editor.
84. Shea, "'Porgy and Bess.'"
85. Winer, review of *The Gershwins' Porgy and Bess*, January 12, 2012.
86. Brown, review of *The Gershwins' Porgy and Bess*, January 12, 2012.
87. Rooney, review of *The Gershwins' Porgy and Bess*, January 12, 2012.
88. Jones, review of *The Gershwins' Porgy and Bess*, January 12, 2012.
89. Vincentelli, review of *The Gershwins' Porgy and Bess*, January 13, 2012.
90. Jensen-Moulton, "Porgy's Cane"
91. Jensen-Moulton, "Porgy's Cane"
92. *Spring Awakening Playbill*, September 2015, 20.
93. Stroker, interview with Young-Howze.
94. Beth Lipari, interview with author.
95. Davis, *Enforcing Normalcy*, xiv.
96. DWSA [CC] Videos, DWSA's 'Broadway Backstory' Episode."
97. Gray, *Living the Dream.*
98. Gray, *Living the Dream.*
99. Gray, *Living the Dream.*
100. Elizabeth, "Ali Stroker on 'Oklahoma!'"
101. Voss, "How Ali Stroker Reps the Bisexual and Disabled Communities with Class."
102. Voss, "How Ali Stroker Reps the Bisexual and Disabled Communities with Class."
103. Sandahl, "The Difference Disability Makes," 92.
104. Guardian News, "Actors Don't Black Up, so Why Do They Still Crip Up?"
105. Sandahl, "The Difference Disability Makes," 91.
106. Sandahl, "Using Our Words," 130–131.
107. Sandahl, "Using Our Words," 141.
108. Flynn, "'Access Is a Human Right.'"
109. This argument is indebted to Sue-Ellen Case's influential article on gender in Greek tragedy. Case, "Classic Drag."

Epilogue: Recasting Broadway

1. Heimans and Timms, "Understanding 'New Power.'"
2. Baayork Lee, interview with author.
3. Baayork Lee, interview with author.
4. Describing its work with P.S. 124's Theatre Club, NAAP's website states, "Arts education for children also builds an awareness of self and self-expression. The earlier children develop an artistic sense, the earlier they see possibilities in their futures." For an in-depth study of the politics of musicals in primary schools, see Stacy Wolf, "Disney Goes to School," in *Beyond Broadway*.

274 NOTES

5. Stephanie Lexis, interview with author.
6. Stephanie Lexis, interview with author.
7. "About," Ring of Keys, accessed February 17, 2021, https://www.ringofkeys.org/about.
8. "#3—Twice! Andrea Prestinario," Thesis on Joan podcast.
9. "#3—Twice! Andrea Prestinario," Thesis on Joan podcast.
10. "About," Deaf Broadway, accessed February 17, 2021, https://www.deafbroadway.com/about.html.
11. "About," Deaf Broadway. l
12. Deaf Broadway, "Deaf Broadway's Rocky Horror Picture Show."
13. Blackwood, "How 'Deaf Broadway' Is Making Musical Theater Loud and Clear."
14. White, "How Deaf Broadway's 'Into the Woods' . . ."
15. Motherway, email with author.
16. Wren, "At Olney Theatre."
17. Gioia, "How this *Beauty*"
18. Gioia, "How this *Beauty*"
19. Wren, "At Olney Theatre."
20. DeJarnette, review of *Disney's Beauty and the Beast*.

Bibliography

Archival Collections

Library of Congress, Washington, DC
    Arthur Laurents Papers (Music Division)
New York Public Library for the Performing Arts
    Billy Rose Theatre Division
    Jerome Robbins Dance Division
    Theatre on Film and Tape Archive
Yale University, New Haven, Connecticut
    Michael Bennett Papers, *YCAL MSS 538* (Beinecke Rare Book and Manuscript Library)
    Harvey Fierstein Papers (Manuscripts and Archives Repository)

Interviews Conducted by Ryan Donovan

Brown, Barry. Digital recording, February 2018.
Burns, Craig. Digital recording, September 2017.
Dideriksen, Katrina Rose. Digital recording, April 2017.
Deitch, Kathy. Digital recording, April 2017.
Engel, David. Digital recording, January 2018.
Lee, Baayork. Digital recording, January 2021.
Lexis, Stephanie. Digital recording, February 2021.
Lipari, Beth. Digital recording, September 2017.
Mercanti, J. V. Digital recording, February 2018.
Motherway, Teresa. Email. January 2019.
Sutton, Charlie. Digital recording, January 2018.
Wallace, Marisha. Digital recording, June 2017.
Woodall, Eric. Digital recording, August 2017.

Articles, Books, Dissertations, Films, and Select Websites

Abramovitch, Seth. "Nathan Lane Recalls 'Terrifying' Moment Oprah Tried to Out Him: 'I Wasn't Ready.'" *Hollywood Reporter*, February 8, 2020. https://www.hollywoodr eporter.com/news/nathan-lane-recalls-terrifying-moment-oprah-tried-him-i-wasnt-ready-1277239.
Actors' Equity Association. "Actors' Equity Association Releases Second-Ever Diversity and Inclusion Report," November 18, 2020. https://www.actorsequity.org/news/PR/DandIReport2020/.
Actors' Equity Association. "Auditions and Job Interviews." Actors' Equity Association. Accessed November 13, 2018. https://www.actorsequity.org/resources/Producers/cast ing-call-how-to/.

276 BIBLIOGRAPHY

Actors' Equity Association. "Diversity Report: 2016–2019 in Review," published November 18, 2020. https://actorsequity.org/news/PR/DandIReport2020/diversity-and-inclusion-report-2020.

Actors' Equity Association. "Equity at a Glance." Actors' Equity Association. Accessed July 27, 2016. http://www.actorsequity.org/docs/about/equity_glance.pdf.

Actors' Equity Association. "Equity Chorus Call Audition Procedures." Actors' Equity Association. Accessed November 13, 2018. https://www.actorsequity.org/resources/Producers/casting-call-how-to/ecc-procedures.pdf.

Actors' Equity Association. "Extraordinary Excellence in Diversity on Broadway Award." Actors' Equity Association. Accessed November 13, 2018. https://www.actorsequity.org/aboutequity/awards/DiversityOnBroadway/?page=1.

Actors' Equity Association. "Looking at Hiring Biases by the Numbers." *Equity News*, Spring 2017. https://www.actorsequity.org/news/PR/DiversityStudy/.

Actors' Equity Association. "2007—110 in the Shade and Les Misérables." Actors' Equity Association. Accessed November 13, 2018. https://www.actorsequity.org/aboutequity/awards/DiversityOnBroadway/110LesMiz/.

Actors' Equity Association. "2009—Billy Elliott." Actors' Equity Association. Accessed November 13, 2018. https://www.actorsequity.org/aboutequity/awards/DiversityOnBroadway/BillyElliot/.

ADA.gov. "The Americans with Disabilities Act of 1990 and Revised ADA Regulations Implementing Title II and Title III." Accessed March 24, 2016. http://www.ada.gov/2010_regs.htm.

Ahmed, Tufayel. Review of *Dreamgirls*. Savoy Theatre, London. *Newsweek*, December 14, 2016. http://www.newsweek.com/dreamgirls-west-end-review-amber-riley-cant-slay-jennifer-holliday-effie-white-531716.

Ainlay, Stephen C., Lerita M. Coleman, and Gaylene Becker, editors. *The Dilemma of Difference: A Multidisciplinary View of Stigma*. New York: Plenum Press, 1986.

Ainlay, Stephen C., Lerita M. Coleman, and Gaylene Becker. "Stigma Reconsidered." In *The Dilemma of Difference: A Multidisciplinary View of Stigma*, edited by Stephen C. Ainlay, Lerita M. Coleman, and Gaylene Becker, 1–13. New York: Plenum Press, 1985.

Aldredge, Theoni. *Dreamgirls* designs and script, *T-Vim 2016-006. Billy Rose Theatre Division, New York Public Library.

Allen, Bonnie. "Dreamgirls Lights Up Broadway." *Essence*, May 1982.

Als, Hilton. Review of *La Cage aux Folles*. Longacre Theatre, New York. *New Yorker*, May 3, 2010.

Altman, Lawrence K. "AIDS Is Now the Leading Killer of Americans from 25 to 44." *New York Times*, January 31, 1995. https://www.nytimes.com/1995/01/31/science/aids-is-now-the-leading-killer-of-americans-from-25-to-44.html.

Anderson, Virginia. "'Something Bad [Was] Happening': *Falsettos* as an Historical Record of the AIDS Epidemic." *Studies in Musical Theatre* 13, no. 3 (2019): 221–234.

Arden, Michael. "Director's Note." *Spring Awakening Playbill*. September 2015.

Arden, Michael. Interview with Ken Davenport. *The Producer's Perspective* (podcast). September 7, 2015. https://www.theproducersperspective.com/my_weblog/2015/09/podcast-episode-transcript-36-michael-arden.html.

Artavia, David. "Think You Know *Wicked*'s Nessarose? Think Again." *Playbill*, July 1, 2016. https://www.playbill.com/article/why-nessarose-is-wickeds-underrated-character.

Association for Psychological Science. "Implicit Attitudes Can Change over the Long Term." January 7, 2019. https://www.psychologicalscience.org/news/releases/implicit-attitudes-long-term-change.html.

BIBLIOGRAPHY 277

Avian, Bob, with Tom Santopietro. *Dancing Man: A Broadway Choreographer's Journey.* Jackson: University Press of Mississippi, 2020.

Avian, Bob. Interview with Roslyn Sulcas. *New York Times*, February 28, 2013. https://ren dezvous.blogs.nytimes.com/2013/02/28/q-and-a-keeping-a-chorus-line-in-step.

awardscrazy. "Marissa Jaret Winokur Wins 2003 Tony Award for Best Actress in a Musical." November 9, 2014. YouTube video, 3:05. https://www.youtube.com/watch?v=aK1dBwhKfng.

Backstage. "A Chorus Line." June 27, 1975.

Backstage. "A Chorus Line," n.d. (2018), expires August 9, 2018. https://www.backstage. com/casting/a-chorus-line-237861.

Backstage. "CASTING- EQUITY STAGE." June 14, 1985.

Backstage. "'Falsettos,' 'Billy Elliot,' and 'Grand Hotel.'" *Backstage*, January 2, 2018. https:// www.backstage.com/casting/falsettos-billy-elliot-and-grand-hotel-200957/.

Backstage. "'Kinky Boots,' B'way." n.d. (2017). Accessed September 24, 2020. https://www. backstage.com/casting/kinky-boots-bway-156821/.

Backstage. "'Kinky Boots' Nonunion National Tour." *Backstage*, n.d. (2017). Accessed September 24, 2020. https://www.backstage.com/casting/kinky-boots-nonunion-national-tour-167932/.

Backstage. "La Cage aux Folles." May 23, 1984.

Backstage. "La Cage aux Folles." February 20, 2004.

Backstage. "La Cage aux Folles." August 27, 2009.

Backstage. "Spring Awakening." 2014.

Backstage. "Spring Awakening." July 9, 2015.

Backstage. "Stage Casting." July 4, 1980.

Bailey, Peter. "Dreams Come True on Broadway for Young Stars in *Dreamgirls.*" *Ebony*, May 1982.

Barnes, Clive. Review of *Ain't Supposed to Die a Natural Death.* Ethel Barrymore Theatre, New York. *New York Times*, October 21, 1971. https://www.nytimes.com/1971/10/21/ archives/stage-ghetto-life-of-aint-supposed-blacks-move-through-gantlet-of.html.

Barnes, Clive. Review of *A Chorus Line.* The Public Theater, New York. *New York Times*, May 22, 1975. https://www.nytimes.com/1975/05/22/archives/a-tremendous-chorus-line-arrives.html.

Barnes, Clive. Review of *A Chorus Line.* Shubert Theatre, New York. *New York Times*, December 18, 1976.

Barnes, Clive. Review of *Dreamgirls.* Imperial Theatre, New York. *New York Post*, December 21, 1981.

Barnes, Clive. Review of *La Cage aux Folles.* Palace Theatre, New York. *New York Post*, August 22, 1983.

Barone, Joshua. "How 'A Chorus Line' Veterans Pass It on to a New Generation." *New York Times*, November 12, 2018. https://www.nytimes.com/2018/11/12/theater/a-chorus-line-new-york-city-center-bob-avian.html.

Bauman, H-Dirksen L., and Joseph J. Murray. "Deaf Studies in the 21st Century: 'Deaf-Gain' and the Future of Human Diversity." In *The Deaf Studies Reader*, 5th ed., edited by Lennard J. Davis, 242–255. London: Routledge, 2017.

Bell, Arthur. "Bell Tells." *Village Voice*, August 30, 1983.

Bellis, Rich. "Here's Everywhere in the U.S. You Can Still Get Fired for Being Gay or Trans." *Fast Company*, August 28, 2017. https://www.fastcompany.com/40456937/ heres-everywhere-in-the-u-s-you-can-still-get-fired-for-being-gay-or-trans.

Bennett, Michael. Interview with John Gruen. *After Dark*, unpublished manuscript, October 2, 1981, MGZMT 3-1038, New York Public Library for the Performing Arts.

278 BIBLIOGRAPHY

Bennett, Michael, James Kirkwood, Nicholas Dante, Marvin Hamlisch, and Edward Kleban. *A Chorus Line: The Book of the Musical*. New York: Applause, 1995.

Bennetts, Leslie. "Harvey Fierstein's Long Journey to the Tony and Beyond." *New York Times*, June 26, 1983.

Bennetts, Leslie. "Here Comes the Musical 'La Cage.'" *New York Times*, August 21, 1983.

Bennetts, Leslie. "How Stars of 'La Cage' Grew into Their Roles." *New York Times*, August 24, 1983.

Beresford, Trilby. "Olaf Gets Gender Swap in Disney's 'Frozen' on Broadway." *Hollywood Reporter*, January 15, 2019. https://www.hollywoodreporter.com/news/frozen-musi cal-new-cast-ryann-redmond-play-olaf-1176267.

Berger, Marilyn. "Ronald Reagan Dies at 93; Fostered Cold-War Might and Curbs on Government." *New York Times*, June 6, 2004.

Bernardo, Melissa Rose. "Reign of Fierstein." *Playbill*, February 2011.

Bialik, Kristen. "7 Facts about Americans with Disabilities." *Pew Research*. "Fact Tank" (blog), July 27, 2017. http://www.pewresearch.org/fact-tank/2017/07/27/7-facts-about-americans-with-disabilities/.

Billings, Alexandra. Interview with Ryan McPhee. *Playbill*, January 4, 2020. https://www.playbill.com/article/making-a-brand-new-madame-morrible-in-broadways-long-running-wicked.

Black, Jonathan. *Making the American Body: The Remarkable Saga of the Men and Women Whose Feats, Feuds, and Passions Shaped Fitness History*. Lincoln: University of Nebraska Press, 2013.

Black Theatre United. "A New Deal for Broadway: Equity, Diversity, Inclusion, Accessibility & Belonging for the Theatrical Industry." Updated May 2022. http://www.blacktheatr eunited.com/wp-content/uploads/2022/05/BTU-New-Deal-For-Broadway.pdf.

Blackwell, Charles, Henry Krieger, and Robert Lorick. *The Tap Dance Kid*. New York: Samuel French, 1988.

Blackwood, Nicole. "How 'Deaf Broadway' Is Making Musical Theater Loud and Clear." *Daily Beast*, November 8, 2020. https://www.thedailybeast.com/how-deaf-broadway-is-making-musical-theater-loud-and-clear.

Blazian2006. "The Life–My Body." August 7, 2008. YouTube video, 4:03. https://www.yout ube.com/watch?v=I-ckNG_hyTY.

Blow, Eleanor. "Broadway." *New York Times*, December 24, 1982.

Bosworth, Patricia. "The Fight to Save 'Seesaw.'" *New York Times*, April 8, 1973. https://www.nytimes.com/1973/04/08/archives/the-fight-to-save-seesaw-the-openings-the-fight-to-save-seesaw-the.html.

Bradford, Shannon. "The National Theatre of the Deaf: Artistic Freedom & Cultural Responsibility in the Use of American Sign Language." In *Bodies in Commotion: Disability & Performance*, edited by Carrie Sandahl and Philip Auslander, 86–94. Ann Arbor: University of Michigan Press, 2005.

Brantley, Ben. Review of *Dreamgirls*. Apollo Theater, New York. *New York Times*, November 23, 2009.

Brantley, Ben. Review of *Fiddler on the Roof*. Minskoff Theater, New York. *New York Times*, January 21, 2005. https://www.nytimes.com/2005/01/21/theater/reviews/an-exotic-tevye-in-old-anatevka.html.

Brantley, Ben. Review of *Hairspray*. Neil Simon Theatre, New York. *New York Times*, August 16, 2002.

BIBLIOGRAPHY 279

Brantley, Ben. Review of *Hedwig and the Angry Inch*. Belasco Theatre, New York. *New York Times*, March 13, 2015. https://www.nytimes.com/2015/03/14/theater/cabaret-and-hedwig-get-tougher-onstage.html.

Brantley, Ben. Review of *La Cage aux Folles*. Marquis Theatre, New York. *New York Times*, December 10, 2004.

Brantley, Ben. Review of *La Cage aux Folles*. Longacre Theatre, New York. *New York Times*, April 18, 2010.

Brantley, Ben. Review of *On the Town*. Delacorte Theater, New York. *New York Times*. August 18, 1997. https://www.nytimes.com/1997/08/18/theater/those-gobs-on-shore-leave-again-prowling-wartime-new-york.html.

Brater, Jessica, Jessica Del Vecchio, Andrew Friedman, Bethany Holmstrom, Eero Laine, Donald Levit, Hillary Miller, David Savran, Carly Griffin Smith, Kenn Watt, Catherine Young, and Peter Zazalli. "'Let Our Freak Flags Fly': *Shrek the Musical* and the Branding of Diversity." *Theatre Journal* 62, no. 2 (2010): 151–172.

Brier, Kathy. Interview with Gordon Cox. *Newsday* (New York), September 28, 2003.

Broadwaycom. "Broadway Legend Tommy Tune on 55 Years in the Biz, His $55 NYC Apt and Tapping His Heart Out." February 10, 2015. YouTube video, 33:21. https://www.youtube.com/watch?v=7W2EUU_UTJs&list=PL4B11C2C085A823B0&index=120&t=0s.

Broadwaycom. "Opening Night of the 2004 Tony Award-Winning Broadway Revival of 'La Cage aux Folles.'" January 9, 2015. YouTube video, 5:23. https://www.youtube.com/watch?v=9Glybc6gMjQ.

Broadwaycom. "Show People with Paul Wontorek: 'Kinky Boots' Star Billy Porter on Life as a Diva." February 14, 2013. YouTube video, 28:27. https://www.youtube.com/watch?v=r0ohH6YBOEA&list=PL4B11C2C085A823B0&index=177&t=0s.

Broadwaycom. "Show People with Paul Wontorek Interview: Tony Winner Marissa Jaret Winokur of 'Hairspray.'" April 1, 2011. YouTube video, 18:14. https://www.youtube.com/watch?v=kqSg00sn0Y&list=PL4B11C2C085A823B0&index=231&t=0s.

Broadway League. "2017–2018 Broadway End-of-Season Statistics." https://www.broadwayleague.com/press/press-releases/2017-2018-broadway-end-of-season-statistics/.

Broadway League. "Research Reports." N.d. Accessed October 12, 2017. https://www.broadwayleague.com/research/research-reports/.

Broadway World. "DREAMGIRLS—Broadway Theatre TBA Auditions." May 2, 2017. https://www.broadwayworld.com/equity-audition/DREAMGIRLS-Broadway-Theatre-TBA-2017-15551.

Broadway World. "IT SHOULDA BEEN YOU—Broadway Theatre TBA Auditions." August 20, 2014. https://www.broadwayworld.com/equity-audition/IT-SHOULDA-BEEN-YOU-Broadway-Theatre-TBA-2014-9296.

Bronski, Michael. *Culture Clash: The Making of Gay Sensibility*. Boston: South End Press, 1984.

Brooks, Daphne. *Bodies in Dissent: Spectacular Performances of Race and Freedom, 1850–1910*. Durham, NC: Duke University Press, 2006.

Brown, Scott. Review of *The Gershwins' Porgy and Bess*. Richard Rodgers Theater, New York. *Vulture*, January 12, 2012. https://www.vulture.com/2012/01/theater-review-porgy-and-bess.html.

280 BIBLIOGRAPHY

Brustein, Robert. Review of *La Cage aux Folles*. Palace Theatre, New York. *New Republic*, September 19, 1983.

Burden, Martin. "Gene Barry Takes Roles in Good Stride." *New York Post*, August 18, 1983.

Burden, Martin. "Marshall's No Square." *New York Post*, August 19, 1987.

Burgard, Deb, Elana Dykewoman, Esther Rothblum, and Pattie Thomas. "Are We Ready to Throw Our Weight Around? Fat Studies and Political Activism." In *The Fat Studies Reader*, edited by Esther Rothblum and Sondra Solovay, 334–340. New York: New York University Press, 2009.

Burns, Crosby. "The Gay and Transgender Wage Gap." Center for American Progress, April 16, 2012. https://www.americanprogress.org/issues/lgbtq-rights/news/2012/04/16/11494/the-gay-and-transgender-wage-gap/.

Burt, Ramsay. *The Male Dancer: Bodies, Spectacle, Sexualities*. London: Routledge, 1995.

BWW News Desk. "Marisha Wallace, Moya Angela, Karen Mav, and More Join DREAMGIRLS; Extends through June 2018." *Broadway World*, October 18, 2017. https://www.broadwayworld.com/article/Marisha-Wallace-Moya-Angela-Karen-Mav-and-More-Join-DREAMGIRLS-Extends-Through-June-2018-20171018.

Carley, Brennan. "Peppermint Is Turning Broadway on Its Head." *GQ*, September 6, 2018. https://www.gq.com/story/peppermint-is-turning-broadway-on-its-head.

Case, Sue-Ellen. "Classic Drag: The Greek Creation of Female Parts." *Theatre Journal* 37, no. 3 (1985): 317–327.

Cassal, Steve. "Dreamgirl Lands a Hefty Role." *Independent Journal* (San Rafael, CA), December 10, 1983.

Catanese, Brandi Wilkins. *The Problem of the Color[Blind]: Racial Transgression and the Politics of Black Performance*. Ann Arbor: University of Michigan Press, 2011.

Celebrity Radio by Alex Belfield. "Hairspray the Musical on Broadway—Tracy Turnblad Kathy Brier." March 15, 2014. YouTube video, 11:35. https://www.youtube.com/watch?v=tpZRQalDPi8.

Centers for Disease Control and Prevention. "Adult Obesity Facts." Last modified June 29, 2020. www.cdc.gov/obesity/data/adult.html.

Centers for Disease Control and Prevention. "CDC: 1 in 4 Adults Live with a Disability." Last modified August 16, 2018. https://www.cdc.gov/media/releases/2018/p0816-disability.html.

Chambers, Andrea. "Gene Barry Sings His Love Songs to a Man in Broadway's *La Cage* and His Family Cheers Him On." *People*, December 5, 1983.

Chemers, Michael. Introduction to "Staging Stigma: A Freak Studies Manifesto." *Disability Studies Quarterly* 25, no.3 (2005). http://dsq-sds.org/article/view/574/751.

Chomsky, Daniel, and Scott Barclay. "The Editor, the Publisher, and His Mother: The Representation of Lesbians and Gays in the *New York Times*." *Journal of Homosexuality* 60 (2013): 1389–1408.

Christel, Deborah A., and Susan C. Dunn. "Average American Women's Clothing Size: Comparing National Health and Nutritional Examination Surveys (1988–2010) to ASTM International Misses & Women's Plus Size Clothing." *International Journal of Fashion Design, Technology and Education* 10, no. 2 (2017): 129–136.

Clarke, Gerald. "Broadway Out of the Closet." *Time*, August 29, 1983.

Clippety. "Harvey Fierstein with Barbara Walters on 20/20 (1983)." October 22, 2011. YouTube video, 11:53. https://youtu.be/wffy5QC40io.

Clum, John. *Something for the Boys: Musical Theater and Gay Culture*. New York: Palgrave, 1999.

BIBLIOGRAPHY   281

Collela, Jenn. Interview with Dana Piccoli. *After Ellen* (blog), March 15, 2013. https://www.afterellen.com/people/106285-jenn-colella-talks-thespianism-and-lesbianism-on-and-off-broadway.

Coleman, Lerita M. "Stigma: An Enigma Demystified." In *The Dilemma of Difference: A Multidisciplinary View of Stigma*, edited by Stephen C. Ainlay, Lerita M. Coleman, and Gaylene Becker, 211–232. New York: Plenum Press, 1985.

Collins-Hughes, Laura. Review of *Smokey Joe's Café*. Stage 42, New York. *New York Times*, July 22, 2018. https://www.nytimes.com/2018/07/22/theater/smokey-joes-cafe-review-leiber-stoller.html.

Collins-Hughes, Laura. "'Spring Awakening' Revival Requires Signing in Lieu of Singing." *New York Times*, July 17, 2015.

Connolly, William. "The Sex Is in the Heel." *Gay Times* (London), December 2016.

Cook, Amy. *Building Character: The Art and Science of Casting*. Ann Arbor: University of Michigan Press, 2018.

Cooper, Nathanael. "'Anyone Should Be Able to Play Hedwig': Creators Defend Show over Casting Controversy." *Sydney Morning Herald*, November 18, 2020. https://www.smh.com.au/culture/musicals/anyone-should-be-able-to-play-hedwig-creators-defend-show-over-casting-controversy-20201118-p56fpy.html.

Cottom, Tressie McMillan. *Thick: And Other Essays*. New York: New Press, 2019.

Coven, Bree. "There's a Place for Us . . . Somewhere." In *Cast Out: Queer Lives in Theater*, edited by Robin Bernstein, 140–149. Ann Arbor: University of Michigan Press, 2006.

Cramer, Lyn. *Creating Musical Theatre: Conversations with Broadway Directors and Choreographers*. London: Bloomsbury, 2013.

Creel, Gavin. Interview with Lynda Sturner. *Wicked Local Truro*, July 4, 2019 (updated July 5, 2019). https://truro.wickedlocal.com/entertainment/20190704/on-heels-of-gay-pride-with-gavin-creel.

Crimp, Douglas. *Melancholia and Moralism: Essays on AIDS and Queer Politics*. Cambridge, MA: MIT Press, 2004.

Crocker, Jennifer, and Diane M. Quinn. "Social Stigma and the Self: Meanings, Situations, and Self-esteem." In *The Social Psychology of Stigma*, edited by Todd F. Heatherton, Robert E. Kleck, Michelle R. Hebl, and Jay G. Hill, 153–183. *The Social Psychology of Stigma*. New York: Guildford Press, 2000.

cunytv75. "Theater Talk: Jennifer Holliday." November 21, 2016. YouTube video, 26:46. https://www.youtube.com/watch?v=IHY4pwx0-Wc.

Currie, Glenne. Review of *La Cage aux Folles*. Palace Theatre, New York. U.P.I., August 21, 1983.

Curtin, Kaier. *"We Can Always Call Them Bulgarians": The Emergence of Lesbians and Gay Men on the American Stage*. Boston: Alyson, 1987.

D'Emilio, John. *Rewriting History: Essays on Gay History, Politics, and the University*. London: Routledge, 1992.

D'Emilio, John. *The World Turned*. Durham, NC: Duke University Press, 2002.

Dace, Tish. Review of *La Cage aux Folles*. Palace Theatre, New York. *Advocate*, August 18, 1983.

Damien Slattery. "Dreamgirls—Audition in LA 1983—Michael Bennet & Michael Peters." June 21, 2016. YouTube video, 5:18. https://www.youtube.com/watch?v=tF0jAthdOHA.

Damien Slattery. "Lillias White—Dreamgirls—1983." March 27, 2017. YouTube video, 7:58. https://www.youtube.com/watch?v=S79C1Kbainc&t=16s.

282 BIBLIOGRAPHY

Davis, Lennard J. *Bending over Backwards: Disability, Dismodernism & Other Difficult Positions*. New York: New York University Press, 2002.

Davis, Lennard J. *The End of Normal: Identity in a Biocultural Era*. Ann Arbor: University of Michigan Press, 2014.

Davis, Lennard J. *Enforcing Normalcy: Disability, Deafness, and the Body*. London: Verso Books, 1995.

de la Garza, Alejandro. "'Don't Ask, Don't Tell' Was a Complicated Turning Point for Gay Rights. 25 Years Later, Many of the Same Issues Remain." *Time*, July 19, 2018. https://time.com/5339634/dont-ask-dont-tell-25-year-anniversary/.

Deaf Broadway. "Deaf Broadway's Rocky Horror Picture Show: Audition Announcement." August 31, 2020. YouTube video, 7:00. https://www.youtube.com/watch?v=4oBYokio JAk&t=6s.

DeafDigest (blog). "DeafDigest Mid-Week edition, October 23, 2015." October 23, 2015. http://deafdigest.net/mid-week-news/20151023/.

Deaf West Theatre. Homepage. Accessed August 8, 2018. www.deafwest.org.

Deaf West Theatre. "Deaf West's Spring Awakening: Casting Call." March 4, 2014. YouTube video, 06:08. https://www.youtube.com/watch?v=sVf21r6330s.

Deaf West Theatre. "Deaf West Theatre Presents Spring Awakening." Kickstarter. Published July 21, 2014. https://www.kickstarter.com/projects/1832685006/deaf-west-theatre-presents-spring-awakening.

Deaf West Theatre. "Deaf West Theatre's Spring Awakening Tony Performance." Kickstarter. Published May 23, 2016. https://www.kickstarter.com/projects/1832685 006/deaf-west-theatres-spring-awakening-tony-performan.

Debruge, Peter. Review of *Spring Awakening*. Brooks Atkinson Theatre, New York. *Variety*, September 27, 2015.

DeJarnette, Darby. Review of *Disney's Beauty and the Beast*, Olney Theatre Center, Olney, MD. *DC Metro Theater Arts*, November 12, 2021.

Del Deo, Adam, and James D. Stern, directors. *Every Little Step*. 2009; New York: Sony Pictures Classics. Film.

DeLaria, Lea. Interview by Jen Gushue. *American Theatre*, August 20, 2018. https://www.americantheatre.org/2018/08/20/lea-delaria-raging-butch/.

Dembart, Lee. "22 Leap at Chance to Join 'A Chorus Line.'" *New York Times*, June 27, 1975. https://www.nytimes.com/1975/06/27/archives/22-leap-at-chance-to-join-a-chorus-line.html.

Deschamps, David, and Bennett Singer. *LGBTQ Stats: Lesbian, Gay, Bisexual, Transgender, and Queer People by the Numbers*. New York: New Press, 2017.

Dinero, Dan. "A Big Black Lady Stops the Show: Black Women, Performances of Excess and the Power of Saying No." *Studies in Musical Theatre* 6, no. 1 (2012): 29-41.

Dodson, P. Claire. "'Mean Girls' Musical Has a New Regina George in 19-Year-Old Renee Rapp." *Teen Vogue*, June 18, 2019. https://www.teenvogue.com/story/mean-girls-musical-regina-george-19-year-old-renee-rapp.

Dolan, Jill. "Practicing Cultural Disruptions: Gay and Lesbian Representation and Sexuality." In *Critical Theory and Performance*, 2nd ed., edited by Janelle G. Reinelt and Joseph R. Roach, 334–354. Ann Arbor, University of Michigan Press, 2007.

Donovan, Ryan. "If You Were Gay, That'd Be Okay: Marketing LGBTQ Musicals from *La Cage* to *The Prom*" In *Gender, Sex, and Sexuality in Musical Theatre: He/She/They Could Have Danced All night*, edited by Kelly Kessler, 155–173. Bristol, UK: Intellect, 2022.

BIBLIOGRAPHY 283

Dovidio, John F., Brenda Major, and Jennifer Crocker. "Stigma: Introduction and Overview." In *The Social Psychology of Stigma*, edited by Todd F. Heatherton, Robert E. Kleck, Michelle R. Hebl, and Jay G. Hill, 1–28. *The Social Psychology of Stigma*. New York: Guildford Press, 2000.

Duggan, Lisa. *The Twilight of Equality? Neoliberalism, Cultural Politics, and the Attack on Democracy*. Boston: Beacon Press, 2003.

Dunning, Jennifer. "High-Stepping into Stardom." *New York Times*, April 2, 1978. https://www.nytimes.com/1978/04/02/archives/highstepping-into-stardom-ann-reinking.html.

DWSA [CC] Videos. "DWSA's 'Broadway Backstory' Episode." January 3, 2017. YouTube video, 54:36. https://www.youtube.com/watch?v=EqxHv7yEHRo.

Dziemianowicz, Joe. "Baby, You're a Big Curl Now." *New York Daily News*, August 14, 2002.

Eder, Richard. Review of *Runaways*. Plymouth Theater, New York. *New York Times*, May 15, 1978.

Eisenbach, David. *Gay Power: An American Revolution*. New York: Carroll & Grad, 2006.

Elizabeth, De. "Ali Stroker on 'Oklahoma!' and Bringing Disability Representation to Another Iconic Musical." *Teen Vogue*, August 6, 2018. https://www.teenvogue.com/story/ali-stroker-oklahoma-disability-representation.

Ellis, Sheila. Interview with A. Peter Bailey. *New York Amsterdam News*, November 6, 1982.

Epstein, Kayla, and Alex Needham. "Spring Awakening on Broadway: Deaf Viewers Give Their Verdict." *The Guardian*, November 2, 2015.

Ernsberger, Paul. "Does Social Class Explain the Connection between Weight and Health?" In *The Fat Studies Reader*, edited by Esther Rothblum and Sondra Solovay, 25–36. New York: New York University Press, 2009.

Rothblum, Esther, and Sondra Solovay, editors. *The Fat Studies Reader*. New York: New York University Press, 2009.

Everett, Rupert. Interview with Carole Cadwalladr. *Guardian*, November 28, 2009. https://www.theguardian.com/film/2009/nov/29/rupert-everett-madonna-carole-cadwalladr.

Eyen, Tom, and Henry Krieger. *Dreamgirls* Final Draft, January 10, 1983. Michael Bennett Papers, YCAL MSS 538. Beinecke Rare Book and Manuscript Library, Yale University.

Fabray, Nanette. Interview by Jennifer Howard (video). Television Academy Foundation, August 12, 2004. https://interviews.televisionacademy.com/interviews/nanette-fabray?clip=17639#interview-clips.

Faderman, Lillian. *The Gay Revolution: The Story of the Struggle*. New York: Simon and Schuster, 2015.

Falk, Gerhard. *Stigma: How We Treat Outsiders*. New York: Prometheus Books, 2001.

Farrell, Amy Erdman. *Fat Shame: Stigma and the Fat Body in American Culture*. New York: New York University Press, 2011.

Fierberg, Ruthie. "After Endless Hours, Spencer Liff Formed a New Language—the Choreography of *Spring Awakening*." *Playbill*, December 29, 2015. http://www.playbill.com/article/after-endless-hours-spencer-liff-formed-a-new-language-u2014-the-choreography-of-spring-awakening-com-376781.

Fierstein, Harvey. *I Was Better Last Night: A Memoir*. New York: Alfred A. Knopf, 2022.

Fierstein, Harvey. Interview. August 8, 2003, VHS (NCOX 2163), Theatre on Film and Tape Archive. New York Public Library, New York, NY.

284 BIBLIOGRAPHY

Fierstein, Harvey. Interview with Gordon Cox. *Variety*, July 1, 2015.

Fierstein, Harvey. Interview with Jesse McKinley. *New York Times*, January 2, 2005. https://www.nytimes.com/2005/01/02/theater/newsandfeatures/fierstein-as-tevye-sounds-crazy-no.html.

Fierstein, Harvey. Interview with Susan Haskins and Michael Riedel. *Theater Talk* (video), 26:47, January 28, 2005. https://theatertalk.org/harvey-fierstein-of-fiddler-on-the-roof/.

Fierstein, Harvey. "Our Prejudices, Ourselves." *New York Times*, April 13, 2007.

Flinn, Denny Martin. *What They Did for Love: The Untold Story Behind the Making of* A CHORUS LINE. New York: Bantam Books, 1989.

Flynn, Isabel. "'Access Is a Human Right': How Deaf and Disabled People Are Transforming Theatre." *Guardian*, January 27, 2020. https://www.theguardian.com/stage/2020/jan/27/theatre-access-actors-writers-directors-theatres-accessibility.

Forth, Christopher E. *Fat: A Cultural History of the Stuff of Life*. London: Reaktion Books, 2019.

Foster, Susan Leigh. "Closets Full of Dances: Modern Dance's Performance of Masculinity and Sexuality." In *Dancing Desires: Choreographing Sexualities On & Off the Stage*, edited by Jane C. Desmond, 147–207. Madison: University of Wisconsin Press, 2001.

Foster, Sutton. Interview with John Horn. *Los Angeles Times*, May 9, 2014. https://www.latimes.com/entertainment/arts/la-et-cm-ca-sutton-foster-20140512-story.html.

Foster, Sutton. Interview with Adrienne Gaffney, *Vanity Fair*, May 30, 2014. https://www.vanityfair.com/culture/2014/05/sutton-foster-violet-no-makeup.

Foulkes, Julia L. *A Place for Us:* West Side Story *and New York*. Chicago: University of Chicago Press, 2016.

Fox, Jen Tesse. "All It Took Was a Text! Learn How Marlee Matlin and Russell Harvard Got on Board for *Spring Awakening*." *Playbill*, October 13, 2015. http://www.playbill.com/article/all-it-took-was-a-text-learn-how-marlee-matlin-and-russell-harvard-got-on-board-for-spring-awakening-com-366787.

Frank, Sandra Mae. "Deafness Is Having a Cultural Moment. So Why Are Deaf Roles Still Handed to Hearing Actors?" *Washington Post*, December 8, 2015.

Fraser, Laura. "The Inner Corset: A Brief History of Fat in the United States." In *The Fat Studies Reader*, edited by Esther Rothblum and Sondra Solovay, 11–14. New York: New York University Press, 2009.

Gajewski, Ryan. "Glee's Amber Riley: Casting Directors Told Me to Lose Weight." *Wetpaint.com*, November 22, 2012. http://www.wetpaint.com/glees-amber-riley-casting-directors-told-me-to-lose-weight-738606/.

Gallela, Donatella. "Racializing the American Revolution." GC *Advocate*, November 16, 2015. http://gcadvocate.com/2015/11/16/racializing-the-american-revolution-review-of-the-broadway-musical-hamilton/.

Gallup. "Gay and Lesbian Rights." Accessed April 20, 2018. http://news.gallup.com/poll/1651/gay-lesbian-rights.aspx.

Garberoglio, Carrie Lou, Stephanie Cawthon, and Mark Bond. "Deaf People and Employment in the United States: 2016." National Deaf Center Report, https://www.nationaldeafcenter.org/sites/default/files/Deaf%20Employment%20Report_final.pdf.

Gardner, Kara Anne. *Agnes de Mille: Telling Stories in Broadway Dance*. New York: Oxford University Press, 2016.

BIBLIOGRAPHY 285

Garland-Thomson, Rosemarie. *Extraordinary Bodies: Figuring Disability in American Culture and Literature*. New York: Columbia University Press, 1997.

Garland-Thomson, Rosemarie. *Freakery: Cultural Spectacles of the Extraordinary Body*, edited by Rosemarie Garland Thomson. New York: New York University Press, 1996.

Garland-Thomson, Rosemarie. *Staring: How We Look*. New York: Oxford University Press, 2009.

Gay, Roxane. *Hunger: A Memoir of (My) Body*. New York: Harper Collins, 2017.

Gelb, Barbara. "Producing—and Reproducing—'A Chorus Line.'" *New York Times*, May 2, 1976. https://www.nytimes.com/1976/05/02/archives/producing-and-reproducing-a-chorus-line.html.

Genius.com. "If a Girl Isn't Pretty" Lyrics. https://genius.com/Original-broadway-cast-of-funny-girl-if-a-girl-isnt-pretty-lyrics.

Gennaro, Liza. "Evolution of Dance in the Golden Age of the American "Book Musical." In *The Oxford Handbook of the American Musical*, edited by Raymond Knapp, Mitchell Morris, and Stacy Wolf, 45–61. New York: Oxford University Press, 2011.

Gerard, Jeremy. "'Dreamgirls,' Revamped for Tour, Is Returning to Broadway." *New York Times*, June 27, 1987.

Gershwin, George, Ira Gershwin, and DuBose Heyward. *Porgy and Bess: Opera Study Guide with Libretto*. Boca Raton, FL: Opera Journeys Publishing, 2019.

Gilford, Barbara. "DANCE; Ballroom Style Glides onto Concert Stage." *New York Times*, July 1, 1990. https://www.nytimes.com/1990/07/01/nyregion/dance-ballroom-style-glides-onto-concert-stage.html.

Gill, Brendan. Review of *La Cage aux Folles*. Palace Theatre, New York. *New Yorker*, September 5, 1983.

Gioia, Michael. "ASL for *Spring Awakening* Tony Performance Was Censored by CBS." *Playbill*, June 12, 2016. http://www.playbill.com/article/asl-for-spring-awakening-tony-performance-was-censored-by-cbs.

Gioia, Michael. "Heavy Character Actress Need Not Apply? Women Get Real on Casting." *Playbill*, August 25, 2016. http://www.playbill.com/article/heavy-character-actresses-need-not-apply-women-get-real-on-casting.

Gioia, Michael. "How This *Beauty and the Beast* Is Reflecting Real Life with 'Different Body Types and Ethnicities.'" *People*, November 24, 2021. https://people.com/theater/how-this-beauty-and-the-beast-is-reflecting-real-life-with-different-body-types-and-ethnicities/.

Gioia, Michael. "Is Weight Just a Number? Acting, Auditioning and Being Authentic at a Bigger Size in This *Gigantic* Business." *Playbill*, December 11, 2015. http://www.playbill.com/article/is-weight-just-a-number-acting-auditioning-and-being-authentic-at-a-bigger-size-in-this-gigantic-business-com-375097.

Gioia, Michael. "The Sounds of Spring." *Playbill*, September 2015.

Gioia, Michael. "Thanksgiving for a Broadway Body! How to Stay Hot and Healthy This Holiday." *Playbill*, November 25, 2015. http://www.playbill.com/article/thanksgiving-for-a-broadway-body-how-to-stay-hot-and-healthy-this-holiday-com-373013.

Goffman, Erving. *Stigma: Notes on the Management of Spoiled Identity*. Englewood Cliffs, NJ: Prentice Hall, 1963.

Goldberg, Carey. "Study: Bias Drops Dramatically for Sexual Orientation and Race—But Not Weight." *WBUR* (blog), January 11, 2019. https://www.wbur.org/commonhealth/2019/01/11/implicit-bias-gay-black-weight?fbclid=IwAR2Id1to_i35P4iz7PRVFhD1xsqPUuDTOnX8L_Mj6BwQN_Pi6kdfhLeDvgU.

286 BIBLIOGRAPHY

Goldfarb, Myra Yellin. "'A Chorus Line' Retains Its Kick to the End." *Morning Call*, March 18, 1990. https://www.mcall.com/news/mc-xpm-1990-03-18-2725448-story.html.

Gonsalves, Gregg, and Peter Staley. "Panic, Paranoia, and Public Health—The AIDS Epidemic's Lessons for Ebola." *New England Journal of Medicine* 371 (December 18, 2014): 2348–2349. https://www.nejm.org/doi/full/10.1056/NEJMp1413425.

Gottschild, Brenda Dixon. *The Black Dancing Body: A Geography from Coon to Cool.* New York: Palgrave Macmillan, 2003.

Gray, Matthew. *Living the Dream. Howlround.* December 11, 2015. Podcast. https://howlround.com/living-dream-podcast-12.

Green, Blake. "Good Hair Days." *Newsday* (New York), August 14, 2002.

Green, Jesse. Review of *Spring Awakening*. Brooks Atkinson Theatre, New York. *New York*, September 27, 2015.

Gross, Larry. *Up from Invisibility: Lesbians, Gay Men, and the Media in America.* New York: Columbia University Press, 2001.

Grumley, Michael. Review of *La Cage aux Folles*. Palace Theatre, New York. *New York Native*, September 26, 1983.

Guardian News. "Actors Don't Black Up, so Why Do They Still Crip Up?" September 10, 2018. YouTube video, 2:37. https://www.youtube.com/watch?v=kwXcMuE4G7M.

Guthman, Julie. "Neoliberalism and the Constitution of Contemporary Bodies." In *The Fat Studies Reader*, edited by Esther Rothblum and Sondra Solovay, 187–196. New York: New York University Press, 2009.

Hall, Richard. "The Pyschometrics of 'La Cage.'" *New York Native*, October 10, 1983.

Hall, Stuart. "What Is This 'Black' in Black Popular Culture?" *Social Justice* 20, no. 1/2 (1993): 104–114.

Hamermesh, Daniel S. *Beauty Pays: Why Attractive People Are More Successful.* Princeton, NJ: Princeton University Press, 2011.

Haplology Kloof. "'Come Up to My Place'—On the Town (Broadway Revival, 1998)." June 10, 2013. YouTube video, 3:27. https://www.youtube.com/watch?v=wZ3wVJATKBY.

Hart, Norman. "The Selling of *La Cage aux Folles*: How Audiences Were Helped to Read Broadway's First Gay Musical." *Theatre History Studies* 23 (June 2003): 5–24.

Harvey, David. *A Brief History of Neoliberalism*. New York: Oxford University Press, 2005.

Healy, Patrick. "It Ain't Necessarily 'Porgy.'" *New York Times*, August 5, 2011. https://www.nytimes.com/2011/08/07/theater/porgy-and-bess-with-audra-mcdonald.html.

Heatherton, Todd F., Robert E. Kleck, Michelle R. Hebl, and Jay G. Hill, editors. *The Social Psychology of Stigma*. New York: Guildford Press, 2000.

Heimans, Jeremy, and Henry Timms. "Understanding 'New Power.'" *Harvard Business Review*, December 2014. https://hbr.org/2014/12/understanding-new-power.

Henderson, Gretchen E. *Ugliness: A Cultural History*. London: Reaktion Books, 2015.

Henerson, Evan. "'The Word of Your Body' Is Reborn in Deaf West's *Spring Awakening*." *Playbill*, September 8, 2014. http://www.playbill.com/article/the-word-of-your-body-is-reborn-in-deaf-wests-spring-awakening-com-329874.

Herrera, Brian Eugenio. "The Best Actor for the Role, or the Mythos of Casting in American Popular Performance." *Journal of American Drama and Theatre* 27, no. 2 (2015). http://jadtjournal.org/2015/04/24/the-best-actor-for-the-role-or-the-mythos-of-casting-in-american-popular-performance/.

Herrera, Brian Eugenio. *Latin Numbers: Playing Latino in Twentieth-Century U.S. Popular Performance*. Ann Arbor: University of Michigan Press, 2015.

Herrera, Brian Eugenio. "Looking at *Hamilton* from Inside the Broadway Bubble." In *Historians on* Hamilton: *How a Blockbuster Musical Is Restaging America's Past*, edited

BIBLIOGRAPHY 287

by Renee C. Romano and Claire Bond Potter, 222–245. New Brunswick, NJ: Rutgers University Press, 2018.

Herman, Jerry. Interview. *Playbill* 121, no. 2 (February 2005).

Herman, Jerry, with Marilyn Stasio. *Showtune*. New York: Donald I. Fine Books, 1996.

Herman, Jerry, and Harvey Fierstein. *La Cage aux Folles*. London: Samuel French, 2014.

Hetrick, Adam. "*Hamilton, Waitress* and *Spring Awakening* Win Equity's Diversity Award." *Playbill*, July 29, 2016. www.playbill.com/article/hamilton-waitress-and-spr ing-awakening-win-equitys-diversity-award.

Hickey, John Benjamin. Interview by Paul Wontorek. *Show People with Paul Wontorek*. Broadway.com (video), (25:08), October 30, 2019. https://www.broadway.com/buzz/ 197039/john-benjamin-hickey-on-the-inheritance-directing-sarah-jessica-parker-matthew-broderick-in-plaza-suite-more-on-show-people/.

Hoffman, Warren. *The Great White Way: Race and the Broadway Musical*. New Brunswick, NJ: Rutgers University Press, 2014.

Hoffman, William M. Introduction to *Gay Plays: The First Collection*, edited by William M. Hoffman, vii–xxxix. New York: Avon Books, 1979.

Hofler, Robert. *Party Animals: A Hollywood Tale of Sex, Drugs, and Rock'n'Roll, Starring the Fabulous Allan Carr*. Boston: DaCapo Press, 2010.

Hofler, Robert. "Straight Talk about Gay Plays." *Variety*, July 23, 2001.

Hofler, Robert. "What's in a Kiss?" *Variety*, November 21, 2004.

Holliday, Jennifer. Interview by Russ Mitchell, *CBS Sunday Morning*, February 22, 2007.

Holliday, Jennifer. Interview by David Edwards Hughes. *Talkin' Broadway*, n.d. Accessed September 10, 2017. https://www.talkinbroadway.com/page/regional/seattle/ se387.html.

Holtcamp, Victor. *Interchangeable Parts: Acting, Industry, and Technology in U.S. Theater*. Ann Arbor: University of Michigan Press, 2019.

hooks, bell. "Continued Devaluation of Black Women." In *Ain't I a Woman? Black Women and Feminism*, 2nd ed., 51–86. New York: Routledge 2015.

hooks, bell. *Feminist Theory: From Margin to Center*, 3rd ed. New York: Routledge, 2015.

Horwitz, Simi. "Rising to the Challenge." *Backstage*, June 18–24, 2009.

Howard, Stuart. Interview with Kevin David Thomas and Robert W. Schneider. *Behind the Curtain: Broadway's Living Legends* (podcast). June 29, 2020. https://broadwaypod castnetwork.com/behind-the-curtain/222-stuart-howard-casting-director/.

Howe, Blake, Stephanie Jensen-Moulton, Neil Lerner, and Joseph Straus, editors. *The Oxford Handbook of Music and Disability*. New York: Oxford University Press, 2015.

Howe, Blake, Stephanie Jensen-Moulton, Neil Lerner, and Joseph Straus. Introduction to *The Oxford Handbook of Music and Disability*. In *The Oxford Handbook of Music and Disability Studies*, edited by Blake Howe, Stephanie Jensen-Moulton, Neil Lerner, and Joseph Straus, 1–11. New York: Oxford University Press, 2015.

HuffPost Live. "'Spring Awakening' Interview: Daniel Durant, Alex Boniello and D. J. Kurs." January 21, 2016. YouTube video, 20:24. https://www.youtube.com/watch?v= ozb5294yxxM.

Hulbert, Dan. "Tony Winner Returns in 'Dreamgirls.'" *Atlanta Journal and Constitution*, July 31, 1994.

Iovannone, Jeffrey J. "Why Is There No Gay Men's Body Liberation Movement?" *Think Queerly* (blog), March 19, 2019. https://medium.com/th-ink/why-is-there-no-gay-mens-body-liberation-movement-af5eabe7acf.

Isherwood, Charles. Review of *Spring Awakening*. Brooks Atkinson Theatre, New York. *New York Times*, September 27, 2015.

288 BIBLIOGRAPHY

Jackman, Hugh. Interview with Jesse Green. *New York Times*, September 5, 2004. https://www.nytimes.com/2004/09/05/theater/arts/theater-debriefing-eight-days-a-week.html.

Jensen-Moulton, Stephanie. "Porgy's Cane: Mediating Disability in A.R.T.'s *Porgy and Bess*." *American Music Review* 41, no. 1 (2011). http://www.brooklyn.cuny.edu/web/academics/centers/hitchcock/publications/amr/v41-1/moulton.php.

Jester, Julia Grace. "Placing Fat Women Center Stage." In *The Fat Studies Reader*, edited by Esther Rothblum and Sondra Solovay, 249–255. New York: New York University Press, 2009.

Joe Windish. "Harvey Fierstein 1983: Torch Song, Letterman & La Cage." April 13, 2007. YouTube video, 5:51. https://www.youtube.com/watch?v=zyW88v5I3Sw.

John Clonts Scottsdale Arizona Real Estate Agent. "The Making of La Cage—Promotional Video—Pittsburgh 1985." January 3, 2020. YouTube video, 23:58. https://www.yout ube.com/watch?v=bQkLRcqjL-M.

Johnson, Jake. "Building the Broadway Voice." In *The Oxford Handbook of Voice Studies*, edited by Nina Sun Eidsheim and Katherine Meizel. New York: Oxford University Press, 2019: 475–491.

Jones, Chris. Review of *The Gershwins' Porgy and Bess*. Richard Rodgers Theater, New York. *Chicago Tribune*, January 12, 2012. https://www.chicagotribune.com/ct-ae-0115-porgy-bess-broadway-review-20120112-column.html.

Jones, Chris. "Welcome to the '60s." *Chicago Tribune*, January 18, 2004.

Jones, Jeffrey. "LGBT Identification Rises to 5.6% in Latest U.S. Estimate." Gallup, February 24, 2021. https://news.gallup.com/poll/329708/lgbt-identification-rises-lat est-estimate.aspx.

Jones, John Bush. *Our Musicals, Ourselves*. Waltham, MA: Brandeis University Press, 2003.

Jordan, Jamal. "Sheryl Lee Ralph Is Glowing." *New York Times*, September 21, 2022. https://www.nytimes.com/2022/09/21/style/sheryl-lee-ralph-abbott-elementary.html.

Kantor, Michael. *Broadway: The American Musical*. Episode 8, "Putting It Together: 1980–Present." PBS, 2004. DVD.

Kauffmann, Stanley. "Homosexual Drama and Its Disguises." *New York Times*, January 23, 1966.

Kauffmann, Stanley. "On the Acceptability of the Homosexual." *New York Times*, February 6, 1966.

Kauffmann, Stanley. Review of *Dreamgirls*. Imperial Theatre, New York. *Saturday Review*, February 1982.

Kauffmann, Stanley. Review of *La Cage aux Folles*. Palace Theatre, New York. *Saturday Review*, November–December 1983.

Kazan, Lainie. Letter to the editor. *New York Times*, April 29, 1973. https://www.nytimes.com/1973/04/29/archives/lainies-seesaw-side-credit-for-kerman.html.

Keating, Joshua. "1987: The Year the *New York Times* Discovered Gay People." *Slate*, October 11, 2013. http://www.slate.com/blogs/outward/2013/10/11/the_new_york_times_discovered_gay_people_in_1987.html.

Kelly, Kevin. *One Singular Sensation: The Michael Bennett Story*. New York: Doubleday, 1990.

Kerr, Walter. Review of *Dreamgirls*. Imperial Theatre, New York. *New York Times*, January 3, 1982.

King, Kelly, and Rebecca Puhl. "Weight Bias: Does It Affect Men and Women Differently?" *Obesity Action*, Spring 2013. https://www.obesityaction.org/community/article-libr ary/weight-bias-does-it-affect-men-and-women-differently/.

BIBLIOGRAPHY   289

Kirle, Bruce. *Unfinished Show Business: Broadway Musicals as Works-in-Process*. Carbondale: Southern Illinois University Press, 2005.

Kitchen, Lee. "'Spring Awakening' from a Hard-of-Hearing Point of View." *Tallahassee Democrat*, January 16, 2016.

Kirkland, Justin. "Billy Porter Arrived a Long Time Ago. The World Finally Caught Up." *Esquire*, June 9, 2019, https://www.esquire.com/entertainment/tv/a27817829/billy-porter-pose-interview-2019/.

Kleban, Edward. "Broadway Boogie Woogie/Edward Kleban." Billy Rose Theatre Division, New York Public Library. New York Public Library Digital Collections. Accessed November 19, 2020. https://digitalcollections.nypl.org/items/734ccc00-8358-0134-4f1c-00505686a51c.

Klein, Alvin. "Lainie Kazan Goes Back to Her Roots." *New York Times*, May 3, 1992. https://www.nytimes.com/1992/05/03/nyregion/lainie-kazan-goes-back-to-her-roots.html.

Knapp, Raymond. The *American Musical and the Formation of National Identity*. Princeton, NJ: Princeton University Press, 2005.

Knapp, Raymond. "'Waitin' for the Light to Shine": Musicals and Disability." In *The Oxford Handbook of Music and Disability Studies*, edited by Blake Howe, Stephanie Jensen-Moulton, Neil Lerner, and Joseph Straus, 814–835. New York: Oxford University Press, 2015.

Kolb, Rachel. "*Spring Awakening* and the Power of Inclusive Art." *The Atlantic*, October 18, 2015.

Kregloe, Karman. "The Problematic History of Lesbians in Musical Theater." *After Ellen* (blog), September 11, 2007. https://www.afterellen.com/more/24247-the-problematic-history-of-lesbians-in-musical-theater.

Kroll, Jack. "Broadway Glitters and Is Oh So Gay." *Newsweek*, August 29, 1983.

Kuchwara, Michael. Review of *Flower Drum Song*. Virginia Theatre, New York. Associated Press, October 16, 2002. https://www.theintelligencer.com/news/article/Flower-Drum-Song-on-Broadway-10498416.php.

Kuppers, Petra. *Disability and Contemporary Performance: Bodies on Edge*. London: Routledge, 2003.

Kurs, DJ. "American Sign Language in Theatre and Its Impact or, Why We Need More Deaf Actors Onstage." *Howlround*, April 5, 2016. http://howlround.com/american-sign-language-in-theatre-and-social-advancement-or-why-we-need-more-deaf-actors-onstage.

Kurth, Peter. "Michael Jeter Takes on Hollywood." *POZ*, January 1, 1998. https://www.poz.com/article/Michael-Jeter-23341-5269.

Kushner, Tony. *Angels in America, Part One: Millennium Approaches*. New York: Theatre Communications Group, 1995.

Kwan, Samantha, and Jennifer Graves. *Framing Fat: Competing Constructions in Contemporary Culture*. New Brunswick, NJ: Rutgers University Press, 2013.

La Cage aux Folles program. "Who They Are: Michael Coveney in Conversation with Jerry Herman and Harvey Fierstein." Playhouse Theatre, London, 2008.

Laurents, Arthur. Interview by David Behrens. *Newsday*, July 24, 1984.

Laurents, Arthur. Interview by Suki Sandler. December 8, 1993. Unpublished transcript, Arthur Laurents Papers, Library of Congress, Washington, D.C.

Laurents, Arthur. Interview by N. Graham Nesmith. *The Dramatist: The Journal of The Dramatists Guild of America, Inc.* (May/June 2003): 7–16.

290 BIBLIOGRAPHY

Laurents, Arthur. *Mainly on Directing: Gypsy, West Side Story, and Other Musicals.* New York: Alfred A. Knopf, 2009.

Laurents, Arthur. *The Rest of the Story: A Life Completed.* New York: Applause, 2011.

LeBesco, Kathleen. "Quest for a Cause: The Fat Gene, the Gay Gene, and the New Eugenics." In *The Fat Studies Reader,* edited by Esther Rothblum and Sondra Solovay, 65–74. New York: New York University Press, 2009.

LeBesco, Kathleen. *Revolting Bodies? The Struggle to Redefine Fat Identity.* Amherst: University of Massachusetts Press, 2003.

LeBesco, Kathleen. "Situating Fat Suits: Blackface, Drag, and the Politics of Performance." *Women & Performance: A Journal of Feminist Theory* 15, no. 2 (2005): 231–242.

Leduc, Amanda. *Disfigured: On Fairy Tales, Disability, and Making Space.* Toronto: Coach House Books, 2020.

Leduc, Amanda. Interview with Disability Visibility Project, February 10, 2020. https://disabilityvisibilityproject.com/2020/02/10/qa-with-amanda-leduc-on-fairy-tales-and-disability/.

Lee, Ashley. "'I Have to Be Thin to Do This Job': Inside the Theater's Long-standing Fatphobia." *Los Angeles Times,* May 15, 2021. https://www.latimes.com/entertainment-arts/story/2021-05-15/broadway-body-theater-fatphobia.

Leong, Nancy. "Racial Capitalism." *Harvard Law Review* 2151 (June 2013): 126. https://harvardlawreview.org/2013/06/racial-capitalism/.

Liff, Spencer. Interview with Ken Davenport. *The Producer's Perspective* (podcast). September 28, 2015. https://dev-the-producersperspective.pantheonsite.io/my_weblog/2015/09/podcast-episode-39-transcript-spencer-liff.html.

Liff, Spencer. "Follow Choreographer Spencer Liff's Workout Routine for a Broadway Body." *Playbill,* August 15, 2018. http://www.playbill.com/article/follow-choreographer-spencer-liffs-workout-routine-for-a-broadway-body.

Lim, Stephanie. "At the Intersection of Deaf and Asian American Performativity in Los Angeles: Deaf West Theatre's and East West Players' Adaptations of *Pippin.*" *Studies in Musical Theatre* 11, no.1 (March 2017): 23–37.

Lim, Stephanie. "Silence, Gesture, and Deaf Identity in Deaf West Theatre's *Spring Awakening.*" *Journal of American Drama and Theatre* 33, no. 1 (2020). https://jadtjournal.org/2020/12/11/silence-gesture-and-deaf-identity-in-deaf-west-theatres-spring-awakening/.

Llana, Jose. Interview with Thirsty. Spring 2016, *Stay Thirsty.* https://www.staythirstymedia.com/201604-092/html/201604-llana.html.

Llana, Jose. Interview with Aaron Hicklin. *Out,* July 4, 2014. https://www.out.com/pride/2014/07/04/my-pride-jose-llana.

Lopez, German. "The Reagan Administration's Unbelievable Response to the HIV/AIDS Epidemic." *Vox,* December 1, 2015, updated December 1, 2016. https://www.vox.com/2015/12/1/9828348/ronald-reagan-hiv-aids.

LuPone, Patti. Interview with Andrew Gans. *Playbill,* March 12, 2010. https://www.playbill.com/article/diva-talk-celebrating-sondheim-with-tony-winner-patti-lupone-com-166701.

Madison, D. Soyini. *Critical Ethnography: Method, Ethics, and Performance.* Los Angeles: SAGE, 2012.

MAKERS. "Cynthia Erivo Performs 'I'm Here' from 'The Color Purple' | 2017 MAKERS Conference." April 4, 2017. YouTube video, 12:18. https://www.youtube.com/watch?v=E-Flmo07ddk.

BIBLIOGRAPHY 291

Malone, Beth. Interview with Adam Hetrick. *Playbill*, June 29, 2015. https://www.playbill. com/article/for-beth-malone-butch-is-a-beautiful-thing-what-this-fun-home-star-learned-playing-lesbian-com-351968.

Malykhina, Elena. "Sizing Them Up." *Newsday* (New York), September 23, 2002.

Mandelbaum, Ken. *A Chorus Line and the Musicals of Michael Bennett*. New York: St. Martin's Press, 1989.

MargoChanning. "Effie White—Does She Have to Be Heavy?'" *Broadway World* message board. June 15, 2005. https://www.broadwayworld.com/board/readmessage.php?thr ead=854590.

Markel, Howard. "The Painful Life of Cole Porter." *MedGenMed* 6, no. 2 (2004). https:// www.ncbi.nlm.nih.gov/pmc/articles/PMC1395752/.

Markel, Howard. "When a Secret President Ran the Country." *PBS Newshour*, October 2, 2015. https://www.pbs.org/newshour/health/woodrow-wilson-stroke.

McElroy, Steven. "A Vulnerable Center-Stage Moment." *New York Times*, August 1, 2012. https://www.nytimes.com/2012/08/05/theater/lindsay-mendez-talks-about-dogfight.html.

McKenzie, Shelly. *Getting Physical: The Rise of Fitness Culture in America*. Lawrence: University Press of Kansas, 2013.

McNally, Terrence. *Selected Works: A Memoir in Plays*. New York: Grove Press, 2015.

McNulty, Charles. "Playwrights Are Calling Out Racism in Theater. Their Art Lights a Path to Justice." *Los Angeles Times*, June 11, 2020. https://www.latimes.com/entertainm ent-arts/story/2020-06-11/playwrights-racism-white-american-theater.

McRuer, Robert. *Crip Theory: Cultural Signs of Queerness and Disability*. New York: New York University Press, 2006.

Mead, Rebecca. "Under the Sea." *New Yorker*, November 19, 2007. https://www.newyor ker.com/magazine/2007/11/26/under-the-sea.

Mechikoff, Robert A., and Steven G. Estes. *A History and Philosophy of Sport and Physical Education: from Ancient Civilizations to the Modern World*, 4th ed. New York: McGraw-Hill, 2006.

Meyers, Joe. "How 'Lord Farquaar' Stops the Show on His Knees." *Connecticut Post*, December 24, 2012. https://www.ctpost.com/news/article/How-Lord-Farquaar-stops-the-show-on-his-knees-4143559.php.

Miller, D. A. *The Novel and the Police*. Berkeley: University of California Press, 1988.

Miller, D. A. *Place for Us: Essay on the Broadway Musical*. Cambridge, MA: Harvard University Press, 1998.

Miller, Terry. Review of *La Cage aux Folles*. Palace Theatre, New York. *New York Native*, September 12, 1983.

Miller, Terry. "'Sing Me a Song with Social Significance,'" *New York Native*, August 1–14, 1983.

MissPoochSmooch. "2000 Tony Awards ~ COMPLETE." January 14, 2014. YouTube video, 2:13:17. https://youtu.be/laSxK51T86s?t=3001.

Mitchell, David, and Sharon Snyder. *Narrative Prosthesis: Disability and the Dependencies of Discourse*. Ann Arbor: University of Michigan Press, 2000.

Mitchellivers. "A Chorus Line on Donahue 2." January 6, 2008. YouTube video, 9:30. https://www.youtube.com/watch?v=bJp7FWujLDA.

Mitchellivers. "A Chorus Line on Donahue 3." January 6, 2008. YouTube video, 8:50. https://www.youtube.com/watch?v=YgdmvMkHw20.

Mitchellivers. "A Chorus Line on Donahue 4." January 6, 2008. YouTube video, 6:26. https://www.youtube.com/watch?v=d-dBgS7_AGU.

292 BIBLIOGRAPHY

Mitchellivers. "A Chorus Line on Donahue 5 January 6, 2008. YouTube video, 7:05. https://www.youtube.com/watch?v=eW6RdLRyJjo.

Mitchell, John Cameron. Interview with Anna Sale. *Death, Sex & Money* (podcast). April 15, 2015. https://www.wnycstudios.org/podcasts/deathsexmoney/episodes/john-cameron-mitchell-death-sex-money.

Mobley, Jennifer-Scott. *Female Bodies on the American Stage: Enter Fat Actress*. New York: Palgrave Macmillan, 2014.

Mobley, Jennifer-Scott. "Staging Fat: Dramaturgy, Female Bodies, and Contemporary American Culture." PhD thesis, Graduate Center, City University of New York, 2010.

Monbiot, George. "Neoliberalism—The Ideology at the Root of All Our Problems." *The Guardian*, April 15, 2016. https://www.theguardian.com/books/2016/apr/15/neoliberalism-ideology-problem-george-monbiot.

Moody, Nekesa Mumbi. "Jennifer Hudson Steals 'Dreamgirls' Show." *Washington Post*, December 12, 2006. http://www.washingtonpost.com/wp-dyn/content/article/2006/12/12/AR2006121200939.html.

Moore, Trudy S. "'Dreamgirls' Tour Cast Loaded with New Talent." *Jet*, June 11, 1984.

Most, Andrea. *Making Americans: Jews and the Broadway Musical*. Cambridge, MA: Harvard University Press, 2004.

MrPoochsmooch. "A Chorus Line 1976 Tony Awards." June 1, 2012. YouTube video, 7:57. https://www.youtube.com/watch?v=htLGQ3CDODY.

MrPoochsmooch. "La Cage aux Folles 1984 Tony Awards." January 20, 2014. YouTube video, 15:15. https://www.youtube.com/watch?v=v4SGTEv1164.

Muñoz, Javier. Interview with Taffy Brodesser-Akner, *GQ*, September 1, 2016. https://www.gq.com/story/javier-munoz-of-hamilton-has-been-reborn.

Muñoz, Javier. Interview with Oriol R. Gutierrez. *POZ*, September 26, 2016. https://www.poz.com/article/spotlight-javier-munoz.

Musto, Michael. "Drag Queens and Gay Sex Back on Broadway Where They Belong!" *Village Voice*, March 6, 2013. https://www.villagevoice.com/2013/03/06/drag-queens-and-gay-sex-back-on-broadway-where-they-belong/.

Nachman, Gerald. Review of *Dreamgirls*. Golden Gate Theatre, San Francisco. *San Francisco Examiner*, December 21, 1983.

Nassour, Ellis. "An Intimate Chat with the Chorus 'Girls.'" *Broadway Bill of Fare*, July 26, 1984.

Nassour, Ellis. "Here Comes Lea DeLaria in *On the Town*—Born to Make People Laugh." *Playbill*, November 19, 2019. https://www.playbill.com/article/here-comes-lea-delaria-born-to-make-people-laugh-com-101256.

Nelsen, Don. "A First Peek Inside 'La Cage aux Folles' . . . the Musical Comedy with a Difference." *New York Daily News*, July 10, 1983.

New York Times. "David Carroll Is Dead; A Broadway Actor, 41." March 13, 1992. https://www.nytimes.com/1992/03/13/obituaries/david-carroll-is-dead-a-broadway-actor-41.html.

New York Times. "George W. Holt 3d, Producer." July 15, 1987. https://www.nytimes.com/1987/07/15/obituaries/george-w-holt-3d-producer-and-director.html.

Newell, Alex. Interview with Jason Pham. *Stylecaster* (blog), n.d. 2017 Accessed July 21, 2020. https://stylecaster.com/alex-newell-glee-sexuality-body-image/.

Newman, Barbara. "*Speaking of Dance: Scott Salmon*." *Dancing Times London*. May 1986.

BIBLIOGRAPHY 293

Norman, Marsha. *The Color Purple*. In *The Color Purple: A Memory Book* by Lise Funderburg. Cambridge, MA: Da Capo Press, 2006.

Norman, Marsha, and Lucy Simon. *The Secret Garden*. New York: Samuel French, 1992.

Novick, Julius. Review of *La Cage aux Folles*. Palace Theatre, New York. *Village Voice*, September 6, 1983.

NYC Pride. "Our Timeline." Accessed April 6, 2018, https://www.nycpride.org/about/.

O'Donnell, Mark, Thomas Meehan, Marc Shaiman, and Scott Wittman. *Hairspray: The Complete Book and Lyrics of the Hit Broadway Musical*. New York: Applause, 2002.

O'Donnell, Mark, Thomas Meehan, Marc Shaiman, and Scott Wittman. *Hairspray: The Roots*. New York: Faber and Faber, 2003.

O'Haire, Patricia. "Dreamgirls II." *New York Daily News*, June 21, 1987.

Oja, Carol J. *Bernstein Meets Broadway: Collaborative Art in a Time of War*. New York: Oxford University Press, 2014.

Oleksinski, Johnny. "When Did Celebs Become No-Talent Hotties?". *New York Post*, August 9, 2019. https://nypost.com/2019/08/09/when-did-celebs-become-no-talent-hotties/.

Original Broadway Cast. *Bring It On: The Musical*. Sh-K-Boom Records, 2012, digital.

Original Broadway Cast. *The Who's Tommy*. RCA Victor, 1993, compact disc.

"Our Towns: A Community Notebook." *Chicago Tribune*, August 27, 1989.

Pacheco, Patrick. "Water's 'Hairspray' Is Beginning to Gel." *Newsday*, December 20, 2001.

Padgett, Donald. "André De Shields, 74, Opens Up about Living with HIV." *Plus*, February 11, 2020. https://www.hivplusmag.com/stigma/2020/2/11/andre-de-shields-74-opens-about-living-hiv.

Pao, Angela C. *No Safe Spaces: Re-casting Race, Ethnicity and Nationality in American Theater*. Ann Arbor: University of Michigan Press, 2010.

Papp, Joseph, and Kenneth Turan. *Free for All: Joe Papp, The Public, and the Greatest Theater Story Ever Told*. New York: Anchor Books, 2010.

Patterson, Richard. "The Secrets to Broadway Bodies: How Performers Stay Trim, Toned, and Tight." *Playbill*, January 31, 2015. http://www.playbill.com/article/the-secrets-to-broadway-bodies-how-performers-stay-trim-toned-and-tight-com-340312.

Paul, Mark, Darrick Hamilton, and William Darity Jr. "Discriminatory Penalties at the Intersection of Race and Gender in the United States." Washington Center for Equitable Growth, August 7, 2018. https://equitablegrowth.org/discriminatory-penalties-at-the-intersection-of-race-and-gender-in-the-united-states/.

Paulson, Michael. "Broadway Is Reopening. But Not Until September." *New York Times*, May 5, 2021 (updated September 14, 2021). https://www.nytimes.com/2021/05/05/theater/broadway-reopening-new-york.html.

Paulson, Michael. "'Fun Home' Recoups on Broadway." *New York Times*, December 13, 2015. https://www.nytimes.com/2015/12/14/theater/fun-home-recoups-on-broadway.html.

Paulson, Michael. "'Hamilton' Producers Will Change Job Posting, but Not Commitment to Diverse Casting." *New York Times*, March 30, 2016. http://www.nytimes.com/2016/03/31/arts/union-criticizes-hamilton-casting-call-seeking-nonwhite-actors.html.

Paulson, Michael. "Lights, Gestures, Action! How to Stage a Broadway Musical with Deaf Actors." *New York Times*, October 2, 2015.

Peikert, Mark. "Broadway's Christian Dante White Wears the Pressure and Responsibility of Being an Out Black Actor with Pride." *Playbill*, June 11, 2019. https://www.playbill.

294 BIBLIOGRAPHY

com/article/broadways-christian-dante-white-wears-the-pressure-and-responsibility-of-being-an-out-black-actor-with-pride.

Peikert, Mark. "With Her 12th Broadway Show, Jenifer Foote Is Happy to Finally Be Herself Onstage." *Playbill*, June 20, 2019. https://www.playbill.com/article/with-her-12th-broadway-show-jenifer-foote-is-happy-to-finally-be-herself-onstage.

People. "Marissa Jaret Winokur: I Had to Call in Fat." August 25, 2009. http://people.com/bodies/marissa-jaret-winokur-i-had-to-call-in-fat/.

Petrzela, Natalia Mehlman. "The Fitness Craze That Changed the Way Women Exercise." *Atlantic*, June 16, 2019. https://www.theatlantic.com/entertainment/archive/2019/06/jazzercise-50-years-women-fitness-culture-judi-sheppard-missett/591349/.

Playbill. "Old Show Queens—Episode 3—On Directors." September 5, 2019. YouTube video, 7:46. https://www.youtube.com/watch?v=TXyzUg_nhfs.

Playbill. "Hey, Johnny! Theatrical Advice—How Important Is a Broadway Body." January 4, 2015. http://www.playbill.com/article/hey-johnny-theatrical-advice-how-important-is-a-broadway-body-com-338298.

Playbill. "*Spring Awakening* Grosses." http://www.playbill.com/production/gross?production=00000150-aea8-d936-a7fd-eefc72fb0000.

Pogrebin, Robin. "Big Hair and Personality to Match; For a Young Actress's Career, A Bouffant Moment in 'Hairspray,'" *New York Times*, August 21, 2002.

Pogrebin, Robin. "Lisa Howard on Her Latest Broadway Show, 'It Shoulda Been You.'" *New York Times*, March 18, 2015.

Porter, Billy. "Billy Porter Breaks a 14-Year Silence: 'This Is What HIV-Positive Looks Like Now.'" *Hollywood Reporter*, May 19, 2021. https://www.hollywoodreporter.com/news/general-news/billy-porter-hiv-positive-diagnosis-1234954742/?fbclid=IwAR3pIWQ84MOmYYPKJGoEwuBt796H8q5mB60wBWJsHbeXULY_F5k-abw6j0w.

Porter, Billy. "The First Time I Refused to Keep Playing a Stereotype." *New York Times*, November 21, 2017. https://www.nytimes.com/2017/11/21/theater/billy-porter-the-first-time-i-refused-to-keep-playing-a-stereotype.html.

Porter, Tom. "How FDR Kept His Partial Paralysis a Secret from the American Public—Even While He Was on the Campaign Trail." *Business Insider*, May 10, 2019. https://www.businessinsider.com/how-fdr-hid-his-paralysis-from-american-public-even-while-campaigning-2019-4.

Powers, John R., James Quinn, and Alaric Jans. *Do Black Patent Leather Shoes Really Reflect Up?* New York: Samuel French, 1988.

Pratt, Mary Louise. "Arts of the Contact Zone." In *Professing in the Contact Zone: Bringing Theory and Practice Together*, edited by Janice M. Wolff, 1–18. Urbana, IL: National Council of Teachers of English, 2002.

Prestinario, Andrea. Interview with Holly Sansom and Meghan Dixon. "#3—Twice! Andrea Prestinario." *Thesis on Joan* (podcast). July 15, 2020. https://broadwaypodcastnetwork.com/podcast/thesis-on-joan/?_page=3.

Preston, Julia. "Obama Lifts a Ban on Entry into U.S. by H.I.V.-Positive People." *New York Times*, October 30, 2009.

Pronger, Brian. *Body Fascism: Salvation in the Technology of Physical Fitness.* Toronto: University of Toronto Press, 2002.

Quinn, Dave. "How Broadway Icon Jennifer Holliday Overcame Depression, Body Issues and Temporary Blindness to Stage a Comeback in *The Color Purple*." *People*, October 26, 2016. http://people.com/theater/how-broadway-icon-jennifer-holliday-overcame-depression-body-issues-and-temporary-blindness-to-stage-a-comeback-in-the-color-purple/.

Rado, James. Interview with Sheela Lambert. *Advocate*, August 13, 2008. https://www.advocate.com/arts-entertainment/theater/2008/08/13/man-behind-hair.

Rapp, Anthony. Interview by Jeff Walsh. *Oasis* (blog), n.d. Accessed July 9, 2020. https://web.archive.org/web/20140714193216/http://oasisjournals.com/Issues/9708/rent-anthony.html.

Reimers, Sara. "Making an Appearance: Exploring Performers' Experiences of Aesthetic Labour." Centre for Contemporary British Theatre, Royal Holloway, University of London, September 12, 2019. https://www.equity.org.uk/media/3339/making-an-appearance-report.pdf.

Reimers, Sara. "'She's Too Big I Hope for Me to Compass': Fat Suits, Costuming and the Construction of Femininity in Contemporary Stagings of Shakespeare's *Comedy of Errors*." *Studies in Costume & Performance* 2:2 (2017): 157–170.

Rian Keating. "Roz Ryan interviewed by Rian Keating, 1984." January 28, 2015. YouTube video, 29:14. https://www.youtube.com/watch?fbclid=IwAR2cLqOolAnp0fj4rxDWdvjsR7BDVpw9y1nfKL1NY6cRyxlMw-tccjVAUXI&v=Xm6ecFqLBtI&feature=youtu.be.

Rich, Frank. Review of *Dreamgirls*. Imperial Theatre, New York. *New York Times*, December 21, 1981.

Rich, Frank. Review of *Dreamgirls*. Imperial Theatre, New York. *New York Times*, September 23, 1983.

Rich, Frank. Review of *Grand Hotel*. Martin Beck Theater, New York. *New York Times*, November 13,1989. https://www.nytimes.com/1989/11/13/theater/review-theater-tune-s-swirling-vision-of-a-grand-hotel.html.

Rich, Frank. Review of *La Cage Aux Folles*. Palace Theatre, New York. *New York Times*, August 22, 1983.

Rich, Frank. Review of *The Secret Garden*. St. James Theatre, New York. *New York Times*, April 26, 1991, https://www.nytimes.com/1991/04/26/theater/review-theater-garden-the-secret-of-death-and-birth.html.

Rich, Frank. "Stage View: 'La Cage' Has That Old-Time Appeal." Palace Theatre, New York. *New York Times*, August 28, 1983.

Richardson, Michael. "The Sign Language Interpreted Performance: A Failure of Access Provision for Deaf Spectators." *Theatre Topics* 28, no. 1 (March 2018): 63–74.

Riedel, Michael. "On Broadway." *New York Post*, November 19, 2004.

Riedel, Michael. "On Broadway." *New York Post*, April 1, 2005.

Riedel, Michael. "On Broadway." *New York Post*, February 25, 2011.

Risner, Doug. "What We Know about Boys Who Dance: The Limitations of Contemporary Masculinity and Dance Education." In *When Men Dance: Choreographing Masculinities across Borders*, edited by Jennifer Fisher and Anthony Shay, 57–77. New York: Oxford University Press, 2009.

Roberts, Sam. "Sammy Williams, Tony Winner in 'A Chorus Line,' Dies at 69." *New York Times*, March 22, 2018. https://www.nytimes.com/2018/03/22/obituaries/sammy-williams-tony-winner-in-a-chorus-line-dies-at-69.html.

Robertson, Campbell. "'Chorus Line' Returns, as Do Regrets over Life Stories Signed Away." *New York Times*, October 1, 2006. https://www.nytimes.com/2006/10/01/theater/01line.html.

Román, David. *Acts of Intervention: Performance, Gay Culture, and AIDS*. Bloomington: University of Indiana Press, 1998.

296 BIBLIOGRAPHY

Román, David. *Performance in America: Contemporary U.S. Culture and the Performing Arts*. Durham, NC: Duke University Press, 2005.

Rooney, David. Review of *Fiddler on the Roof*. Minskoff Theater, New York. *Variety*, October 13, 2005. https://variety.com/2005/legit/reviews/fiddler-on-the-roof-7-120 0521019/.

Rooney, David. Review of *The Gershwins' Porgy and Bess*. Richard Rodgers Theater, New York. *Hollywood Reporter*, January 12, 2012. https://www.hollywoodreporter.com/review/broadway-gershwins-porgy-bess-theater-review-280994.

Rooney, David. Review of *Hedwig and the Angry Inch*. Belasco Theatre, New York. *Hollywood Reporter*, March 13, 2015. https://www.hollywoodreporter.com/news/crit ics-notebook-john-cameron-mitchell-781336.

Rooney, David. Review of *La Cage aux Folles*. Marquis Theatre, New York. *Variety*, December 9, 2004.

Rooney, David. Review of *Spring Awakening*. Brooks Atkinson Theatre, New York. *Hollywood Reporter*, September 27, 2015.

Rorke, Robert. "'Hair' She Is!" *New York Post*, June 8, 2016.

Rose, Sarah F. *No Right to Be Idle: The Invention of Disability, 1840s–1930s*. Chapel Hill: University of North Carolina Press, 2017.

Rosenfield, Paul. "Arthur Laurents, Uncaged." *Los Angeles Times*, September 2, 1984.

Rosenthal, David N. "Visions Dance Out of Dreamboy's Mind." *Mercury News* (San Jose, CA), December 18, 1983.

Rothblum, Esther, and Sondra Solovay, editors. *The Fat Studies Reader*. New York: New York University Press, 2009.

Roundabout Theatre Company. "Waiting for the Light." *Upstage*, Spring 2003, 1.

Rowan, Tom. A Chorus Line *FAQ: All That's Left to Know about Broadway's Singular Sensation*. New York: Applause, 2015.

Rozentsvit, Aleksandr. "How Broadway's New *Spring Awakening* Is Resonating for a Deaf Theatre Lover." *Playbill*, December 16, 2015. http://www.playbill.com/article/how-broadways-new-spring-awakening-is-resonating-for-a-deaf-theatre-lover-com-375499.

runneryoshi105. "Jennifer Holliday 'And I Am Telling You.'" December 9, 2006. YouTube video, 8:34. https://www.youtube.com/watch?v=rtnKI3ztz9w.

Ryan, Dietrich. "Not Just for Gays Anymore Lyrics-Neil Patrick Harris." *FIM* Fiction (blog). Accessed March 14, 2018. https://www.fimfiction.net/blog/502511/not-just-for-gays-anymore-lyrics-neil-patrick-harris.

Sater, Steven. *A Purple Summer: Notes on the Lyrics of* Spring Awakening. New York: Applause.

Sandahl, Carrie, and Philip Auslander, editors. *Bodies in Commotion: Disability & Performance*. Ann Arbor: University of Michigan Press, 2005.

Sandahl, Carrie, and Philip Auslander. Introduction to *Bodies in Commotion: Disability & Performance*, edited by Carrie Sandahl and Philip Auslander, 1–12 Ann Arbor: University of Michigan Press, 2005.

Sandahl, Carrie. "The Difference Disability Makes." In *Casting a Movement: The Welcome Table Initiative*, edited by Claire Syler and Daniel Banks, 88–99. New York: Routledge, 2019.

Sandahl, Carrie. "Using Our Words: Exploring Representational Conundrums in Disability Drama and Performance." *Journal of Literary & Cultural Disability Studies* 12, no. 2 (2018): 129–144.

BIBLIOGRAPHY 297

Sandahl, Carrie. "Why Disability Identity Matters: From Dramaturgy to Casting in John Belluso's *Pyretown*." In *The Disability Studies Reader* 5th ed., edited by Lennard J. Davis, 454–469. New York: Routledge, 2017.

Sandoval-Sánchez, Alberto. *José, Can You See? Latinos on and off Broadway.* Madison: University of Wisconsin Press, 1999.

San Pablo Burns, Lucy. "'How in the Light of One Night Did We Come So Far?' Working Miss Saigon." In *Puro Arte: Filipinos on the Stages of Empire*, 126–131. New York: New York University Press Press, 2013.

Sater, Steven, and Duncan Sheik. *Spring Awakening.* New York: Theatre Communications Group, 2007.

SaveLiveMusic. "I ♥ New York 70s Broadway Ad." June 17, 2011.YouTube video, 1:03. https://www.youtube.com/watch?v=vS_H9ak7asQ.

Savran, David. *A Queer Sort of Materialism: Recontextualizing American Theater.* Ann Arbor: University of Michigan Press, 2003.

Savran, David. "Queer Theater and the Disarticulation of Identity." In *The Queerest Art: Essays on Lesbian and Gay Theater*, edited by Alisa Solomon and Framji Minwalla, 152–167. New York: New York University Press, 2002.

Savran, David. "*Rent's* Due: Multiculturalism and the Spectacle of Difference." *Journal of American Drama and Theatre* 14, no. 1 (2002): 1–14.

Savran, David. "You've Got That Thing": Cole Porter, Stephen Sondheim, and the Erotics of the List Song." *Theatre Journal* 64, no. 4 (2012): 533–548.

Schechner, Richard. "Casting wthout Limits." *American Theatre*, December 2010.

Schildcrout, Jordan. "Drama and the New Sexualities." In *The Oxford Handbook of American Drama*, edited by Jeffrey H. Richards and Heather S. Nathans, 455–459. New York: Oxford University Press, 2014.

Schulman, Sarah. *The Gentrification of the Mind: Witness to a Lost Imagination.* Berkeley: University of California Press, 2012.

Schulman, Sarah. *Stage Struck: Theater, AIDS, and the Marketing of Gay America.* Durham, NC: Duke University Press, 1998.

Schulman, Sarah. *Ties That Bind: Familial Homophobia and Its Consequences.* New York: New Press, 2012.

Schwarz, Jeffrey, director. *The Fabulous Allan Carr.* Los Angeles: Automat Pictures, 2017. Advance screening copy.

Scott, Robert A., and Dale T. Miller. Foreword to *The Dilemma of Difference: A Multidisciplinary View of Stigma*, edited by Stephen C. Ainlay, Lerita M. Coleman, and Gaylene Becker, ix–xiii. New York: Plenum Press, 1985.

Sedgwick, Eve Kosofsky. *Epistemology of the Closet.* Berkeley: University of California Press, 1990.

Sedgwick, Eve Kosofsky, and Michael Moon. "Divinity: A Dossier, A Performance Piece, A Little-Understood Emotion." In Eve Kosofsky Sedgwick, *Tendencies*, 215–251. Durham, NC: Duke University Press, 1993.

Senelick, Laurence. *The Changing Room: Sex, Drag and Theatre.* London: Routledge, 2000.

Seth Rudetsky. "Camryn Manheim Talks Career & Spring Awakening on Seth Speaks." March 12, 2016. YouTube video, 20:25. https://www.youtube.com/watch?v=o1qdMbdviTs.

Seth Rudetsky. "Spring Awakening's Krysta Rodriguez and Ali Stroker Interview on Seth Speaks." December 16, 2015. YouTube video, 13:34. https://www.youtube.com/watch?v=I-CMPvptROY.

298 BIBLIOGRAPHY

Seth Rudetsky. "Tony Nominated Director Michael Arden on Seth Speaks." June 8, 2016. YouTube video, 09:57. https://www.youtube.com/watch?v=cirkgwS1XA8.

Settle, Keala. Interview with Patrick Hinds. *Theater People* 31 (podcast). February 8, 2015. https://www.buzzsprout.com/19639.rss.

"The Shape of the Fitness Industry." *South Source.* May 2012. source.southuniversity.edu/the-shape-of-the-fitness-industry-85375.aspx.

Shapiro, Eddie. *Nothing Like a Dame: Conversations with the Great Women of Musical Theater.* New York: Oxford University Press, 2014.

Shapiro, Eddie. *A Wonderful Guy: Conversations with the Great Men of Musical Theater.* New York: Oxford University Press, 2021.

Shapiro, Marc. "Jennifer Holliday: The Lady Does Things Her Way." *Stanley Bennett Clay's Hollywood,* October–November 1983.

Shaw, Helen. "*The Book of Mormon* and *Hamilton* Already Feel Like They're from Another Time." Brooks Atkinson Theatre and Richard Rodgers Theater, New York. *Vulture,* December 16, 2019. https://www.vulture.com/2019/12/re-reviewing-the-book-of-mormon-and-hamilton-in-2019.html.

Shea, Andrea. "'Porgy and Bess': Messing with A Classic." *NPR,* August 20, 2011. https://www.npr.org/2011/08/21/139784251/porgy-and-bess-messing-with-a-classic.

Shewey, Don. "The It Boy." *Advocate,* January 19, 1999. https://www.donshewey.com/theater_articles/john_cameron_mitchell.html.

Shewey, Don. "The Musical According to Bennett." *New York Times,* September 25, 1983. https://www.nytimes.com/1983/09/25/arts/the-musical-according-to-bennett.html.

Shinall, Jennifer Bennett. "Occupational Characteristics and the Obesity Wage Penalty." *Vanderbilt Law and Economics Research Paper* 16–12 (2015): https://ssrn.com/abstract=2379575.

Shinn, Christopher. "Disability Is Not Just a Metaphor." *Atlantic,* July 23, 2014. https://www.theatlantic.com/entertainment/archive/2014/07/why-disabled-characters-are-never-played-by-disabled-actors/374822/.

Shirley Herz & Associates. Press Release for national tour of *La Cage Aux Folles,* n.d. Theatre Collection, New York Public Library.

Sieber, Christopher. "'Yes, My Knees Are Fine. . . . Thanks for Asking.'" *Broadway.com,* February 10, 2009. https://www.broadway.com/buzz/6317/christopher-sieber-yes-my-knees-are-finethanks-for-asking/.

Siebers, Tobin. *Disability Aesthetics.* Ann Arbor: University of Michigan Press, 2010.

Siebers, Tobin. *Disability Theory.* Ann Arbor: University of Michigan Press, 2008.

Signorile, Michaelangelo. "Harvey Fierstein on 'Kinky Boots,' Working with Cyndi Lauper and His Show's Big Surprise." *Huffington Post,* May 17, 2013 (updated February 2, 2016). Accessed April 16, 2018, https://www.huffingtonpost.com/2013/05/17/harvey-fierstein-kinky-boots_n_3292504.html.

Silverman, Stephen M. "Broadway's Dream Boy." *New York Post,* June 27, 1987.

Simon, John. Review of *La Cage aux Folles.* Palace Theatre, New York. *New York,* September 5, 1983.

Simon, John. Review of *La Cage aux Folles.* Marquis Theatre, New York. *New York,* December 20, 2004.

Simon, Sarah. "The Feminist History of Fat Liberation." *Ms. Magazine,* October 18, 2019. https://msmagazine.com/2019/10/18/the-feminist-history-of-fat-liberation/.

Simonson, Robert. "Law Is the Law, but Producing Is His Life." *New York Times,* May 25, 2008.

BIBLIOGRAPHY   299

Smart, Jack. "The Broadway Body Revolution of Mark Fisher Fitness." *Backstage*. February 9, 2016. http://www.backstage.com/interview/broadway-body-revolution-mark-fisher-fitness/.

Smith, Liz. "Liz Smith." *New York Daily News*, August 23, 1983.

Snook, Raven. "Big, Blonde and Beautiful in Her Broadway Debut." *TDF Stages* (blog), July 24, 2018. http://bway.ly/4o61zu/#https://www.tdf.org/stages/article/1960/big-blonde-and-beautiful-in-her-broadway-debut.

Snow, Georgia. "Amber Riley Misses Dreamgirls Performances after Being Diagnosed with Pneumonia." *The Stage*, January 4, 2017. https://www.thestage.co.uk/news/2017/amber-riley-misses-dreamgirls-performances-after-being-diagnosed-with-pneumonia/.

Solovay, Sondra. *Tipping the Scales of Justice: Fighting Weight-Based Discrimination*. Amherst, NY: Prometheus Books, 2000.

Solovay, Sondra, and Esther Rothblum. Introduction to *The Fat Studies Reader*, edited by Esther Rothblum and Sondra Solovay, 1–7. New York: New York University Press, 2009.

Sondheim, Stephen. Letter to the editor. *New York Times*, August 10, 2011. https://artsbeat.blogs.nytimes.com/2011/08/10/stephen-sondheim-takes-issue-with-plan-for-revamped-porgy-and-bess/.

Spring Awakening Playbill. "A Note about the ASL Translation." September 2015.

Stamberg, Susan. "Backstage of 'A Chorus Line' with Its Least Known Creator." NPR, May 22, 2000, https://www.npr.org/2000/05/22/1074450/npr-100-i-a-chorus-line-i.

Stanton, Ali. Review of *Dreamgirls*. Imperial Theatre, New York. *New York Amsterdam News*, January 23, 1982.

Stars in the House. "Everything Effie | Stars in the House, Saturday, 1/9/21 at 8PM ET." January 9, 2021. YouTube video, 2:10:10. https://www.youtube.com/watch?v=i_0WPONs3g4.

Steketee, Martha Wade. "Introduction and Background." National Endowment for the Arts Roundtable Report: Creating Opportunities for Deaf Theater Artists." Washington, DC, 2016.

Stein, Ruthie. "Tony Winner Aldredge Talks Tricks of the Trade." *San Francisco Chronicle*, June 5, 1984.

Stern, Gary. "The Real Gals in 'La Cage aux Folles' Admit That It Ain't Such a Drag!" *Backstage*, May 11, 1984.

Sternbergh, Adam. "Ladies and Gentlemen, Your Next Republican President." *New York*, March 21, 2010.

Sternfeld, Jessica. "'Pitiful Creature of Darkness': The Subhuman and the Superhuman in *The Phantom of the Opera*." In *The Oxford Handbook of Music and Disability Studies*, edited by Blake Howe, Stephanie Jensen-Moulton, Neil Lerner, and Joseph Straus, 795–813. New York: Oxford University Press, 2015.

Stevens, Gary, and Alan George. *The Longest Line: Broadway's Most Singular Sensation: A Chorus Line*. New York: Applause Books, 1995.

Straube, Trenton. "R.I.P. Broadway Legend Jerry Herman, Who Lived Openly with HIV Since 1992 [VIDEOS]." *POZ*, January 2, 2020. https://www.poz.com/article/rip-broadway-legend-jerry-herman-lived-openly-hiv-since-1992-videos.

Stroker, Ali. Interview with Ricky Young-Howze. *Howlround*, July 23, 2016. http://howlround.com/six-lessons-i-learned-from-ali-stroker.

Strings, Sabrina. *Fearing the Black Body: The Racial Origins of Fat Phobia*. New York: New York University Press, 2019.

300 BIBLIOGRAPHY

Svich, Caridad. *Mitchell and Trask's* Hedwig and the Angry Inch. London: Routledge, 2019.

Syna, Sy. Review of *La Cage aux Folles*. Palace Theatre, New York. *New York Tribune*, August 22, 1983.

Talcove, Rick. "'Dreamgirls' Turns into Financial Nightmare, Closes." *Los Angeles Daily News*, November 20, 1983.

Talks at Google. "Spring Awakening (Broadway revival cast) | Talks at Google." November 10, 2015. YouTube video, 45:07. https://www.youtube.com/watch?v=-utX-pB8Odg.

Taubman, Howard. "Modern Primer: Helpful Hints to Tell Appearances vs. Truth." *New York Times*, April 28, 1963.

Taubman, Howard. Not What It Seems: Homosexual Motif Gets Heterosexual Guise." *New York Times*, November 5, 1961.

Taylor, Millie. "Singing and Dancing Ourselves: The Politics of the Ensemble in *A Chorus Line* (1975)." In *Gestures of Music Theatre*, edited by Dominic Symonds and Millie Taylor, 276–292. New York: Oxford University Press, 2014.

Taylor, Robert. "A Hot Roadshow Sells Its Sizzle." *Tribune* (Oakland, CA), December 11, 1983.

Tesori, Jeanine, and Lisa Kron. *Fun Home*. New York: Samuel French, 2014.

theatergeek1122. "Walter Charles 'I Am What I Am.'" February 1, 2012. YouTube video, 6:02. https://www.youtube.com/watch?v=Kih_pV6ohPQ.

theatertalk. "Harvey Fierstein Discusses 'La Cage aux Folles.'" April 19, 2016. YouTube video, 26:44. https://www.youtube.com/watch?v=MAElqKusf3Y.

Thomas, Aaron C. "The Pink Elephant in the Room." In *The Routledge Companion to the Contemporary Musical*, edited by Jessica Sternfeld and Elizabeth L. Wollman, 163–172. New York: Routledge, 2020.

Time, "How Gay Is Gay? Homosexual Men and Women Are Making Progress Toward Equality," April 23, 1979.

TimesSquared. "La Cage Aux Folles 1987 Tour with Larry Kert and Harvey Evans." *Broadway World* message board. May 19, 2013. https://www.broadwayworld.com/board/readmessage.php?thread=1060068&page=2.

Tiwary, Vivek J., Arvind Ethan David, and Eva Price. "Impact and Action." *Jagged Little Pill*, Broadway production website, September 17, 2021. https://jaggedlittlepill.com/resources/.

Tony Awards. "Fun Home Performance Tony Awards 2015." July 18, 2015.YouTube video, 3:59. https://www.youtube.com/watch?v=pMAuesRJm1E.

Tune, Tommy. *Footnotes: A Memoir*. New York: Simon and Schuster, 1997.

Tunstall, A. J. Letter to the editor. *The Stage and Television Today*, November 20, 1986.

UN AIDS. "Global HIV& AIDS statistics—2020 fact sheet." Accessed February 4, 2021. https://www.unaids.org/en/resources/fact-sheet#:~:text=75.7%20million%20%5B55.9%20million%E2%80%93100,the%20epidemic%20(end%202019)).

United States Census Bureau. "Statistical Abstract of the United States." Accessed July 9, 2016, www.census.gov/library/publications/timre-series/statistical_abstracts.html.

United States Department of Justice, Civil Rights Division. "The Americans with Disabilities Act of 1990 and Revised ADA Regulations Implementing Title II and Title III." ADA.gov. Accessed March 24, 2016. http://www.ada.gov/2010_regs.htm.

United States Department of Labor. "Persons With A Disability: Labor Force Characteristics—2017." News Release, Bureau of Labor Statistics. June 21, 2018. https://www.bls.gov/news.release/pdf/disabl.pdf.

Variety. "La Cage aux Folles." September 12, 1984.

Variety. "Legitimate: Shubert-CLO Share Subscribers for 'Chorus' & 'Wiz,' on Coast; Original 'Chorus' Cast to Tour." December 03, 1975.

Variety. "London Critics Pan West End 'La Cage.'" May 14, 1986.

Variety. "Spotlight: *Hairspray*." April 21–27, 2003.

Ventura, Michael P. "Working Miracles with Disabled Actors." *Backstage*, February 11–17, 2010.

Viagas, Robert, Baayork Lee, and Thommie Walsh with the entire original cast. *On the Line: The Creation of* A Chorus Line. 2nd ed. Lanham, MD: Limelight Editions, 2006.

Viertel, Jack. "Waiting in the Wings." *Herald Examiner* (Los Angeles), May 22, 1983.

Vincentelli, Elisabeth. "The Boys in the Band Get to Broadway. Why Not the Girls?" *New York Times*, July 5, 2019. https://www.nytimes.com/2019/07/05/theater/broad way-lesbian-theater.html.

Vincentelli, Elisabeth. Review of *The Gershwins' Porgy and Bess*. Richard Rodgers Theater, New York. *New York Post*, January 13, 2012. https://nypost.com/2012/01/13/revam ped-porgy-aint-necessarily-so-fine/.

Voss, Brandon. "How Ali Stroker Reps the Bisexual and Disabled Communities with Class." *New Now Next*, October 1, 2017. http://www.newnownext.com/ali-stroker-ten-days-in-the-valley/10/2017/.

Walters, Suzanna Danuta. *All the Rage: The Story of Gay Visibility in America*. Chicago: University of Chicago Press, 2001.

Wann, Marilyn. Foreword to *The Fat Studies Reader*, edited by Esther Rothblum and Sondra Solovay, xi–xxv. New York: New York University Press, 2009.

Warren, Michael John, director. *Shrek the Musical*. 2013; New York: Netflix. Streaming.

Waters, John. "Finally, Footlights on the Fat Girls." *New York Times*, August 11, 2002. http://www.nytimes.com/2002/08/11/theater/theater-finally-footlights-on-the-fat-girls.html.

Waters, John. *Mr. Know-It-All: The Tarnished Wisdom of a Filth Elder*. New York: Farrar, Straus and Giroux, 2019.

Weber, Bruce. "A Minimalist Actor Now Warns to Excess." *New York Times*, November 4, 1992. https://www.nytimes.com/1992/11/04/theater/a-minimalist-actor-now-warms-to-excess.html.

Weil. Review of *La Cage aux Folles*. Palace Theatre, New York. *Variety*, August 22, 1983.

Weinstein, Farrah. "Worth the Weight." *New York Post*, August 8, 2002.

Weinstein, Steve. "Just in Time: 'La Cage' Returns." *New York Blade*, December 10, 2004.

West, Lindy. *Shrill*. New York: Hachette Books, 2016.

Wetzsteon, Ross. "'La Cage aux Folles' Comes to Broadway." *New York*, August 22, 1983.

White, Abbey. "How Deaf Broadway's 'Into the Woods' Offers a Clear Vision for Accessible Musical Theater." *Hollywood Reporter*, September 14, 2021. https://www.hollyw oodreporter.com/lifestyle/arts/deaf-broadway-lincoln-center-into-the-woods-123 5013345/.

White, Edmund. "Four Geniuses, Gone to AIDS, as They Might Be Today." *T Magazine*, April 19, 2018.

Whitfield, Sarah. "A Space Has Been Made: Bisexual+ Stories in Musical Theatre." In "Queer Pedagogy in Theatre and Performance," special issue of *Theatre Topics* 30, no. 2 (2020). https://jhuptheatre.org/theatre-topics/online-content/issue/volume-30-issue-2-july-2020/space-has-been-made-bisexual.

Whitesel, Jason. *Fat Gay Men: Girth, Mirth, and the Politics of Stigma*. New York: New York University Press, 2014.

302 BIBLIOGRAPHY

Willson, Meredith. *"But He Doesn't Know the Territory."* New York: G. P. Putnam's Sons, 1959. Reprint, Minneapolis: University of Minnesota Press, 2009.

Windman, Matt. Review of *Spring Awakening*. Brooks Atkinson Theatre, New York. *am New York*, September 27, 2015.

Winer, Linda. Review of *The Gershwins' Porgy and Bess*. Richard Rodgers Theater, New York. *Newsday*, January 12, 2012. https://www.newsday.com/entertainment/theater/a-porgy-and-bess-made-for-broadway-1.3445473.

Winkler, Kevin. *Big Deal: Bob Fosse and Dance in the American Musical*. New York: Oxford University Press, 2018.

Wolf, Stacy. *Beyond Broadway: The Pleasure and Promise of Musical Theatre across America*. New York: Oxford University Press, 2020.

Wolf, Stacy. *Changed for Good: A Feminist History of the Broadway Musical*. New York: Oxford University Press, 2011.

Wolf, Stacy. *A Problem Like Maria: Gender and Sexuality in the American Musical*. Ann Arbor: University of Michigan Press, 2002.

Wollman, Elizabeth. *A Critical Companion to the American Stage Musical*. London: Bloomsbury, 2017.

Wollman, Elizabeth. *Hard Times: The Adult Musical in 1970s New York City*. New York: Oxford University Press, 2013.

Wren, Celia. "At Olney Theatre, casting 'Beauty and the Beast' with an eye to inclusion." *Washington Post*, November 2, 2021. https://www.washingtonpost.com/goingoutgu ide/theater-dance/olney-theatre-disneys-beauty-and-the-beast/2021/11/01/9dbca 940-3827-11ec-8be3-e14aaacfa8ac_story.html?fbclid=IwAR14GkLKCW93kl4nzR7P ULwQYZUBqJyoMNty9mRdCFnAs6L0JPhSBgVfsmg.

Yates, Samuel. "Disability and the American Stage Musical." In *The Routledge Companion to Literature and Disability*, edited by Alice Hall, 265–275. London: Routledge, 2020.

Yates, Siena. "How Maori Actress Keala Settle Became the Heart of a Hollywood Blockbuster." *New Zealand Herald*, December 26, 2017. https://www.nzherald.co.nz/entertainment/news/article.cfm?c_id=1501119&objectid=11964062.

Zahifito. "Donna Mckechnie Sings 'Broadway Boogie Woogie Blues,' a Cut Song from A Chorus Line Workshop." April 6, 2020. YouTube video, 2:35. https://www.youtube.com/watch?v=mP2qXoCjKPw.

Zailan, Marian. "'La Cage' Stars Play It Straight." *San Francisco Chronicle*, June 10, 1984.

Zara, Christopher. "It's 2019, and Your Boss Can Still Fire You for Being Gay in These States." *Fast Company*, June 25, 2019. https://www.fastcompany.com/90369004/lgbt-employee-protections-by-state-map-shows-where-gay-workers-can-be-fired.

Zazzali, Peter. "Star Struck! The Phenomenological Affect of Celebrity on Broadway." *Journal of American Drama and Theatre* 28, no. 1 (Winter 2016). https://jadtjournal.org/2016/03/23/star-struck-the-phenomenological-affect-of-celebrity-on-broadway.

Index

For the benefit of digital users, indexed terms that span two pages (e.g., 52–53) may, on occasion, appear on only one of those pages.
Figures and boxes are indicated by *f* and *b* following the page number

"10th and Greenwich" (*Ain't Supposed to Die a Natural Death*), 120–21
110 in the Shade (Schmidt, Jones, Nash), 9–10, 98–99

ableism, 3–4, 18, 31, 172, 207, 210–11, 232, 233, 234, 237–38
Actors' Equity Association (AEA), 8–11, 26, 77–78, 111, 172, 212–13, 239. *See also* Diverity Report; Equal Employment Opportunity Committee; Extraordinary Excellence in Diversity on Broadway Award
  Equal Employment Opportunity Committee, 9–10
ACT UP (AIDS Coalition to Unleash Power), 142
AIDS, 17, 76–77, 124, 127, 128, 140–43, 146–47, 149–50, 155–60, 162, 166–67, 172, 179
Ailey, Alvin, 30
Ain't Supposed to Die a Natural Death (Van Peebles), 120–21
  "10th and Greenwich," 120–21
Aldredge, Theoni V., 43, 68*b*–69, 79–80, 125–26
Allard, Martine, 88–89
Allegro (Rodgers, Hammerstein), 30
Allen, Bonnie, 59
Allen, Peter, 166–67
American Sign Language (ASL), 25, 179–84, 185–86, 188, 189–90, 191–93, 194–98, 199, 204–5, 206, 242–43. *See also* ASL Masters; ASL musicals

Americans with Disabilities Act of 1990 (ADA) [1990], 212, 213
"And I Am Telling You I'm Not Going" (*Dreamgirls*), 58–59, 66*b*–69*b*, 68*f*, 69–71, 76, 137*b*–38
Angela, Moya, 83–84
Angels in America (Kushner), 148, 158
Annie (Strouse, Charnin, Meehan), 211
Apollo Theater, 69*b*
Applause (Strouse, Adams, Comden, Green), 115, 121
Arden, Michael, 180–81, 184, 186, 187, 189–93, 194–95, 199–200, 202*b*, 205
Ashman, Howard, 156
ASL Masters, 186, 194–95, 199
ASL musicals, 179–206. See also *Big River*; Deaf West Theatre; *Oliver!*; *Spring Awakening*
  labor issues, 186, 188–89, 195
Astin, Skylar, 199
"At the Ballet" (*A Chorus Line*), 33–34
Avenue Q (Lopez, Marks, Whitty), 154*b*–55
Avian, Bob, 27, 32–33, 42–43, 44–46, 47–49, 51, 52–53, 69–70, 86–87

Bacall, Lauren, 115
Ballets Russes, 133–34
Barnes, Clive, 27, 50, 70–71, 120–21
Barnum (Coleman, Stewart, Bramble), 215
Barry, Gene, 117*f*, 128–31, 138*b*, 141, 169
Bassey, Shirley, 139*b*
Bauman, H-Dirksen L., 181
Be More Chill (Iconis, Tracz), 150–51
Beach, Gary, 167, 169

304 INDEX

Beauty and the Beast (Menken, Ashman, Rice, Woolverton), 213–14, 220
  Olney Theatre Center revival [2021], 244–46, 245f
Bechdel, Alison, 152b
Bennett, Michael, 31–33, 37–40, 44–45, 47–50, 51–52, 53–54, 66b, 67b, 68b–69, 69–70, 71–72, 73–74, 75–77, 82, 84, 86–87, 112, 121, 156, 240
"Big Black Lady Stops the Show, A" (*Martin Short: Fame Becomes Me*), 98–99
"Big, Blonde, and Beautiful" (*Hairspray*), 99–101
Big River (Miller, Hauptman), 179
  Deaf West Theatre Broadway revival [2003], 179, 180, 182, 184–85, 187–88, 189, 191–93, 195, 198–99, 203–5
  "Waitin' for the Light to Shine," 179
"Big Spender" (*Sweet Charity*), 92b
Billings, Alexandra, 170–71
Billy Elliott (John, Hall), 9–10, 105, 149
bisexuality, 118–19, 150–51, 162–63, 164, 173, 176
"Bitch of Living, The" (*Spring Awakening*), 200b–2b
Bitter-Sweet (Coward), 119–20
Black Lives Matter, 8
Black musicals, 37
Blair, Pamela, 34f, 45, 52
Bloody Bloody Andrew Jackson (Friedman, Timbers), 216–17
Bockus, Royer, 241–42
body shaming, 63–66, 172. *See also* *Dreamgirls*; Holliday, Jennifer; size
Boeck, Katie, 191, 192f, 200b–1
Bogen, Ben, 176
Boniello, Alex, 187
Book of Mormon, The (Parker, Stone, Lopez), 118, 149, 159–60
  "Turn It Off," 149
Bosworth, Patricia, 86–87
Boy from Oz, The (Allen, Sherman, Enright), 159, 166–68
Boy Meets Boy (Solly, Ward), 121
Bradford, Shannon, 194
Brady, Wayne, 164–66

Brantley, Ben, 167–68, 170–72, 229
Brice, Fanny, 4–5, 70
Brier, Kathy, 103–4
Bring It On (Miranda, Kitt, Green), 89, 150–51
Broadway Bares (fundraiser), 17, 158
Broadway Body, the, 12–22, 243–44
  ability/disability and, 207
  aesthetics, 15–17
  Cage Aux Folles, La, in, 133–34
  Chorus Line, A, in, 27–28
  conformity, 12–15
  definition, 4–6
  gay culture and, 21–23, 146–47, 173–76
  labor and, 18–20, 53
  labor market, in, 109
  neoliberalism and, 20–21
  outdatedness of, 241
  persistence of, 243
Broadway Body, the Positivity Project (BBPP), 239, 241–42
"Broadway Boogie Woogie" (*A Chorus Line*), 3
Broadway Cares/ Equity Fights AIDS, 17, 158, 159
Brooks, Daphne, 64
Brown, Barry, 128, 132–33, 136, 140, 141–42
Brown, Candy, 37–38
Brown, Scott, 232–33
Brown, Sharon, 72, 76, 84
Brustein, Robert, 132
Burge, Gregg, 156
Burns, Craig, 94, 96–97, 101, 102–3, 105–6, 110
"But Alive!" (*Applause*), 115

Cabaret (Kander, Ebb, Masteroff), 31–32
  Broadway revival [1998], 150–51, 162–63, 164
Cage Aux Folles, La (Herman, Fierstein), 25, 115–44, 117f, 130f, 135f, 137b–39b, 146, 148–49, 150, 158, 161–62, 167, 169, 176
  audience response, 142–44
  Cagelles, the (dancers), 133–37
  casting, 116–17, 123, 128–37

drag in, 115, 116, 121–22, 125–26, 130–31, 133–37
gay liberation movement and, 123–26, 127, 140–42
"I Am What I Am," 25, 26, 125, 127, 137, 137*b*–39*b*, 169
"Look Over There," 143
race and ethnicity, 126
"Song on the Sand," 130–31, 142–43
Cagelles, the (dancers in *La Cage Aux Folles*), 133–37
casting, 133–37
Calhoun, Jeff, 182–83, 195
capitalism, 12, 20, 59, 62, 123–24, 144, 225–26
Caroline, or Change (Tesori, Kushner), 64–65, 98–99
Carousel (Rodgers, Hammerstein), 90
Carr, Allan, 126–27, 128, 136–37
Carrie (Gore, Pitchford, Cohen), 94, 215
Carroll, David, 156–58, 157*f*
Carter, Lynne, 132
Carter, Nell, 78
Cason, Yvette, 78–79, 84
Cassal, Steve, 75
casting, 5–12, 57–58
  Cage Aux Folles, La, 116–17, 123, 128–37
  Chorus Line, A, 45–51
  Color Purple, The, 225–26
  d/Deaf actors, 8, 184–94
  disability, 8, 208–9, 212–13, 216–17, 221–25, 232–38
  Effie White (*Dreamgirls*), 69–85
  equity in, 8–12
  fat phobia and, 59–62
  labor, as, 5–6, 7, 18, 30–31, 57–58, 63, 65–66, 132–33
  LGBTQ+, 8, 160–76
  race and ethnicity, 6–7
  size, 7, 8, 63–66, 86–91
  size-blindness, 8
  Tracy Turnblad (*Hairspray*), 94–97
celebrity, 225–37
Center for American Progress, 160
Chaplin: The Musical (Curtis), 170
Charles, Walter, 132, 138*b*

Chicago (Kander, Ebb, Fosse), 32–33, 37–38, 106–7, 120–21
Children's Hour, The (Hellman), 148
Chorus Line, A (Hamlisch, Kleban, Kirkwood, Dante), 3, 25, 27–29, 31–54, 34*f*, 35*b*–36*b*, 41*f*, 50*f*, 115, 121, 126, 133–34, 136, 150–51, 156, 213–14, 216, 240
  "At the Ballet," 33–34
  Broadway Body, the, in, 27–28
  "Broadway Boogie Woogie," 3
  Broadway revival [2006], 37, 42, 48–49, 50–51, 53
  casting and recasting, 41–51
  concept, 33–35
  "Dance: Ten, Looks: Three" (*A Chorus Line*), 26, 33–34, 53–54
  dancers, demands on, 51–54
  genesis, 31–33
  "Hello Twelve, Hello Thirteen, Hello Love," 33–34, 38–39
  homophobia in, 39–42
  "I Can Do That," 33–34
  "I Hope I Get It," 33, 35*b*–36*b*
  identity, depiction, 37–45
  individual vs. collective, 43–45, 53
  LGBTQ+ representation, 39–42
  merchandising, 51–54
  "Music and the Mirror, The," 33–34
  "Nothing," 33–34
  "One," 34–35, 43
  race and ethnicity, 38–40
  representation in, 38–45
  sexuality, depictions, 42
  structure, 34–35
  "What I Did for Love," 34–35
Cilento, Wayne, 37, 41–42, 49–50, 51–52
Civil Rights Act [1964], 147–48
Clinton, Bill, 147
Clum, John, 117–18, 134
Cole, Jack, 30
Coleman, Cy, 86–87, 92*b*
Collela, Jenn, 170
Collins-Hughes, Laura, 91, 187–88
Color Purple, The (Russell, Willis, Bray, Norman), 106–7, 150–51, 208–9, 225, 226–27
  "I'm Here," 226

306 INDEX

Color Purple, The (*cont.*)
  "Too Beautiful for Words," 226
Come from Away (Sankoff, Hein), 170
coming out, 23–24, 40, 42, 62, 128–29,
    145, 146–47, 150, 156–58, 160–
    72, 221–22
  labor issue, as, 147, 156–58,
    173–74
  musicals, in, 150
Company (Sondheim, Furth), 31,
    32, 242–43
compulsory heterosexuality, 18
Cook, Amy, 9
Corey, Rita, 187–88
Cottom, Tressie McMillan, 61
Coven, Bree, 175–76
Covid-19, 4–5
Coward, Noël, 119–20
Crawford, Michael, 21–22
Creel, Gavin, 169–70
Crimp, Douglas, 159–60
Criss, Darren, 227–28
Cumming, Alan, 164
Curtis, Keane, 169

DaCosta, Morton, 208
Dance a Little Closer (Strouse, Lerner),
    120, 148–49
"Dance: Ten, Looks: Three" (*A Chorus
    Line*), 26, 33–34, 53–54
dancer training, 52–53
Dante, Nicholas, 32–33, 39–41, 156
D'Arcy James, Brian, 221
Davenport, Ken, 187, 198, 199–200,
    204, 206
Davis, Daniel, 167
Davis, Lennard J., 11, 20, 180, 182–
    83, 209–10
Davis, Mary Bond, 99–101, 100*f*
d/Deaf actors, 6, 23–24, 179–206. See
    also *Big River*; Deaf West Theatre;
    Spring Awakening
  casting, 8, 184–94
Deaf Broadway (advocacy group),
    239, 242–43
deaf studies, 24–25
Deaf West Theatre, 6, 179–206, 200*b*–
    2*b*, 208–9

Big River Broadway revival [2003], 179,
    180, 182, 184–85, 187–88, 189, 191–
    93, 195, 198–99, 203–5
  Spring Awakening Broadway revival
    [2015], 9–10, 25, 179–82, 183, 184–
    85, 186–206, 192*f*, 196*f*, 200*b*–2*b*,
    202*f*, 208–9, 234–36
deBose, Ariana, 171–72
Defense of Marriage Act, 147–48
DeGeneres, Ellen, 162
Deitch, Kathy, 97, 108, 109–10
DeJarnette, Darby, 245–46
DeJesus, Robin, 126
DeLaria, Lea, 91, 163, 164, 165*f*,
    170, 216–17
de Lavallade, Carmen, 30
de Mille, Agnes, 29–30
Dennis, Ron, 37–38, 126
De Shields, André, 172
Destiny of Me, The (Kramer), 163
Devine, Loretta, 58*f*, 73*f*
Dideriksen, Katrina Rose, 102, 105–6
Diggs, Taye, 227–28
Dinero, Dan, 76
disability, 3–4, 6, 7, 10–11, 18, 22–23,
    24, 209–38
  casting, 6–7, 8, 10–11, 208–9, 212–13,
    216–17, 221–25, 232–38
  compulsory able-bodiedness, 18
  disability rights movement, 211
  fairy tales as expression of, 217–25
  labor issues, 208–9, 210–13, 233–
    34, 236
  musicals, in, 213–17, 225–38 (see
    also *Barnum*; *Color Purple, The*;
    Gershwins' Porgy and Bess, The;
    Hedwig and the Angry Inch;
    Light in the Piazza, The; *Newsies*;
    Rocky Horror Show, The; *Secret
    Garden, The*; *Shrek the Musical*;
    Violet; *Wicked*)
  onstage depiction, 207–17, 225–38
  politics and, 211–12
  social construct, as, 210–11
  stigmatization and, 210
  terminology, 209–10
disability studies, 24–25, 180, 209–11
Diversity Report (AEA), 10–11

Divine (né Harris Glenn Milstead), 94
Do Black Patent Leather Shoes Really Reflect Up? (Quinn, Jans), 87–88
Dodge, Marcia Milgrom, 244–46
Dogfight (Pasek, Paul, Duchin), 90
Dolan, Jill, 146
"Don't Ask, Don't Tell," 147
Donahue, Phil, 27–28, 33–34, 38–39, 52
drag, 94, 95, 115, 116, 118–19, 121–22, 125–26, 130–31, 133–37, 149, 150–51
  Billy Elliott, in, 149
  Cage Aux Folles, La, in, 115, 116, 121–22, 125–26, 130–31, 133–37
  Hairspray, in, 94, 95
  Kinky Boots, in, 174–75
Drag, The (West), 119–20
Dreamgirls (Krieger, Eyen), 53–54, 57–59, 58f, 66b–69b, 68f, 69–85, 73f, 80f, 86, 87–88, 92b, 95, 101–2, 106–8, 109, 112
  "And I Am Telling You I'm Not Going," 58–59, 66b–69b, 68f, 69–71, 76, 137b–38
  casting, 69–85
  Effie White (character), 57–59, 69–85, 87, 106–8, 111–12
  "I Am Changing," 79
  size issues in, 57–59
  West End production [2016], 82–83
Duggan, Lisa, 21
Durant, Daniel, 186, 191–93, 203

Ebony (magazine), 71
Eder, Richard, 179
Edmond, Treshelle, 203
Effie White (character in *Dreamgirls*), 57–59, 69–85, 87, 106–8, 111–12
Ellis, Fraser, 47
Ellis, Sheila, 83–84
Eng, Stephen, 240–41
Engel, David, 134, 136–37, 138b–39, 140–41
Erivo, Cynthia, 226
Escape to Margaritaville (Buffett, Garcia), 90–91
Essence (magazine), 59
eugenics, 22–24, 60–61, 210–11
Everett, Rupert, 162–63

"Everything's Coming Up Roses" (*Gypsy*) [Styne, Sondheim], 137b–38
Extraordinary Excellence in Diversity on Broadway Award (AEA), 9–10, 111
Eyen, Tom, 66b, 70, 76–77

Faggot, The (Carmines), 121
fairy tales on stage, 217–25
Falk, Gerhard, 127
Falsettos (Finn, Lapine), 146, 150, 158, 159–60
Fat Camp. See *Gigantic*
fat phobia, 3–5, 57–58, 63, 64, 87, 91, 99, 103, 104–5
  casting and, 59–61
fat shaming
  race and ethnicity, 57–59, 60–61
fat studies, 23–25, 59–62, 88–89
Fela! (Kuti, Jones, Lewis), 159–60
Feldstein, Beanie, 4–5, 171–72
Ferguson, Jesse Tyler, 164, 165f
Fiddler on the Roof (Bock, Harnick, Stein), 31–32, 203
  Broadway revival [2004], 167–68
Fierstein, Harvey, 94, 95–96, 106, 116, 121–23, 124, 125, 126–27, 128, 144, 148, 161–62, 167–68, 169
Finian's Rainbow (Lane, Harburg, Saidy), 213–14
Fish, Daniel, 235–36
Fisher, Mark, 13–14. See also fitness companies, Broadway-focused; Mark Fisher Fitness; MyBroadwayBody. com; *Playbill*
Fishman, Shirley, 204
fitness companies, Broadway-focused, 12–15, 13f
Five Guys Named Moe (Peters, Jordan, etc.), 89
Flinn, Denny Martin, 32–33
Flower Drum Song (Rodgers, Hammerstein), 38–39
  Broadway revival [2002], 149
Follies (Sondheim, Goldman), 32
Foote, Jenifer, 171–72
Forbes (magazine), 13
Forth, Christopher E., 175

308 INDEX

Fosse, Bob, 30, 31–33, 37–38, 92*b*–93*b*, 133–34, See also *Pippin*
Foster, Sutton, 221, 227
Foulkes, Julia, 5–6
Frank, Barney, 162
Frank, Sandra Mae, 186, 188, 191, 192*f*, 200*b*–1, 203
Friedman, Sonia, 83
Friedman's, Michael, 156
Frozen (Anderson-Lopez, Lopez, Lee), 89
Frühlings Erwachen [*Spring Awakening*] (Wedekind), 180–81, 191–93
Full Monty, The (Yazbek, McNally), 148–49
Fun Home (Tesori, Kron), 150, 152*b*–55*b*, 153*f*, 170, 175, 203, 242
  "Ring of Keys," 152*b*–55*b*, 153*f*, 242
Funny Girl (Styne, Merrill), 3, 4–5, 86

Gad, Josh, 89
Gamache, Laurie, 44–45, 49–50
Garland-Thomson, Rosemarie, 19–20, 22–23
Garza, Troy, 47–48
Gault, Ken, 17
gay liberation movement, 123–25, 127, 142–43
Gaynor, Gloria, 139*b*
Gennaro, Liza, 29
Geraghty, Katy, 108–9
Gershwins' Porgy and Bess, The (Gershwin, Heyward), 207
  Broadway revival [2014, adapted Parks, Murray], 208–9, 225, 230–34, 231*f*
Gigantic [AKA *Fat Camp*] (Blair, Drucker, Berger), 14–15, 89
Gill, Brendan, 132
Goffman, Erving, 18, 22–23, 210
Gold, Sam, 203
Gonsalves, Gregg, 155–56
Goodwin, Deidre, 51
Gottfried, Martin, 50
Grammer, Kelsey, 169
Grammy Awards, 138*b*–39
Grand Hotel (Forrest, Wright, Davis), 148–49, 150, 156–58, 157*f*, 213–14, 216–17

Graves, Jennifer, 20–21, 61–62
Grease (Jacobs, Casey), 31–32, 106–7, 164–66
  Jan (character), 88–89, 90, 103–4
Greatest Showman, The (2017 film), 91
Green, Jesse, 195–97
Grenfell, Katy, 92*b*, 93*b*
Groff, Jonathan, 10–11, 199
Grumley, Michael, 123
Guys and Dolls (Loesser, Swerling, Burrows), 30, 37
Gypsy (Styne, Sondheim, Laurents), 33, 64–65, 87, 198

Haberman, Linda, 129
Hair (MacDermot, Rado, Ragni), 150–51
Hairspray (Shaiman, Wittman, O'Donnel, Meehan), 6, 14, 63–65, 87, 90, 93*b*, 94–106, 100*f*, 104*f*, 122, 170–71
  "Big, Blonde, and Beautiful," 99–101
  drag in, 94, 95
  live telecast [2016], 95–96
  Motormouth Maybelle (character), 95, 99–101, 102, 107–8, 109, 175
  race and ethnicity, 97–101
  size issues in, 101–6
  "Tracy Camp," 105–6
  Tracy Turnblad (character), 59–60, 63–64, 84, 87, 91, 94–106, 108–9
Hall, Michael C., 227–28
Hamermesh, Daniel S., 218–19
Hamilton (Miranda), 8, 9–11, 105, 172, 195, 198
Hamlisch, Marvin, 32–33
Hands on a Hardbody (Anastasio, Green, Wright), 91
Hanks, Tom, 162
Harada, Ann, 240
Harney, Ben, 67*b*
Harris, Neil Patrick, 117–18, 227–28
Harvard, Russell, 188, 203
Hayes, Sean, 168–69
Head Over Heels (Go-Gos, Whitty, Magruder), 14–15, 89, 111, 112, 150–51
Hearn, George, 25, 117*f*, 128–31, 130*f*, 138*b*–39*b*, 169

Hedwig and the Angry Inch (Trask, Mitchell), 163–64, 208–9, 216, 225, 227–31, 228f
Heimans, Jeremy, 239
"Hello Twelve, Hello Thirteen, Hello Love " (*A Chorus Line*), 33–34, 38–39
Hello, Dolly! (Herman, Stewart), 31–32, 37
Hemingway, Geoff, 14
Herman, Jerry, 120, 125–26, 128–29, 142–43, 144, 148
Herrera, Brian Eugenio, 5–6, 132–33
Herz, Shirley, 141
Hickey, John Benjamin, 162–63
Hildreth, Gregg, 89
Hirschfeld, Al, 138b
Hlibok, Bruce, 179
Hodge, Douglas, 169
Hoffman, Warren, 39
Hoffman, William M., 116
Holder, Geoffrey, 30
Holliday, Jennifer, 57–58, 58f, 66b, 67b–69b, 68f, 69–81, 106–8
Hollywood Reporter, 195–97, 229, 232–33
Holt, Fritz, 156
Holt, George W. "Fritz," 141–42
Holtcamp, Victor, 46, 48
Homma, Robert, 156
homogeneity, 21–22, 53, 122–23, 125
homophobia, 4, 17, 39–42, 115–16, 118–19, 120, 126–27, 133–35, 140–41, 142–43, 144, 146, 147–48, 159, 160–63, 164–66, 169–70, 172, 174–75, 210–11
homosexuality, 22–23, 37, 40–41, 115–76, 207–8. *See also* AIDS; bisexuality; *Cage Aux Folles, La*; casting; *Chorus Line, A*; drag; *Fun Home*; lesbianism; LGBTQ+; transgender
Broadway Body, and the, 21–24
casting, 8 (see also *Cage Aux Folles, La*)
Chorus Line, A, representation in, 39–42
coming out, 160–72
onstage depictions, 115–21, 142–44, 145–51
society, in, 146–48
House of Flowers (Arlen, Capote), 30
Howard, Lisa, 7, 90–91
Howard, Stuart, 128–29, 136–37

Hudson, Jennifer, 70, 106–8
Hudson, Rock, 162
Humans of Broadway (Instagram account), 108–9
Hwang, David Henry, 149

"I Am Changing" (*Dreamgirls*), 79
"I Am What I Am" (*La Cage Aux Folles*), 25, 26, 125, 127, 137, 137b–39b, 169
"I Cain't Say No" (*Oklahoma!*), 235–36
"I Can Cook Too" (*On the Town*), 88–89
"I Can Do That" (*A Chorus Line*), 33–34
"I Hope I Get It" (*A Chorus Line*), 33, 35b–36b
"I Love New York" ad campaign, 28
"I'm Here" (*The Color Purple*), 226
If/Then (Kitt, Yorkey), 9–10, 150–51, 170
Into the Woods (Sondheim, Lapine), 217–18, 242–43
Iovannone, Jeffry J., 15–17
Isherwood, Charles, 195–97
It Shoulda Been You (Anselmi, Hargrove), 9–10, 90–91, 150

Jackman, Hugh, 166–68
Jacobs, Bernard B., 71–72
Jagged Little Pill (Morissette, Kitt, Ballard, Cody), 148–49, 150–51, 173
Jan (character in *Grease*), 88–89, 90, 103–4
Jazzercise, 52
Jensen-Moulton, Stephanie, 233
Jersey Boys (Gaudio, Crewe, Elice, Brickman), 105, 148–49
Jeter, Michael, 156–58, 157f
Jibson, Carly, 95–96
John, Elton, 162
Johnson, Jake, 15, 48
Jones, Bill T., 200b–2b
Jones, Chris, 232–33
Jones, Jade, 244–46, 245f

Kamlot, Bob, 47
Kauffman, Stanley, 70–71
Kazan, Lainie, 86–87, 112
"Keep It Gay" (*The Producers*), 149
Kelly, Kevin, 44
Kerr, Walter, 70–71
Kert, Larry, 128–29, 156

310   INDEX

King and I, The (Rodgers, Hammerstein),
  38–39, 240–41
  Broadway revival [1996], 169–70
King, Billie Jean, 162
Kinky Boots (Lauper, Fierstein), 164–
  66, 174–75
  drag in, 174–75
Kinnunen, Caitlin, 171–72
Kirkwood, James, 32–33, 39–40
Kirle, Bruce, 43–44, 166–67
Kismet (Wright, Forrest), 30
Kiss of the Spiderwoman (Kander, Ebb,
  McNally), 148–49
Kleban, Edward, 32–33
Knapp, Raymond, 179–80, 208
Kolb, Rachel, 197
Kramer, Larry, 126–27
Krieger, Henry, 66*b*, 88
Krieger, Mitchell, 70
Kron, Lisa, 152*b*
Kuchwara, Michael, 149
Kurs, DJ, 181–82, 183, 184, 185–86, 190–
  91, 199, 205–6
Kushner, Tony, 148
Kuti, Fela, 159–60
Kwan, Samantha, 20–21, 61–62

La Cage Aux Folles (Herman, Fierstein).
  See *Cage Aux Folles, La*
La Master, Monique, 71
labor. *See* ASL musicals; Broadway Body,
  the; casting; coming out; disability;
  race and ethnicity; size
LaChanze, 226
Lady in the Dark (Weill, Gershwin,
  Hart), 119–20
Lake, Ricki, 95–96, 103, 107–8
Lam, Nina Zoie, 240–41
Lane, Nathan, 145–46
Lansbury, Angela, 13, 198
Lapine, James, 158, 217–18
Latessa, Dick, 100*f*
Laurents, Arthur, 115, 119, 125–27, 128–
  29, 132, 134–35, 137*b*–38, 140–41,
  142–44, 148, 161–62
"Laurey Makes Up Her Mind" (*Oklahoma!*
  ballet), 29
Lavender Scare, 147

Lawrence v. Texas [2003], 147–48
Lawrence, Carol, 13
Leap of Faith (Menken, Slater,
  Cercone), 217
LeBesco, Kathleen, 23–24, 62
Leduc, Amanda, 227
Lee, Baayork, 27, 28–29, 37, 38–39,
  42, 45–46, 47, 48–51, 53,
  239, 240–41
Lee, Michele, 86
Legally Blonde (O'Keefe, Benjamin, Hach),
  149, 150, 242–43
  "There! Right There!" 149
Leong, Nancy, 59
Les Misérables (Schönberg, Boublil,
  Kretzmer). See *Misérables, Les*
lesbianism, 23, 24, 62, 116, 118–21, 145–
  46, 147–51, 158, 162, 164, 167–68,
  170, 173–74, 175–76, 241–42.
  See also bisexuality; coming out;
  Color Purple, The; *Fun Home*; gay
  liberation movement; *Grand Hotel*;
  homosexuality; transgender
"Let Your Freak Flag Fly" (*Shrek the
  Musical*), 220
Leung, Telly, 240
Lewis, Edwina, 84
Lewis, Jenifer, 69–70
Lewis, Kecia, 73–74, 84
Lewis, Norm, 231, 231*f*, 232–34
Lexis, Stephanie, 241–42
LGBTQ+. *See* AIDS; bisexuality; *Cage
  Aux Folles, La*; casting; *Chorus Line,
  A*; drag; *Fun Home*; homosexuality;
  lesbianism; LGBTQ+; transgender
LGBTQ+ studies, 24–25
Life, The (Coleman, Gasman, Newman),
  84, 91, 92*b*–93*b*, 93*f*
  "My Body," 92*b*–93*b*
  "Oldest Profession, The," 92*b*
Liff, Spencer, 14, 183, 190, 201*b*–2*b*, 203
Light in the Piazza, The (Guettel,
  Lucas), 214–15
Lim, Stephanie, 179
Lion King, The (John, Taymor, Allers,
  Mecchi), 220
Lion, Margo, 101
Lipari, Beth, 185–86, 205–6, 234–35

INDEX 311

Little Mermaid, The (Menken, Ashman, Slater, Wright), 219–20
Little Night Music, A (Sondheim, Wheeler), 216–17
"Little People" (*Les Misérables*), 224–25
Llana, Jose, 169–70
"Look Over There" (*La Cage Aux Folles*), 143
Lopez, Priscilla, 38–39
Love! Valour! Compassion! (McNally), 148
Lucas, Craig, 203
Lucas, Sydney, 153*b*–54, 153*f*
LuPone, Bob, 45
LuPone, Patti, 21–22, 83–84, 110

M. Butterfly (Hwang), 126
MacDonald, Audra, 231*f*
Mackenzie, Austin, 186, 191
Madame Thénardier (character in *Les Misérables*), 88–89
Madison, D. Soyini, 9
Malone, Beth, 152*b*, 153*f*, 154*b*, 170
"Mama Who Bore Me" (*Spring Awakening*), 193, 200*b*–1
"Mama Will Provide" (*Once on This Island*), 170–71
Mame (Herman, Lawrence, Lee), 31–32, 120, 121–22
Man of La Mancha (Leigh, Darion, Wasserman), 31–32
Manheim, Camryn, 188, 190, 194
Marceau, Yvonne, 213–14
Marcos, J. Elaine, 51
Mark Fisher Fitness, 13–14
Marriner, Christopher, 224*b*
Marshall, Peter, 131, 135–36
Matera, Barbara, 79–80
Matlin, Marlee, 188, 194, 195
Mav, Karen, 83–84
McColl, Mary, 10–11
McDonald, Audra, 98–99
McGillin, Howard, 162
McGirt, Julia, 84
McKechnie, Donna, 31, 44, 45–46, 47, 49–50, 52
McKellen, Ian, 162, 169
McKneely, Joey, 92*b*
McNally, Terrence, 148, 161

McNulty, Charles, 26
McRuer, Robert, 18, 176
Mean Girls (Richmond, Benjamin, Fey), 89–90, 118, 149
Meat Loaf (né Marvin Lee Aday), 216–17
Meehan, Thomas, 94
Mendez, Lindsey, 90
Michele, Lea, 200*b*–1
Michell, Keith, 132
Midler, Bette, 110
Mientus, Andy, 187, 200*b*
Milan Conference (1880), 180–81, 189–90
Milk, Harvey, 127
Miller, D.A., 117–18, 139*b*, 142–43
Miller, Terry, 119–20, 123
Milligan, Bonnie, 14–15, 89, 111
Minnelli, Liza, 110
Misérables, Les (Schönberg, Boublil, Kretzmer), 9–10, 88–89, 101–2, 242–43
  "Little People," 224–25
Miss Saigon (Schönberg, Boublil, Maltby), 6–7, 105
Mitchell, Arthur, 30
Mitchell, David, 213–14
Mitchell, Jerry, 13, 17, 94, 106
Mitchell, John Cameron, 163–64, 227–31, 228*f*
Mitchell, Russ, 70
Mobley, Jennifer-Scott, 88–89
Monbiot, George, 20
Moore, Maureen, 87–88
Moss, Kathi, 57
Mostel, Zero, 21–22
Motormouth Maybelle (character in *Hairspray*), 95, 99–101, 102, 107–8, 109, 175
Muñoz, Javier, 172
Murray, Joseph J., 181
"Music and the Mirror, The" (*A Chorus Line*), 33–34
Music Man, The (Willson, Lacey), 208
"My Body" (*The Life*), 92*b*–93*b*
MyBroadwayBody.com, 13, 13*f*

Nachtman, Gerald, 74–75
National Asian Artists Project (NAAP), 239, 240

312 INDEX

National Deaf Center, 188–89
National Endowment for the Arts
    (NEA), 204
Navratilova, Martina, 162
Nederlander Jr., James, 141–42
Nelson, Joe, 47–48
neoliberal capitalism, 12, 20, 62
neoliberalism, 4, 20–22, 62
New Brain, A (Finn, Lapine), 89
New York Amsterdam News, 71
New York Native, 123
New York Post, 21–22, 50, 76–77, 95–96,
    103, 232–33
New York Times, 4–5, 7, 27–28, 45–46, 48,
    50–51, 61–62, 73–74, 76–77, 86–87,
    90, 91, 103–4, 107–8, 120–21, 122–
    23, 129, 130–31, 150, 156, 163, 164,
    167–68, 187–88, 195–97, 198–99,
    217, 229, 231–32
Newell, Alex, 170–71, 174–75
Newsies (Menken, Feldman,
    Fierstein), 214–15
Nick & Nora (Strouse, Maltby, Laurents),
    148–49, 150
Nicola, Jim, 204
Nielsen, Kristine, 216–17
Nijinksy, Vaslav, 133–34
Nine (Yeston, Kopit), 57, 66*b*
"Nothing" (*A Chorus Line*), 33–34
Novick, Julius, 116, 123

Obergefell vs. Hodges [2015], 147–
    48, 154*b*
O'Brien, Bill, 189
O'Brien, Jack, 94, 97, 101, 103–5
O'Donnell, Mark, 94
O'Donnell, Rosie, 145–46, 167–68
Oedipus Rex (Sophocles), 217–18
Oklahoma! (Rodgers,
    Hammerstein), 28–31
    Broadway revival [2019], 235*f*
    "I Cain't Say No," 235–36
    "Laurey Makes Up Her Mind" (de Mille
    ballet), 29
"Oldest Profession, The" (*The Life*), 92*b*
Oleksinski, Johnny, 21–22
Oliver! (Bart), 182

Olney Theatre Center, 245*f*
O'Malley, Rory, 10–11
On a Clear Day You Can See Forever (Lane,
    Lerner), 149
On the Town (Bernstein, Comden,
    Green), 88–89
    Broadway revivals, 91, 164, 165*f*
    "I Can Cook, Too," 88–89
Once on This Island (Flaherty, Ahrens),
    170–71, 174
Once upon a Mattress (Rodgers, Barer,
    Thompson, Fuller), 213–14
"One" (*A Chorus Line*), 34–35, 43
Orientalization, 38–39
Owens, Larry, 89

Page, Patrick, 188
Pajama Game, The (Adler, Ross), 30
Pal Joey (Rodgers, Hart, O'Hara), 149
Pao, Angela C., 7
Parks, Suzan-Lori, 230–33
Passing Strange (Stew), 146, 148–49
Patinkin, Mandy, 217
Patten, Lauren, 171–72
Paulson, Michael, 4–5
Paulus, Diane, 230–33
Peacock, Michon, 31–33, 43–44
People (magazine), 129, 130–31
Peppermint (performer), 111, 170–71
Peters, Bernadette, 110, 217–18
Peters, Michael, 66*b*, 76–77
Phantom of the Opera, The (Lloyd Webber,
    Hart, Stilgoe), 162, 214–15, 220–21
Phelan, Deborah, 135, 136–37
Pippin (Schwartz, Hirson), 31–32, 133–34
Playbill, 13–15, 30, 108, 150, 170–72, 180–
    81, 188, 193, 194–95, 196*f*, 197–99,
    216–17, 234
Poiret, Jean, 121–22
Porgy and Bess. See *Gershwins' Porgy and
    Bess, The*
Porter, Billy, 163, 164–66, 172
Porter, Cole, 119–20, 207–8
Pose (TV series), 166
Pratt, Mary Louise, 180
Pressley, Brenda, 79–80, 84
Prestinario, Andrea, 241–42

Priscilla, Queen of the Desert (Elliott, Scott), 150–51
Producers, The (Brooks, Kelly, Meehan), 148–49
"Keep It Gay," 149
Prom, The (Sklar, Beguelin, Martin), 150
Promises, Promises (Bacharach, David, Simon), 31–32, 38–39
Broadway revival [2010], 168–69
Pryce, Jonathan, 6–7
Public Theater, 32–33
Purlie (Geld, Udell, Davis, Rose), 31, 37

Quilley, Dennis, 131

race and ethnicity, 3–4, 6–7, 22–23, 24. *See also* casting; *Dreamgirls*; Lee, Baayork; National Asian Artists Project (NAAP)
Cage Aux Folles, La, in, 126
Chorus Line, A, in, 37–42
fat shaming and, 57–59, 60–61
Hairspray, in, 94–95, 97–101
labor and, 61, 83–84, 98–99, 109
Rachael Lily Rosenbloom (And Don't You Ever Forget It) (Jabara, Eyen), 31–32
racial capitalism, 59
racism, 3–4, 8, 38–39, 57–58, 61, 126, 155–56, 159, 164–66, 172, 174–75, 210–11, 230–31
Ralph, Sheryl Lee, 58*f*, 73*f*
Rapp, Anthony, 163, 164
Rapp, Renée, 89–90
Reagan, Ronald, 140–41, 155–56
Reams, Lee Roy, 169
Redmond, Ryann, 89, 108
Reed, Alaina, 69–70
Reinking, Ann, 13, 44–46, 52
Rent (Larson), 148–49, 150, 158
representation, 6–7, 8, 9–10, 11, 12, 18, 19, 25, 26, 28
Chorus Line, A, in, 38–45
Rich, Adrienne, 18
Rich, Frank, 67*b*–68, 71, 73–75, 122–23, 150, 217
Richardson, Michael, 204–5

Riley, Amber, 72, 82–84
Ring of Keys (queer advocacy group), 239, 241–42
"Ring of Keys" (*Fun Home*), 152*b*–55*b*, 153*f*, 242
Robbins, Jerome, 29–30, 45
Rock of Ages (D'Arienzo), 149
Rocky Horror Show, The (O'Brien), 216–17, 242–43
Román, David, 39, 126, 159–60
Rooney, David, 168, 169–70, 195–97, 232–33
Roosevelt, Franklin D., 211
Rose, Sarah F., 19–20, 211–12
Ross, Herbert, 30
Ross, Jamie, 138*b*
Roundabout Theatre Company, 179, 187–88, 198–99, 204–5
"Round-Shouldered Man" (*The Secret Garden*), 217
Ruggiero, Evan, 244–46, 245*f*
Runaways (Swados), 179
Rupert, Michael, 158
Ryan, Roz, 75, 84

Salmon, Scott, 136, 137
Sandahl, Carrie, 11, 24, 208–9, 225, 237
Sandoval-Sánchez, Alberto, 42
Sater, Steven, 189, 191–93
Savran, David, 158
Schulman, Sarah, 118, 126–27, 143–44, 159
Schumacher, Thomas, 219
Screen Actors Guild, 212–13
Secret Garden, The (Simon, Norman), 162, 163, 217
"Round-Shouldered Man," 217
Sedgwick, Eve Kosofsky, 23
Seesaw (Coleman, Fields, Bennett), 38–39, 86–87, 112, 121
Senelick, Laurence, 125, 132
Serrecchia, Michael, 47
Settle, Keala, 91, 95–96, 104–5
Sextet (Hurwit, Goldsmith, Perr), 120, 121
sexuality. *See* bisexuality; casting; coming out; homosexuality; transgender

314   INDEX

Shaiman, Marc, 94, 98–101
Shaw, Helen, 159
Sheik, Duncan, 189, 191–93
Shinn, Christopher, 225–26
Shirley, Don, 76
Shrek the Musical (Tesori, Lindsay-
    Abaire), 208–9, 220–25, 222*b*–24*b*,
    223*f*, 227
  "Let Your Freak Flag Fly," 220
  "What's Up, Duloc?," 222*b*–24*b*, 223*f*
Side Show (Krieger, Russell), 215
Sieber, Christopher, 221–25, 222*b*–
    24*b*, 223*f*
Sign-language interpreted performances
    (SLIPs), 204–5
SimCom (Simultaneous Communication),
    194, 197
Simon, Neil, 32–33
size, 3–4, 24, 57–112. See also *Dreamgirls*;
    fat-phobia; fat studies; *Hairspray*;
    Broadway shows, in, 57–58
  casting, 7, 8, 86–91
  labor and, 60, 107–8, 109, 112
  size-blindness, 8
Smokey Joe's Café (Leiber, Stoller), 91
Snyder, Sharon, 213–14
Solovay, Sandra, 103–4
Some Like It Hot (Wilder film), 126
"Somewhere" (*West Side Story* dream
    ballet), 30–31
Sondheim, Stephen, 217–18, 231–32
"Song of Purple Summer, The" (*Spring
    Awakening*), 193
"Song on the Sand" (*La Cage Aux Folles*),
    130–31, 142–43
South Pacific (Rodgers,
    Hammerstein), 213–14
Spring Awakening (Sheik, Sater), 150–51
  Deaf West Theatre Broadway revival
    [2015], 9–10, 25, 179–82, 183, 184–
    85, 186–206, 192*f*, 196*f*, 200*b*–2*b*,
    202*f*, 208–9, 234–36
  "Mama Who Bore Me," 193, 200*b*–1
  "Song of Purple Summer, The," 193
  "Totally Fucked," 200*b*
Staley, Peter, 155–56
Stanton, Ali, 71

Sterling, Lynn, 92*b*
Stern, Shoshannah, 183, 186, 199
Sternberg, Adam, 169
Sternfeld, Jessica, 214–15
Stevens, Athena, 237–38
Stevens, Tony, 31–33, 37–38, 43–44
Strange Loop, A (Jackson), 89
Streetcar Named Desire, A (Williams),
    119–20, 148
Streisand, Barbra, 70, 86
Strings, Sabrina, 60–61
Stroker, Ali, 171–72, 188, 202*b*, 202*f*, 208–
    9, 234–38, 235*f*, 244
Stuart, Michel, 121
Sugar (Styne, Merrill, Stone), 126
Summer, Donna, 159–60
Summer: The Donna Summer Musical
    (Moroder, Jabara, Summer, McAnuff,
    Cary), 159–60
Sunday in the Park with George
    (Sondheim, Lapine), 216–17
Svich, Caridad, 229–30
Swados, Elizabeth, 179
Sweeney Todd (Sondheim,
    Wheeler), 242–43
Sweet Charity (Coleman, Fields,
    Simon), 92*b*

Taboo (O'Dowd, Davies Markham,
    Busch), 159, 216
Tam, Jason, 42
Tap Dance Kid, The (Krieger, Lorick,
    Blackwell), 88–89
Taylor, Millie, 43
Tesori, Jeanine, 152*b*, 227
"There! Right There!" (*Legally Blonde*), 149
Thomas Jr., William, 126
Time (magazine), 115
Time Out New York, 243–44
Timms, Henry, 239
[title of show] (Bowen, Bell), 148–49
Tony Awards, 25, 41–42, 57, 66*b*, 67*b*,
    77–78, 80–81, 84, 90, 91, 92*b*, 110,
    117–18, 121, 129, 138*b*–39, 145, 152*b*,
    154*b*–55*b*, 156–58, 166, 169–70,
    199–204, 200*b*–2*b*, 208–9, 235–37,
    235*f*, 240–41

"Too Beautiful for Words" (*The Color Purple*), 226
Tootsie (Yazbek, Horn), 150–51, 173
Torch Song Trilogy (Fierstein), 40, 126, 148, 161–62
"Totally Fucked" (*Spring Awakening*), 200*b*
Townsell, Vanessa, 73–74, 73*f*, 79, 84
Toy Johnson, Christine, 9–10
Tracy Turnblad (character in *Hairspray*), 14, 59–60, 84, 87, 91, 92*b*, 93*b*, 94–106, 108–9
  casting, 94–97, 101–6
transformation trope, 217–27
transgender, 10–11, 118–19, 144, 150–51, 160, 163–64, 170–74, 176, 229–30, 241–42
Trask, Stephen, 163–64
triple-threat performers (actor-singer-dancers), 4, 18, 25, 28–29, 30–31, 53–54, 57, 179–80, 183, 207, 214–15, 234–35
Trump, Donald [AKA 45], 172
Tune, Tommy, 47, 121, 141–42, 150, 160–61
"Turn It Off" (*The Book of Mormon*), 149
Twitter, 91, 111

Umphress, Alysha, 91

Valentine, Lisette, 101–2
Van Peebles, Melvin, 120–21
Variety, 90, 168
Viagas, Robert, 52
Viertel, Jack, 74–75
Vietti, Alejo, 91
Village Voice, 116, 123
Vincentelli, Elisabeth, 151, 232–33
Violet (Tesori, Crawley), 208–9, 225, 227

Wailes, Alexandria, 183
"Waitin' for the Light to Shine" (*Big River*), 179
Waitress (Bareilles, Nelson), 9–10, 88–89, 91, 109–10
Wales Padlock Law, 119–20
Wallace, Marisha, 64, 82, 83, 109

Walsh, Thommie, 42, 47
Walters, Barbara, 161
Wann, Marilyn, 109
Washington, Michael Benjamin, 126
Waters, John, 95, 96, 98, 99, 102–3
Waterstreet, Ed, 181–82
Wedekind, Frank, 180–81, 191–93
Weight Watchers, 78–79, 107–8
West Side Story (Bernstein, Sondheim, Laurents, Robbins), 28–31, 42, 213–14
  "Somewhere" (dream ballet), 30–31
West, Lindy, 61–62
West, Mae, 119–20
Wetzsteon, Ross, 115
"What I Did for Love" (*A Chorus Line*), 34–35
"What's Up, Duloc?" (*Shrek the Musical*), 222*b*–24*b*, 223*f*
White, Christian Dante, 171–72
White, Edmund, 140
White, Lillias, 71–72, 74–75, 76–77, 78–80, 80*f*, 84, 92*b*
Whitesel, Jason, 17
Who's Tommy, The (Townshend, McAnuff), 203, 214–15
Wicked (Schwartz, Holzman), 90, 170–71, 207, 216–17
Wild Party, The (LaChiusa, Wolfe), 148–49, 150
Wilkins, Sharon, 92*b*–93*b*
Will and Grace (TV series), 162, 168–69
Williams, Sammy, 41–42, 41*f*
Willson, Meredith, 208–9
Wilson, Flip, 138*b*
Wilson, Woodrow, 211
Winer, Linda, 232
Winkler, Kevin, 31
Winokur, Marissa Jaret, 59–60, 101, 103–5, 104*f*, 107–8, 110, See also *Hairspray*
Wittman, Scott, 94, 98–99
Wiz, The (Smalls, Brown, etc.), 37, 64
Wolf, Stacy, 24, 64, 116–17
Wolfe, George C., 164
Woll, Allen, 24
Wollman, Elizabeth L., 118, 120

316 INDEX

Wonderful Town (Bernstein, Comden, Green), 30
Wong, Janet, 47
Woodall, Eric, 82
Wright, Pamela, 243
Wylie, John, 216–17

Yates, Samuel, 207
"You Can't Stop the Beat" (*Hairspray*), 95
YouTube, 184, 242–43

Zuercher, Garrett, 242–43

The manufacturer's authorised representative in the EU for product safety is Oxford
University Press España S.A. of El Parque Empresarial San Fernando de Henares,
Avenida de Castilla, 2 – 28830 Madrid (www.oup.es/en or product.safety@oup.com).
OUP España S.A. also acts as importer into Spain of products made by the manufacturer.

Printed in the USA/Agawam, MA
May 16, 2025

887590.002